Refugees and
International Rela

Refugees and International Relations

EDITED BY

GIL LOESCHER

AND

LAILA MONAHAN

CLARENDON PRESS · OXFORD

1990

Oxford University Press, Walton Street, Oxford OX2 6DP
Oxford New York Toronto
Delhi Bombay Calcutta Madras Karachi
Petaling Jaya Singapore Hong Kong Tokyo
Nairobi Dar es Salaam Cape Town
Melbourne Auckland
and associated companies in
Berlin Ibadan

Oxford is a trade mark of Oxford University Press

Published in the United States
by Oxford University Press, New York

First published in hardback 1989
First published in Clarendon Paperbacks 1990

British Library Cataloguing in Publication Data
Refugees and international relations.
1. Refugees
I. Loescher, Gil, 1945– II. Monahan,
Laila, 1944–
325'.21
ISBN 0–19–827858–6

Library of Congress Cataloging in Publication Data
Refugees and international relations/edited by Gil Loescher and
Laila Monahan.
p. cm.
Bibliography: p.
Includes index.
1. Refugees—Government policy. 2. International relations.
I. Loescher, Gil. II. Monahan, Laila, 1944– .
HV640.R4318 1989 362.8'7—dc19 88–28813
ISBN 0–19–827858–6

Printed and bound in
Great Britain by Biddles Ltd,
Guildford and King's Lynn

Contents

Contributors

ROBERT L. BACH is an Associate Professor of Sociology at the State University of New York at Binghamton. He is also the Chairperson of an Advisory Group of a Ford Foundation research and service programme on Relations between Newcomers and Established Residents in the United States. Co-author of *Latin Journey: Mexican and Cuban Immigrants in the United States* and author of numerous articles and reports on international migration and world economic development, the economic and political integration of immigrants in the United States, and refugee resettlement in countries of permanent asylum, he is currently completing book-length manuscripts on Cuban Migration to the United States and Refugee Resettlement in the United States.

GENEVIÈVE CAMUS-JACQUES has been responsible for the Human Rights Programme of the World Young Women's Christian Association in Geneva since 1982. She has visited refugee camps in the Middle East, Pakistan, Thailand, Malaysia, Papua New Guinea, Austria, Mexico, and Honduras; worked with National YWCAs to implement programmes for women and children; worked, under the auspices of CIMADE, with refugees settled in France; served as co-convenor of the Refugee–Migrant Women issue during the preparation for and at the 1985 NGO Forum in Nairobi, and is currently convenor of an NGO working group on refugee women. She has published several articles on refugees and refugee women and collaborated with her husband André Jacques on two books, *Les Déracinés* and *Stranger within your Gates*.

JOHAN CELS has been a Visiting Research Fellow at Queen Elizabeth House, Oxford University and a Ph.D. student at the University of Notre Dame, for which he is completing his dissertation on the European refugee regime. As a Research Consultant to the European Consultation on Refugees and Exile (ECRE), he was commissioned to carry out a major study on *de facto* refugees in Europe. His publications include articles on European refugee policy in *Human Rights and Foreign Policy*, Dilys

Hill (ed.), and *Refugees in the Age of Total War: Europe and the Middle East*, Anna Bramwell (ed.).

GERVASE COLES, formerly an Australian Foreign Service Officer, is a noted specialist on international refugee policy. From 1981 to 1985 he was seconded to the Office of the United Nations High Commission for Refugees as Senior Legal Adviser, and Chief of Conferences and Promotion of the Refugee Law and Doctrine Division. He served as Co-ordinator of Study and Research at the International Institute of Humanitarian Law at San Remo, Italy, where he also edited the Institute's *Yearbook*. He is the author of numerous publications on refugee law and policy issues and has recently rejoined UNCHR.

JACQUES CUÉNOD was Executive Director of ACORD (formerly Euro-Action ACORD) until February 1988. He previously worked for UNHCR as Deputy Director of Assistance, Regional Representative for Indo-China, Inter-Agency Programme Co-ordinator, and Regional Representative for Africa. He also worked for UNWRA in the Middle East for eight years. Within UNHCR, he was responsible for developing the concept of 'Refugee Aid and Development', a task he pursued with ACORD at the request of the International Council of Voluntary Agencies (ICVA).

FRED CUNY is the Chairman of INTERTECT, a professional disaster management consultancy firm, based in Dallas, Texas. An acknowledged expert on relief issues in both natural disasters and refugee emergencies, he is the author of numerous publications and training materials, including *Refugee Camps and Camp Planning: The State of the Art* and *Disasters and Development*.

PATRICIA WEISS-FAGEN, a past Associate of the Refugee Policy Group, with primary responsibility for the area of mass exodus, asylum, and protection, has recently joined the staff of UNHCR in Washington, DC. She is an Associate Professor of History at San José State University (California) and is the former Vice Chair of Amnesty International, USA. A specialist on US Human Rights and Asylum Policy, she has numerous publications to her name, which include *Exiles and Citizens: Spanish Republicans in Mexico*.

ELIZABETH G. FERRIS is the Information and Interpretation Secretary of the World Council of Churches' Refugee Service. In this capacity she carries out research and provides analyses of global refugee situations. She is also in charge of administering WCC support for refugee projects in Latin America and North America. Prior to joining the WCC in 1985 she was an Assistant Professor of Political Science at several US universities, including Lafayette College and Miami University (Ohio). From 1981 to 1982 she was a Fulbright professor at UNAM (Universidad Nacional Autónoma de México). She is the author of *The Central American Refugees* and editor/co-editor of *Refugees in World Politics, The Dynamics of Latin American Foreign Policies*, and *Latin American Foreign Policies: Global and Regional Dimensions.*

DENNIS GALLAGHER founded the Refugee Policy Group in 1982, and currently serves as its Executive Director. RPG, based in Washington, DC, is a centre for policy analysis and research on domestic and international refugee issues. Formerly he was the Director of the Office of Refugee Resettlement in the Department of Health and Human Services. He edited the *International Migration Review* special issue 'Refugees: Issues and Directions'.

GUY GOODWIN-GILL is currently a Visiting Fellow of Osgoode Hall Law School, York University, Toronto. He is on leave from the Office of the United Nations High Commissioner for Refugees, in which he has served as Legal Adviser and Senior Research Officer. He is the author of two major works on refugee and migrant law, *The Refugee in International Law* (1983) and *International Law and the Movement of Persons Between States* (1978), as well as many articles. He is also Editor-in-Chief of the *International Journal of Refugee Law*.

LEON GORDENKER is Professor of International Organizations at the Graduate Institute of International Studies in Geneva and Professor Emeritus of Princeton University. He is the author of *Refugees in International Politics, The United Nations in International Politics, The UN Secretary General and the Maintenance of Peace*, and *International Aid and National Decisions.*

ARTHUR C. HELTON, a US lawyer, is the Director of the Political Asylum Project for the Lawyers Committee for Human Rights, which is based in New York City. Among his numerous articles is 'Political Asylum Under the 1980 Refugee Act: An Unfulfilled Promise', which appeared in the University of Michigan *Journal of Law Reform.*

JEAN-PIERRE HOCKÉ was elected United Nations High Commissioner for Refugees in December 1985. From 1973 he was head of the Operations Department and, from 1981, a member of the Directorate of the International Committee of the Red Cross (ICRC). With ICRC, he was responsible for the launching of large-scale humanitarian operations during many major conflicts, including those in the Middle East and, in particular, the Lebanon and Cyprus, and also in Angola, Vietnam, Kampuchea, Iran and Iraq, Central America, and Ethiopia. He was also responsible for the definition of the aims which ICRC intends to pursue in the next ten years.

RANDOLPH KENT is a Visiting Research Fellow at the Refugee Studies Programme, Queen Elizabeth House, Oxford University, and Director of the School of International Relations (UK Graduate Programme), University of Southern California. From 1982 to 1985 he led a project on 'Disasters, Disaster Relief, and the International System', funded by the British Economic and Social Research Council, and in 1986 he was awarded a Nuffield Foundation grant to evaluate the performance of the UN Office for Emergency Operations in Africa. His most recent publication, *Anatomy of Disaster Relief: the International Network in Action*, was published in 1987. He is the author of the annual *Disaster Monitor* for *Third World Affairs* and is Review Editor for the *Journal of Refugee Studies*.

GIL LOESCHER (Co-editor) is Associate Professor of Government and member of the Kellogg Institute for International Studies at the University of Notre Dame. His most recent book with John Scanlan is *Calculated Kindness: Refugees and America's Half-Open Door: 1945 to Present*. He has co-edited a number of other related books, including *The Moral Nation: Humanitarianism and U.S. Foreign Policy Today*, *The Global Refugee Problem: US and World Response*, and *Human Rights and American Foreign Policy*. From 1987 to 1989 he has been a Visiting Research Fellow at Queen Elizabeth House, Oxford University, where he has been writing a Twentieth Century Fund study on international co-operation and the management of refugee problems.

SUSAN FORBES MARTIN is a Senior Associate of the Refugee Policy Group where she has primary responsibility for policy-related research concerning refugees in industrialized countries. Prior to joining the RPG she served as Research Director of the US Select Commission on Immigration and Refugee Policy. She is also author of numerous articles on US refugee resettlement and asylum policies.

ROY MCDOWALL. From 1972 to 1987 he was responsible for the Refugee Section in the Immigration Department of the Home Office and, in this capacity, served as the UK representative on the Council of Europe *ad hoc* Committee on Asylum, Refugees/Stateless Persons (CAHAR). From 1977 he was a member of the UK Delegation to UNHCR's Executive Committee and its Protection Sub-Committee.

DENNIS MCNAMARA is a Deputy Director of UNHCR's Division of Law and Doctrine. He was previously UNHCR's Legal Adviser in Asia and was later Chief of UNHCR's South and South-east Asia Section in Geneva. In 1986–7, during a sabbatical year, he was a Visiting Fellow at the Centre of International Studies at the London School of Economics, where he conducted research for a study of the international response to the Indo-Chinese refugee crisis in South-east Asia.

LAILA MONAHAN (Co-editor) is Publications Officer of the Refugee Studies Programme, Queen Elizabeth House, Oxford University. She is Co-editor of *War and Refugees: The Western Sahara Conflict*, and of a special refugee issue of *Current Sociology*. Formerly she lectured in English in the United States, Finland, and England.

ELLY-ELIKUNDA MTANGO is Minister Counsellor at the Tanzanian Permanent Mission to the United Nations, Geneva. He serves as a member of the UN Human Rights Commission Working Group of Experts on Southern Africa and as a delegate to the UNHCR Executive Committee Sessions, where he has taken an active role in UNHCR deliberations on the issue of armed attacks on refugee camps. He was formerly Head of Legal and International Law Sections of the Ministry of Foreign Affairs, Tanzania.

BARRY STEIN is a Professor of Social Science and a core faculty member of the Center for Advanced Study in International Development, African Studies Center, and the Women in International Development Program at Michigan State University. Since 1975 he has taught courses on refugees, displaced persons, exiles, and on refugee issues and has published widely in the field.

A founder of the Refugee Policy Group, he served from 1982 to 1985 as senior associate responsible for policy-related research concerning refugee assistance in developing countries. He has co-edited a special issue of the *International Migration Review* entitled 'Refugees Today' and has conducted research for the Select Commission on Immigration and Refugee Policy and on older refugee settlements in Africa for the US Agency for International Development. He is currently studying voluntary repatriation.

Jonas Widgren joined UNHCR in Geneva in 1987 as Co-ordinator of Inter-Governmental Consultations on Asylum Seekers and refugees in Europe and North America. Before this, from 1967, he was active in Swedish immigration policy as secretary of various task forces and as Director of Immigration in the Ministry of Labour, 1979–82. He was appointed Under-Secretary of State for Immigration in 1982 and Chairman of the OECD Working Party on Migration from 1983 to 1987. He has been active in European refugee affairs since 1984.

Introduction

Refugee Issues in International Relations

GIL LOESCHER

WE live in a rapidly changing and basically violent world. If we do not directly suffer from wars, military coups, poverty, famine, and natural disasters, modern technology ensures that we cannot ignore the human toll they exact. We watch as millions of people are forced into exile, looking for food, for safety, for hope for the future. Refugees are everywhere—a by-product of every crisis. Millions of Afghans sit in camps in Pakistan and Iran. Thousands of Iranians have sought asylum in Turkey, Pakistan, the Persian Gulf, Europe, and North America. Africa, riddled with wars and famine, provides a sad catalogue of refugees. Poverty, repression, and wars in Central America have fed a steady stream of refugees northwards. Camps in Hong Kong and Thailand house thousands of Vietnamese, Cambodians, and Laotians behind barbed wire. Forty years on, the Palestinians have yet to find a home.

For the majority of these refugees, life in exile is as bad as or even worse than the conditions experienced in the countries from which they have fled. Many are confined to camps or ramshackle settlements close to the borders of their home countries where, deprived of opportunities to work or farm their own land, they depend on international charity for survival. Refugees are often separated from members of their families, exposed to the danger of armed attack, subject to many forms of exploitation and degradation, and haunted by the constant fear of expulsion, and the forced return to their countries of origin. Vast numbers of children have spent all their lives in refugee camps. The longer they live there, the

The author would like to acknowledge permission from the Macmillan Press Ltd. to use material from his contribution entitled 'Refugees and Foreign Policy', which appears in Dilys M. Hill (ed.), *Human Rights and Foreign Policy* (London: Southampton Studies in International Policy, 1988).

less chance they have of ever experiencing some semblance of a normal life. Refugees who are fortunate enough to resettle in third countries can rebuild their lives and start afresh, but many are unsuccessful, never emerging from the socially marginalized sectors of society. Unfamiliarity with different cultures and climates, depression, often profound alienation, and unemployment have devastating effects on many resettled refugees.

Refugee situations are not merely problems calling for humanitarian concern. They can be a potential threat to the social, economic, and political fabric of host states, and ultimately a threat to peace. Unfortunately, no ready solutions to the seemingly interminable refugee problems present themselves. The major refugee problems in Afghanistan, South-east Asia, Central America, and the Horn of Africa all began eight or more years ago and, with few exceptions, political solutions to these regional conflicts remain difficult. There is little to suggest that the trend will be reversed in the near future, particularly in the poorer areas of the world. Population growth, economic stagnation, famine, political instability, superpower rivalry, the ever-growing arms trade, increased militarism, and ethnic conflicts all signal greater mass movements of populations in the future.

Traditionally, the United Nations High Commissioner for Refugees (UNHCR), together with numerous other governmental and non-governmental agencies, has taken initiatives only after a situation has reached such magnitude as to command international attention. Whereas this 'post-event' action may have sufficed in the past, now, as geopolitical features and the character of refugee flows have changed, many observers question the viability of the UNHCR and the existing organized structures to cope with, much less resolve, these difficulties.

What is commonly recognized is that, since refugees are a global problem, the search for solutions must also be global. Also, it is becoming clear that the view that refugee movements pose humanitarian problems marginal to the central issues of war and peace, or that they are unique and isolated events, must be superseded by a serious consideration of refugee problems as an integral part of international politics and relations.

The fact that refugees do make a substantial impact on world politics and on the domestic affairs of many countries is evident. In recent years refugees have appeared in massive numbers and in unexpected places. According to the UNHCR, some twelve million refugees are to be found, on all continents, with both industralized and developing countries directly affected by the arrival of desperate people seeking safety and assistance.

The pressures created by the presence of refugees in receiving countries, particularly those in the Third World, can be enormous. Governments walk a tightrope in trying to balance economic, national security, and humanitarian interests. Most are extremely reluctant to accord legal status to refugees from neighbouring countries for fear of damaging diplomatic relations, encouraging a mass influx of people seeking refuge, or offering protection to an ideologically incompatible group of persons. Refugees often place unacceptably heavy economic burdens on host governments. The fact that refugees require jobs and social services at a time when an increased number of nationals within host societies are also in desperate need of such jobs and services creates popular resentment towards refugees, and pressure on governments to restrict immigration. Refugees are also intimately linked to their nations' security problems. Refugees often live on, or very near, disputed borders; they either reside among combatants in an ongoing conflict, or are perceived to be materially assisting guerrilla forces attempting to overthrow the government from which they have fled. Host governments have alternatively viewed refugees as freedom fighters, guerrillas, subversives, or illegal immigrants.

For these reasons, among others, the increased occurrence and very real threat of further large movements of refugees have given rise to increased protectionism on the part of Western governments, which in turn has led to increased pressure on Third World governments. As a consequence, on various occasions, some countries of asylum and host governments have closed their borders to refugees, have treated all who attempted to enter or travel through as illegal immigrants, have expelled new arrivals, have incarcerated and harassed those in detention centres and border camps, and have denied journalists and voluntary agencies access to these areas. It is clear that this unjust and untenable situation must be dealt with by a concerted effort on the part of all the actors, the industrialized and the developing countries, the rich and the poor nations.

But yet, despite the growing acknowledgement that something must be done about refugee problems, these are still among the least considered major international issues. Until recently little attempt has been made to understand refugee issues within their national and international political contexts. The relationships between foreign policy concerns and refugees have been and remain little explored in both the international relations literature and in studies of refugee movements. Little systematic research has been done into either the political causes of different types of refugee movements or the political, strategic, and economic factors that determine the policy responses of states to refugee crises. Nor has any comprehensive theoretical framework been developed to explain and compare government policies, to analyse the policy-making process in individual countries, or to assess the relationship between international norms and national compliance with these legal standards. Until recently, there was neither a real data base on refugees, nor any particular coherence in such refugee literature as did exist.

Refugee literature and research

Much of the extant literature is descriptive, with scholars generally concentrating on the refugee situations and policies of individual countries. Researchers have focused especially on European, African, Cuban, and Indo-Chinese refugees and on the resettlement, integration, and economic impact of refugees.[1] Thus, in these areas, the data and the analysis are increasingly more developed than in other areas of refugee studies. Less than adequate treatment, however, has been accorded to the process of refugee policy-making at the national or international levels, to an examination of underlying causes of refugee flows, or to the general issue of solutions to refugee problems.

Legal scholars have focused their analyses principally on the UNHCR statute and the legal provisions of national and international refugee instruments pertaining to refugee definition,

[1] For a current sampling of this literature see Dennis Gallagher (ed.), 'Refugees: Issues and Directions', International Migration Review, 20 (summer 1986), 137–501. Some of the major bibliographical references pertaining to refugees include *International Bibliography of Refugee Literature* (Geneva: International Refugee Integration Resource Center, 1985) and the bibliography in Barry Stein and Sylvano Tomasi (eds.), 'Refugees Today', *International Migration Review*, 15 (spring–summer 1981), 331–93. The new *Journal of Refugee Studies* and the new *International Journal of Refugee Law* (both by Oxford University Press) will include up-to-date research on refugees.

asylum, and protection.[2] This literature is often limited in that frequently insufficient attention is given to the national interests, domestic and foreign policy constraints, and ideological concerns of states which must be taken into account together with legal and humanitarian principles in order to understand both the reasons for and the responses of states to refugee crises. Recently, however, some legal scholars have adopted a much broader policy-orientated approach in their writings. In particular, comparative legal analyses which take into account domestic- and foreign-policy influences have been made of American and European refugee determination procedures. These studies provide important insights into the effectiveness of refugee decision-making procedures, the role of UNHCR, and the impact of domestic and foreign-policy factors on the implementation of refugee legal instruments.[3]

Historians too have made detailed examinations of refugee movements and the role of international organizations during and after both World Wars.[4] Some of these studies were sponsored or commissioned by the post-war refugee institutions and have the shortcoming of being insufficiently critical of either the states or the

[2] Some of the standard works include Atle Grahl-Madsen, *The Status of Refugees in International Law* (2 vols.; Leiden: A. W. Sijthoff, 1966, 1972), and *Territorial Asylum* (Dobbs Ferry, NY: Oceana Publications, 1980); Guy Goodwin-Gill, *The Refugee in International Law* (Oxford: Clarendon Press, 1983); Paul Weis, 'Human Rights and Refugees', *Israel Yearbook on Human Rights*, 1 (1971), 35–50; 'Territorial Asylum', *The Indian Journal of International Law*, 6 (1966), 173–94; 'The 1967 Protocol Relating to the Status of Refugees and some Questions of the Law of Treaties', *The British Yearbook of International Law* (1967), 39–70; Gilbert Jaeger, *Status and International Protection of Refugees* (San Remo: International Institute of Human Rights, 1978); Peter MacAlister-Smith, *International Humanitarian Assistance: Disaster Relief Organizations in International Law and Organization* (Dordrecht: Martinus Nijhoff, 1985).

[3] Christopher Avery, 'Refugee Status Decision-Making in Ten Countries', *Stanford Journal of International Law*, 17 (winter 1984), 183–241. Other examples of legal scholars adopting somewhat broader policy-oriented approaches include David Kennedy, 'International Refugee Protection', *Human Rights Quarterly*, 8 (Feb. 1986), 9–69; David A. Martin, 'Large-Scale Migrations of Asylum-Seekers', *American Journal of International Law*, 76 (1982), 598–609.

[4] Some of the standard works include Louise Holborn, *Refugees, A Problem of Our Time: The Work of the United Nations High Commissioner for Refugees* (2 vols.; Metuchen, NJ: Scarecrow Press, 1975), and *The International Refugee Organization: A Specialized Agency of the United Nations, its History and Work, 1946–52* (London: Oxford University Press, 1956); Malcolm. J. Proudfoot, *European Refugees, 1939–1952: A Study in Forced Population Movement* (London: Faber and Faber, 1957); John Hope Simpson, *The Refugee Problem* (London: Oxford University Press, 1939); Jacques Vernant, *The Refugee in the Post-War World* (New Haven, Conn.: Yale University Press, 1953). John Stoessinger, *The Refugee in the World Community* (Minneapolis: University of Minnesota Press, 1956), is one early work that is critical of governmental attitudes to post-war refugee problems.

intergovernmental agencies which formed the international refugee regime during that period. They do none the less provide detailed information both about refugee movements and about the international agencies established to protect and assist refugees. However, several recent studies by historians of World War II and the post-war refugee situation[5] are much more frank in their analysis of both states and intergovernmental agencies, and underline the conflicting economic, political, and humanitarian interests of these principal actors. A group of historians in Sweden are currently researching the impact of the cold war on the refugee policies of major European states and the United States.[6] Moreover, through the scrutiny of the archives of international organizations and of major Western governments, individual scholars are reassessing some of the conventional interpretations of past and present refugee problems. From this re-examination we may hope to learn from former attempts to solve refugee problems so that we do not repeat the same mistakes.[7]

Thus, whereas there is a growing and important literature on the causes of refugee flows,[8] on emergency assistance programmes for

[5] Michael R. Marrus, *The Unwanted: European Refugees in the Twentieth Century* (Oxford: Oxford University Press, 1985); Michael R. Marrus and Robert O. Paxton, *Vichy France and the Jews* (New York: Basic Books, 1981); Bernard Wasserstein, *Britain and the Jews of Britain, 1939–1945* (Oxford: Clarendon Press, 1979); Nikolai Tolstoy, *Victims of Yalta* (London: Hodder and Stoughton, 1977); David S. Wyman, *The Abandonment of the Jews: America and the Holocaust 1941–45* (New York: Pantheon, 1985); Alfred M. de Zayas, *Nemesis at Potsdam: The Anglo-Americans and the Expulsions of the Germans* (London: Routledge and Kegan Paul, 1979); Leonard Dinnerstein, *America and the Survivors of the Holocaust, 1941–1945* (New York: Columbia University Press, 1982).

[6] The results of this research, which is being undertaken under the direction of Professor Goran Rystad, University of Lund, Sweden, should be available in 1990.

[7] See e.g. Anna Bramwell, (ed.), *Refugees in the Age of Total War* (London: Unwin-Hyman, 1988). Archival research by Howard Adelman at York University, Toronto, will result in a new history and evaluation of UNWRA and the Palestinians. I am writing a Twentieth Century Fund book describing the evolution of international co-operation concerning refugees and identifying alternative responses for handling refugee flows within the international system.

[8] See the forthcoming study by a team of political scientists: Aristide Zolberg, Astri Suhrke, and Sergio Aguayo, *Escape from Violence: Globalized Social Conflict and the Refugee Crisis in the Developing World* (New York: Oxford University Press, 1989). For their preliminary findings see A. Zolberg, A. Suhrke and S. Aguayo, 'International Factors in the Formation of Refugee Movements', *International Migration Review*, 20 (summer 1986), 151–69. Also relevant is a report for the UN High Commission on Human Rights by Prince Sadruddin Aga Khan, who formerly served as UN High Commissioner for Refugees, detailing the linkages between mass exoduses and human rights violations (UN Doc. E/CN.4/1503).

refugees,[9] on transnational networks to assist refugees,[10] and on the policy responses of particular states to refugee movements,[11] political scientists and international relations scholars have on the whole paid insufficient attention to the refugee issue and its relationship to foreign-policy formation. This would seem to be a serious omission which researchers must remedy if refugee issues are to be understood fully and if solutions, even partial ones, are to be found.

Refugees and international relations

The study of refugees offers valuable insights into the functioning of international relations in several respects. Refugee policy analysis incorporates many of the most basic issues of international political analysis: the roles of various decision- and policy-makers at the

[9] Recent studies which critically examine international assistance programmes for refugees are William Shawcross, *Quality of Mercy* (New York: Simon and Schuster, 1984); Linda Mason and Roger Brown, *Rice, Rivalry and Politics* (Notre Dame, Ind., and London: University of Notre Dame Press, 1983); Barbara Harrell-Bond, *Imposing Aid: Emergency Assistance to Refugees* (Oxford: Oxford University Press, 1986); Jason Clay and Bonnie Holcombe, *Politics and the Ethiopian Famine, 1984–85* (Cambridge, Mass.: Cultural Survival, Dec. 1985); Randolph Kent, *The Anatomy of Disaster Relief: The International Network in Action* (London: Frances Pinter, 1987); Bruce Nichols, *The Uneasy Alliance: Religion, Refugee Work, and US Foreign Policy* (New York: Oxford University Press, 1988); and Jason Clay, 'The West and the Ethiopian Famine: Implications for Humanitarian Assistance', in Gil Loescher and Bruce Nichols (eds.), *The Moral Nation: Humanitarianism and US Foreign Policy Today* (Notre Dame, Ind., and London: University of Notre Dame Press, 1989). Pioneering studies of refugee assistance programmes have been carried out by T. F. Betts, Robert Chambers, and Art Hansen. See, for example, T. F. Betts, 'Evolution and Promotion of the Integrated Rural Development Approach to Refugee Policy in Africa', *Africa Today*, 31 (1984), 7–24; Robert Chambers, 'Rural Refugees in Africa: What the Eye Does Not See', *Disasters*, 3 (1979), 381–92; and Art Hansen, 'Managing Refugees: Zambia's Response to Angolan Refugees, 1966–1977', *Disasters*, 3 (1979), 375–80.

[10] Leon Gordenker, *Refugees in International Politics* (London: Croom Helm, 1987); Elizabeth Ferris (ed.), *Refugees and World Politics* (New York: Praeger, 1985); Robert Gorman, *Private Voluntary Organizations as Agents of Development* (Boulder, Colo.: Westview Press, 1984; Independent Commission on International Humanitarian Issues, *Refugees: The Dynamics of Displacement* (London: Zed Books, 1986); and W. R. Smyser, *Refugees: Extended Exile* (New York: Praeger, 1987).

[11] Gil Loescher and John A. Scanlan, *Calculated Kindness: Refugees and America's Half-Open Door* (New York and London: The Free Press and Macmillan, 1986), Norman L. Zucker and Naomi Flink Zucker, *The Guarded Gate: The Reality of American Refugee Policy* (San Diego: Harcourt Brace Jovanovich, 1987); Gilburt D. Loescher and John A. Scanlan (eds.), *The Global Refugee Problem: US and World Response* (Beverly Hills, Calif., and London: Sage Publications, 1983); Elizabeth Ferris, *Central American Refugees and the Politics of Protection* (New York: Praeger, 1987); Charles B. Keely, *Global Refugee Policy: The Case for a Development-Orientated Strategy* (New York: The Population Council, 1981).

national and international level, the recognition and implementation of human rights standards, the adherence of states to domestic and international legal norms, the role of transnational forces and organizations, the transnational dynamics of social and political conflict, the role of ideology and ethnic groups in foreign policy-making, the considerations of economic development, and other issues. The formulation of refugee policy involves a complex interplay of domestic and international factors at the policy-making level and illustrates the conflict between international humanitarian norms and the sometimes narrow self-interest calculations of sovereign nation states.

Refugees are usually created as the direct result of political decisions taken by sovereign states, with consequences that extend beyond national borders. The existence of refugees affects foreign policy, exacerbates inter-state conflicts, and influences international attitudes. Several of the authors of the following chapters argue convincingly that demographic, economic, and political trends indicate that refugee influxes will probably feature largely in foreign and domestic policy issues over the next generation. It also appears likely that states will continue to protect their sovereignty by strictly controlling the entry of foreigners. Given these probable developments, there is an urgent need to move from the descriptive and legal to broader analytical studies which focus on causes of refugee movements and determinants of public policy—studies that will place refugee issues firmly in their proper context of international relations.

Refugees—regimes and structures

Recognizing the considerable effect of mass movements of refugees on the international political system, the international community has specified refugees as a unique category of human rights victims which should be accorded special protection and benefits. The principal international definitions of refugee at present are the United Nations concepts, formulated in the immediate post-World War II period, codified in the 1951 United Nations Convention Relating to the Status of Refugees, and expanded in the 1967 Protocol. According to the definition, refugees are people who are forced, for political, racial, or ideological reasons, to flee their home countries. Refugees should not be compelled to return home by the authorities in those nations where they seek refuge if to do so would place them in danger of persecution. Refugees have the right to apply for asylum and to demonstrate the political nature of their plight, according to internationally recognized criteria for securing refugee status. During this process, refugees should be treated fairly and be given adequate assistance to sustain them physically, psychologically, and socially. It is the state's own business, however, just how much it makes available to refugees in terms of material assistance and administrative and legal aid aimed at rendering them self-sufficient again and able to regain a sense of identity and self-respect. International law seeks to define the minimum that should be offered to refugees.

Over the past three and a half decades since the Convention was formulated a transnational response to the world refugee phenomenon has been institutionalized in the refugee-receiving nations and in an extensive structure of private and public international organizations, geared to provide refugee protection, aid, and resettlement. The international refugee regime was created by the leading Western powers and was acceptable only in so far as the system served, or did not run counter to, their particular interests or needs. At the time of the regime's creation, the Western powers, particularly the United States, were ill-disposed towards yielding authority to international institutions like the UNHCR, and imposed considerable limitations on their activities. Nevertheless, over time the UNHCR and the network of international agencies, national governments, and voluntary organizations have developed a response strategy which permits some refugees to remain in their countries of first asylum, enables others to be resettled in third countries, and arranges for others to be repatriated to their countries of origin. Moreover, in response to a growing international refugee problem, the responsibilities of the UNHCR have been expanded so that protection is accorded to a progressively larger group of people in refugee-like situations across the world.

Despite this broadened mandate, and humanitarian concerns notwithstanding, refugee groups are not treated equally within the international regime, nor do all states respond similarly to refugee problems. The international treatment of refugees and their selection for special aid or resettlement in other countries depend on a shifting combination of factors which include: the domestic support for certain refugees in the receiving country; the publicity afforded to particular instances of persecution; the financial strain likely to be incurred; but especially those foreign policy concerns involving the relationship of the receiving country to the country of origin, countries of first asylum, and other countries with an interest in a particular refugee migration. Even the most patently generous admissions or aid decisions are thus tinged with political considerations. Refugees receive protection and assistance either because, by their very presence, they pose political, economic, and social difficulties, or because of media publicity which captures the public attention and sympathy.

The international refugee regime has also not been able to escape political colouration. International refugee officials have realized for some time that whatever power they exercise depends largely on the financial and political support of the United States government and other large donor countries. The policies of the regime therefore primarily reflect the interests and priorities of the major donor countries in Europe, North America, Japan, and Australia. The UNHCR and voluntary agencies simply lack the financial independence and institutional strength to challenge their largest benefactors.

Thus, although the international mechanism geared to respond to refugee problems is in theory highly systematic, it is neither apolitical nor proving able to respond adequately to many of today's refugee situations. Many reasons are posited for this state of affairs. The UNHCR has been criticized by humanitarian agencies dealing with refugees, as well as by representatives of some governments which finance UNHCR programmes, for its inability to provide protection for all groups of refugees. These agencies are particularly concerned about such recent situations as the safety of refugees involved in recent repatriations in Central America, forced round-ups of refugees in Djibouti, the reduction of the UNHCR presence in Washington, DC, and UNHCR reluctance to assume an active protection role on the Thai–Kampuchean border. Voluntary agencies are concerned at the lack of an absolutely clear definition of UNHCR's responsibility for protection on all levels, and at the lack of a clear, consistent response to specific refugee situations. These problems also largely reflect governments' unwillingness to seek and to obtain political solutions to long-standing refugee problems. UN or regional peace agendas to terminate hostilities and to deal with political conflict in major refugee-producing regions do exist, but both a willingness to make foreign-policy adjustments and a commitment to a necessary multilateralism are difficult to achieve. Neither are Western governments willing to share the burdens of recent refugee flows. Alarmed at the uncontrolled arrival of increasing numbers of asylum-seekers, Western governments have increasingly resorted to unilateral measures to keep refugees out rather than to international co-operation to respond positively to contemporary refugee incidents.

Refugees and *realpolitik*

Both the difficulties facing UNHCR and the responses of countries highlight the political considerations which closely link refugee incidents and the conduct of international relations. Foreign-policy factors are involved in both the international responses to refugees and in the root causes of refugee flows. Human rights abuses within one nation often have direct consequences on others, especially when the nation's citizens pour into neighbouring countries in search of safety. Not surprisingly, sudden massive movements of usually unwelcome refugees can adversely affect relationships between nations. Government responses to refugee movements from neighbouring or distant countries are greatly influenced by the relations between sending and receiving nations. In the same way, political and economic tensions between host countries and countries of origin can directly influence the way refugees are treated. Politically or militarily active refugees can cause strategic and political difficulties for the government of the country of origin, as well as complicate relations between sending and receiving countries. Conversely, refugees can also be used and exploited by governments in pursuit of larger geopolitical and ideological objectives.

The refugee crises of recent decades have often taken place in areas where local conflicts have been drawn into the broader superpower struggle for global influence. This jockeying for influence has been seen in the Horn of Africa, Indo-China, Central Asia, the Middle East, Southern Africa and Central America where millions of refugees have been created. The United States and other major donor governments provide refugee aid for reasons of national interest as well as humanitarian concern. The former US Coordinator for Refugee Affairs, Eugene Douglas, argued that US refugee policy helped to counter Soviet expansion and influence by 'wean[ing] away client states from Soviet domination'.[12] In this statement, Douglas expressed the principal attitude towards refugees that has prevailed not only in the Reagan administration but also in the US government since World War II.[13]

Geopolitical and ideological considerations similarly help to explain the positive response shown towards refugees in those regions where the West has perceived its vital interest to be at stake. In some of the more remote areas of the globe, where the West has not been geopolitically involved, this generosity has been less forthcoming. Thus, it is not coincidental that the West has not accepted a significant number of refugees from Africa or from South Asia. Even where Western security interests are perceived to be at stake, as in the Horn of Africa or the Middle East, but where other political considerations prevail, expedients such as intensified relief aid rather than secondary settlement are usually favoured. Even so, preoccupations with the strategic balance during the entire era of East-West confrontation have tended to favour resettlement, into Europe as well as the United States, whenever the stability of allies or sympathetic neutral countries has been threatened by the presence of large numbers of involuntary or politically motivated immigrants. Thus, for example, over the years the industrialized countries have advocated and effected programmes aimed at relieving pressures caused by mass influxes of Hungarians, Czechs, and Poles into Austria, and large numbers of Indo-Chinese into Thailand, Malaysia, and the rest of South-east Asia.

Refugees as instruments of foreign policy

The rationale of refugee policy has not been limited to preserving political and military stability. Refugees are often used, both symbolically and instrumentally, to pursue foreign-policy objectives. Symbolically, refugees 'vote with their feet', thereby demonstrating the bankruptcy of their nation's political and economic system. Refugee policy also can be used to embarrass or destabilize enemy governments. Not only can a refugee exodus

[12] Eugene Douglas, 'The Problem of Refugees in a Strategic Perspective', *Strategic Review* (fall 1982), 11–20.

[13] Loescher and Scanlan, *Calculated Kindness*; and Zucker and Zucker, *The Guarded Gate*.

drain another state of its manpower skills and legitimacy, it can at the same time empower any opposition in exile. However, refugee policy can be a double-edged foreign-policy instrument. Communist and other regimes have effected mass expulsions to rid themselves of political dissidents and other 'undesirables' and to destabilize and embarrass Western adversaries.[14] ASEAN officials claim that the expulsion by Vietnam of hundreds of thousands of Vietnamese nationals of Chinese origin by Vietnam was a veiled attempt to create racial and economic problems in South-east Asia and to infiltrate enemy agents into the region. Similarly, Fidel Castro's deliberate expulsion of a number of criminals and psychotics during the 1980 Mariel boatlift to Key West, Florida, was an attempt to embarrass the United States. Until 1986 the East German government facilitated the entry into West Berlin of tens of thousands of Third World asylum applicants, anticipating that West Berlin and West German reception facilities and judicial systems would be unable to cope with such massive numbers of arrivals.[15]

Refugees also have been used instrumentally as so-called 'freedom fighters' and guerrillas to wage wars of liberation on all continents. In regions of intense superpower conflict and competition, these refugees have been armed and their counter-revolutions supported, both materially and ideologically. In the Horn of Africa the West supports a variety of regional secessionist groups, including refugees, in their national liberation struggles. The interests of the West in maintaining pressure on Ethiopia, and, through Ethiopia, on the Soviet Union, are served by the continued struggles for national self-determination in that region. In South-east Asia, where US refugee policy has linked humanitarian concerns to strategic interests, refugees have been used to serve larger American foreign policy objectives. The plight of the Vietnamese boat people, and the Cambodian and Laotian refugee crises of 1978–80, generated considerable anti-communist publicity. While the outflow of over a million refugees discredited the new Indo-Chinese communist governments, it also caused new foreign-policy problems for Vietnam and its client regimes. In the

[14] On this point see Michael S. Teitelbaum, 'Immigration, Refugees and Foreign Policy', *International Organization*, 38 (summer 1984), 429–50.

[15] Philip Rudge, 'Fortress Europe', *World Refugee Survey 1986 in Review* (New York: US Committee for Refugees, 1987), 5–12.

United States and in Europe Vietnamese exile groups have formed a network dedicated to destabilizing communist control of their country. Along the Thai–Cambodian border, China, the United States, and the ASEAN nations support the Khmer resistance front as a way of maintaining political pressure on the Soviet Union's clients, the Vietnamese government. In Afghanistan the nearly three million refugees who have fled to Pakistan—a close ally of the United States—form a base for Afghan *mujahidin* resistance to Soviet and Soviet-backed Afghan control. As in the Horn of Africa and Indo-China, refugee assistance simultaneously aids both the victims and the pursuit of long-term US strategic objectives. In Central America the United States labels Salvadorean refugees as guerrillas in disguise, and demonstrates suspicion if not hostility towards the international and voluntary agencies working with refugees in Salvadorean camps in Honduras.[16] Nicaraguan refugees in Honduras, Costa Rica, and Miami on the other hand have been seen as 'freedom fighters' and as such have been encouraged to wage a war of resistance in Nicaragua.

The practice of using refugees for foreign policy or military objectives is by no means limited to the United States or its allies. To give but a few examples, the Soviet Union considers Muslim refugee groups an important factor in the pursuit of its regional and global strategic objectives. The Soviet Union may either generously assist or else abandon groups it has long sponsored—depending on its perception of Soviet national interests. Algeria provides a base for the Polisario guerrillas who are claiming the West Sahara. Ethiopia offers sanctuary to southern Sudanese fighters who are opposed to Islamic rule in Khartoum, and Sudan, in turn, provides refuge to Eritreans, Tigrayans, and other ethnic groups who oppose the Mengistu regime in Addis Ababa. In order to neutralize Mozambique's capacity to serve as a base for anti-apartheid movements and to destabilize the government in Maputo, South Africa has actively supported Renamo, a band of guerrillas renowned for its atrocities. There are numerous other examples of states employing refugees and so-called freedom fighters as foreign-policy instruments. Although refugees have more typically been pawns manipulated by and sometimes sacrificed to larger foreign-

[16] Gil Loescher, 'Humanitarianism and Politics in Central America', *Political Science Quarterly*, 103 (summer 1988), 295–320.

policy objectives, refugees and their leaders are not always passive. Freedom fighters have leaders who are very politically aware and armed forces engaged in warfare for clearly articulated political objectives. In recognition of their use as foreign-policy instruments and symbols, these fighters frequently receive diplomatic recognition and considerable support from external patrons. In some instances refugees have used their countries of asylum as bases for guerrilla warfare, and have even been supplied with arms while still receiving refugee assistance. The provision of humanitarian assistance to armed refugee communities has greatly complicated aid policy and has been highly controversial. The actions of refugees also help to shape the terms on which international and regional political agreements are structured. The presence of Afghan exiles in Pakistan or of Nicaraguan *contras* in Honduras, for example, has created obstacles to ceasefires and peace agreements in Afghanistan and Central America.

Foreign policy and admissions policies

Foreign-policy considerations can also markedly influence decisions on refugee admissions, in particular the determination of which persons should be granted and which denied refugee status. The decision to bestow formal refugee status on citizens of a particular state usually implies condemnation of the 'sending' government for persecuting its citizens. A generous admissions policy towards a certain group may in fact encourage them to flee; this flight can then be used as propaganda to demonstrate that people are 'voting with their feet' or 'choosing sides' in an ideological conflict. Conversely, a decision not to accord refugee status will often imply support for the sending government. Such foreign-policy considerations explain, for example, the different treatment accorded by the United States to Salvadoreans and Haitians, as opposed to Cubans, Indo-Chinese, and Nicaraguans.[17] Although foreign-policy factors appear to play a less important role elsewhere than they do in the United States, an element of selection based on foreign policy and ideological considerations is observable in all countries. In Pakistan, for

[17] Loescher and Scanlan, *Calculated Kindness*; and Zucker and Zucker, *The Guarded Gate*.

example, Afghans are the beneficiaries of a massive relief effort and are given almost complete freedom of movement, while Iranians are given tenuous temporary asylum and receive virtually no government assistance. Depending on the political stance of receiving countries in the West, most refugees from poor countries are variously labelled economic migrants, illegal immigrants, or persons with manifestly unfounded claims to asylum. In the majority of Western European nations a significantly larger proportion of refugees during the past four decades have been admitted from Eastern European countries than from developing countries. In Germany asylum applicants from Third World countries may be subject to long-term detention, whereas Eastern European applicants are not.

Refugees as 'symbols' of foreign policy

Until the early 1970s the great majority of refugees fleeing to the West were from Eastern and Central Europe. During the immediate aftermath of World War II, not only did the Western states recognize the connection between the large uprooted populations of Eastern and Central Europe and future stability in the region, but as East–West tensions grew in the 1950s, the West also began to see refugees as *symbols* of foreign policy, to be exploited as part of a continuing propaganda campaign. The terms 'refugee' and 'defector' became synonymous. Each defection, each crossing into Austria or West Berlin, was construed as a 'ballot for freedom'. Refugees from communist bloc countries were also of particular instrumental interest to Western intelligence agencies, which were based at the federal agency for recognition of refugees in Zirndorf, West Germany, where these refugees were debriefed—an arrangement that continues to the present day. In the heyday of the 'Rollback of Communism', refugees and defectors also were infiltrated back behind the Iron Curtain to encourage resistance movements in communist regimes. Relatively large numbers of communist bloc refugees were accepted into Europe without question and without close investigation into their motives for leaving. During the 1950s and 1960s, most European governments never envisaged a large-scale movement of refugees from the poor countries northwards to Europe.

The changing face of European and North American refugee flows

By the early 1970s, however, the character of the refugee flow into Europe and North America began to change. As countries behind the Iron Curtain consolidated their rule, fewer people were able to flee to the West. At the same time, larger numbers of so-called 'Third World' nationals began fleeing politically repressive and desperately poor regimes to seek refuge in Europe and North America. Unlike the treatment accorded to Eastern Europeans, no presumptive refugee status was granted to these groups. Rather, as the number of asylum applicants from the Third World grew, European and North American states became increasingly restrictive in their admissions policies. Important exceptions to this practice included, in the early and mid-1970s, the Chileans and other 'southern cone' Latin American refugees into Europe and, in the late 1970s and early 1980s, the Indo-Chinese into the United States and Europe. The admission of these groups, however, depended to a large extent on the formation of broad coalitions of interested politicians, church representatives, labour leaders, and ordinary people, many of whom had no tie with Latin America or South-east Asia except that of sympathy. Most prospective entrants from the poor countries have not been the beneficiaries of this kind of sentiment and support. Although part of this disparity can be explained by economic pressures within and xenophobic attitudes among European states, foreign policy considerations too have played an important role, particularly in the United States.

Root causes and foreign policy

Foreign-policy factors also figure prominently in any kind of causal analysis of contemporary refugee incidents. As suggested earlier, the origins of contemporary refugee flows are closely connected to the conduct of international relations, and in recent decades the great majority of refugee movements have taken place among the poor countries. The more than one hundred new states that have gained independence in the post-war period have inherited often arbitrarily determined boundaries, fragile national unities, and uncertain economies. The dissolution of colonial empires and the creation of nation states, with the consequent social and economic changes, have been major sources of instability and refugee movements in Asia and Africa. Many new states face acute problems of ethnic minorities, regional discontent, religious hostilities, class conflicts and cultural separatisms. The easy availability of low-cost, highly destructive weapons on the international arms market enables nationalistic and often brutal politicians to retain power and to suppress demands for self-determination among these groups and to repress other domestic opposition movements. In a world where liberal democracies are few in number, more governments than ever before have sought to enforce authoritarian or totalitarian order by coercive means, thus producing greater outflows of refugees. Internal heterogeneity, political repression, and economic deprivation have made many states into potential powder kegs. In many instances, domestic instability has invited foreign intervention, and external powers have taken advantage of unsettled situations in geopolitically important regions of the world. The underlying forces of nationalism, ethnic conflict, foreign intervention, arms sales, incompetent government, and widespread human rights violations overlap, and it is difficult if not impossible to determine the exact 'root causes' of different refugee outflows.

Root causes and the refugee regime

To date the international refugee regime has been largely ineffective in dealing with the root causes of refugee problems. The regime was not originally designed for that purpose, and international agencies have traditionally refrained from examining the causes of refugee flows and from dealing directly with countries of origin because these agencies wanted to appear to be non-political, strictly humanitarian actors. In recent years, however, several initiatives[18] have been taken within the UN to try to prevent the conditions that cause the mass exodus of refugees, rather than to treat the symptoms or effects, and to make countries of origin more accountable for their actions. In identifying the causes of refugee

[18] The first initiative was taken by West Germany when it introduced a resolution in the UN General Assembly to investigate forms of co-operation needed to prevent mass exoduses (UN General Assembly Resolution 24/124, 11 Dec. 1980). The second initiative, a report for the UN Human Rights Commission by Prince Sadruddin Aga Khan (UN Doc. E/CN.4/1503), examined the linkages between human rights violations and mass exoduses.

flows, however, most governments emphasize the internal weaknesses of states rather than the involvement of external powers. While refugee flows often originate as a result of persecution at the hands of brutal rulers or because of indiscriminate violence, external powers can significantly influence the factors which generate these flows. Until the international dimensions of the causes of refugee flows are fully recognized, little headway will be made towards a resolution of refugee problems. Moreover, the international community has little ability to take preventive action in countries of origin because the root causes of contemporary refugee situations require political intervention against those governments that violate human rights, preferably *before* people need to flee. For the most part, UN institutions are unable either to prevent human rights violations or to punish those responsible.[19] In some measure, this is because prevention of human rights abuses depends on overcoming the barrier of national sovereignty, something no international organization has yet managed to accomplish consistently.

Furthermore, the international organization that has the mandate to protect refugees, the UNHCR, cannot intervene to protest against the cause of refugee outflows since this mandate takes effect only after flight has occurred. Decisions on asylum and the quality of care for refugees remain the prerogatives of individual states. National states remain the decisive actors in refugee affairs. The UNHCR can call attention to the legal obligations undertaken by governments that have adhered to the UN Refugee Convention and Protocol, but it is limited in its power to change the course of action of a government that is determined to violate treaty commitments to aid and protect refugees. The UNHCR is further constrained in that, in order to mount refugee relief operations, it must not only secure permission from countries of asylum to operate within their territories, but also raise money from donor governments. As a result the world's principal refugee protection agency is prevented from unduly criticizing either host or donor governments' policies towards refugees. UNHCR officials are therefore inclined to avoid raising delicate political questions when dealing with humanitarian issues for fear of overstepping their mandate or damaging relations

[19] Jack Donnelly, 'International Human Rights: A Regime Analysis', *International Organization*, 40 (summer 1986), 598–64; David P. Forsythe, 'The United Nations and Human Rights, 1945–1985', *Political Science Quarterly*, 100 (summer 1985), 249–70.

with sensitive governments, most of which would consider such intervention to be interference in their internal affairs.

The book

Given the political realities and limitations described above, what can be done to alleviate the current refugee stalemate, to further the resolution of the problem of refugees, and to prepare for the almost inevitable refugee problems of tomorrow? In October 1986 Jean-Pierre Hocké, the UN High Commissioner for Refugees, gave the first Joyce Pearce Memorial Lecture for the Refugee Studies Programme at Oxford University. This lecture was followed by a seminar series sponsored by the Programme on many of the most pressing refugee issues facing the UNHCR and the international community in the 1980s and beyond. Officials of the UN High Commissioner for Refugees, foreign and civil service officials from industrialized and developing countries, administrators of major voluntary and church agencies, immigration lawyers, social workers, refugees, volunteers, students, and academic specialists came together in Oxford during the winter of 1986–7 to discuss the protection and assistance of refugees and the question of refugees in international relations. Additional papers were specially commissioned by the editors.

This book, which is largely the product of these seminars, examines the general failure to resolve refugee situations and explores ways in which the current crisis in solutions to refugee problems might be overcome. Focusing on the causes of refugee movements and the determinants of public policy affecting international responses to the refugee problem, it is divided into three sections, covering the international framework, the dimensions of the refugee problem, and the search for appropriate responses to the refugee problem. The initial chapters establish the international context in which the discussion of contemporary refugee problems must take place.

The international framework

The initial chapter by Jean-Pierre Hocké outlines the major characteristics of the international refugee situation as he sees them today. The causes of refugee flows have become increasingly complex and are interwoven with other major international problems, such as population growth, unemployment, internal conflict, and widespread political and economic repression. The majority of refugees are at present confined in camps and settlements where they have an idle, depressing existence. Since refugee groups mostly form parts of mass movements, solutions to their problems must be found for them as groups, not as individuals. Because there appears to be no ready solution to this situation, government and public hostility to refugees world-wide has reached an alarming level. The High Commissioner calls on his readers to recognize the interdependence of refugee problems on these other international problems, and to realize that the refugee situation requires a global strategy, that it can no longer be addressed merely as a humanitarian problem adequately dealt with by international assistance and adherence to legal norms. Hocké argues for an international approach involving co-ordinated and collective action by states to address root causes of refugee flows, to assign responsibility to states for causing refugee movements, to improve human rights within countries of origin, and to define and discover appropriate political responses to refugee problems. With this framework within which to address and resolve refugee problems, the High Commissioner sets the stage for many of the chapters that follow.

Jonas Widgren maintains that during recent years a growing link has been observable between refugee movements and the pattern of global migration from South to North. As a result the problem of refugees can be perceived correctly as part of the more general issue of international migration. Like Hocké, he believes that only by considering refugees in the context of other problems such as population pressure, economic under-development, wars, and ecological disasters can the international community begin to fashion more comprehensive and effective means of response to what is arguably the most pressing humanitarian problem facing the international political system. Recalling how past large-scale migrations have substantially 'contributed to European dynamism and development', Widgren points towards a solution with a concept of 'free zones of circulation' in which human resources could be used and expanded for the benefit of people in an increasing number of places around the world.

By its very nature, a sudden mass movement of refugees requires an immediate, rapid response on the part of international organizations, states, and voluntary agencies. Randolph Kent looks at the political process involved in generating international and national responses within the context of disaster relief in general. He paints a picture of how the various governments, agencies, and hierarchies within this disaster response system function, often at cross purposes to one another. In doing so, he makes a clear case for the need for a reliable and consistent mechanism for dealing with the frequently 'predictable' disasters which often include or create refugees.

Deterrence, detention, and special needs

The second section of the book defines several current dimensions of the refugee problem. Elly-Elikunda Mtango addresses the disturbing and widespread problem of military attacks on refugee camps and settlements. Armed attacks on refugees in places as diverse as Southern Africa, Central America, the Middle East, and South-east Asia have increased in recent years, and dramatically underscore the need for more effective physical protection of refugees and displaced persons. National armies attack with impunity both refugees and civilian communities based near refugee camps and settlements. South Africa, for example, has regularly attacked camps in Angola, Botswana, Zambia, and Lesotho, and the Vietnamese armed forces have repeatedly attacked Cambodian refugees encamped along the Thai border. As Mtango indicates, however, neither UNHCR nor any other humanitarian agency is adequately equipped to ensure the physical safety of these refugees. Although for many years nation states have given considerable attention to this issue within the context of the UNHCR Executive Committee, a variety of political interests which Mtango documents have prevented agreement on a comprehensive set of principles. Indeed, governments have only recently reached agreement on a set of 'Conclusions'. However, Mtango feels that these Conclusions fall short of the solemn declaration and international legal instrument required to guarantee the physical security of refugees. He reiterates the need for continued political attention to this critical issue, and the need to adopt new legal standards and norms to deal with it.

Another related but even more alarming development is the steady erosion of those international norms of refugee protection and basic principles of human rights which have evolved as a result of such enormous effort since World War II. As indicated earlier, government responses to refugees are becoming more restrictive throughout the world, with deterrents being used to make it impossible for people to seek asylum easily. The adoption of these repugnant but now commonplace responses threatens all the gains made over previous decades in raising the level of international respect for human rights. Using the case of South-east Asia, Dennis McNamara describes the evolution and use of the policy of so-called 'humane deterrence' which has been adopted by governments in the region to deter potential refugees or asylum-seekers by means of harsh treatment. Initially implemented against Kampuchean refugees in Thailand, 'humane deterrence' became the policy adopted throughout South-east Asia and in Hong Kong. There is little evidence that these inhumane measures have any deterrent effect. McNamara argues, for example, that even after years of the rigid closed camp policy in Hong Kong, it has yet to be proved that 'humane deterrence' has had any effect in discouraging people from leaving Vietnam. Indeed, frustrated by the ineffectiveness of these measures to deter new arrivals, the Hong Kong authorities introduced even stricter measures in June 1988. All Vietnamese boat people arriving in Hong Kong would be treated as illegal immigrants and most of them would face repatriation to Vietnam when and if Hanoi agreed to take them back. Unfortunately, 'humane deterrence' is not confined to Asian countries. European and North American governments have also adopted measures which include the imposition of visas; the fining of airline companies for carrying undocumented aliens; detention; severe limitations on the right of residence, accommodation, employment, social welfare benefits, and counselling and advice services in order to discourage the arrival of new asylum-seekers. These measures are described in several of the chapters.

Arthur Helton, as a human rights lawyer, examines the nature of and the rationale behind one of these deterrent measures, detention, which is widely practised in different forms by nearly all governments. Prolonged detention in camps and prisons, often in dirty and humiliating conditions, has a dramatic effect on the psychological state, morale, and integration capacities of asylum-seekers. These practices are inconsistent with basic guarantees of dignity, supposedly upheld by law and by official government policies. Helton argues that detention is an extremely dubious practice under the terms of international law and that the failure to develop a more serious and positive policy towards the complexities of global mass forced migration constitutes an inappropriate response to the international dimensions of the refugee problem.

Women are particularly traumatized by life in exile. They face both physical dangers and difficulties particular to their traditional roles, which take different forms according to the various stages of refugee movement. In transit, women are vulnerable to physical attack and even abduction. Even in the relative safety of the camps and settlements, problems persist. Life in exile is characterized by the fragmentation of families and communities. The lack of privacy and the impossibility of maintaining the culture and values that once shaped their identity have had a grave effect on refugee women's morale and psychological state. Fundamental social changes have taken place among many refugee women who have been forced by circumstances to take on a more independent role. They have become important income earners, and in some cases household heads and the main providers. Geneviève Camus-Jacques discusses these special problems of women refugees, describing their plight and identifying their special needs for protection and assistance. She argues that more concerted action is needed to deal with their specific problems and to allow women to participate more fully in decision-making that affects them.

Closely related, and also neglected, is the issue of refugee children. Children make up over 50 per cent of the world's refugee population and, like women, they have special need for protection and assistance which are often unmet or overlooked. There is now a compelling case to be made for recognizing the specific protection, material, and psychological needs of both groups under international law. The High Commissioner's October 1987 Note on Refugee Children and the subsequent Conclusions reached in the sub-committee on International Protection seem to offer hope that, in the case of children at least, this need is beginning to be acknowledged. The special but entirely separate problems faced by women refugees, however, are only beginning to receive sufficient attention by UNHCR and governments.

Non-governmental organizations (NGOs) have always played an important role in refugee policy matters, but to date the considerable influence of NGOs on refugee policy-making has been largely ignored by scholars. International public law does not regulate the establishment of NGOs, nor does it provide a legal status for them to operate within the territory of states in which they carry out their activities. NGOs' role can sometimes be wider than that of international government organizations, especially in matters of protection. As concern for the refugee is their paramount commitment, if not their *raison d'être*, they serve as both a promoter of existing instruments and an advocate of humanitarian change in process and practice. The scale of private resources to which NGOs have access each year is enormous. Nevertheless, in most instances, it is governments and UNHCR and not NGOs which establish the framework for relief and development activities.

Elizabeth Ferris, of the World Council of Churches, examines the changing-role of Church-related NGOs. She argues that in the past NGOs saw themselves as humanitarian, non-partisan organizations which co-operated with governments to extend relief or to resettle refugees world-wide. In today's increasingly politicized refugee environment, however, at least some Church-related NGOs no longer perceive themselves as non-partisan actors and are frequently in direct conflict with international organizations and governments. Moreover, Ferris maintains that the potential of NGOs to affect the contemporary refugee situation is great, whether it be by providing information, assistance, protection, or networking and conflict resolution skills. Church-related NGOs in particular are upgrading their collective analysis of refugee problems and their advocacy work at national and international levels to promote more humane refugee policies. In the belief that they speak with more weight and influence when they speak collectively rather than as individual entities, Churches have been co-operating with their national and regional partners and across faiths to pursue a more active advocacy role on refugee issues.

Asylum crisis in Europe and North America

The last two chapters of this section focus on the asylum crisis in Europe. Roy McDowall, a former British government official and an active participant in the Council of Europe's deliberations over refugee policy during the past fifteen years, examines the erosion of refugee protection and the lack of co-ordination among European states concerning refugee policy. In the past Europe responded generously to the resettlement of Hungarians and Czechs and to the refugee influxes from outside Europe such as those from Chile and Vietnam. McDowall argues, however, that the refugees resulting from recent wars and civil disturbances in the Third World today increasingly migrate to Europe and North America in a 'less orderly fashion', often bypassing established refugee processing channels. European governments, he maintains, seriously question whether their societies can absorb such large influxes of foreigners, and have reacted in both disparate and unilateral ways to restrict the entry of asylum-seekers. Like several of the other contributors, McDowall argues for a more global approach to the refugee problem, to include in particular the linking of development aid with regional resettlement. At the same time, he maintains that states should exercise their sovereign right to return persons denied asylum or refugee status to their countries of origin or embarkation. This attitude, typical of a growing number of states, contrasts markedly with the position taken by UNHCR. The UNHCR recommends that Western governments offer at least temporary refuge to the large numbers of persons fleeing civil conflict and man-made disaster, even though they do not meet the narrow refugee definition contained in the 1951 Convention and 1967 Protocol. To act otherwise would represent a striking reversal of the entire concept and structure of refugee protection as it has developed during the past four decades. Many governments, however, are opposed to this point of view, and as they have become progressively more restrictive in their policies towards asylum-seekers, they have tended to exclude UNHCR from their consultations and joint actions concerning refugees.

The situation of these *de facto* refugees in Europe, that is groups such as Tamils, Iranians, Palestinians, Lebanese, and Ghanaians, is examined by Johan Cels. He argues that the current restrictive measures being adopted by European states are based on a misrepresentation of the nature and scale of the problem of *de facto* refugees. Cels points out that the combined number of refugees in Western Europe amounts to less than 5 per cent of the total estimated world refugee population. The main burden of refugee movements falls on developing countries. Moreover, Cels argues that European states are responding in excessively negative and counter-productive ways, and are retreating from hitherto agreed and observed norms of humanitarian law and convention. By so doing, it is clear that governments are ignoring the real issues posed by the global refugee crisis: repression, poverty, unchecked demographic growth, superpower rivalries, local wars, arms sales, natural disasters, and famines. These are the issues that press for a concerted, global attack on the root causes of the mass flows of forced migrants. European governments must fulfil their humanitarian and legal obligations by playing an active role on economic and diplomatic fronts in this attack.

Appropriate responses

The third section of the book concerns the search for appropriate responses to refugee problems. Many of these problems are closely linked to seemingly politically intractable regional conflicts. A large percentage of the world's refugee population consists of persons who have been refugees and have lived in camps for many years. As a result of this stalemate the bulk of UNHCR's resources is now spent in many instances on care and maintenance programmes in refugee camps in the Third World rather than on finding alternative solutions to refugee situations or on protecting the rights of refugees. This failure to resolve refugee problems has led to what has been termed a 'crisis in durable solutions'. The chapters in the third section, therefore, examine the prospects for those traditional durable solutions to refugee problems employed by the international community over the past four decades—repatriation, resettlement, and local integration—and offer more imaginative ways of dealing with refugee problems for the future.

The chapter by Jacques Cuénod, recently of ACORD, a leading consortium of development agencies, which opens this section presents proposals which figure, in some form or other, in many of the other chapters. Cuénod offers a practical plan of action, in which he analyses the way in which refugee aid can be orientated more towards long-term development objectives. Arguing against prolonged relief programmes for refugees, Cuénod proposes a reorientation of refugee assistance programmes towards development and integration schemes. He believes that aid should be directed towards people on the basis of their need rather than as a category, 'refugees'. In this way the presence of refugees can have a positive impact on host countries. Because most countries which host the majority of the world's refugees are poor, it is unrealistic to expect them to bear the brunt of the resettlement burden when they cannot even adequately provide for their own nationals. Cuénod details the way in which an international fund could be established and implemented to promote a development programme designed to help refugees and host nationals alike.

The repatriation of refugees, a current priority of industrialized states and of the UNHCR, has become a major source of contention between UNHCR and voluntary agencies and human rights NGOs. Several of the contributors here believe voluntary repatriation to be the most satisfactory solution for refugees, and programmes to return refugees to states which have overthrown repressive regimes are relatively uncontroversial. However, the promotion of repatriation to those countries which are still ruled by regimes whose policies of terror were the original cause of the refugees' flight is highly controversial and is the subject of heated debate and polarized opinion. Repatriation depends on the refugees' willingness to return home and on substantial changes in those conditions in the country of origin which led to the refugees' flight in the first place. Guy Goodwin-Gill highlights several of the critical issues concerning voluntary repatriation, including the question of information regarding conditions in the country of origin; the use of 'coercion' or active 'encouragement' to be repatriated; the cessation or revocation of refugee status; and the means of ensuring the security of refugees once they have returned home. While acknowledging the difficulty of determining whether circumstances in a country of origin have changed sufficiently to warrant return and national reconciliation, Goodwin-Gill argues that international law and human rights norms fully support voluntary repatriation as the preferred international solution to refugee problems. Other authors, such as Gervase Coles, argue that repatriation is the most humane and realistic solution since most refugees want to return home above everything else.

Nevertheless, many human rights organizations and voluntary agencies continue to express concern about the conception of and rationale behind many current repatriation programmes, including the repatriation of Ethiopian refugees from Djibouti, Chadian refugees from the Sudan, and several other situations. To many observers, current programmes to repatriate Ethiopians, Chadians, Ugandans, Mozambicans, Salvadoreans, and Guatemalans, among others, seem to be extremely risky for the refugees concerned, given the lack of physical and economic security existing in the countries of origin. Concern has been voiced that repatriation is promoted by

UNHCR and governments as a means to at least partially 'resolve' the financial burdens imposed by long-standing refugee populations. The obligation to support returnees to their home countries is shorter-lived and less expensive than are programmes for maintaining refugees in their country of asylum. In his chapter, Guy Goodwin-Gill makes a detailed analysis of the legal and political dimensions of voluntary repatriation and discusses the background and events of one of the more controversial repatriations in recent years—that of Ethiopian refugees from Djibouti.

A key feature of many repatriations is that they are spontaneous, rather than being prompted by any international agency or government. In numerical terms alone, spontaneous movements have been far more significant than planned repatriations. Refugees have always returned to their homes when conditions allowed, even in the most unpropitious circumstances, and yet it is difficult to find adequate information about these repatriations. Fred Cuny and Barry Stein examine the history of spontaneous repatriation and outline the conditions under which it can be facilitated. For repatriation—whether planned or spontaneous—to be successful, most of the contributors to this volume would agree that development assistance, in order to create a favourable economic and social environment, must be channelled into those areas to which the refugees wish to return.

Resettlement

Third country resettlement is no longer a favoured solution to refugee problems. In the aftermath of World War II and the Hungarian Uprising, the majority of the refugees who were resettled were, generally speaking, culturally homogeneous with the major settlement countries, which were largely the industrialized societies. A quick survey of the current refugee populations indicates that this is no longer the case. Coupled with their own economic difficulties and a growing xenophobia in many countries, Western nations are increasingly reluctant to take in large groups of people who are not easily assimilable. In the view of many observers, the movement in recent years of well over a million Indo-Chinese refugees from South-east Asia to the industrialized countries, and the difficulties that have been encountered, have contributed to 'compassion fatigue' and the unwillingness of industrialized states to take on such seemingly open-ended commitments again.

Robert Bach discusses the difficulties surrounding resettlement. In particular he points to the domestic problems of resettlement, such as the social, economic, and cultural interactions of refugees with the people of the industrialized countries. Because refugees today often have fewer political and cultural links with the receiving countries, legal and political concepts and practices, which have been tried and tested for more homogeneous and Westernized groups of refugees in the past, are no longer directly applicable to new arrivals. A new restrictive attitude towards asylum-seekers has emerged in the West generally; local authorities protest at the adverse financial impact of refugee resettlement; and the perception among governments, particularly that of the United States, that refugees are unduly dependent on welfare 'handouts', is widespread. According to Bach, the major difficulty confronting resettled refugees, and the principal issue to which policy-makers should address themselves in the future, is the uncertain or insecure legal status which makes full access to the host countries' institutions and economic opportunities impossible. Without this minimum of human and civil rights, resettled refugees face economic and other hardships and are unable to participate fully in their new countries.

Despite a growing disenchantment with overseas resettlement, some level of commitment to this kind of response seems necessary, particularly if a major refugee crisis, requiring resettlement as a solution, were to occur in the future. For first-asylum countries already suffering from massive unemployment or from acute cultural and ethnic divisions, resettlement means that asylum can continue to be extended to new arrivals because the refugee burden will eventually be shared. In addition, expansion of resettlement opportunities in Western states through a quota system might help to reduce the uncertainties surrounding the arrival of unexpected asylum-seekers and limit the incidence of irregular entrants. In sum, resettlement remains an important way of responding (humanely and equitably) to certain refugee problems.

Another prominent feature of the contemporary refugee situation is that an increasingly large proportion of the world's refugees are the victims of civil and social unrest and conflict. As several authors in this volume have illustrated, many in these groups, such as Tamils from Sri Lanka, and Central Americans, do not easily fall within the definition of 'refugee' set forth in the 1951 Convention, but are nevertheless in need of temporary protection since they cannot be returned to their home countries under present circumstances. Dennis Gallagher, Susan Forbes Martin, and Patricia Weiss-Fagen examine the history of safe haven responses in the industrialized countries and argue for greater use of these mechanisms, especially in the short term, to improve the capacity of the international community to respond effectively and humanely to the sudden arrival of political exiles in North America and Western Europe.

One of the commonly stressed priorities for UNHCR and other international aid agencies is the need to establish mechanisms to make timely responses to future refugee emergencies. It is now fashionable to speak about devising early warning systems to anticipate forced migrations. Although developing sophisticated methods of predicting emergencies could be helpful in the future, in many situations local sources of information about impending disasters or migrations are already available and are routinely ignored. Moreover, no matter how advanced the early warning system, political obstacles will frequently make it impossible to react quickly enough to minimize suffering and problems. As researchers have pointed out, the Ethiopian government and international agencies had warned of the impending 1985 famine as early as 1981, but governments chose to ignore these warnings, mainly for political reasons,[20] and international agencies were not able to raise the money to respond to the famine at a time when it was still manageable.

Leon Gordenker provides a case for the plausibility and value of early warning systems that would give time to improve the conditions that cause a refugee exodus in the first place, and provide the opportunity for contingency planning and emergency assistance to be mobilized. Although Gordenker recognizes the formidable obstacles involved in any such system, he feels that, on some scale, this kind of predictive model could be workable. He carefully and systematically analyses these obstacles at every stage of the refugee process and response mechanism. In his analysis of the issues involved in enlisting co-operation, he presents a picture of the

[20] See Fred Cuny's chapter in Gil Loescher and Bruce Nichols (eds.), *The Moral Nation: Humanitarianism and US Foreign Policy Today* (Notre Dame, Ind., and London: University of Notre Dame Press, 1989).

realpolitik of refugee matters in general. It seems that, in the absence of sufficient political will to resolve refugee problems, measures that might be taken to prevent or to prepare for future refugee flows, such as the institution of an early warning system, are likely to be of only marginal relevance. The value of such measures depends largely on the political will of states and international organizations to take the necessary concerted action.

In the concluding chapter of the book, Gervase Coles outlines the weaknesses of the present international refugee regime, which have prevented it from finding solutions to refugee situations, and offers proposals for taking initiatives designed to obtain these solutions. Since its inception over thirty-five years ago, UNHCR has relied to a great extent on resettlement in the traditional immigration countries as the normal solution to these problems. In the process UNHCR downplayed or ignored altogether the question of developing relations with the creators of refugees, the countries of origin. In the absence of any such relations, voluntary repatriation programmes were difficult to negotiate, and the burden of the refugee problem fell on neighbouring host countries or resettlement nations overseas. In recent years the sheer size of many refugee movements has made permanent local settlement or resettlement elsewhere difficult and even unacceptable to some countries. In addition, Coles maintains that the majority of refugees now flee countries where armed conflicts rage and living conditions have radically deteriorated. The fact that the danger facing many of these refugees often does not affect individuals as such and is not discriminatory in nature makes permanent external resettlement neither necessary nor appropriate. The almost sole reliance on external resettlement, Coles argues, is untenable and provides neither a humane nor a realistic approach to contemporary problems. Thus, the question of determining appropriate responses has inevitably become more pertinent and pressing.

A more general, flexible, and cosmopolitan response is needed which both reflects the diversity and complexity of the causes of refugee movements and provides for greater international co-operation on this issue. What is needed in particular is many more efforts at collective management and strengthening existing international refugee institutions. Coles outlines a number of political and administrative measures which, if taken, would alleviate the plight of millions of refugees, as well as help resolve some of today's seemingly intractable political problems. However, given the nature, size, and complexity of today's refugee problem, no overall permanent solution, or 'quick fix', can be expected. Rather, the aim of this introductory chapter, and indeed of the entire book, is to indicate directions for more effective approaches to refugee situations at present and in the future.

I

The International Framework

1. Beyond Humanitarianism

The Need for Political Will to Resolve Today's Refugee Problem

JEAN-PIERRE HOCKÉ

THERE are today some 12 million refugees spread all over the world. No region is spared the agony of the tragic movements of scores of men, women, and children, uprooted from their homes and land because of armed conflict and intolerance. They seek either temporary refuge, pending a change of circumstances that will allow their return home in safety and dignity, or new homes where they can re-establish their lives in peace and security. Whether viewed in terms of numbers, causes, or geography, the world today is faced with a refugee problem, the dimensions of which have never been experienced before and the consequences of which, if left unchecked, will be profound.

The overwhelming majority of the world's refugees both originate and are found in the developing countries of the Third World, which are least able, because of their own population pressures and economic difficulties, to assume this added burden. Consider the fact that there are some 3 million refugees in Pakistan, 2 million in Iran, over a million in Sudan, hundreds of thousands in Somalia, and tens of thousands in various other countries in Asia, Africa, and Central America, not to mention the tragic situation of millions of Palestinian refugees still awaiting a solution to their plight almost forty years after becoming homeless. The numbers continue to rise as new groups of asylum-seekers emerge before solutions are found for the old.

Unlike the not too distant past when most refugees had the opportunity to integrate into and become useful and productive members of their host societies, today's refugees often find themselves confined in overcrowded refugee camps and settlements. For many people this has become the normal way of life. Its perpetuation crushes human dignity and reduces the human capacity for hope and regeneration. This must necessarily be a blot on the human conscience. Another aspect of this situation is that among today's refugees we often find entire communities, tribes, or other groups who have moved *en masse* and for whom solutions must be found not individually but as groups.

The technological revolution in particular has added a whole new dimension to the refugee problem, for today's refugees not only cross land borders but also travel by sea and by air. The spontaneous movement of large numbers of asylum-seekers from one continent to another, particularly from the developing countries to the developed, industrialized nations of the West, helped by easily available air transport, has given rise to new tensions and hostilities towards refugees and asylum-seekers. These asylum-seekers either come directly from their countries of origin or via a country of first asylum in their region of origin. These movements, more than anything else in recent years, have severely shaken existing refugee law and practice in the West. Governments have reacted to these unscheduled arrivals with refugee policies which are defensive in nature and determined by the imperative of deterrence.

In my view the above perspectives provide but a faint picture of the major problems of today. It is now established that the world population is growing at the rate of over one million every five days, with nine-tenths of this increase in the poorer countries of the Third World. The strain this puts on to scarce natural resources, on to economies, and on to the social structures of these countries is well known. Unemployment increases rapidly, giving rise first to internal migrations and then to movements abroad. With exhausted economies and accumulating foreign debts, the developing countries continue to struggle with underdevelopment, unable to cope with the increasing needs and rising expectations of their growing populations.

Taken together, these factors constitute a perfect breeding ground for social tension and unrest. Internal conflicts may give rise in turn to international tension, armed conflict, and sometimes external threat, which often serve as a justification for internal repression, leading to the infringement of human rights. This then triggers the exodus of refugees. And so the chain continues.

Because the major problems of the world today are intertwined in this way, they have to be tackled globally, with joint efforts by all countries, rich and poor, north and south, east and west. The refugee problem can no longer be treated in isolation but must be addressed within the context of an international strategy which addresses all of the relevant factors. No purpose would seem to be served by continuing to look at today's refugee movements solely in the context of the existing legal framework, which does not begin to cover the entire spectrum of involuntary movement.

Let me dwell a little on the last point. The Office of the United Nations High Commissioner for Refugees was set up in 1951, against the backdrop of refugee movements from Eastern Europe. These refugees were received, integrated, and resettled mainly in the Western industrialized states. The wave of sympathy and the ancient cultural and ethnic affinities between the populations of the receiving countries and these European refugees made their reception and integration relatively smooth. This experience led to the development and adoption of international standards according to which refugees should be treated. These standards are embodied in the 1951 United Nations Convention Relating to the Status of Refugees.

In the 1960s emphasis shifted to the Third World, to decolonization, and to wars of national liberation. The sense of brotherhood forged through common experience and suffering, particularly on the African continent, and the generous humanitarian assistance from the international community as a whole, made the reception and maintenance of hundreds of thousands of refugees a relatively easy affair. Moreover, on the attainment of their countries' independence, it was the task of the High Commissioner to help them return home to rebuild their lives and their newly independent countries. A fine example of a regional approach in developing normative standards for the treatment of refugees was the adoption of the 1969 OAU Convention Governing the Specific Aspects of Refugee Problems in Africa.

In the 1970s refugee movements became increasingly complex. First, the numbers were much larger than before. Who can forget the staggering 10 million East Pakistani refugees in India in 1971. Second, the movements were caused mainly by political and armed conflicts in existing independent nation states. Unlike during the period of decolonization, the prospects for political solutions and for removing the root causes of flight became more problematic. The East Pakistani refugee problem ended successfully with the creation of Bangladesh and the return of the refugees to their newly independent state, but the problems of other important refugee groups, such as those from the Indo-Chinese countries, continue to fester. After almost fifteen years the Indo-Chinese refugee problem is still with us, even though over 1.2 million persons have been resettled in third countries during this period. Third, the problems which gave rise to refugee movements during this decade were further complicated by the socio-economic factors to which I have already referred.

The situation in the present decade has been aggravated not only by the dramatic rise in the number of refugees and asylum-seekers in the developing world but also by the growing movement of asylum-seekers from the Third World to the developed, industrialized states in the West. Liberal asylum traditions have been jolted by the new reality of asylum-seekers who come straight from distant lands on the wings of a revolutionized air transport system. These are the 'jet people' of the 1980s, who have succeeded the 'boat people' of the 1970s. There is a growing perception in Western countries that their generosity in providing homes not only for refugees emanating from their own region, but also for large numbers of refugees from other areas, is being overstrained and in some cases abused by common 'fortune-seekers'. The expression 'compassion fatigue' is now common coinage.

Although this deterioration in attitude towards refugees and asylum-seekers may, under the circumstances, be understandable, it does not make it any less serious a concern for all those who believe in an international humanitarian order. If the human capacity for compassion declines, man's worth is diminished and humanitarian action is threatened.

I am particularly concerned about the growing negative public opinion in the West *vis-à-vis* refugees and asylum-seekers from the Third World. Many governments in the West have responded to the recent influxes of refugees by adopting restrictive practices, a reaction that has tended to prove contagious. Humanitarian principles, so carefully nurtured in the West over the past few decades, are under threat. Basic standards of refugee protection are being lowered. Refugees are being used as political tools in domestic party politics. In this process the basic human values which serve as the reference point for all humanitarian activities are being devalued. This erosion of values must be checked, and I am sure it can be done, provided that states exercise their political judgement and will to do so, bearing in mind the immeasurably serious consequences of acting otherwise.

Given both the size and complexity of the world refugee problem, it is time that the international community took a fresh look at the legal instruments available, and identified a political means to address the problem more effectively. The academic community can play a very useful role here: I have no doubt that the development of a body of critical and independent literature encompassing the crucial areas of concern would be of great assistance, not only to my Office but also to the international community as a whole, in charting new directions both in policy and practice. To this process, my presentation is but a modest contribution.

So far I have mainly tried to set the context of today's refugee problem. My basic premiss is that the refugee problem is a world-wide phenomenon, and that it is inextricably linked with the other major international problems of the present time. Hence, because it can no longer be seen as a problem particular to a country or region, a common, global approach to it has become imperative. The refugee problem should therefore be of concern to governments and peoples everywhere, and its solution should be considered to be in the best interests of all states.

My second premiss is that the law relating to the contemporary refugee situation must amount to more than a law relating to the legal status and protection of refugees—it must be a law encompassing the refugee problem as a whole. The primary concern of this law should be the refugee or asylum-seeker—the victim of persecution or violence. I call this a victim-orientated approach. The needs of the victim should guide the search for appropriate solutions.

My third premiss is that the refugee problem concerns not only individuals in their relations with states, but also states in their relations with one another. As long as the emphasis is put on the former, the refugee problem is bound to remain on the periphery of international relations. Today's refugee problem demands that it be brought into the mainstream of international concern so that more attention can be given to solutions, whether they are to be found in the country of final destination, in intermediate countries, or in the country of origin. Such an approach will enable countries of origin to be associated with efforts to find comprehensive solutions, especially in establishing conditions favourable to voluntary repatriation and in limiting the causes of refugee movements. Humanitarian interventions on behalf of refugees are no longer sufficient if made without reference to the political situations which have given rise to the refugees' flight. The humanitarian objectives and the political will of governments to seek out the root causes of refugee movements must converge. States must be ready to take a collective and responsible approach to all refugee problems. The Office of the High Commissioner, which is a creation of states, can fulfil its mandate only with the full co-operation of states. The UNHCR can only be as effective as states are willing to make it. Gone is the time when states could feel good by just contributing financially to the High Commissioner's humanitarian programmes and work with refugees. Today's High Commissioner needs more than the humanitarian support of governments: he also needs their collective political will to explore solutions to refugee situations. While the High Commissioner undertakes the necessary humanitarian action, states should also explore all possible political initiatives.

Let me now elaborate on the above premisses. What do we mean by a global approach? As I stated earlier, today's refugee problem affects all regions. The same refugee groups are found throughout the world; for example, Afghans, Iranians and Sri Lankan Tamils have sought asylum not only in those countries bordering their region of origin, but also in various countries in the West. Responses based on purely national interest and domestic considerations only deflect the problem from one country to another. These may serve short-term national goals but are no solution to the underlying humanitarian problem. What is needed is a co-ordinated global approach which addresses the problem in all its aspects. In the short run, this co-ordinated policy would mean that, when faced with similar refugee problems, states should consult with each other and with UNHCR and adopt an approach which takes full account of all the aspects of a given refugee situation, its implications for the various states affected, and the extent to which it can be dealt with by combined action. In recognition of the need for this kind of approach, a number of

Western governments have been participating in consultations which have been organized by my Office in recent years. The same kind of co-ordinated global approach should also be undertaken to address the root causes of refugee movements, a subject to which I shall return later.

Now, what do I mean by a victim-orientated approach? I believe that the basic principle guiding all humanitarian action should be the principle of humanity. In refugee affairs this means that the interests of the refugee or asylum-seeker as a human being should take precedence over the possibly conflicting interests of states. By putting humanitarian principles first, states will discover it is in this way that they can also safeguard their true political interests. Humanitarian need must be acknowledged before all others. Given the complexity of circumstances that cause refugee movements today, it should not be possible for governments to deny humanitarian treatment just because a person or group of people are unable to meet the qualifications set down in the 1951 Convention. This would be a legalistic and static approach, doctrinaire rather than doctrinal. If the people concerned are unable to show 'a well-founded fear of persecution' to qualify as refugees, as required by the 1951 Convention, but nevertheless have valid reasons for not wanting to go back home, they must still qualify at least for temporary asylum and humane treatment. Governments must continue to assume responsibility for them until they can return home. In my view large numbers of asylum-seekers today fall into the grey zone—those who do not fully qualify under the international legal instruments, but nevertheless need international protection. I call them the extra-Conventional refugees, who may not be entitled to receive the status provided for under the 1951 Convention but who must nevertheless receive humanitarian treatment until a co-ordinated international effort leads to an appropriate solution to their problems, including the possibility, eventually, of returning home in safety and dignity.

As we have already seen, the vast majority of today's refugees and asylum-seekers in the developing countries of the Third World do not correspond to the formal definition of a refugee provided for in the 1951 Refugee Convention. In other words, they are not all victims of persecution because of race, religion, nationality, or political opinion. They belong to the wider category of people who leave their countries because of the danger to their lives and livelihood caused by armed conflict and other forms of violence. The recognition by the international community that such persons are in need of international protection is evident in the various resolutions adopted by the General Assembly, and in its assistance to my Office on their behalf. If such persons move to other regions they must remain of concern to the international community until appropriate solutions are found for them. There cannot be different standards for different regions. The main criterion for enlisting the help of the High Commissioner, and equally of states, should be *the existence of a need for international protection.*

I would urge, however, that, given the seriousness of the current situation, we do not get bogged down in controversy over the definition of who is, or who is not, a 'real' refugee. Let us recognize that the 1951 Convention definition, based on the concept of 'individual persecution', is no longer adequate to address all facets of today's refugee problem. It was not framed to respond to the large-scale influxes we frequently encounter today. It is moreover an instrument intended to facilitate lasting or permanent settlement/asylum within a country outside the country of origin, whereas with many of today's large-scale influxes, where entire communities or tribes are involved, there is no alternative but to try to achieve voluntary repatriation under appropriate conditions. Therefore in my view states should, as a matter of course, allow those who fulfil the criteria to receive the care provided for by the Convention. But states, with the active support of the international community, must also assume responsibility fot the extra-Conventional category until an appropriate solution is found to their problems.

Given the present restrictive mood of states, I do not think, however, that we should talk about a formal legal regime for this category. On the other hand, states must also realize that they cannot simply legislate their way out of the present predicament. You cannot prevent people who have compelling reasons for leaving their country from fleeing to another country for refuge. You must address the reasons which prompted their flight. In the meantime there is a need for co-ordinated efforts by governments and by UNHCR and its partners to develop practices which are both humane and socially responsible. Once such practices are applied generally, they will develop into an agreed doctrine; over time the doctrine will evolve into law. In my view this is the most natural way of developing humanitarian law.

Let me now turn to my third premiss. What do I mean by the political will of states to address root causes? As I said earlier, today's refugee problem can no longer be tackled through humanitarian assistance alone. For those large numbers of people who belong to the extra-Conventional category, the only solution lies in attending to the root cause, first to remove the reason for further flows where refugee movements appear likely to continue, and then to reverse the flow through the creation of appropriate conditions for the voluntary repatriation of those who have already left. I realize that this is not an easy task and may not succeed in many cases but an effort must be made and initiatives must be taken, for, invariably, the causes of a problem and the solution to that problem are integrally linked.

When I talk about addressing root causes, let me also make it clear that it is primarily the community of states which must take initiatives in the matter. The UNHCR is willing to play the role that governments themselves wish it to play in order to facilitate such initiatives.

An analysis of the root causes of the major refugee movements of today would reveal two main contributory factors: armed conflicts or serious internal disturbances, and human rights violations. These are themselves only too often the result of disparities between rich and poor countries, which have existed for many years, with all the manifold consequences inherent in this disparity.

I believe that a collective approach by the international community can have a decisive impact on armed conflicts and serious internal disturbances. Similarly, any international approach towards durable or permanent solutions must also include action to improve the human rights situation within the country of origin and to ensure that country accepts the responsibilities of statehood. The acceptance of the law of state responsibility in the field of refugee law is seriously deficient. This is a particular area in which more attention is called for from the international community. The concept of state responsibility will bring the country of origin more fully into the international system of response.

The root causes approach should apply not only to the country of origin but to intermediate receiving countries also. As I indicated earlier, we are often confronted today with what one might call 'two-step refugee flows'; that is, refugees who first move to a neighbouring country in the region and, thereafter, because of unsatisfactory conditions there, move to another country, usually outside the region, where conditions are perceived to be more satisfactory. In such situations too it is of crucial importance that states exercise the political will to look into the root causes of the second movement, while at the same time making available appropriate financial and other assistance to the countries of first asylum in order to enable them to continue to provide temporary asylum to refugees in their territories.

There are two schools of thought about UNHCR's role *vis-à-vis* the root causes of refugee movement. Some believe that, for UNHCR to be effective in the handling of refugee problems and in finding appropriate solutions, it must take an active interest in all major disruptions which could or do lead to refugee flows across frontiers, and that it must try to contribute to their resolution. Others fear that, if UNHCR follows this line of action, it may become entangled in political controversy, and its humanitarian work may be blocked.

Although both concerns may be valid, I think it is possible to take a middle path. The UNHCR is, of course, bound by the statutory provisions of a 'humanitarian and non-political' organization. But where does one draw the line between the 'humanitarian' and the 'political'? Sometimes a facile distinction is made by referring to all actions aimed at the situation in the country of asylum as 'humanitarian' and any action aimed at the causes of the situation in the country of origin as 'political'. I reject this distinction. To me, any action which is aimed at and motivated by a concern for the well-being of human beings is 'humanitarian', whether this action relates to the country of asylum or the country of origin.

This being said, UNHCR must of course avoid any action that could be perceived as being incompatible with its strictly non-political, humanitarian mandate. The UNHCR must not take sides in hostilities or engage at any time in controversy, whether political, racial, religious, or ideological. On the other hand, UNHCR must be concerned with the question of root causes in order to be aware of the precise reasons for refugee flows, and thus be able to identify solutions in a more appropriate manner. Beyond this, UNHCR should, while preserving its non-political, humanitarian mandate, encourage governments to adopt a more active approach in considering the root causes of refugee flows.

Once we recognize that root causes are an essential factor to be taken into account, this will necessarily have an impact on our approach to refugee problems as they arise, while appropriate solutions are being sought, and until these solutions are finally implemented.

In all refugee situations, particularly those involving large numbers, two parallel and simultaneous actions should be taken by the international community right from the beginning. One is humanitarian, directed primarily towards alleviating human suffering and providing protection. The other is political, directed primarily towards attenuating the root causes and providing solutions. While UNHCR should concern itself with humanitarian action, it is the community of states which must undertake action in the political arena. The two actions must go hand-in-hand and complement each other.

As I stated earlier, in many of today's large-scale influxes, where entire communities or groups have fled, voluntary repatriation is the only realistic alternative to an indefinite dependence on charity. It is to this, therefore, that states must turn their attention first. The objective will be to secure a general improvement in the situation in the country of origin in order to create the necessary conditions for the voluntary return of refugees. I am aware that there is no easy formula for achieving this. Large-scale repatriations normally occur in response to clear-cut changes in the refugees' countries of origin—a change of regime, an end to armed conflict, a withdrawal of an occupying or colonial power, etc. I believe, however, that co-ordinated efforts by the community of states can also have a beneficial effect in other kinds of situations. The collective will of states and the political influence that they may be able to exert are certainly factors which cannot be disregarded. It should be pointed out here that promoting conditions favourable to voluntary repatriation is a dimension which is hardly ever taken into account in current international development aid programmes. There can be no doubt that if the impressive sum of some $1–3 billion made available annually by the international community for all kinds of humanitarian activity the world over were partly to be used for development aid, with particular reference to creating conditions conducive to voluntary repatriation, this could indeed go a long way to making that solution feasible.

It also should be recognized that efforts to implement voluntary repatriation, even if initially on a modest scale, may in themselves promote conditions for a more far-reaching solution. If, for example, a country of origin and a country of asylum could agree, despite their political differences, to the voluntary repatriation, say, of only the most vulnerable groups, such as the elderly, the handicapped, unaccompanied minors, etc., this would demonstrate in political terms that, despite the continuation of the conflict, the two states were willing to at least partially address the humanitarian problem. This in turn could help to alleviate the situation, to restore confidence, and to pave the way for the eventual voluntary repatriation of the entire group.

This example leads to a further reflection, which is relevant not only to voluntary repatriation but to the right approach to refugee problems in general. It must be recognized that the longer a refugee problem is allowed to stagnate, the more difficult the solutions are going to become. It has been observed in many refugee situations that over a period of time the refugees themselves become an integral part of the overall political problem, and may thus impede any solution. If human problems are not solved, there exists the real danger of exacerbating political tension. If humanitarian issues are ignored, states will only pay a higher political price at a later date.

From what I have said it follows that a constructive approach to refugee problems calls for parallel efforts to deal with both their humanitarian and their political aspects. These areas are closely interrelated and the attainment of positive results in one cannot but have a favourable impact on the other.

If the main emphasis of this chapter has been on the causes of and comprehensive solutions to refugee movements, it is because I believe that the international protection of refugees, for which my Office was created, can no longer be perceived in isolation from these factors. The humanitarian principles established for the treatment of refugees, together with the mechanisms for their implementation, represent an achievement of which the whole civilized world has reason to be proud. But, in order to ensure that this achievement is preserved, we need to look beyond humanitarianism and to find the political will to resolve today's refugee problems.

2. Europe and International Migration in the Future

The Necessity for Merging Migration, Refugee, and Development Policies

JONAS WIDGREN

DURING the four years I have been involved in European refugee affairs I have been struck by the lack of academic debate about and research into this burning issue. This stands in sharp contrast to the abundance of studies and the extensive international research co-operation in the field of labour migration in Europe, a field with which I have been associated during the last fifteen years. Given that these fields are two sides of the same coin—i.e. emigration from one's own country—it is only natural that practitioners in one field should draw upon the experience of the other.

However, there is another reason for linking research and policy in the field of humanitarian and refugee affairs with research relating to economically-based international migration. These two patterns of human migration have shown an increasing tendency to converge, given the present world situation which is characterized by denial of human rights, under-development, wars, and ecological disaster. These factors, among others, increasingly mesh together, but our tools for counteracting these disasters—which have already forced millions to move, and may well force many millions more in the future—are disparate, and we use them in an uncoordinated manner.

In this context I record a passage from the lecture given in Oxford by the new UN High Commissioner for Refugees M. Jean-Pierre Hocké:

> The major problems of the world today are [thus] intertwined . . . they have to be tackled globally, with joint efforts by all countries, rich and poor, North and South, East and West. The refugee problem can no

longer be treated in isolation but must be addressed within the context of an international strategy which addresses all of the relevant factors. No useful purpose would seem to be served by continuing to look at today's refugee movements solely in the context of the existing legal framework, which may not begin to cover the entire spectrum of involuntary movement.[1]

This quotation makes a good starting-point for this present exercise. What I shall try to do is (1) to indicate some past and future challenges to Europe in the field of international migration; (2) to enumerate existing mechanisms used to try to meet these challenges; and (3) briefly to launch some ideas for new European strategies in this area.

The chain of events

What precisely is 'this area'? The crucial problem is that the area has never been defined, since perspectives have changed so quickly. During the past thirty-five years European governments have more or less been involved in attacking only one problem at a time in the field of international migration, irrespective of the interrelationship of these problems. Roughly speaking, the chain of events has been as follows.[2]

The economic reconstruction of war-ravaged Europe quickly absorbed what in the 1950s was termed 'over-population', i.e. the refugees and the displaced persons from eastern and central Europe. One major problem for the Western European governments of the 1960s was the shortage of manpower and, as a result, some 10 million guestworkers were recruited from southern Europe. During this period of mass migration (1960–74) many refugees from the right-wing dictatorships of Greece, Spain, and Portugal were received under the name of guestworkers. But the oil shock of 1973–4 led to a halt in immigration, which is still in force, and nearly a million foreign workers were sent back home. The keyword for this period was *lack of labour*.

Democratization in southern Europe, along with some willing-

[1] Jean-Pierre Hocké, *Beyond Humanitarianism: The Need for Political Will to Resolve Today's Refugee Problems* (Lecture delivered at Oxford University, 29 Oct. 1986).

[2] See Jonas Widgren, *International Migration, New Challenges to Europe* (Strasbourg: Council of Europe, 1987).

ness by immigration countries to compensate for the earlier access to cheap labour, and also to prevent further out-migration, led to a European North–South dialogue on how to create jobs in southern Europe. At meetings of the Organization for Economic Co-operation and Development, the International Labour Organization, and the Council of Europe, national policy-makers discussed the need to attack the root causes of emigration in the countries surrounding the Mediterranean basin. The keyword here was *job creation in sending countries*.

By the late 1970s and the beginning of the 1980s the process of reuniting the refugee families of the 1940s and 1950s, and of integrating the guestworkers of the 1960s and early 1970s, had been completed, and they and their children had become permanent settlers. Thereafter discussions concentrated on improving their inferior legal and social status, for which the keyword was *social integration*.

At this point (1978–9) a refugee crisis in South-east Asia called for immediate international action. Western European governments had been dutifully paying their annual contributions to the UNHCR, many seeing the latter as an international agency which simply provided material support for refugees in *other* parts of the world, and arranged for high-level analytical exercises in the field of refugee law and policy. When hundreds of thousands of people fled Vietnam in small boats it was only natural for the countries of the Western world to take their fair share, in a well-organized transfer programme, based upon an agreed system of national quotas. As regards this particular Third World refugee problem at least, *humanitarian responsibility* was the keyword.

However, the steep rise in unemployment in Western Europe (from 9 million in 1979 to 19 million in 1985, many of whom were foreign workers), combined with high immigration levels, despite increased border control, gave rise to popular concern. In fact, in terms of annual registered immigration, Europe leads the whole OECD area. At present the Western European countries accept as many immigrants annually as the immigration countries of North America and Oceania admit together. In the mid-1980s the total European intake for one year amounted to 850,000, compared with that for the United States of 600,000, or for Canada of 100,000. Europe has never opted for immigration on demographic grounds, but it will certainly become a leading area of immigration in the future, whether it likes it or not. The way in which the European countries now react to the changes in migratory patterns is therefore extremely short-sighted.

What are the characteristics of these changes in migratory patterns? First, during the 1980s there has been a distinct increase in Third World immigration, mainly from Asia (of the total number of immigrants in Europe, non-European countries now account for 45 per cent). Second, whereas roughly 70 per cent of total immigration until the mid-1970s was accepted on economic grounds, the proportions are now reversed. As much as 80–5 per cent of legal immigration today is of a non-economic character and is accepted on social and humanitarian grounds, i.e. cases of family reunion, and refugees. The year 1985 seems to mark an historic turning-point because, since that year, the number of asylum-seekers has exceeded the number of legally admitted foreign workers. The number of asylum-seekers has increased from 50,000 in 1983 to 180,000 in 1986. Also, southern Europe is now experiencing increasing immigration pressures from non-European countries, and probably has a total of 2 million foreigners, of whom one-half are illegal. One reason for this pressure is that the 'employment safety valve' which the expanding Middle East oil-producing economies have provided for Mediterranean as well as Asian migrants since the mid-1970s is now being drastically reduced, as a result of falling oil prices (the oil-producing countries of the Persian Gulf have lost approximately $80 billion as a result of this fall in prices).

Increasing pressure of Third World immigration has had two effects on Europe. One has been a marked tendency of governments to reinforce border controls: *stricter immigration control* is the keyword. This is discussed in other chapters in this volume and I do not need to dwell on the matter further. I need only refer to the flood of unilateral measures in this field, which began to be undertaken by a number of European countries in the autumn of 1986.

The other effect has been the problem of xenophobia. There is a general feeling in all the immigration countries of Western Europe that hostile tendencies towards immigrants have been growing during recent years. Representatives of the various ethnic groups concerned energetically claim this to be the case. There are increasing reports in the media of racially motivated attacks against individual immigrants. Furthermore, there has been a resurgence of extreme right-wing parties in Western Europe, which base their appeal on anti-immigrant feeling. Responsible governments cannot but take this very seriously indeed, given the experience of history. The *combating of xenophobia* is an appropriate keyword here.

This tense situation has prompted European governments to look beyond the mounting problems of border control and the administration of asylum cases, of which some fit the refugee criteria, but still more do not. Contacts were established among the receiving countries most concerned which resulted in the 1985 Geneva consultations on the arrivals of refugees and asylum-seekers to Europe, and the ensuing meetings in Stockholm and The Hague. This consultative mechanism was to develop, together with the UNHCR, a scheme for increased UNHCR presence in the Third World, increased support to (mainly) non-European countries of first asylum, the organized transfer of emergency cases to Europe, continued respect for and application of the Geneva Convention, and long-term policies for the combating of root causes of emigration. The keywords became *burden-sharing and regionalization.*

Finally, to those of us responsible for policy-making in the field of international migration, still another phenomenon has quickly grown in significance over recent years. The keyword here is *international terrorism.* It is no coincidence that asylum policies are being discussed simultaneously these days at meetings of the UNHCR and in confidential meetings of ministers of the interior. International terrorism is a real threat, and terrorism must be combated. (It is typical, that, as Swedish Under-Secretary of State for Immigration, I was myself responsible for the areas of border control, asylum policies, refugee co-ordination, social and cultural integration of immigrants, ethnic discrimination, and terrorism at one and the same time.) There is a danger that European refugee policies may be dominated by nation states' joint concern with the threat of terrorism.

Policy targets

Following this quick review of policy developments, where do we stand now? What can we expect in the future? And what measures ought to be taken? The tasks that lie ahead of us are enormous. In a situation where pressures and perspectives are shifting so quickly, we must do everything possible to maintain Europe as a stronghold of human rights. We must abide by the Geneva Convention on refugees, and apply it generously. We must improve our administrative machinery to implement our immigration and refugee legislation. Immigration and asylum applicants should receive government decisions more quickly. We must develop a system of international burden-sharing *vis-à-vis* those refugees heading for Europe. We must work for the further social integration of those who have already been admitted to our countries. We must simultaneously combat discrimination, xenophobia, and terrorism. We must work for the further integration of Europe and for an extension of the right of free movement. Finally, we must increase our development aid to refugees (including our contributions to UNHCR and UNRWA), and improve our co-ordination of international measures to tackle root causes of Third World emigration.

This is the general perspective facing governments in Europe in the area of international migration, including refugee affairs. Many of the policy objectives mentioned are, at first glance, incompatible, but it is the task of governments to balance different interests and to make them as compatible as possible. But, is there a true willingness on the part of governments to tackle these rapidly emerging problems, which are such a sensitive issue in the minds of the general public? Do governments have proper national administrative machinery for this? And what about the existing intergovernmental machinery?

What first gives rise for concern, to my mind, is the lack of insight into the necessity for more efficient planning in order to tackle root causes of involuntary emigration. During the decades to come there is every reason to believe that we shall witness a rise in international migration among those seeking safety and employment. The present number of migrants in the world is estimated at some 80 million (or 1.7 per cent of the world population). This figure includes the number of foreign workers legally employed (20 million), the UNHCR and UNRWA refugees (16 million), and persons living in refugee-type situations (4 million). Of this total of 80 million, Western Europe accounts for nearly 25 per cent, the equivalent of 5 per cent of the total European population. However, of the UNHCR refugees, Europe accounts for only one million.

Why do we have reason to believe that this figure of 20 million migrants in Europe, and migration trends in general, will increase?

Root causes

It is clear that international migration is presently increasing as a result of war, structural global inequality, and repression. Two-thirds of the countries of the world infringe the human rights of their citizens. A large part of the present inflow to Europe stems from such countries. Currently forty or so armed conflicts in the world claim civilians as a major share of the victims. Most Third World countries are experiencing massive internal migration, caused by dramatic population increases, and the growth of mega-cities. In just a few decades Calcutta will have some 20 million inhabitants, and the population of Nigeria will be equal to that of all of Western Europe.

Europe itself is undergoing significant demographic changes. The population of Europe is ageing; at present in two states (Germany and Sweden) more than 15 per cent of the population is over 65. By the year 2000 this group of countries will have increased to nine, and by the year 2020 only Turkey and Ireland will have less than one-tenth of their total population in the older age-group. Many European countries (including Germany) should envisage a decrease of total population around the year 2000, and the population of industrialized Europe will account for only 3 per cent of the world's population, as compared to 6 per cent now. In a mere thirty years the population of Sub-Saharan Africa is expected to have grown from 180 million in 1950 to one or two billion. The Maghreb will by then have a population of 150 million, Egypt 90 million, and Turkey 90 million. North Africa will have a population larger than that of Europe.

The proportion of the world's population living in the developed countries has fallen from one-third in 1960 to one-quarter in 1985. According to UN projections this proportion will drop still further, to around one-fifth, by the year 2000. Meanwhile, the average age of the population in the more-developed regions will be increasing, whereas that of the less-developed regions will be falling, as a result of differences both in fertility rates and life expectancy. Whereas the average fertility rate (number of children per woman) of the less-developed regions approached 4.0 in 1985, that of the more-developed regions was slightly under the reproduction level. Meanwhile, the expectation of life (at birth) in less-developed areas is at present 57.3 years, whereas that in more-developed areas is 73.1 years. As a result, the difference in the growth-rates of the population of working age (15–64 years) will be even more marked than that of the total population. In absolute terms, the working-age population of the less-developed areas may rise by around 825 million between now and the end of the century, while that of the more-developed areas may increase by only about 70 million. These differences will become more marked during the first half of the twenty-first century, if there is no increase in the fertility level in the developed countries and no decline in demographic growth in the less-developed countries.

One of the many excellent studies prepared for the OECD Conference on the Future of Migration in May 1986 indicates that 60 million young people enter the labour markets of the least developed countries in the world *each year*. The study provides ample evidence that pressure for migration—given this and other demographic, economic, and political trends—will increase. And it summarizes as follows:

> Even if the receiving countries were to show the maximum willingness to accept new immigrants, no more than 1.0–1.2 million new arrivals per year could possibly be taken up by the three OECD immigration areas. And even this figure would require enormous efforts on their part, and in numerical terms it would be only a drop in the ocean, considering the magnitude of the employment problem in the sending countries, which need to create 35 million to 40 million new jobs every year to solve it.[3]

At the same time, the firm trend towards urbanization in the less-developed countries seems likely to continue. In just a few decades half the world's population will live in towns and more than 60 per cent of the world's urban population will live in towns of over one million inhabitants. The number of conurbations of more than 5 million inhabitants (there are twenty-three at present) may double between now and the end of the century. Virtually all new urban areas seem likely to emerge in the less-developed countries. This rapid urbanization of the less-developed areas is somewhat different in character from that which took place in more-developed areas

[3] Antonio Golini and Corrado Bonifazi, *Demographic Trends and International Migration* (Paris: OECD, 1986), 57.

in the past. Urbanization in the developed world resulted primarily from more rapid industrialization and the ensuing manpower needs. By contrast, present and projected development in the less-developed countries is the result in large part of over-population in rural areas. However, urbanization without sufficient industrialization as a counterpart is almost certain to lead to increasing problems of poverty and urban decay. Rural–urban migration under these conditions will therefore tend to induce migration towards more prosperous urban-industrial centres outside the country, i.e. emigration.

To these perspectives should be added the starvation that is rife in many parts of the world as a result of crop failures and the abuse of natural resources. Estimates state that some 600 million people will be suffering from malnutrition by the year 2000. Moreover, ecological changes will force many to move; we all remember the situation in the Sudan and Ethiopia in 1984, and we know that each year the Sahara increases in area equal to the size of Hungary. Another factor to be considered is the rapidly growing international transport and communications links between continents, which increasingly facilitate inter-continental travel and migration.

Finally, and most importantly, the overall economic imbalance between developed and developing countries persists. Debt burdens and the general misuse of money on armaments rather than on basic necessities can only aggravate these imbalances. Not only are standards of living widely disparate in these countries and needs in the social, educational, health, and nutritional fields acute in many developing countries, but the situation threatens to become even worse, if we do not act now. In a world where resources are scarce and unevenly distributed, the arms race is sheer madness. It not only threatens humanity with destruction, it also consumes such immense sums of money that the world has to make a choice—*either* to arm *or* to develop; we cannot finance both at the same time.

Current military expenditures represent well over 5 per cent of total world output. They are over twenty-five times as large as all official development assistance to poor countries. The close connection between disarmament and development has been on the UN agenda for some years, and a few years ago the General Assembly also recommended that member nations should initiate national studies. We have done this in Sweden—showing the possibility of transforming the armaments industry into civil industry—but unfortunately we have so far been the only nation to do so.

Is it really a question of both economy and peace? Arms are intrinsic evidence of the distrust that exists among nations and, as long as this is not transformed into confidence and a recognition of the fact that we in the world are mutually interdependent, for our security as much as anything, then the world will remain in a dangerous state. Arms consume money which, if invested in social, educational, and other civil fields, would contribute to a better way of life for millions of people, thus lessening the strains and tensions in society that cause migratory flows and—ultimately—threaten the peace of the world.

What the world needs is a kind of new Marshall Plan—a massive transfer of resources from the North to the South. This was the main proposal of the Brandt Commission, which concluded that a first priority must be to meet the needs of the poorest countries and regions. The report states: 'We recognize that the removal of poverty requires both substantial resource transfers from the developed countries and an increased determination of the developing countries to improve economic management and deal with social and economic inequalities.' The burden of rapid population growth and the consequent pressure on the environment are aggravated by the present debt crisis. Today the developing countries together are some $1,000 billion in debt. Since the middle of the 1970s the debt has risen fivefold.

Of course this cannot continue. The heavy debt burden of the developing countries constitutes not only a threat to social and economic development, but to the stability of the whole world. There is evidence of a growing acceptance of the need for co-ordinated international undertakings, undertakings effected within the framework of a joint strategy covering economic, financial, trade, and development aid policies.

Along with the worsening economies of the countries of the South, there has unfortunately been a decrease in international development assistance, at least during the first years of the 1980s. The United Nations has set as a goal the payment by each donor country of at least 0.7 per cent of its gross national product as development aid. The only OECD countries that have reached this goal are the four traditional donor countries—The Netherlands, Norway, Denmark, and Sweden. For many other countries reports show either a static situation or a decrease in development aid as part of the gross national product.

This is extremely serious since the economic crisis of the 1980s hit the poorest countries more severely than had earlier, post-war crises. Per capita real income of developing countries as a whole is at present below the level reached in the late 1970s. Dozens of countries have lost a decade or more of development. Some of the economic and social achievements of the developing countries over the last twenty years are in real danger of being lost. The countries most severely affected are no longer able adequately to provide the basic needs of food, safe water, health care, and education for their populations, let alone find additional resources for development.

We can never, in the long-term perspective, properly handle the new European migration situation if we do not try to attack the root causes of migration more effectively. But so far European countries have not acted as though they really recognize the link between joint international action and national border control.

Intergovernment machinery

It is obvious that the existing international system is not adapted to deal with all the problems involved in modern mass migration and its causes. A number of intergovernmental agencies are involved in various aspects of international migration: the UN itself; the ILO when it comes to labour migration; UNESCO in so far as education is concerned; the UNHCR as the principal refugee agency; UNRWA to deal with the Palestinian refugees; the Intergovernmental Committee for Migration (ICM) in the field of transport assistance; OECD as regards the analysis of economic and migration trends; the European Community, and the Council of Europe, in various other ways. There are of course also numerous other international bodies involved.

However, what is lacking is a joint conceptual framework. The world has changed, and so has the pattern of human migration. What is needed more than ever is effective intergovernmental machinery to deal with all the new challenges of the future. This does not, to my mind, imply the setting up of new systems or new agencies. What is needed is an awareness of the new situation, flexibility, and an honest willingness to co-operate, both between

European governments and the intergovernmental agencies they once established, and between those agencies themselves.

The UNHCR

When it comes to the UNHCR, it is clear that the agency is in a difficult position. On the one hand, there is the Mandate and the UN Refugee Convention which place limits on its actions; on the other, the reality of the situation which requires that the UNHCR takes greater action. If the UNHCR cannot find its way through this dilemma, European governments might be tempted to act unilaterally on refugee policy matters. This would be a highly dangerous development since the UNHCR is the only world-wide agency among those mentioned whose brief is to deal with migration issues from the humanitarian aspect. What M. Hocké mentioned in his lecture on the interplay between governments and the UNHCR, and the way in which the UNHCR could act as a catalyst, gives cause for hope for the future.

The series of European consultations on asylum-seekers which began nearly two years ago has not yet produced any tangible results. They will be the first real test of our willingness to go further in solving the problems of the future. These consultations deal with the present serious refugee situation and what could be done in a systematic manner to improve things. I am not pessimistic, but it seems as though refugee issues have now become as complex as those relating to disarmament and other pressing international issues. One must move very slowly, very carefully, in order not to lose what has already been achieved.

Hopes for the future

In the past Europe experienced large-scale migration, and this contributed substantially to its dynamism and development. The present inflow of some 0.2 million asylum-seekers annually, or the roughly 20 million immigrants now living in Europe, should be compared with the 40 million who once left for America, the tens of millions who returned to Europe from there, the 10 million guestworkers in Europe before World War II, and the 7 million of them who left for countries overseas. All this has happened during a mere century. I remain confident that we shall also manage to solve the present problems that face us.

Let me just mention the issue of free zones of circulation as another piece of historical evidence of relevance here. Only some thirty-five years ago the idea of establishing a joint European labour market was considered to be Utopian. However, such a joint labour market exists today within the European Community. New or potential Southern European members of the Community are gradually being included in this labour circulation free zone. In addition, a free labour market has existed in the northern part of Europe since 1954, when the Nordic labour market agreement was concluded. And zones of free circulation of labour have been established and are under development in other parts of the world.

What has this notion of zones of free circulation to do with refugees? As a matter of fact it has a lot to do with the efforts to find solutions to the new problems posed by the refugee situation in Europe. Only some ten to fifteen years ago three of the new members of the European Community were dictatorships, producing thousands of political refugees. Now they are democracies, and full partners in the process of European integration. And the process of European integration will—ideally—in the long term gradually spread to countries and regimes (presently areas of origin of refugees) in the immediate neighbourhood of the existing Community.

In summary what is needed more than ever is effective government willingness to deal with the following three issues:

—the long-term tackling of root causes, be they infringement of human rights, ecological disasters, or poverty;

—the maintenance of liberal refugee policies in combination with a new system of burden-sharing and of increased support to non-European countries of first asylum;

—the further development of free zones of circulation, not only in Europe, but in other parts of the world, to give people new hope in terms of the richness and dynamism brought by the migration of human resources.

3. Emergency Aid

*Politics and Priorities**

RANDOLPH KENT

Introduction

REFLECTING upon the 1971 flight of almost 10 million East Pakistani refugees to the safety of India's borders, P. N. Haksar, then Principal Secretary to the Indian Prime Minister, commented that 'there is no system which can move in a humanitarian rather than a political fashion. There are two streams in society: emotions of conscience and the state system. The first is prevented by the second.'[1]

Time and again, politics is blamed for the ways in which responses to disaster-afflicted peoples are made. This is certainly so in cases of emergencies involving refugees or mass distressed migrants.[2] To outside observers, the causes of refugee emergencies are from the very outset ostensibly far more political than those which create victims of so-called natural disasters. Such perceptions of causation clearly spill over into views about the ways refugee emergencies are handled. And yet, whether an emergency involves a sudden mass migration of peoples or a natural disaster, politics is regarded as the key determinant of who gets what, when, and where.

'If politics is not the decisive factor in determining who gets what

* Material for this chapter has been drawn from the author's book, *Anatomy of Disaster Relief* (London: Pinter Publishers, 1987).

[1] Interview with P. N. Haksar, former Principal Secretary to the Prime Minister of India, 1971–3, New Delhi, 16 Mar. 1983.

[2] The terms 'refugees' and 'mass distressed migrants' are used here interchangeably, despite their legal distinctions. Robert Chambers, before the British Parliament's Foreign Affairs Committee in Jan. 1985, described the difference in this way: 'the term "refugee" has a technical sense which, strictly speaking, limits it to those who cross international boundaries for reasons of fear and persecution. It can also be used for a single person who flees alone. The phenomenon to be faced now is the mass movement of desperate and destitute people. [This latter term] covers a broader spectrum of conditions than the older

and when [in disasters],' contended D'Souza, 'then how do you explain why the Gambia received $11.5 million worth of aid in a matter of a few weeks during [UN Secretary-General] Waldheim's attempt to get re-elected or why the Afghan refugees are awash with assistance, or why the US Congress in a matter of days appropriated $50 million for the Italian relief operation? It is all political.'[3] It was 'power politics playing its usual role' which, according to Michael Harris, then Oxfam's Overseas Director, explained the failure of the international community to respond to the plight of Ethiopia in 1984. For Sir Robert Jackson, who acted as the UN Secretary-General's Special Representative in several major disasters from 1972 to 1983, the Kampuchean relief operation demonstrated 'deep superpower politics'.[4] And in a telling vignette, Jackson quotes Waldheim as saying that 'four years ago [1974] I believed that humanitarian relief was above politics. Now I know that humanitarian relief is politics.'[5]

If the plight of refugees and other victims of disasters is so intertwined with political calculations, then it seems necessary to explore the term 'politics'. I shall view politics in the more general context of humanitarian assistance; for while refugee issues are specifically the principal concern of this volume, political processes affecting donor responses to refugee emergencies are consistent with response patterns to emergencies in general.

Politics is a process primarily concerned with the allocation of values and resources. One predominant view of politics is that states, in the Palmerstonian sense, are devoid of sentiment and have no friends. States only have interests. State behaviour and, hence, the allocative process in international relations, is assumed to be motivated by the pursuit of national interests. While Morgenthau—the founder of the modern school of political realism—accepts that 'political reality is replete with contingencies and systematic irrationalities', he and his many adherents maintain that

terms "refugee influx" and "refugee", useful though these remain. MDMs occur wherever people move or are moved in distress and *en masse* in thousands, whether within or between countries, and whatever the immediate cause, whether international or civil war, persecution, expulsion, famine, forcible resettlement, or some combination of these or other disasters or conditions.' Foreign Affairs Committee, Session 1984–5, 'Famine in Africa' (London: HMSO, April 1985), 143.

[3] Interview with Frances D'Souza, Director of International Disaster Institute, London, 30 Sept. 1982.

[4] Interview with Sir Robert Jackson, UN, New York, 21 Nov. 1980.

[5] Ibid.

state actions reflect a persistent drive to enhance or preserve power and prestige.[6] It is a view assumed by Morris Davis when he wrote that 'real or potential donor nations habitually put their perceived national interests over humanitarian concerns'.[7]

This predominant and enduring view, or 'realist paradigm', assumes both a rational and a holistic conception of state behaviour. Statecraft is holistic in that it reflects a persistent and relatively consistent consensus—as reflected by the actions of states—about the objectives of the state. State activities are deemed to be rational because policy options are continually assessed in terms of those choices that will maximize and ensure power.[8]

However, such assumptions about politics are open to challenge if one looks at the processes by which those in authority within the state make decisions. True, there are certain precepts which form consistent themes in state policies.[9] Later we shall refer to these as norms. Nevertheless, it would be mistaken to assume that such themes serve as predictable standards upon which individual decisions are made. An alternative way of understanding state behaviour and resource allocation is to view politics as a process.

Groups both within and outside government constantly promote and compete for particular values and resources. The values and resources which each seeks to garner are not necessarily devoid of emotions of conscience, but the ways that they must be sought are inherently political; for, in the final analysis, politics is about the strategies and tactics, the trade-offs and linkages, employed to promote what contending groups regard as priorities.

Ultimately, priorities are determined by those decision-makers with allocative authority. However, as there are many different

[6] H. J. Morgenthau, *Politics Among Nations*, 5th edn. (New York: Alfred A. Knopf, 1973), 8.

[7] M. Davis (ed.), *Civil Wars and the Politics of International Relief: Africa, South Asia and the Caribbean* (New York: Praeger Publishers, 1975), 91.

[8] For a description as well as a critique of the 'realist paradigm', see J. Vasquez, *The Power of Power Politics: A Critique* (London: Frances Pinter Publishers, 1983).

[9] This may be due in part to the ways that those in one nation view those in others; see e.g. W. Buchanan and H. Cantril, *How Nations See Each Other* (Urbana: University of Illinois Press, 1983), 51–2. It might reflect the kinds of educational and professional orientation of particular societies, as suggested by H. Kissinger in 'Domestic Structure and Foreign Policy', in J. Rosenau (ed.) *International Politics and Foreign Policy* (New York: Free Press, 1969). The consistency of precepts might also reflect a tradition of dealing with problems in certain sorts of ways. A. Bozeman suggests this when comparing African attitudes towards conflict with those of American or European cultures, in *Conflict in Africa* (Princeton: Princeton University Press, 1976).

types of allocative issues, so, too, are there many levels of allocative decision-makers, each with its own agenda determined by decisional roles and guidelines and each affected by the impact of contending interests. Yet, this point should not leave one with the impression that allocative decisions are necessarily handled in a predictable or orderly way, or that they progress up a hierarchical ladder on top of which is an ultimate decisional authority. This view ignores the intense interactive dynamics present throughout the decisional process.

Allocative policies emerge from many quarters. Some may be triggered by senior decision-makers, or may descend or move laterally to other levels, but never be acted upon. Some issues which would normally be handled by lower-level decision-makers may find their way into the upper reaches of policy-making. Other issues that might well deserve the attention of senior-level decision-makers may never emerge past lower levels, with the consequence that significant policy initiatives may be made without the awareness of those who should know.

If such allocative dynamics suggest a political process out of control, then the image is too strong. If, on the other hand, the image portrayed is one in which frequently unpredictable and incomplete agendas, in a constant state of flux, are placed before decision-makers, then the picture seems to reflect more clearly the realities of political processes. In that sense, the political process is analagous to a cascade where conflicting pressures collide at various junctures with seemingly endless inputs and outputs.[10]

One way to view the political process from this perspective is to assess the impact of roles, norms, and contending interests as they affect allocative functions.

Roles

Lloyd Jensen has written that 'one might anticipate that the higher in the role hierarchy a decision is made, the more likely it is that

[10] The unpredictability of the process also bears a resemblance to Prigogine's view of change in the physical sciences. His concept of chemical organization might serve as a useful analogue for the dynamics affecting political agendas: 'all systems contain subsystems, which are continually "fluctuating". At times, a single fluctuation or a combination of them becomes so powerful, as a result of positive feedback, that it shatters the preexisting organization. At this revolutionary moment . . . it is impossible to determine in advance which direction change will take.' The quotation is taken from I. Prigogine and I. Stengers, *Order Out of Chaos: Man's New Dialogue with Nature* (London: Flamingo, 1984), xv.

broader and longer-range interests will be reflected'.[11] Yet, as he and many others have demonstrated, the assumption is flawed.[12] As one traverses up the hierarchy, one by no means finds a broadening of perspectives, but rather just differing perspectives reflecting different sorts of roles. In the oft-quoted phrase found in Allison, 'where one sits is where one stands'; or, in other words, the diverse demands upon each (political) player shape his priorities, perceptions and issues. 'For larger classes of issues—e.g. budgets and procurement decisions—the stance of a particular player can be predicted with high reliability from information about his seat.'[13]

All who are directly involved in the allocative process (e.g. Parliamentarians, dictators, members of executive and legislative branches of governments) take office with certain assumptions about their responsibilities or roles. An individual's role is determined by a combination of role clarity and role consensus, the former referring to a person's perception of what kind of behaviour is expected and the latter to the degree to which others agree to that kind of behaviour.[14]

It is essential for the decision-maker to maintain role consensus, and this normally depends upon balancing a variety of competing interests, each seeking allocative decisions. There are constant tensions in any individual's role, and most policy choices present the decision-maker with imperfect options, which are made more acute by the fact that the roles of others are equally complex, and each must find some way to accommodate or reduce the threat posed by others.

The former British Prime Minister Harold Wilson suggested as much during the furore over Britain's failure to provide relief for starving Biafra in 1968. 'The head of government', he wrote in his memoirs, 'has to face these problems not singly or single-mindedly, but simultaneously, against the background of a hundred other issues, economic, financial, and political. The headlines, however sensationalized or selective, fail to measure even the tip of the

[11] L. Jensen, *Explaining Foreign Policy* (Englewood Cliffs, NJ: Prentice-Hall Inc., 1982), 37.

[12] Ibid. 8; and see e.g. G. Fisher, *Public Diplomacy and the Behavioural Sciences* (Bloomington, Ind.: Indiana University Press, 1972), 66.

[13] G. Allison, *Essence of Decision: Explaining the Cuban Missile Crisis* (Boston: Little, Brown and Co., 1971), 176.

[14] R. Bauer and K. Gergen, *The Study of Policy Formation* (New York: Free Press, 1968), 228.

iceberg in the sea of democratic government, where the heaviest and most lethal pressures are below the surface, sometimes concentrated within the heart of the individual.'[15]

The cascading impact of roles upon the political process can be demonstrated by viewing episodes in the US response to the 1983 'Andean creeping disaster'.[16] Ostensibly, the political element of a proposal to assist El Niño-affected nations was uncomplicated. There was proven need, and the five relevant bureaux (namely, the Office for Foreign Disaster Assistance, US AID's Program and Policy Coordination division, its Latin-American Bureau, the State Department desk, and the Food for Peace programme) were all convinced that action to assist should be taken. However, funds were not available, and the Congress had to be approached for additional allocations.

The head of AID's Office for Program and Policy Coordination (PPC) was responsible for seeking Congressional authorization for additional allocations. Yet he could do so only by first convincing the Office for Management and Budget (OMB), the Congressional watchdog for governmental expenditures, that further funds were required. His OMB counterpart was convinced there was a problem, but said that he did not want AID to approach Congress because of end-of-year fiscal problems 'which would probably negate AID efforts'.

The OMB's reactions presented an immediate role conflict for the PPC official. On the one hand, he had to be sure that US AID was and was seen to be fiscally responsible. On the other hand, it was his responsibility to find funds. The latter role was affected by his colleagues from the four other bureaux, the former was being emphasized by the OMB.

To the PPC official, one way to resolve the conflict between his two roles was to seek means to reobligate funds from what were called 'failed projects' to emergency relief. Reobligation meant that unspent funds initially designated for development projects in those Andean countries now suffering from drought would be allocated to emergency relief. This seemingly straightforward

[15] H. Wilson, *The Labour Government, 1964–1970: A Personal Record* (London: Weidenfeld and Nicolson and Michael Joseph, 1971), 559.

[16] The narrative is based upon interviews with members of US Congressional staffs and various officials within US AID and the US State Department during the second and third weeks of Sept. 1983.

matter, however, was complicated by the fact that all unspent US federal allocations have to be returned to the US Treasury. Reobligation would be contrary to the most fundamental budgetary principles of the US government.

Both end-of-year fiscal problems and the constitutional hazards of reobligation meant that OMB for one was unwilling to support the reobligation solution which the PPC official saw as a means to resolve his own role conflict. OMB instead suggested ways in which US Aid could rejuggle other AID funds without risking the problems implicit in reobligation. However, to follow the rejuggling recommendations of OMB would mean that uncommitted funds in other AID divisions might be threatened, and therefore the PPC felt unable to draw from these for the Andean emergency. Role consensus in this instance meant that the PPC could not be seen to be undermining allocations within other AID departments.

The only solution remaining to PPC was to seek Congressional approval for AID's proposed reobligation scheme. This would mean incurring the wrath of OMB by bypassing it and going directly to Congress—by the back door—to persuade Congress to provide a legal basis for reobligating funds.

To maintain role consensus, the PPC chose to put its responsibilities of budgetary scepticism aside and pursue funding in ways that the OMB clearly found unorthodox. US AID's lawyers worked in the back corridors with various Congressional staffs to find a reobligation formula. Finally, four months after the five bureaux had agreed to contribute to the Andean disaster, Congress had approved PL98/63, allowing AID to reobligate failed project funds for purposes of disaster relief.

Of course, reobligation authorization in this instance did not lead automatically to assistance, for the impact of roles was felt once again as various agencies sought out how these reobligated funds were to be allocated. Who should do what?, became a fundamental management issue. 'Food for Peace wants to know whether ports can handle food'; the Office for Foreign Disaster Assistance felt that the operation should come within its own purview; while the Latin-American Bureau regarded the disaster as falling outside OFDA's competence. All these stances reflected the particular roles to which the individual decision-makers were committed. Where one sits determines where one stands. And in the case of the Andean creeping disaster, it took two further months to reconcile these contending roles before the bulk of relief aid began to flow to the disaster-stricken people.[17]

Norms

Joseph Sisco, a former Assistant Secretary of State under President Richard Nixon, once remarked that 'no bureaucracy resists policy changes. What happens is that administrations rely upon the specifics of policy which provide in turn for continuity.'[18] However, policy is not merely handed down from a political apex to bureaucracies below. There is what Sisco has called an 'inherent tension' between policy-makers and implementers. Roles constrain the degree to which radical changes can be made, and both roles and policy change are conducted within a framework of overall contextual consensus, which refers to the norms—the political *Zeitgeist*—within which policy is formulated. Where roles reflect institutional standards of behaviour, norms as we are defining them suggest the general parameters that limit the context in which all policy-makers in Western defence and foreign affairs ministries operate; no one would view capitulation to Soviet power as an acceptable option. There are, in other words, certain norms which are taken as given in the policy-making context. However, it is within those norms that the tensions between roles are felt.

The problem for policy-makers is often that even norms are not necessarily clear. Whereas capitulation to the Soviet Union may be an extreme example of an unambiguous norm, assisting a communist country in a disaster may not be. In this sort of situation, ambiguous norms and roles may come into conflict: United States provision of relief assistance to Angola is a case in point.

During the latter part of 1982 and early 1983, officials in US AID's Office of Refugees, Emergencies, Disasters, and Food Aid in

[17] Interview with Len Rogers, Office of Program and Policy Coordination, US AID, Washington, DC, 14 Sept. 1983.

[18] Interview with Joseph Sisco, former Assistant Secretary of State for Near Eastern and South Asian Affairs, Washington, DC, 12 Sept. 1983. Of Sisco, Henry Kissinger commented that he was 'enormously inventive, with a talent for the stratagems that are the lifeblood of Middle East diplomacy . . . He was adroit in the ways of Washington and quickly established a personal relationship with me, perceiving that in the Nixon Administration Presidential authority would be the ultimate arbiter . . . After I became Secretary of State I made him Under Secretary of State for Political Affairs, the highest career policymaking position in the Department.' H. Kissinger, *White House Years* (Boston: Little, Brown and Co., 1979), 349.

Africa were faced with the portent of serious food shortages in Angola and Mozambique. Both countries were regarded as communist and not of immediate interest to the United States. This certainly was the position taken by members of the National Security Council (NSC), which advises the President on foreign policy matters. The Kirkpatrick–Helms lobby was making every effort to ensure that US assistance of any kind would not reach nations that were not aligned with US interests,[19] a norm that pervaded many senior-level policy positions within the administration.

However, for middle-level policy-makers within the Agency for International Development, the Kirkpatrick–Helms norms were far more ambiguous than they were, for example, for certain NSC staff members.[20] There was genuine disagreement about the way such rigid posturing would scuttle any US efforts at some form of dialogue in Southern Africa—a view shared with State Department desk officers—and there was also genuine concern that the United States could not continue to ignore the mounting consequences of food shortages in Angola and Mozambique in particular. There were, therefore, serious tensions between the policy norms of the administration and the roles of middle-grade officials within the Agency.

Faced with these tensions, the officials within USA AID decided to avoid a direct confrontation with senior-level officials and resorted to alternative assistance channels. Allocations for assistance to the two countries were funnelled through intergovernmental organizations—principally UNICEF—and emergency assistance continued to be so directed for well over a year, despite the established norms that circumscribed the policy postures of those in the White House.[21]

The consequence of tensions between policy norms and roles is by no means unique to the United States. A consistent theme of officials in the eight donor nations interviewed for this study expressed the complexities of fulfilling role obligations that were consistent with policy milieu. The officer in charge of West Germany's Section 301, which deals with humanitarian assistance,

[19] Interviews with officials from US AID, Washington, DC, second and third weeks of Sept. 1983.

[20] Ibid.

[21] Ibid.

for example, spoke of the difficulty of ascertaining a policy norm when emergency assistance may at any one time involve three different ministerial interpretations of policy, namely, the Ministry of Foreign Affairs, the Ministry of the Interior, and the Ministry of Economic Co-operation.[22]

For a senior official within the Dutch Ministry of Foreign Affairs, there were rarely overall policy norms that determined the fate of a disaster response. More often than not, the norm was a direct result of the interpretation of which department within which ministry was handling the matter.[23] And for that official's counterpart in the Emergency Relief and Humanitarian Assistance Unit within the Foreign Ministry, policy was a function of the way 'I will decide how to route it [the request for disaster assistance]'.[24]

In the dilemmas created between norms and roles, the key factor is often clarity. An issue which fits starkly into the context of policy norms more often than not easily coheres with appropriate guidelines and roles. The greater the ambiguity inherent in an issue, the greater the possibility that policy formulation will reflect strains between norms and decision roles. Such tensions intensify the potential for unpredictable and disjointed allocative decisions.

Interest groups

Clarity for the purposes of this discussion concerning the policy process has far less to do with accuracy of information and far more to do with explicitness. Explicit information is that which clarifies both roles and norms. If there is any single all-abiding function of interest groups, it is that of promoting clarity. It is important to emphasize that one is not talking of accuracy but rather of removing ambiguity.

The purpose of any single interest group—be it directly within the decisional structure or outside it—is to urge upon those with allocative functions the urgency and priority of its own particular interest. This is accomplished in a host of ways. Parliamentarians are urged by outside groups to press ministers; junior as well as

[22] Interview with Dr Ekkehard Hallensleben, Section 301, Humanitarian Assistance, Ministry of Foreign Affairs, Federal Republic of Germany, Bonn, 24 May 1984.

[23] Interview with J. Van Bosse, Head of North Africa Desk, Dutch Ministry of Foreign Affairs, The Hague, 29 May 1984.

[24] Interview with J. F. L. Blankenberg, Department for Development Co-operation, Dutch Ministry of Foreign Affairs, The Hague, 29 May 1984.

senior officials 'nobble' legislators; middle-level officials may use outside groups to influence more senior policy echelons. The routes of interest groups are numerous, but the purpose is consistent: to ensure that issues reflecting particular interests gain priority consideration and, in so doing, gain the clarity which is needed to mobilize roles without creating conflicts within accepted norms.

Take, for example, the effect of the actions of a variety of US interest groups in the case of the Ethiopian famine disaster in early 1983. The policy norm was that Ethiopia was a problem for the Soviets to handle. This, according the the US Chargé d'Affaires in Ethiopia at the time, was reflected in the arm's-length position adopted by the State Department's Africa Desk in response to the Chargé's occasional famine warnings.[25]

Nevertheless, US AID officials had by late 1982 established an interagency Task Force on Ethiopia and the Sudan (IGETSU) to monitor the effects of the famine. Ironically, at the same time that IGETSU began its activities, AID's programme assistance for Catholic Relief Services' (CRS) activities in Ethiopia was severely cut. CRS—eventually joined by Bread for the World and the Lutheran World Services—used this cut as a reason to begin to lobby sympathetic Congressmen to restore CRS's programme assistance and to increase general assistance allocations to Ethiopia.

One of these Congressmen was Howard Wolpe, Chairman of the House Sub-Committee on Africa, who had been pressed by the then Ethiopian Chargé d'Affaires in Washington, Tesfaye Demeke, to visit Ethiopia, in part to witness the famine for himself. Wolpe's increasing interest in Ethiopia made his office a natural conduit for back-channelled information from officials from AID's IGETSU, who were becoming convinced by mid-1983 that larger amounts of assistance would be required than was being acknowledge by the State Department. By 1 June 1983 the informal coalition being formed between Wolpe and his Committee members and middle-level officials from US AID was aided by an unusual event. The Association for Ethiopian Jews—in part as a result of fears of the drought's effect on the Falashas[26]—'undertook an enormous

[25] Interview with David Korn, former US Chargé d'Affaires, 1982–5, US Embassy in Addis Ababa, London, 22 Jan. 1986.

[26] The Falashas are a small peasant community in north-western Ethiopia that practises a unique form of Judaism. In 1984 a large number of the Falashas were airlifted to Israel in a massive secret operation.

mailing campaign to the Congress which led to considerable pressure on the [Reagan] Administration'.[27] McPherson, US AID's Administrator, came under intense pressure to explain why US assistance to Ethiopia was being cut back at a time of growing need.

On 13 July 1983 McPherson wrote to Wolpe that the 'American people have always wanted the US to respond to disasters without regard to politics . . . Ethiopia is no exception.'[28] What in effect McPherson was admitting was that he had not anticipated the ferment of the 'sub-systems' within and outside the Administration to press for restoration of assistance to Ethiopia. In effect, he was caught off guard by the tensions being created between the roles of his own officials and the policy norms of the Reagan Administration. Nor, for that matter, could he or did he anticipate the clarity which a variety of disparate interest groups—the Association for Ethiopian Jews, the Congressional Sub-Committee on Africa, Catholic Relief Services, US AID's Africa emergency office—gave to that specific issue.

Yet, the situation in which McPherson found himself was not an unusual example of the policy process. The cascading effect of diverse interests establishing agendas, modifying them, mobilizing various roles, and pushing at the bounds of established norms represents the political process. It suggests why the political result is often disjointed, inconsistent, and unpredictable.

If inconsistency, disjointedness, and unpredictability are often the hallmarks of the policy process, then one must ask how issues involving disasters and disaster relief enter into allocative decision-making. How, in other words, do disasters gain access to the priority formulation process? To some extent we have already suggested certain kinds of pressures that influence the fate of disaster decisions. Yet there are particular characteristics of disasters which one should consider as one attempts to understand the dynamics of the international relief network in action.

Disasters and priority formulation

The additional complexities affecting the ways disasters gain access to the priority formulation process are fourfold: (1) limited

[27] Interview with Allison Rosenberg, Staff of the Republican Majority, US Senate Foreign Relations Committee, Washington, DC, 16 Sept. 1983.

[28] Letter from M. Peter McPherson to the Hon. Howard Wolpe, 13 July 1983.

constituencies; (2) information loading; (3) *ad hoc* coalitions, and (4) trade-offs and linkages. In total, they suggest not only why some disasters gain priority attention and others do not, but also why particular kinds of relief responses actually emerge.

Limited constituencies

Disasters are viewed essentially as aberrations—events distinct and isolated from what is usually regarded as normal life.[29] To a very significant extent this view of disasters rebounds upon the political process, which affects the attention that disasters are given.

The constituencies which take an interest in issues concerning disasters and disaster relief are limited. Institutionally, they lack bargaining power and are isolated from issues in which the struggle for more enduring interests take place. This point has importance—as we shall see in a later section of this paper—both in terms of organizational behaviour and for our immediate discussion on political processes.

Whether it is in the US Office for Foreign Disaster Assistance, West Germany's Section 301, Sweden's Emergency Office, or Great Britain's Disaster Unit, what might logically be regarded as key rungs in the disaster response ladder—namely those cells with defined relief responsibilities—are more often than not out of the mainstream of allocative action. They all have limited funds at their disposal;[30] but when it comes to a major disaster requiring substantial assistance they only too often take a back seat in the formulation of priorities.

This reality introduces four points that explain the very limited constituency which can be consistently relied upon to support aid to those affected by disaster. The first of these four points stems from the fact that disasters are perceived, or, for the most part, treated as isolated and distinct phenomena. Those with formal responsibility for dealing with disasters are essentially cut off from any enduring interests which would allow for consistent bargaining power. Links with those interest groups involved in development or with agricultural policies, for example, are for the most part tenuous. Such limited constituencies have no permanent interest groups to

[29] See e.g. the excellent discussion by Hewitt in K. Hewitt (ed.), *Interpretations of Calamity* (London and Boston: Allen and Unwin, 1983), chap. 1.

[30] Most governments require that, for amounts exceeding a relatively small contribution, e.g. $100,000, reference to Cabinet or some other senior decision-making body must be made.

build upon, nor do they have sufficient allocative authority to give them a stake in the allocative game. There are, of course, exceptions to this general rule. Every disaster unit has its stories of 'ambulance chasers', seeking to sell their fish, boats, or tents to disaster agencies. However, they are relatively minor when compared with the more enduring interest groups, such as those found in development, where agricultural inputs, turn-key industries, and the like constantly interact with those which have far greater resources at hand.

Second, since disaster units generally lack sufficient resources to make any significant impact upon most major disasters that occur, resources depend upon those that do. This in turn means that disaster responses often depend upon institutions, e.g. agricultural ministries, which might have adequate supplies but which also have priorities other than disasters. At this point one returns to that frequent refrain—'where one sits is where one stands'. The posture that one takes on an issue depends upon the pressures being exerted in terms of roles and norms. While officials within the US Department of Agriculture or its Canadian counterpart may be aware of a disaster, their responses will be determined by the costs and benefits to their respective institutions in the light of issues extraneous to the disaster, e.g. legislators' pressures to off-load certain types of surplus commodities.

The third point, which naturally flows from the second, is that of linkage. The size of a constituency focusing upon any particular disaster depends upon the kinds of links with which they are immediately concerned. Morton Halperin, a former senior official on the US National Security Council, once remarked that disasters rarely grab the attention of presidents. 'They lack the time or inclination to concern themselves with such issues. A president might link a particular policy with a particular disaster, but the bottom line is that the president is just too busy to focus upon anything but the larger strategic issues.'[31] Former OFDA Co-ordinator Stephen Tripp came to the same conclusion. The reason

[31] Interview with Morton Halperin, former staff member of the National Security Council during the Nixon Administration and author of *Bureaucratic Politics and Foreign Policy* (Washington, DC: The Brookings Institution, 1974), Washington, DC, 14 Sept. 1983. Maurice Williams, who, as Deputy Administrator of US AID, had been the 'President's relief coordinator six times', told this writer that 'Presidents do get involved where there are sensitive political issues. Sometimes the President is concerned, sometimes he isn't. I was called by the President to deal with the Managua earthquake because the President was afraid

that President Richard Nixon took cognizance of the 1970 East Pakistan cyclone disaster was because Pakistan was a key component in his China policy and, at the time of the disaster, Nixon was focusing considerable attention upon Pakistan. For the same kind of reason Jordan received $5 million worth of relief assistance in the wake of the 1971 Jordanian–Palestinian conflict (despite the fact that Tripp had believed that only one-tenth of that amount was needed) because the White House at that particular time was concentrating upon improving US–Jordanian relations.[32]

Finally, the disaster relief constituency within the political spectrum is limited because the attention which sustains relief issues within the political process is short-lived. Disasters are not only regarded as aberrant and isolated phenomena, they are also assumed to be of short duration. They are viewed, in the words of one Swedish NGO representative, as 'unwarranted interference in the normal course of affairs'.[33]

Beyond instant demonstrations of sympathy and the kudos that may be derived from such demonstrations, prolonged involvements in disasters are constantly challenged by the pressures emanating from more enduring issues. Normal priorities constantly push their way into the agendas of decision-makers, agendas which constantly fluctuate in the face of shifting pressures.

When one US AID official spoke of the fear of being 'mousetrapped' by disaster relief into long-range commitments, he was acknowledging two kinds of concern. The first was the more obvious worry about a recipient assuming that emergency assistance implied more than just short-term involvement. The second, however, reflects the fact that any form of prolonged commitment would divert resources and attention away from those interests which ensure his role consensus. There are, in other words, few within the political process who have vested interests in the world of disaster relief.

that, because of the corruption, the Left might take over. Disasters get all wrapped up in politics. With the Sahel operation, the operation reflected the emergence of Black Americans increasingly becoming a political force. There is a question of visibility in matters of relief efforts . . . Each case is quite specific in a political and country context.' (Interview with Maurice Williams, New York, 29 Sept. 1983).

[32] Interview with Stephen Tripp, former Coordinator, Office of US Foreign Disaster Assistance, Washington, DC, 15 Sept. 1983. This was also a position suggested by Joseph Farland, US Ambassador to Pakistan during the 1970 cyclone and 1971 refugee crises. (Interview with Joseph Farland, Washington, DC, 18 Sept. 1983.)

[33] Interview with official from the Swedish Red Cross, Stockholm, 6 June 1984.

Information loading

Between May 1985 and April 1986 there were at least eighty major disasters which led to assistance from the international community.[34] Information about these disasters enters into the priority formulation process in a variety of ways, ways that are rarely consistent or predictable. A field-worker from an NGO may alert his or her headquarters to the onset of a disaster, or an ambassador from a potential donor country may be informed by a host government official that a serious disaster has occurred, or someone in a government agency in some distant capital might have read about a disaster in a newspaper or heard about it in a radio or television broadcast. Given the variety of ways in which disaster information enters the system, a response depends upon the routes through which the information is channelled. As that information progresses through channels, it becomes 'loaded' with matters that are frequently extraneous to the plight of the disaster victims themselves, but which naturally follow from the ways that information is processed. Information loading becomes a fundamental factor in the interrelationship between roles, guidelines, contending interests, and the priority formulation process.

The more incomplete and ambiguous the informational input, the more that information is moulded by recipients according to their own referents. Such referents are a function of perceptions, of institutional behaviour, but, for our purposes here, they will be described as a function of roles and norms.

In a political process in which disaster issues find limited constituency with limited allocative authority, the roles and norms of those in the mainstream of allocative responsibilities become crucial determinants in weighing the importance of any single disaster. However, these people must be persuaded or must recognize that a particular disaster issue falls within their competence or sphere of interest.

For an officer on the Ethiopia–Somalia desk in the British Foreign and Commonwealth Office in August 1984, the FCO's responsibility was to ensure that aid to Ethiopia was consistent with certain fundamental objectives, e.g. compensation for nationalized British property. This objective was reinforced by what she

[34] This figure derives from statistics provided by UNDRO and the Office of US Foreign Disaster Assistance.

referred to as 'the general political philosophy of the new Thatcher government'.[35] For her and her colleagues, information about an impending food crisis in Ethiopia was weighed in terms of their ability to achieve their role responsibilities and to remain consistent with the ethos of the administration. Her colleagues at the Overseas Development Administration had different ways of assessing the information which they were receiving from Ethiopia. They accepted that the impact of the drought was becoming increasingly severe in Ethiopia, but, given ODA's particular concern with the Sudan, ODA officials responded to the information in terms of the drought's impact upon movements of peoples from northern Ethiopia into the Sudan.[36]

Information is either screened out of the process or accepted, depending upon the extent to which it is consistent with roles and norms. If and when it is accepted, information is processed in terms of how it is seen as fitting into the particular roles of those who process it. Thus, for example, in 1985 the US Department of Defense accepted US AID's proposal for airlift operations in Ethiopia providing US military aircraft could be used.[37] In 1971, according to a White House official, reports about millions of refugees crossing into India from East Pakistan were given scant attention. The White House was concerned only about presenting Pakistan as a stable regime.[38] Two miles away, at the US Department of State, senior officials, who had no direct responsibility for refugees, took the position that the refugee influx represented one of the most serious threats to South Asian regional stability since Indian independence. These State Department representatives felt that India—not Pakistan—was the critical component to South Asian security.[39]

[35] Interview with official from Ethiopia/Somalia Desk, Foreign and Commonwealth Office, London, 21 Aug. 1984.

[36] Interview with official from the Overseas Development Administration, Foreign and Commonwealth Office, Khartoum, 31 Nov. 1984.

[37] Interview with John Kelly, US Agency for International Development, Washington, DC, Apr. 1985.

[38] Interview with Hal Saunders, former staff member of the National Security Council under the Nixon Administration, Washington, DC, Sept. 1983.

[39] Interview with Christopher Van Hollen, US Deputy Assistant Secretary of State for Near Eastern and South Asian Affairs from 1969 to 1972, Washington, DC, 19 Nov. 1980. For an intriguing analysis of the 'White House versus Bureaucracy', see C. Van Hollen, 'The Tilt Policy Revisited: Nixon–Kissinger Geopolitics and South Asia', *Asian Survey*, 20/4 (Apr. 1980), 339–61.

Such differences exemplify the ways that information becomes loaded by the roles and norms that decision-makers assume. How such differences are reconciled or accommodated depends in part upon the impact of the *ad hoc* coalitions formed by interest groups.

Ad hoc coalitions

Earlier we suggested that the function of interest groups is to add clarity to issues in which ambiguity arises between roles and guidelines. The term 'clarity' has little to do with accuracy, and far more to do with reducing ambiguity—for our purposes an important distinction.

According to the FCO official cited above, when MPs and the Jewish lobby concerned with Falashas began to exert enormous pressure, the FCO's stance on Ethiopian assistance came under review.[40] Of course, in the study of politics, there is nothing new in suggesting the impact of pressure groups upon the political process. Every minister, government official, and legislator is more than amply attuned to the influences of special interests.

However, what is important to bear in mind in the study of disasters in the context of political processes is that—as opposed to many forms of representation both within and outside governments—disasters and disaster relief do not have their own permanent lobbyists. The kind of response which a disaster receives all too often depends on the *ad hoc* coalitions which may adopt a particular disaster issue at any one time. The limited constituences which may be more predictably at the forefront of promoting the cause of disaster relief, those within the non-governmental sector or disaster relief cells in governments or IGOs, normally rely on coalition partners—those with no specific relief mandates—who have their own particular interests to promote to join them in pushing the priority importance of a particular disaster issue.

These latter members of *ad hoc* coalitions may participate for a myriad of reasons. In Sweden one MP said, with a certain degree of embarrassment, that he was on occasion prodded by the housing industry to ensure that the Swedish government responded to a disaster with supplies of Swedish housing material.[41] There is also

[40] See above, n. 35.

[41] The comment arose in an interview with Peter Ekelund, Disaster Section, Swedish International Development Association, Stockholm, 8 June 1984.

the apocryphal Agriculture Minister who feels compelled by his role to ensure that a disaster operation is supported with his nation's wheat, a role priority which may take precedence over policy norms. There is also the middle-level diplomatic official who, as Halperin has noted, 'pushes these issues because of a particular interest or concern in a particular geographic area'.

The *ad hoc* coalitions which form to push a particular disaster relief decision to the fore are not necessarily self-serving in their concerns. The mutual interests which prompt individual components of such coalitions should not be confused with lack of emotions of conscience. Yet, in the political process, disasters in many respects are orphans, depending all too often upon being adopted by those with role and norm perspectives that have no ostensible responsibility for responding.

Though the force of such *ad hoc* coalitions may push a particular issue to those levels where allocative decisions might be made, the disaster issue for the most part sustains its priority hold with considerable precariousness. Since *ad hoc* coalitions normally comprise those with limited responsibilities for disasters, the tendency is for coalitions to dissipate rapidly as a result of changing individual agendas that reflect pressures more consistent with expected role performance. Hence, even if a Prime Minister becomes part of or the object of an *ad hoc* coalition seeking to intervene in a disaster, his or her attention is short-term at best. As former British Prime Minister Edward Heath recalled, 'Matters of disaster relief may arise during Cabinet discussion, but if they do, it is because they are part of a general foreign policy discussion determined by those within the Foreign Office who prepare the Foreign Minister's brief.'[42] The attention span given to an emergency is indeed short.

Trade-offs and linkages

Disasters, as an issue within the political process, depend very often upon factors that are extraneous to the issue itself. Response to a disaster frequently depends upon trade-offs and linkages amongst an array of differing roles to gain access to the priority formulation process. Without the prospect for such trade-offs and linkages,

[42] Interview with Edward Heath, former British Prime Minister, London, 27 June 1985.

those with allocative authority may never actually focus upon the disaster. Yet the effect of trade-offs and linkages may, on the other hand, distort the response that is eventually made.

By trade-offs, we mean the compromises which have to be made within the formulation of policy that will allow any single component within the allocative process to perceive a vested interest. For example, the head of the Natural Disasters Section of the Norwegian Ministry of Development Co-operation commented that 'there are enormous surpluses of dried fish and salted fish, and we're under certain pressures to use them. I've had chairmen of the Fisheries Committee in Parliament calling me on the phone to get me to use such surpluses for relief.'[43] Such pressures are often hard to resist—even though those afflicted by the disaster may be unaccustomed to dried or salted fish—because that Parliamentarian's influence may help in mobilizing greater support for the disaster relief operation.

One of the problems which hampered US AID's attempt to support transport assistance to the Ethiopian relief operation in 1984 was the fear that US automobile manufacturers would object to US dollars being used to purchase spare parts and trucks for foreign-made vehicles.[44] The possibility of a trade-off for those with influence within the allocative process was indeed limited on this particular issue. Giving assistance to non-governmental organizations is indeed regarded as a convenient trade-off within the political process by many officials in Europe with responsibilities for disaster relief; for, in the words of one Dutchman, 'it allows us to satisfy the religious-based domestic constituencies which they represent'.[45]

Trade-offs, both large and small, are a normal part of the political process. For disaster issues, however, where those with responsibilities for disasters have limited bases from which to bargain, the potential for bargaining is more often than not in the hands of those who have their own particular views of what might or might not be gained from some form of involvement in disaster relief. The trade-offs, in other words, are all too often out of the direct control of

[43] Interview with Nils Dahl, National Disasters Section, Norwegian Ministry of Development Co-operation, Oslo, 5 June 1984.

[44] Interview with Dr Martin Howell, Director, Office of US Foreign Disaster Assistance, Washington, DC, 13 Sept. 1983.

[45] See above, n. 24.

those who have direct responsibilities for relief. Yet the trade-offs must be determined, if the pressure from those who can directly influence the allocative process is to be mobilized towards constructive action.

Halperin, in describing the ways that disasters gain the attention of senior decision-makers in the United States, suggested that 'disasters get the attention of junior officials. Who really cares becomes a matter of a quirk. What turns junior people on to particular issues . . .'[46] His point is not that senior officials are necessarily indifferent to the plight of the afflicted, but rather that—as mentioned above—the roles which they seek to fulfil isolate their attention to particular sorts of matters. Only when such matters might be 'linked' with a particular disaster does the possibility arise that the disaster will gain their priority attention. The role of the junior official with a quirk about a particular disaster is to find that linkage.

However, as examples cited earlier of Nixon's response to the East Pakistan cyclone and the Jordanian–Palestinian conflict suggest, the President was sensitive to these disasters because they were both linked to particular aspects of policy upon which he had been focusing at the time. The issue for the junior official, as he attempts to promote a particular relief response up the decisional ladder, frequently depends upon finding ways to link the response with other policy priorities.

Yet disaster initiatives are by no means always the result of the ways junior officials link such initiatives with the prevailing concerns of senior policy-makers. Senior policy-makers can indeed make their own links. A member of SIDA's emergency unit explained that Swedish disaster relief to Bolivia was prompted by the Swedish Cabinet, which wished to demonstrate solidarity with another socialist government. Similarly, assistance to Vietnamese hurricane victims around the same time was also prompted by a desire to expand contacts with the Vietnamese government.[47]

The head of Norway's Natural Disaster Section in the Ministry of Development Co-operation referred to the same sort of linkage in discussing relief aid contributions to Benin: 'When the Minister of Industry for Benin was coming to Norway, our minister [of Development Co-operation] asked if there was anything we could

[46] See above, n. 31. [47] See above, n. 41.

do for that country. We telexed the United Nations Disaster Relief Office that we had $50,000, and UNDRO replied that they were looking for funds to cover an operation involving $27,000 for the salary of a specialist, and we sent the money to UNDRO for Benin.'[48]

Such trade-offs and linkages are by no means unusual phenomena in the policy formulation process. What kinds of trade-offs and linkages may push one issue into the fore and leave others behind adds to the unpredictability of political results. In the realm of disaster relief initiatives, as well as responses to refugee crises, the unpredictable consequence of trade-offs and linkages means that criteria of needs, kinds of interventions, and which afflicted populations might receive assistance all too frequently become hostages to matters extraneous to the plight of afflicted peoples.

However unfortunate the conclusion, it does nevertheless reflect the workings of politics. Of course, to a very significant extent the resort to linkages and trade-offs depends in large part upon the clarity—both in terms of roles and norms—that surrounds any single issue. This too is a factor inherent in the political process.

Conclusion

Disasters, whether caused by political conflicts, environmental deterioration, or natural catastrophes, are subject to the same process factors. As perceived aberrations, they lack the support of more permanent interest groups that would give them greater access to those with allocative responsibilities. Disaster and refugee relief is too often dependent upon limited constituencies, and only when such constituencies are supported by *ad hoc* coalitions does relief permeate the priority formulation process. Highly susceptible to 'loading', disaster issues frequently engender tensions between roles and norms, ultimately making the recourse to linkages and trade-offs the only way to move a disaster initiative up the priority queue. In the final analysis, it is not that the political process is necessarily devoid of emotions of conscience; rather it is that emotions of conscience cannot be separated from the ways that roles, norms, and interest groups interact to determine national priorities regarding humanitarian crises.

[48] Interview with official from the Norwegian Ministry of Development Co-operation, Oslo, 5 June 1984.

II

Dimensions of the Refugee Problem

4. Military and Armed Attacks on Refugee Camps

ELLY-ELIKUNDA MTANGO

THE Statute of the Office of the United Nations High Commissioner for Refugees (UNHCR Statute)[1] and the 1951 Convention Relating to the Status of Refugees (Refugee Convention)[2] refer to the protection mandate and function of the United Nations High Commissioner for Refugees (UNHCR) without specifically mentioning his competence on matters relating to the physical safety of refugees. A possible explanation for this omission could be that these instruments were drafted at a time when the serious threat to physical safety during World War II had passed. The war was over, the United Nations had been established to ensure durable peace, and the 1949 Geneva Conventions[3] already agreed to regulate the conduct of war. The drafters of the two refugee instruments would have felt, therefore, that the United Nations mechanism, the law of armed conflicts, and the national laws of asylum would be adequate to ensure the physical integrity of refugees. They thus concentrated on issues relating to the economic and social well-being of refugees. States were left free to negotiate and agree on additional provisions for the protection of refugees and the UNHCR had to promote such agreements (Statute, Article 8(a)). Only the 1969 OAU Convention[4] covers specific measures relating to the security of

[1] UN General Assembly Res. 428 (V); UN Doc. HCR/INF/48, UNHCR Statute.

[2] 189 United Nations Treaty Service (UNTS) 137 (Convention relating to the Status of Refugees); 606 UNTS 267 (Protocol relating to the Status of Refugees, 31 Jan. 1967).

[3] 75 UNTS 31, 85, 135, 287.

[4] OAU Convention governing the specific aspects of refugee problems in Africa, 1969: Collection of International Instruments Concerning Refugees (UNHCR Publications, 1979), 193–200; 8 International Legal Materials 1288, 1292 (1969).

refugees, countries of asylum, and countries of origin. This Convention, however, applies only to its signatories *inter se* within Africa and is not intended to contradict the commitment of African states to liberate their continent from colonialism and oppression. Furthermore, the African Charter for Human and Peoples' Rights now in force specifically spells out the obligation of state parties to support the armed struggle conducted by national liberation movements.[5]

It is necessary, therefore, to search for legal principles proscribing armed attacks on refugees in the Law of Armed Conflicts, human rights law, and fundamental principles of international law contained primarily in the United Nations Charter and the relevant resolutions of the United Nations General Assembly, such as resolution A/Res. 2625 (XXV).[6] The fact that the relevant legal instruments and declarations of the General Assembly largely reflect established rules of customary international law makes it possible to suggest that the problem is not so much one of lack of rules but lack of will by governments to recognize the applicability of the law and the obligation to abide by international law.[7]

Today, however, armed attacks on refugees take various forms in various parts of the world. The culprits can be countries of origin, countries of asylum, or armed groups within these countries. Attacks may be simply indiscriminate or may be directed at specific refugee camps or locations. In one region, states of asylum may separate armed refugees from non-combatant refugees, while in another region combatants and civilians may exist side by side in the same camp.

The ability of asylum countries to protect refugees from attack or to control their activities in order to ensure their safety also differs from one country to another. Thus, there are cases where refugee camps and settlements are attacked and yet, because of the

[5] Article 20 (2) and (3) of the African Charter for Human Rights and Peoples' Rights, Published in the *International Commission of Jurists Review*, 27 (Dec. 1981).

[6] United Nations Declaration on Principles of International Law concerning Friendly Relations and Co-operation among States, 1970.

[7] See the similar view in an article by René Korsinik, 'Droit international humanitaire et protection des camps de réfugiés', in C. Swinarski (ed.), '*Études et essais sur le droit international humanitaire et sur les principles de la Croix-Rouge*', (International Committee of the Red Cross: Martinus Nijhoff, 1984).

particular circumstances, it becomes rather difficult to determine which principles of international humanitarian law are specifically applicable.[8] One explanation for this is that the situation of refugees may sometimes differ from that of civilian populations. Another is that, because the Law of Armed Conflicts which forms the bulk of international humanitarian law is primarily intended to regulate the conduct of combatants, the protection of civilians may not have been a major concern of the law-makers. This goes some way to explain why there are so few provisions for the protection of civilians in the hundreds of articles of the 1949 Geneva Conventions and their additional Protocols of 1977.

As armed attacks on civilian refugee populations increase in number, the need for a new refugee instrument to deal more specifically with the problem of the physical safety of refugees—in particular the protection from military or armed attacks—becomes more compelling. Such a refugee instrument should establish a minimum legal standard to serve as a yardstick for state behaviour. Of course, along with this effort, it is also necessary to institute a variety of political measures to tackle the root causes of refugee situations and to create conditions which make armed attacks on refugees less likely to occur.

This study will highlight the gravity of the problem of military and armed attacks on refugee camps and settlements and the ways in which the international community has reacted to these developments. I shall also review the actual negotiations in the Executive Committee of the UNHCR by examining the conflicting viewpoints of member states, the problems posed by legal ambiguities, and the *realpolitik* interests of specific governments. The body of law which guides international conduct concerning the physical safety of refugees is reviewed and an outline of possible measures to alleviate the problem is suggested.

[8] Most writers, including Korsinik, Patrnogic, and Dinstein, over-emphasize the importance of the provisions of the 1949 Conventions and 1977 Protocols, which, strictly speaking, apply to the subject of the present study only to the extent that they reflect established rules of customary international law. What is needed is a specific refugee instrument inspired by both customary international law of armed conflict and human rights law. See also below, n.12.

The notion of 'armed attack'

In the context of international humanitarian law and this study, an attack constitutes an act of violence,[9] and an armed attack refers to 'an action by regular forces across international borders and also the sending by or on behalf of a State, of armed bands, groups, irregulars, or mercenaries which carry out acts of armed force against another State of such gravity as to amount to (*inter alia*) an actual armed attack conducted by regular forces, or its substantial involvement therein'.[10] Attacks against refugees have taken the form of armed attacks as defined above, but there have also been cases of military attacks against refugee camps carried out by agents of the state of asylum or refuge within its own territory, as in Honduras in 1985. Some attacks within the state of asylum or refuge have also been attributed to armed groups or individuals pursuing political motives, as is often the case in Lebanon. The United Nations system and its institutions, particularly the Executive Committee of the UNHCR, while recognizing the wider problem of military and armed attacks on refugees, have focused attention on the prohibition of armed attacks *sensu stricto* on refugee camps and settlements.[11] In this study, therefore, emphasis will be given to such state-sponsored armed attacks across international borders in particular because in this case the culprits are either self-professed or can be easily identified. International action including condemnation is therefore possible even though an international consensus for such action has so far been difficult to achieve.

The notion of 'refugee'

I do not intend to dwell on the complexities relating to the concept of refugees, but in what follows I refer to political refugees, particularly those who do not have the rights and obligations usually attached to possession of nationality of the country of

[9] Protocols additional to the Geneva Conventions of 12 August 1949, Protocol I Article 49 (1) published by the Geneva International Committee of the Red Cross (Geneva, 1977). See also Adam Roberts and Richard Guelf, (eds.) *Documents on the Laws of War,* (Oxford: Clarendon Press, 1982), 387 and 447.

[10] *Nicaragua* v. *United States of America* (Merits), The Hague: *ICJ Reports* (1986), 103.

[11] See e.g. UNHCR Report on International Protection 1985 (Doc. A/AC.96/671).

asylum or refuge. Although many writers[12] focus their attention on refugees who fall within the mandate of UNHCR, military or armed attacks have affected refugees generally and hence some reference has to be made to all refugees; those of concern to the UNHCR and those outside its mandate. However, it will be remembered, in connection with international protection, that no UN agency has a defined mandate to protect refugees except the UNHCR.[13] Notwithstanding this limitation, the international community has to be concerned with any refugee who has left his country of regular residence, of which he may or may not be a national, as a result of political events in that country which render his continued residence impossible or intolerable, and has taken refuge in another country or, if already absent from his home, is unable to return without the threat of danger to life or liberty, as a direct consequence of the political conditions existing there. Thus, included in this notion of refugee are not only those refugees covered by the 1951 Refugee Convention and the 1967 Protocol,[14] but also those covered by the 1969 OAU Convention,[15] Palestinian refugees, and any refugee recognized as such under relevant international instruments or under the national legislation of the state of refuge or state of residence.[16] Such a liberal treatment of the notion of refugee, however, should not complicate this examination of the problem. Most attacks, whether on Convention or non-Convention refugees, are directed against zones set aside specifically to shelter refugees (zones commonly known as camps, settlements, or refugee reception centres).

The reality and seriousness of the problem

Although the granting of asylum is, in principle, a humanitarian act which should not be considered as an unfriendly act towards the country of origin,[17] the countries of origin have, in practice,

[12] e.g. M. Veuthey, 'Réfugiés et conflits armés', mimeo. (Geneva: ICRC, 28 Oct. 1983); J. Patrnogic, 'International Protection of Refugees in Armed Conflicts', *Annales de droit international médical*, 29 (July 1982); Y. Dinstein, 'Refugees and the Law of Armed Conflict', *Israel Year-book of Human Rights*, vol. 12 (1982).

[13] See above, n. 1.

[14] See above, n. 2

[15] See above, n. 4.

[16] See Protocols additional to the Geneva Conventions of 12 Aug. 1949, Protocol 1, Article 73 (above, n. 9).

[17] See United Nations Declaration of Territorial Asylum, 1967 (A/Res. 2313 (XXII)).

considered refugees as a potential threat to their security and have harboured suspicions that they are plotting against the country from which they have fled. Because refugees often come from politically active opposition elements in the country of origin, they are easily blamed—rightly or wrongly—for any acts of sabotage. When this happens, demands are made to the host country for their extradition or expulsion, and if this does not occur, punitive raids are carried out. These raids generally occur in areas where refugees are sheltered, but they also take place indiscriminately in areas where they may be sporadically settled. Such incursions, which violate the sovereignty and territorial integrity of the asylum country, have claimed many victims among refugees and nationals alike and have caused tremendous loss of property. They thus have had a destabilizing effect and have exacerbated international discord by further aggravating tensions among states. At the same time, the fear and insecurity created by such attacks negatively influence the asylum policy of the refugee receiving country, making the country less willing to admit asylum-seekers, or even inclined to expel those already admitted. In certain cases, asylum countries have forcibly repatriated refugees to their countries of origin or have acquiesced in their abduction, in violation of the principle of *non-refoulement* enshrined in the Refugee Convention. Article 33 of the Convention contains an absolute obligation on states not to forcibly return refugees to countries where their lives or freedom would be threatened. This is a fundamental principle of international law from which no state should derogate.[18]

International awareness of the gravity of military or armed attacks on refugee camps and settlements was primarily aroused by the attention of the media[19] on the attack by South African armed forces on the refugee camp of Kassinga in Huila Province, Angola, on 4 May 1978, when six hundred refugees were massacred and four hundred others wounded, and the massacre of Palestinian refugees in Sabra and Shatila camps in Beirut, Lebanon, in September 1982.[20] But these were by no means the first incidents or

[18] Guy Goodwin-Gill, *The Refugee in International Law* (Oxford: Clarendon Press, 1983), 97–100.

[19] e.g. *Le Monde* of 19 Sept. 1982 stated: 'Shatila was a camp. Now it is only a charnel-house. It was a main street and a hive of small alleyways. Now it is death under the sky' (trans. in *Refugee Magazine*, UNHCR (Aug. 1983), 21).

[20] *Refugee Magazine* (Aug. 1983), 18, 21.

the most serious in terms of the magnitude of loss of life or destruction of property. As far back as May 1940, French, Belgian, and Dutch refugees were bombed by Nazi forces at La Charité-sur-Loire in France, and thousands of lives were lost. As the *Refugee Magazine* of August 1983 put it, 'Alas, they were the forerunners of other refugees who, thirty years later, were in their turn to be attacked, machine-gunned, persecuted elsewhere in the world.'[21] At the height of the Zimbabwe liberation war, in August 1976 and November and December 1977, Rhodesian forces repeatedly attacked Zimbabwean refugee camps in Manica Province, Mozambique, killing over 3,600 refugees, wounding thousands of others, and causing extensive material damage. Raids by South African armed forces on refugee camps in Angola, Mozambique, and Zambia and commando-style attacks on refugee homes and places of residence in Botswana, Lesotho, Swaziland, and Zimbabwe have been increasing since 1974, thus making the security of refugees in Southern Africa a priority problem for the region and the international community.[22] Unofficial figures obtained from sources close to the UNHCR indicated that 5,212 refugees and 41 nationals were killed and several thousand wounded in Southern Africa alone between 1974 and 1986.

The Republic of South Africa has admitted to having carried out only some of the attacks on South African and Namibian refugees (e.g. the Kassinga (Angola) attack of May 1978 and that on the Makeni (Zambia) Refugee Reception/Transit Centre on 19 May 1986). However, all available evidence clearly points to that country as being the principal, if not exclusive, perpetrator of all the reported attacks in Angola, Botswana, Lesotho, Mozambique, Swaziland, Zambia, and Zimbabwe. South Africa's explanation for attacking refugees living in neighbouring countries has always been that the refugees (many of them sympathetic to national liberation movements) were involved in subversive activities against South Africa itself or against the Namibian (South West Africa) territory which it has illegally occupied and ruled. It has thus justified the attacks either by reference to the right of self-defence or that of hot pursuit, without demonstrating that the essential elements justifying the exercise of such rights under international law existed. It has

[21] Ibid. 38.

[22] Ibid. (Dec. 1983), 19.

instead relied on the basis of 'might is right', and indeed none of the states neighbouring South Africa is strong enough to defend itself militarily against South Africa. African governments are faced with a conflict between the reality of the military power of South Africa and the necessity to fulfil their international obligations. Governments perceive that they have a duty to provide sanctuary and physical protection to refugees of South African or Namibian origin and a duty to fulfil their obligations under the OAU Charter and the 1981 African Charter on Human Rights and Peoples' Rights to assist colonized or oppressed peoples in their liberation from foreign domination.[23]

This dilemma is particularly pronounced in the cases of Botswana, Lesotho, and Swaziland, which are caught politically and diplomatically between the millstones of White South Africa and Black nationalism. This has earned them the title 'captive states' of Southern Africa.[24] Of particular significance, however, is that each of the three states has been victim to devastating armed attacks on its refugee populations, perpetrated by the South African Defence Force. In one such attack, on Maseru (Lesotho), which occurred on 9 December 1982, forty-two people, including Lesotho nationals, were killed, thirty of them South African refugees. In another South African attack, on Gabarone, Botswana, on 14 June 1985, twelve people were killed. A South African General, Constand Viljoen, claimed that the targets were certain key activists of the 'control centre of the Transvaal sabotage organization of the African National Congress'.[25] In Swaziland, various detentions, deportations, and expulsions are reported to have taken place between 1981 and 1986, with the explanation that 'by continuing to deport [South] African National Congress refugees, Swaziland will hope to ensure that Mbabane [the capital city] is not invaded as Gabarone and Maseru have been . . . '.[26]

The situation facing refugees in Southern Africa typifies the destabilizing effect of armed attacks on asylum countries and their damaging impact on the principle of *non-refoulement*. Asylum

[23] See above, n. 5.

[24] Lesotho, Botswana and Swaziland: 'Captive States', by Rok Ajulu and Diana Cammack, in *Destructive Engagement: Southern Africa at War*, ed. Phyllis Johnson and David Martin (Harare: Zimbabwe Publishing House, 1986), ch. 5.

[25] *African Research Bulletin* (Exeter), 22/6 (1985), 7668–9.

[26] Johnson and Martin (eds.), *Destructive Engagement*, p.165.

countries have made extensive efforts to ensure that refugee camps and settlements are exclusively civilian and have made public pronouncements that they would not permit their territories to be used as staging grounds for subversive attacks against South Africa. Armed attacks against them have continued, however, and, because of their inability to defend themselves, they have been inclined instead to return refugees to South Africa or force them to seek resettlement in other countries. This practice has consequently precipitated the need for an adequate international response to the problem. A similar situation has also faced refugee populations in the Middle East, where Israel plays the same role as South Africa plays in Southern Africa. In the Middle East, however, Israel acts both directly and through surrogate militias and armed bands, while in Southern Africa there is hardly any evidence of involvement of forces other than military, para-military, or mercenary commanded directly by the South African armed forces.

It is not possible to obtain clear evidence of what occurs in all the refugee camps in Pakistan and South-east Asia, particularly since the UNHCR does not have free access to some of them. Oral testimony provided by UNHCR officials raises doubts about whether some refugee camps in these regions provide shelter to civilians only or are occasionally infiltrated by fighters, thus distinguishing them from refugee camps and settlements in Southern Africa. Whatever the situation may be, refugees have in fact been victims of attacks in the Thai–Kampuchean border and Waziristan and Kurram districts of Pakistan. The attack on Kurram district on 27 February 1987 killed more than forty-two people, mostly Afghan refugees.[27] There is no justification for attacking refugees on the mere suspicion that (from time to time) some guerrilla fighters may be living among the civilian refugees. International humanitarian law provides that a site used primarily for civilian purposes should, even in case of doubt, be presumed to be used for that purpose and should not therefore be the object of an armed attack.[28] The frequency with which this principle is violated does not encourage liberal asylum policies for asylum countries in South-east Asia (e.g. Thailand).

In Central America in the early 1980s, attacks similar to those in

[27] *La Suisse* (28 Feb. 1987).

[28] See Protocol I, Article 52 (1) and (3) (above, n. 9).

Southern Africa occurred involving Salvadorean refugees in Honduras and Guatemalan refugees in Mexico. There have been some attacks which did not involve the crossing of international borders, such as that on Colomoncagua refugee camps in Honduras in 1985, which is alleged to have been carried out by Honduran armed forces. If this allegation could be proved, then the question of responsibility of an asylum country as culprit rather than victim (as is usually the case) would arise.

Another situation, equally exceptional, is that of armed attacks by criminal bands against Ugandan refugees in southern Sudan in 1986 and Zaïrean refugees in Angola in 1985. In these cases the asylum country is neither victim nor culprit but may have a general responsibility for the safety of aliens living in its territory. The international responsibility of the attacking state, be it the country of origin or the asylum state itself, is examined below.

International response

The thirtieth session of the Executive Committee of the UNHCR (1979) severely condemned armed attacks on refugee camps in Southern Africa in which numerous refugees, including women and children, were killed and others permanently incapacitated. It expressed the hope that the necessary steps would be taken to protect refugees from such attacks and to assist the victims (Conclusion No. 14 (XXX)). At its thirty-second session, in 1981, the Executive Committee

> noted with grave concern the inhuman military attacks on refugee camps in Southern Africa and elsewhere, involving extreme and indescribable hardships to refugees and called upon the [United Nations] High Commissioner [for refugees] to examine the serious humanitarian problems resulting from Military Attacks on refugee camps and settlements which are the concern of the UNHCR, and the need for special measures to protect and ensure the safety of such refugees, and to report thereon at the earliest possible date to the Executive Committee.[29]

The High Commissioner mandated Ambassador Felix Schnyder, High Commissioner for Refugees from 1961 to 1965, to carry out a survey of the various aspects of the problem. Reacting to

[29] UNHCR Doc. EC/SCP/26, 15 Mar. 1983, p. 1.

a preliminary report by Ambassador Schnyder, the Executive Committee at its thirty-third session, in October 1982, expressed the hope that his report 'would lead to the adoption of measures which would make refugee camps and settlements safer from military attacks than they have so far been'.[30] Ambassador Schnyder reported *inter alia* that

> [the] various attacks have involved incursions by regular or paramilitary armed forces, indiscriminate bombardments and brutal killing or abductions of refugees including women, children and aged persons. Apart from the grave harm caused to refugees, such attacks may also endanger the national population of asylum countries and thus lead to the risk of the governments of these countries adopting a more restrictive attitude towards asylum seekers in general. In such situations respect for the essential principle of *non refoulement* could be endangered.[31]

The Schnyder report also pointed out the limitations of the UNHCR in dealing with armed attacks, particularly because its international protection mandate, seemed to be aimed essentially at ensuring that refugees were treated in conformity with basic standards recognized by the international community rather than providing actual physical protection to refugees. The report noted that armed attacks on refugee camps and settlements across international borders constituted first and foremost a violation of the sovereignty and territorial integrity of asylum countries, which was a matter outside the scope of the High Commissioner's competence.[32] While underlining the duty of the High Commissioner to seek to arouse the widest possible international interest in the problem of physical safety of refugees, Ambassador Schnyder argued that the prevention of armed attacks on refugees would normally call for action on the political plane and that the High Commissioner, after voicing his concern on behalf of the international community, would need to have recourse to the competent political organs of the United Nations.[33]

Nevertheless, Ambassador Schnyder proposed to the Executive Committee a Draft Declaration on the Prohibition of Military or Armed Attacks against Refugee Camps and Settlements which

[30] UNHCR Doc. EC/SCP/26, p. 1, para. 3.
[31] EC/SCP/26, p. 2, para. 5.
[32] EC/SCP/26, p. 2, para. 7.
[33] EC/SCP/26, p. 4, para. 14.

would be submitted for adoption as a solemn declaration of the United Nations General Assembly. When this draft declaration was examined by the Executive Committee in October 1982, political and strategic considerations prevailed over humanitarian concern and all that emerged was the underlining of the urgency of the question.[34] Members of the Executive Committee for developing countries (particularly Algeria, China, Nigeria, Tanzania, and Thailand) insisted on outright condemnation of armed attacks on refugee camps and settlements. Western industrialized countries generally agreed but failed to prevail on one or two influential members (believed to be the United Kingdom and the United States) who preferred not to jeopardize the interests of friendly states (Israel and South Africa) who were among the known main culprits. They argued that certain refugee camps were used to prepare and direct subversive activities against those countries from which the refugees had fled and consequently that the armed attacks were justifiable as legitimate acts of self-defence. Various attempts to reach a consensus on the draft declaration at each subsequent session of the Executive Committee suffered the same fate. The delegations from developing countries whose territories were actual or potential targets of armed attacks tried in vain to demonstrate flexibility by agreeing to formulate a mere set of principles or conclusions to be adopted by the Executive Committee instead of the Draft Solemn Declaration proposed by Ambassador Schnyder. At its thirty-seventh session, in October 1986, the Executive Committee reiterated its grave concern that military and armed attacks on refugee camps and settlements continued to occur world-wide in violation of basic rights of refugees.[35] The Committee stressed the urgency and importance of reaching agreement on a set of principles or conclusions dealing with the question of military or armed attacks on refugee camps and settlements in order to reinforce the protection of refugees, and requested its Chairman and the High Commissioner for Refugees to continue consultations on the matter and to report to the thirty-eighth session of the Executive Committee.[36]

The issue did not only feature at the Executive Committee of the UNHCR. The gravity of the problem of armed attacks on refugees

[34] UN General Assembly Doc. A/AC.96/613, 12 Oct. 1982, p. 7.
[35] UN General Assembly Doc. A/AC.96/618, 15 Oct. 1986, p. 30, para. 129.
[36] Ibid., para. 129 (*a*).

was also recognized and serious concern expressed in various other forums. The conclusions of the Eighth Round Table of the International Institute of Humanitarian Law, in September 1982, deplored the fact that in many cases refugees were being subjected to inhuman attacks carried out by military forces, resulting in the death or grievous suffering of large numbers of innocent people.[37] It drew attention to the obligation to respect fundamental principles governing the relations between states contained in the United Nations Charter and the Declaration of Principles of International Law on Friendly Relations (A 2625 (XXX)) and considered that the international community should examine those further measures necessary to ensure the better protection of victims of armed conflicts by such means as the clarification and elaboration of principles of refugee law. The Ninth Round Table of the San Remo Institute addressed itself to current problems in international humanitarian law relating to the activities of refugees, their physical safety, and national security. In its conclusions the Round Table underlined that, while a satisfactory, lasting solution to the problem of armed attacks may require a solution of the basic problem represented by a refugee situation, 'the issue of the responsibility of the country of origin for a refugee situation should be a fundamental element in determining the appropriate over-all response'.

The International Red Cross has similarly taken an interest in the subject. In order to contribute to the development of doctrine on the subject of military and armed attacks on refugee camps and settlements, the International Committee of the Red Cross (ICRC) published an article which dealt with some of the legal considerations relating to the question.[38] The Twenty-fifth International Conference of the Red Cross (1986), for its part, called upon governments to continue their efforts to find a speedy solution to the problem of military and armed attacks on refugee camps and settlements and reaffirmed the willingness of the Red Cross movement to assist in that endeavour.[39] It also condemned any act leading to forced involuntary disappearance of individuals or

[37] Publication of the International Institute of Humanitarian Law (San Remo, 1982).

[38] See Korsinik, 'Droit international humanitaire et protection des camps de réfugiés', p. 387.

[39] See Commission II Report of the XXVth International Conference of the Red Cross, Resolution on Refugees (Annex 15).

groups of individuals and urged governments to endeavour to prevent them. It recommended 'a universal campaign to make the rights of civilians according to international law known by all'.[40]

The United Nations Security Council too has expressed grave concern about various incidences of armed attacks on refugees, among them the attacks on refugees living in Lesotho (Res. 2406 of 14 December 1982 and 2707 of 15 December 1982, among others). In its resolution 39/140, dated 14 December 1984, the United Nations General Assembly condemned 'all violations of the right and safety of refugees and asylum-seekers, in particular those perpetrated through military or armed attacks against refugee camps and settlements . . .' (para. 3).

Factors militating against an agreed set of principles on the prohibition of military and armed attacks on refugee camps and settlements

Contending schools of thought

The predominant view advocated by the refugee-receiving countries (popularly known as asylum countries)—in particular Algeria, China, Nigeria, Sudan, Tanzania, Thailand, and Uganda—is that any future set of principles prohibiting military and armed attacks against refugee camps and settlements should make it clear that such attacks are contrary to international law since they violate the rights and safety of refugees and sovereignty and territorial integrity of asylum countries, and constitute attacks against civilians.[41] These countries also insist on the inclusion of an absolute prohibition against military and armed attacks on refugee camps and settlements, contending that these cannot be justified under any circumstances (e.g. on the grounds of self-defence or hot pursuit). They acknowledge that as long as the principles contain such a clear condemnation of armed attacks and state the obligation on states to refrain from such attacks, they should also require new responsibilities on the part of refugees, the countries of asylum or refuge, and the relevant United Nations bodies to ensure that the

[40] See Commission II Report of the XXVth International Conference of the Red Cross, Resolution on Refugees (Annex 15).

[41] See e.g. the statement of the Tanzania delegation on International Protection in the Summary Records of the thirty-sixth session of the UNHCR Executive Committee, Oct. 1985.

civilian and humanitarian character of the camps and settlements is maintained. These countries recognize the desirability of granting UNHCR access to the camps as one measure to ensure that their civilian character is always preserved. The proponents of this viewpoint argue, however, that in order to avoid the possibility that the principles (particularly those relating to the character of the camps) may themselves be used as a pretext for an attack or as an excuse following an attack, the prohibition against armed attacks should not be made conditional on the need for such camps and settlements to be exclusively civilian and humanitarian.[42]

According to a second school of thought, composed of a small group of countries (the Federal Republic of Germany, Israel, the United Kingdom, the United States), refugee camps and settlements must only be used for civilian and humanitarian purposes, and refugees, countries of asylum or refuge, and the relevant United Nations bodies should do all within their power to ensure that such camps and settlements are exclusively civilian and humanitarian. They argue that this is necessary to establish the conditions which are most likely to have the effect of preventing military and armed attacks and that the protected status of refugee camps and settlements must not be abused or jeopardized by those who would introduce into them activities or elements inconsistent with their civilian and humanitarian character. The proponents of this view are reluctant to condemn military or armed attacks when they occur unless the above-mentioned elements are clearly reflected in a set of agreed principles on this subject.

Realpolitik and legal ambiguity

Despite intensive efforts within the UNHCR Executive Committee to reach an agreement on a Declaration of Principles on the Prohibition of Military and Armed Attacks on Refugee Camps and Settlements, it has not been possible to arrive at a consensus during six years of negotiations. As attacks have become widespread, so have the political obstacles. The principal perpetrators continue to be Israel and South Africa, both of which are allies or countries of strategic importance to the United States, an influential participant in the negotiations on the Declaration of Principles, and without whose consent no consensus is possible. In the case of Central

[42] *Refugee Magazine* (Dec. 1985), 5.

America the political sensitivity of the situation makes it difficult for the United States to take a position against attacks on Salvadorean or Guatemalan refugee camps. Similar considerations would apply in relation to Afghan and Kampuchean refugees, but since most of the countries involved in these situations (Afghanistan, Pakistan, the Soviet Union, and Vietnam) are not members of the Executive Committee, they could not obstruct an agreement. Israel and the United States are members of the Executive Committee, and considerations of *realpolitik*—in particular the desire to shelter strategic allies or to keep open the option to use force as a viable instrument of diplomacy—have outweighed humanitarian considerations. Moreover, the recent tendency by the United States to use force against countries such as Libya and Nicaragua in order to coerce changes in their policies does not provide the necessary incentive to outlaw the use of force in other circumstances and is likely to have a negative effect on the negotiations for the prohibition of armed attacks on refugee camps and settlements.

The problem of determining which principles of international law are applicable to the problem of armed attacks on refugees has also caused a lot of confusion. There is no single body of law that deals adequately with the problem. Refugee law does not cover the question of physical protection of refugees, and the law of armed conflicts expressed in the Geneva Conventions of 1949 and its additional Protocols of 1977 covers situations facing refugees in other circumstances and has little to do with armed attacks on refugee camps and settlements. The international law relating to the use of force, human rights, or protection of aliens can be applied to this problem only by analogy since the concepts were developed before the phenomenon of military and armed attacks on refugees manifested itself and became a matter of great concern to the international community.

The problem arises both from the unwillingness of states to recognize and respect the existing law and from the ambiguity of the law which might be applicable to certain concrete situations in which refugee camps and settlements are attacked.[43] It is necessary, therefore, that existing law be interpreted in the light of specific situations in which refugees find themselves, and that specific additional measures be taken to reinforce the security of refugee

[43] Korsinik, 'Droit international humanitaire et protection des camps de réfugiés', p. 38.

camps and settlements. The following part of this study will examine the applicable principles of international law with a view to identifying where such principles need to be consolidated and strengthened.

The relevant principles of international law

Despite the lengthy discussions on the problem of military and armed attacks that have been taking place in the Executive Committee of the UNHCR, the principle that such attacks on refugees cannot be justified under conventional and customary international law has been questioned by some of the participants, the most vocal of whom are the United States, the United Kingdom, and Israel. This minority group has contended that some of these attacks can be justified on grounds of the exercise of the right of self-defence. Arguments of this kind are based on political rather than legal premisses. Attacks on refugees who are civilians and non-combatants and who are generally housed in specially designated areas under the care of international agencies such as the UNHCR or the United Nations Relief and Works Agency (UNRWA) are illegal. Nevertheless, the issue of the illegality of military and armed attacks needs to be considered. In particular, two fundamental questions should be examined: one must determine whether military and armed attacks are proscribed under conventional or customary international law, and if so, whether the law relating to the exercise of the right of self-defence provides an exception to the general prohibition. In order to respond to the two questions, it is necessary to examine briefly the relevant bodies of law relating to armed conflicts, use of force by states, the right of self-defence, and human rights and refugee law.

Armed conflicts

The international humanitarian law on armed conflicts, also known as the law of Geneva, aims at safeguarding military personnel who are no longer in combat (*hors de combat*), as well as persons not taking part in hostilities.[44] Its provisions are embodied in the four

[44] Jean Pictet, 'The Principles of International Humanitarian Law', *International Review of the Red Cross* (1966), 455.

Geneva Conventions of 1949 (of which Convention No. IV deals with the protection of civilian persons in time of war) and their Additional Protocols of 1977 (Protocols I and II).[45] They are relevant to the character of refugees as persons not taking part in hostilities, or who are at least ex-combatants. Although the Geneva Conventions and Protocols are not directly concerned with the problem of armed attacks on refugees, they contain certain rules which could be applied by analogy. For example, Common Article 3 of the 1949 Geneva Conventions contains the minimum standard for treatment of persons not taking active part in hostilities. According to the article, these persons must in all circumstances be treated humanely, without any adverse distinction founded on race, colour, religion or faith, sex, birth, or wealth, or any other similar criteria.[46] The article prohibits, among other things, violence to life and person, in particular murder, mutilation, cruel treatment, and torture.

Under Common Article 3, military and armed attacks on refugees would be prohibited as acts involving violence to life and person etc. Every single attack on refugees to date has involved one or more of the prohibited acts, including the 'taking of hostages', 'outrages upon personal dignity, in particular humiliating and degrading treatment and summary sentencing and execution'.[47] Even assuming that combatants might be present in the refugee camps and settlements, visiting relatives, or recuperating, they should be entitled to better treatment than being summarily killed.[48] Furthermore, their presence could not justify an indiscriminate attack on a camp or settlement whose inhabitants are mostly civilians, including women and children.

As to the Fourth Geneva Convention of 1949, it appears that the articles containing specific references to refugees (Articles 26, 44, and 70) are not of much assistance since they refer only to exemption from treatment as enemy aliens or protection from arrest, prosecution, conviction, or deportation where the refugees in question became refugees before the outbreak of hostilities. On

[45] See above, nn. 3, 9.

[46] See above, n. 3.

[47] This view and a few other ideas expressed in this chapter have been developed in part from discussions with officials of the Directorate of Refugee Law and Doctrine of the UNHCR Office, Geneva. I am indebted in particular to Anders Johnson for his ideas, some of which I have adopted.

[48] Ibid.

the other hand, refugees could benefit from the protection provided under Article 4 of the Fourth Convention, following the adoption of additional Protocol I. Article 73 of this protocol accords to persons who became refugees before the outbreak of hostilities the status of 'protected persons' under the 1949 Geneva Conventions.[49] The protocol also extends the protection of the 1949 Geneva Conventions to situations of armed conflicts involving the struggle of peoples against colonial domination and alien occupation, and against racist regimes in the exercise of their right of self-determination.[50] Refugees from such conflicts would benefit from the protection of the 1949 Geneva Conventions and their additional protocols even if they were not nationals of states party to these instruments.[51]

Although Article 73 is emphasized by some authorities,[52] others contend that its applicability is limited to refugees who are recognized as such before the outbreak of hostilities, and thus does not apply to persons who become refugees after the outbreak of hostilities or in peacetime. Most incidents of armed attacks on refugees in the Middle East do take place in a situation of existing hostilities since all Arab countries except Egypt are technically at war with Israel. In Southern Africa, because armed attacks on refugees take place in peacetime, protection is derived from established customs, principles of humanity, and dictates of public conscience referred to in Article 2 of Protocol I. It has also been argued that refugees who do not qualify as protected persons under Article 4 of the Fourth Convention would be entitled to enjoy the safeguards provided by Article 75 of Protocol I.[53]

Thus, there exist certain gaps in the law of armed conflicts, particularly as it may be applied to military and armed attacks on refugees. The foregoing illustration makes clear that not all categories of refugees qualify as protected persons entitled to benefit from Article 4 of the Fourth Geneva Convention of 1949. Second, the fact that the 1974–7 Diplomatic Conference rejected

[49] Patrnogic, 'International Protection of Refugees in Armed Conflicts' (San Remo: International Institute for Humanitarian Law, 1985).

[50] Article 1 (4); see n. 9.

[51] See 'Basic Rules of the Geneva Conventions and their additional Protocols Chapter I.V Section II (2)', ed. ICRC, Geneva (Sept. 1983).

[52] e.g. Patrnogic, 'International Protection of Refugees in Armed Conflicts'.

[53] M. Bothe, *et al.*, *New Rules for Victims of Armed Conflict* (Dordrecht: Martinus Nijhoff, 1982), 449. See also Veuthey, 'Réfugiés et conflits armés', p. 33.

the proposal by Syria to extend the protection of Additional Protocol I to refugees who flee after the beginning of an armed conflict is further evidence of a gap remaining to be filled. In that case, Syria was invited (by the Conference) 'to continue its efforts in connection with the law of refugees outside the specialized field of the laws of war'.[54]

The use of force by states

As indicated earlier, most states that attack refugees attempt to justify their actions by claiming the right of self-defence. It is true that the use or threat of force is illegal unless carried out in self-defence or with the authority of an organ of the United Nations.[55] This principle, which is reflected in the Kellogg–Briand Pact of 1928, where it was provided that 'settlements or solutions of all disputes or conflicts of whatever origin they may be which may arise among them [states] shall never be sought except by peaceful means',[56] has a foundation in both customary law and state practice. It has also been enshrined and strengthened by the United Nations Charter, in Articles 2, 3, and 4. Its current validity has been underlined by the International Court of Justice in its recent judgment concerning military and para-military activities against Nicaragua. The Court states:

> far from having constituted a marked departure from a customary international law which still exists unmodified, the [United Nations] Charter gave expression in this field to principles already present in customary international law, and that law has in the subsequent four decades developed under the influence of the Charter, to such an extent that a number of rules contained in the Charter have acquired a status independent of it. The essential consideration is that both Charter and the customary international law flow from a common fundamental principle outlawing the use of force in international relations.[57]

There is no doubt that an armed attack constitutes a use of force. The International Court of Justice has suggested that, in addition

[54] Bothe, *New Rules for Victims of Armed Conflict*.

[55] I. Brownlie, *International Law and the Use of Force by States* (Oxford: Clarendon Press, 1963), 367.

[56] 94 League of Nations Treaty Series 57; see also Brownlie *International Law and the Use of Force*, p. 79.

[57] *Military and Paramilitary Activities in and against Nicaragua* (*Nicaragua* v. *United States of America*) (*Merits*), Judgement, *ICJ Reports* (1986), 96–7.

to an 'armed attack', the use of force includes other less serious forms of attack, such as the 'organizing or encouraging the organization of irregular forces or armed bands . . . for the incursion into the territory of another State'.[58] The illegality of armed attacks on refugee camps and settlements therefore would be clear and uncontested except where such attacks are in the exercise of the legal right of individual or collective self-defence as provided for under customary international law and in Article 51 of the United Nations Charter.[59]

The right of self-defence

The question is not whether states can resort to force in the exercise of the right of self-defence. Many authorities[60] have cited cases where force could be used, provided that 'the principles of good faith and international law are complied with, including the requirement that necessity of self-defence, instant, overwhelming, leaving no choice of deliberation must be established'.[61] Our intention is rather to determine whether armed attacks on refugees could form a legitimate exercise of the right of self-defence.

The right of self-defence can be exercised and justified only where it is permitted by international law, including customary law,[62] but even in this case the *onus probandi* rests on the state to assert the necessity of self-defence.[63] There is always a presumption of illegality when force is used.[64] The state using force has to establish that it has been the victim of an armed attack and that the reaction is proportionate to the apparent threat.[65] Furthermore, the right of self-defence in international law contemplates action against states only.[66] Although the right of anticipatory action was recognized in cases of the pursuit of armed bands,[67] this rule would

[58] Ibid., 102.

[59] Ibid.

[60] See e.g. Brownlie *International Law and the Use of Force*, pp. 214, 238; D. W. Bowett, *Self Defence in International Law* (Manchester: Manchester University Press, 1958).

[61] See Bowett, *Self Defence in International Law*, p. 59.

[62] See Lauterpacht, 20 Grot Soc. (L934), pp. 178, 188–9, 198–201; Brownlie, *International Law and the Use of Force*, p. 238; Bowett, *Self Defence in International Law*.

[63] Brownlie, *International Law and the Use of Force*, p. 252.

[64] Ibid.

[65] Ibid.

[66] See Corfu Channel Case (Merits), *ICJ Reports* (1949).

[67] Soviet Union in Outer Mongolia (1921) and Manchuria (1929). Cases discussed by Brownlie, 7 ICLQ (1958), 732–3.

only apply where their acts could be imputed to the state of asylum or refuge,[68] or where the support given constituted an armed attack. Concerning the rendering of assistance to rebels, the International Court of Justice held that 'the Court does not believe that the concept of "armed attack" includes not only acts by armed bands where such acts occur on a significant scale but also assistance to rebels in the form of provision of weapons or logistical or other support'.[69] It has also been argued that the rule in favour of the right of anticipatory action is incorrect since Article 51 of the United Nations Charter excludes it. It was suggested that preparations for an attack could be countered only by preparations to resist attack. Ian Brownlie argues that 'The State which considers itself to be the object of military preparations [is not] forced to remain supine but may take all necessary precautions short of commencing an attack: it may also appeal to the competent organs of the United Nations or of a regional defence organization.'[70]

Second, the right of self-defence cannot be invoked by a state that acts in violation of international humanitarian law. This body of law prohibits attacks on civilian persons and civilian property, including all acts of violence, whether committed in offence or defence. Attacks or threats of violence intended to terrorize the civilian population are also prohibited.[71] Thus, it should not make any difference if those attacks are alleged to be an act of self-defence. There could be no justification even if the refugees have themselves acted in violation of international law. Bothe and others[72] have argued that 'Prohibition of inhuman treatment by acts such as those of Common Article 3 [of the 1949 Geneva Conventions] is absolute and permanent and does not leave room for any violations in response to violations by the adverse party.'[73]

Third, no attack on refugees could be excusable as being an act of reprisal. Article 73 of Additional Protocol I[74] applies 'in all circumstances and without any distinction', and Article 51 (Protocol I) prohibits both indiscriminate attacks and attacks

[68] Michael Akehurst, *A Modern Introduction to International Law*, 5th edn. (London: George Allen and Unwin, 1984), 87.

[69] *ICJ Reports* (1986), 104.

[70] Brownlie, *International Law and the Use of Force*, pp. 366, 367.

[71] Article 51 of Additional Protocol I (see above, n. 9).

[72] Above, n. 53.

[73] Bothe *et al.*, *New Rules for Victims of Armed Conflict*, p. 636.

[74] Above, n. 9.

against civilian populations generally or by way of reprisal. Furthermore, the Declaration on Principles of International Law Concerning Friendly Relations among States, which reflects *opinio juris* as to customary international law on the subjects it covers, provides that states have a duty to refrain from reprisals involving the use of force.[75]

Human rights law

It has been shown in the preceding account that the illegality of armed attacks on refugees involving incursions across international borders could be established on the basis of the law of armed conflicts as well as the law relating to the use of force by states. Not all attacks on refugees fall within these categories, however. Military attacks have occurred in situations of non-international armed conflicts such as in Lebanon and Sudan. They have also taken place in non-conflict situations—e.g. the 1985 Honduran Army attack on the refugee camp Colomoncagua in Honduras, apparently on the pretext of flushing out Salvadorean guerrillas hiding there. The Lebanon and Sudan cases could be covered by the provisions of Common Article 3 of the 1949 Conventions since this has been held to apply to non-international conflicts such as in Guatemala (1954), Algeria (1955), Hungary (1955), Lebanon (1982),[76] and, according to the recent judgment of the International Court of Justice, also Nicaragua.[77] The illegality of the Honduran attack can only be established, however, by resorting to human rights law.

Human rights principles, whether based on religious or ideological concepts, uniformly reflect respect for the right to life and security of the person. In terms of international law, this right is considered to be basic and universal.[78] Its universality manifests itself in the enshrinement of the right to life and security of persons in all major human rights instruments, such as the Universal Declaration of Human Rights, the International Covenants on Civil and Political Rights, the European and American Conventions, and

[75] *ICJ Reports* (1986) 101–2.

[76] Veuthey, 'Réfugiés et conflits armés', p. 13–14.

[77] *ICJ Reports* (1986), 114.

[78] For a detailed analysis of the right to life and security in international law, see R. J. Vincent, *Human Rights and International Relations* (Cambridge: Cambridge University Press, 1986).

the African Charter for Human Rights and Peoples' Rights. Military and armed attacks which involve violence, indiscriminate killings, abductions, and torture thus constitute violations of international human rights law.

The defence of human rights could also be invoked to justify certain activities of refugees against their countries of origin. For example, Namibian, South African, and Palestinian refugees could justify their military activities against their countries of origin on the basis of the legitimate struggle for the realization of their right to self-determination. Grahl-Madsen has considered this question in relation to the concept of a 'just war'[79] as well as in the context of the principles of human rights law. He feels that international condemnation should not be incurred by the state of asylum which tolerates military activities in defence of the human rights of refugees: 'If an activity merely constitutes an exercise of a Human Right as defined in the Universal Declaration of Human Rights or other Human Rights instrument which is trod underfoot by an oppressive regime, toleration by the State granting asylum will hardly incur international responsibility.'[80]

The right to self-determination is just such a human right, as Grahl-Madsen states. It is provided for under Article 1 of the International Covenant of Civil and Political Rights. Furthermore, its significance is underlined in the United Nations Declaration A/Res.1514(XV) on the Independence of Colonial Countries and Peoples, which the International Court of Justice has held to be an accurate statement of modern international law (South West Africa and Western Sahara judgments).[81] There seems also to be a general agreement that peoples who have a legal right to self-determination are entitled to fight a war of national liberation. It has been observed that 'even western States do not dissent from this view . . . although they consider United Nations General Assembly resolutions encouraging wars of national liberation as politically undesirable'.[82] The General Assembly resolution goes further and invites all states

[79] See A. Grahl-Madsen, 'Decolonization, The Modern Version of a Just War', *German Year Book of International Law*, 22 (1979), 255–73; id., *The Status of Refugees in International Law* (Leiden: A. W. Sijthoff, 1966, 1972), ii. 173–87. Note also that the International Convention on the Suppression and Punishment of the Crime of Apartheid declares that the practices of apartheid constitute a crime against humanity.

[80] Grahl-Madsen, *The Status of Refugees*, vol. ii. 173–87.

[81] South West Africa Case, *ICJ Reports* (1971), 16, 31; Western Sahara Case, *ICJ Reports* (1975), 31–3, 121.

[82] Akehurst, *A Modern Introduction to International Law*, p. 256.

to provide material and moral assistance to the national liberation movements in colonial territories.[83] In the Definition of Aggression, the General Assembly has also recognized (in Article 7) the right of all peoples struggling against colonial rule to receive support from other states.[84]

I would argue further that the provisions in the United Nations Declaration on Friendly Relations Among States (A2625 (XXV)), imposing the duty to refrain from the organization of armed bands or to tolerate armed activities against another state, apply to situations other than struggles of colonial peoples to achieve self-determination. This is why Article 4 of the United Nations Declaration on Territorial Asylum prohibits states from permitting only those activities contrary to the purposes and principles of the United Nations. Thus, *a contrario*, activities outside this category are not prohibited. The argument that refugees should generally refrain from armed activities[85] could only be based on pragmatic considerations and not on legal obligations as such.

In connection with the provision of the 1969 OAU Convention, on the question of subversive activities (Article III), it is submitted that it refers to activities against member states of the OAU only and cannot benefit non-members, including South Africa. More important, the provision is not intended to preclude activities in pursuance of the right of self-determination.[86] It is significant to note in this connection that Article 20 of the 1981 African Charter for Human Rights and Peoples' Rights, which came into force in October 1986, provides *inter alia* that:

2. Colonized or oppressed peoples shall have the right to free themselves from the bond of domination by resorting to all means recognized by the international community;
3. All peoples shall have the right to assistance of the States Parties to the present Charter in their liberation against foreign domination, be it political, economic or cultural.[87]

The OAU has demonstrated its resolve to support the right to self-determination even when its member states are involved in the

[83] See e.g. GA Res. 2105 (XX), 20 Dec. 1965.

[84] *American Journal of International Law* (1975), 480.

[85] Grahl-Madsen, *The Status of Refugees*, ii, 147; see also the principles suggested below under the heading 'Some possible approaches to the problem'.

[86] It would otherwise be in conflict with Article 20 of the African Charter on Human Rights and Peoples' Rights.

[87] See above, n. 5.

dispute. It has recognized SADR and its Polisario government-in-exile which is at war with Morocco, an OAU member state, over the disputed territory of the Western Sahara.[88]

Grahl-Madsen has reviewed in detail this question of international responsibility of countries of asylum or refuge and considered the applicability of the relevant provisions of the Havana Convention, the Montevideo Treaty, and the OAU Refugee Convention.[89] He concludes that 'there cannot be seen to exist any rule of international law outside Africa and Latin America, that is obliging a State to take special measures to ensure that refugees . . . do not engage in any activity which may be prejudicial to the interests of the country of origin'.[90] The rules applicable to the parties to the regional instruments cannot be considered as rules of international law of general application, such as the rule that international responsibility may not be incurred by the exercise by refugees of recognized human rights.[91]

It appears that military organizations with purposes other than the exercise of recognized human rights[92] are not automatically outlawed either: 'The law is not entirely clear in this respect. It seems that one cannot out of hand declare such an organization illegal . . . In the final test, it is the organs of the United Nations Security Council or the General Assembly, as the case may be, to decide whether a threat to peace or international security really may be said to exist.'[93] Furthermore, it appears that, where a state could be held responsible, it may not be demanded of it that it ends the asylum by expelling the refugees or by extraditing them to the offended state.[94] The bias in favour of protecting the rights and safety of refugees is quite clear.

Refugee law

There is a direct link between refugee law, human rights law, and the United Nations Charter. The three main refugee instruments,

[88] Note that Morocco withdrew from the OAU in protest at the recognition of the Polisario (Saharawi Republic) government. 'POLISARIO' is the name for the Movement for the Liberation of Western Sahara.

[89] Grahl-Madsen, *The Status of Refugees*, ii. 134–87.

[90] Ibid. 147.

[91] Ibid. 184.

[92] e.g. guerrilla organizations fighting to change the political system of their country of origin.

[93] Grahl-Madsen, *The Status of Refugees*, ii. 185–6.

[94] Ibid. 187.

the 1950 UNHCR Statute,[95] the 1951 Refugee Convention and its 1967 Protocol,[96] and the 1967 United Nations Declaration on Territorial Asylum, all refer to the principles of the United Nations and the Universal Declaration of Human Rights. Thus, members of the United Nations and Parties to the International Covenants on Human Rights have an obligation to protect the human rights of refugees. Article 55 of the United Nations Charter obliges member states to promote 'universal respect for, and observance of, human rights and fundamental freedoms for all without distinction as to race, sex, language or religion'. Also, all members of the United Nations have pledged themselves (under Article 56) 'to take joint and separate action, in co-operation with the organization, for the achievement of the purposes set forth in Article 55'. Furthermore, Article 2 (1) of the International Human Rights covenants obliges state parties to respect and ensure to all individuals within their territories and subject to their jurisdiction the rights recognized in those instruments.[97]

Refugee law, however, lacks explicit provisions on the question of the physical safety of refugees. The UNHCR Statute refers to international protection in general terms, suggesting that the main concern is legal rather than physical protection. The applicability of the Statute in relation to the security of refugees only arose during the debate preceding the adoption of the Statute by the United Nations General Assembly. At that time, a view was expressed that 'it would be the duty of the High Commissioner to intervene with governments in order that refugees might be afforded minimum rights and privileges essential to their existence and security'.[98] Similarly, the 1951 Refugee Convention and the 1967 Protocol did not contain explicit reference to the physical safety of refugees in their enumeration of the rights to be accorded either on an equal basis with nationals or with other aliens.[99] Although refugees should be entitled to the same treatment as ordinary aliens, in regard to the protection of physical safety, the law applicable to

[95] See above, n. 1.

[96] See above, n. 2.

[97] See Universal Declaration, Article 3; International Covenant on Civil and Political Rights, Article 6; and Article 2 (1) of the two 1966 Human Rights Covenants.

[98] GAOR, C. III, p. 363 (1950), Mrs Roosevelt (USA).

[99] Convention Relating to the Status of Refugees, 28 July 1951, 189 United Nations Treaty Series and Protocol Relating to the Status of Refugees, 16 Dec. 1966, see General Assembly Res. 2198 (XXI) 1966 and 606 United Nations Treaty Series.

aliens is unsatisfactory since the duty to protect aliens is owed by the alien's national state. The situation of refugees is thus anomalous since they do not enjoy the protection of the country of their nationality.[100]

A central provision of the 1967 Declaration on Territorial Asylum is that the granting of asylum is a humanitarian, non-political act and that, once asylum is granted, it must be respected by all other states, including the state from whose territory the refugees have fled.[101] This provision is intended to ensure the security of refugees and countries of asylum. In practice, however, countries of origin of refugees do not perceive the granting of asylum in that way. Refugee policy is often an intensely political matter, and refugee problems, therefore, are a major source of tension between states.

Some possible approaches to the problem

I have provided an abundance of legal authority in support of the prohibition of military and armed attacks on refugee camps and settlements, but the legal grounds are often ambiguous and indirect. The 1951 Refugee Convention does not directly cover the question of the physical protection of refugees and asylum seekers. The obligation to ensure the safety of refugees should not rest on asylum countries alone since these may not always have the ability to ensure it. The obligation should be imposed on all states, both individually and collectively. The custodian of the right to safety and security of refugees should be the international community as a whole, with the High Commissioner as its principal agent or Refugee Ambassador.[102] Unfortunately, however, the High Commissioner has regretted that he does not have the means or the competence to ensure physical protection.[103] It is necessary, therefore, to strengthen the hand of the High Commissioner by adopting new legal and political measures to reinforce the physical safety and security of refugees.

[100] See Akehurst, *A Modern Introduction to International Law*, p. 87.

[101] Grahl-Madsen, *The Status of Refugees*, ii. 191.

[102] L. W. Holborn, *Refugees: A Problem of Our Time*, 2 vols. (Metuchen, NJ: Scarecrow Press, 1975), i. 153–73.

[103] See report to ECOSOC-E/1983/43, part IV, p. 24–8.

Legal measures

It is necessary to draw up a new international convention dealing with the problem of the physical safety of refugees, and particularly with the prohibition of armed attacks on refugees. This idea is not new; it was first mooted at the Ninth Round Table of the Institute of International Humanitarian Law at San Remo which concluded that 'the progressive development of refugee law through the elaboration of an appropriate and comprehensive international instrument is required to define more adequately the rights and obligations of all the various parties to a refugee situation and to obtain a satisfactory overall response from the international community as a whole'.[104] The new instrument to be drawn up should clarify, specify, and consolidate the principles and rules of international law applicable to the whole question of the security of refugees in order to improve the understanding and acceptance of such principles and rules. It should specifically strengthen the competence of the High Commissioner on all issues pertaining to physical safety, including the importance of maintaining an international presence in refugee camps and settlements to guarantee their civilian character. The High Commissioner's mandate in this respect should extend to all refugees, whether or not they fall under the notion of 'refugee' provided under the 1951 Refugee Convention. The instrument should clarify the international responsibility of all forces attacking refugees, including organizations other than states. It should also underline the collective responsibility of all in the protection of refugees, including the duty of international solidarity and burden-sharing in responding to the needs of the victims of attacks.

In order to arrive at the proposed international legal instrument, a lengthy period of deliberation would be necessary to articulate carefully all the principles to be included. A sequential approach is therefore recommended. The first stage should be to build on the work already initiated in order to agree on the declaration of a set of principles on the prohibition of military or armed attacks on refugee camps and settlements. Encouraged by the recent procedural conclusions emphasizing the importance of reaching an agreement,[105] the Executive Committee should focus its attention

[104] Publication, San Remo, International Institute of Humanitarian Law (Sept. 1983).
[105] UN General Assembly Doc. A/AC. 96/618, 15 Oct. 1986, p. 30, para. 129.

on the following principles and recommendations, which are suggested with a view to overcoming previous difficulties in the negotiations.

Principles

1. Refugees, including those in camps and settlements, shall not be an object of a military or armed attack. Such attacks must be condemned by the international community if and when they occur.

Explanation. This principle is in line with Article 51 of Protocol I and Article 13 (1) and (2) of Protocol II additional to the 1949 Geneva Conventions. Although the principle is not specific on whether under existing principles of international law military or armed attacks on refugee camps and settlements are proscribed, such a conclusion is inevitable once the principle is agreed. A further elaboration of this principle may spell out the right of the country of asylum and of refugees themselves to demand compensation for damages caused, as well as to demand punishment of the individual culprits.

2. Refugee camps and settlements are civilian places. Their civilian character shall not be abused by anyone.

Explanation. This principle prohibits any state, group, or individual from abusing the non-military character of refugee camps and settlements. It is a safeguard for those states that allege that certain refugee camps and settlements could be used for military purposes.

3. The UNHCR's access to all refugee camps and settlements of its concern shall be facilitated, taking into account the importance of maintaining the highest degree of co-operation with the country of asylum or refuge.

Explanation. This principle provides a further safeguard that refugee establishments will remain non-military. UNHCR's presence would enable it to monitor refugee activities which appear suspicious to the country of origin. The UNHCR would also be empowered to demand the removal of any military elements whenever they were identified. In doing so, however, UNHCR must co-operate with countries of asylum which are naturally sensitive on matters bearing on their sovereignty.

4. Reprisal attacks on refugee camps and settlements or

indiscriminate attacks or acts of terrorism against refugees shall be forbidden.

Explanation. This principle is in line with the rules of international humanitarian law. It is based on the premiss that refugee camps and settlements are civilian places and actions by refugees against their countries of origin do not justify reprisal attacks on civilians. States make reprisal attacks on refugees in neighbouring countries in order to appease public opinion in the country of origin or to create an appearance of invincibility.

5. No state shall tolerate, condone, or encourage any state, or agents thereof, to launch attacks on refugees or to give any other form of assistance to an attacking force. This also includes the obligation of all states to take measures to prevent such attacks.

6. States shall respect all the humanitarian principles and ideals, and in particular abide by the applicable rules of international law, including international humanitarian law.

Explanation. This is a 'catch-all' clause intended to strengthen the respect for international law and encourage its implementation. It is based on the concept that a solution to the problem of military and armed attacks can only be the result of strict compliance with the principles of international law.

Recommendations

Several pragmatic considerations which, though not legal obligations *per se*, are nevertheless essential for the promotion of the physical safety of refugees in countries of asylum or refuge. They are listed only as recommendations since they are matters falling essentially within the realm of national sovereignty and in certain cases could only be observed where the state concerned has the means and is able to do so. The idea of specific recommendations has not been considered in the past, although attempts have been made to frame some provisions in a non-mandatory format. A clear distinction between obligations and recommendations is useful to the extent that it may allay unnecessary fears of encroachment on matters strictly within the national sovereignty of states. Such a clarification may render the draft declaration of principles more easily acceptable to governments. The following recommendations are proposed.

1. Refugee camps and settlements should be established at a reasonable distance from the border of the country from which the refugees have fled.[106]
2. Countries of asylum or refuge should not tolerate within their borders activities of refugees which are contrary to the purpose and principles of the United Nations.
3. The UNHCR and other international agencies should assist countries of asylum or refuge to promote conditions of safety for refugees.
4. The international community shares with countries of asylum or refuge the moral obligations to protect refugees from attacks endangering their physical integrity and well-being.
5. Refugees have a duty to abide by the laws and regulations of the countries of asylum or refuge, including the duty to respect rules for the protection of national security which encompass their own security.

General

The above principles and recommendations should form the basis of a solemn declaration to be adopted by the United Nations General Assembly. The adoption of the declaration should be followed by a diplomatic conference to negotiate an international treaty or convention on the physical safety of refugees which will transform the agreed principles into concrete legal norms to bind all states.

Political and other measures

The protection of refugees from armed attacks and other forms of physical violence cannot be achieved through further efforts at codification and progressive development of law alone. The latter would only provide a juridical basis for political action, including the need for states and international organizations to voice public consternation when attacks on refugees occur. Yet, regional and international arrangements should be agreed at a political level in order to ease inter-state tensions which are the usual prelude to an

[106] Grahl-Madsen *The Status of Refugees*, ii. 146–7, observes that the practice by governments of removing refugees from certain areas contiguous to their countries of origin does not reflect a belief that they are bound to do so by any consideration of international law or even international comity.

armed attack on refugees. The OAU Convention[107] is a typical example of such regional arrangements resulting in a legal instrument concerned with a regional problem. The convention contains provisions similar to those being proposed in the recommendations suggested above. In September 1986 the leaders of Burundi, Rwanda, Tanzania, Uganda, and Zaïre agreed that refugees in each other's territory should be kept at least 50 kilometres away from their countries of origin. Similar measures should be encouraged in other regions.[108]

The UNHCR and other humanitarian organizations should also strive to arouse the widest possible international interest in the problem of armed attacks on refugees. This should be achieved by publicizing the attacks and the serious loss of life and property that they cause. Publicity about and public indignation at such attacks should be so forceful that even the most brutal regimes cannot ignore the criticism. As well as the appeal to the conscience of international public opinion, the United Nations political organs should be called upon to assume their responsibilities. The Secretary-General of the United Nations should bring the matter of armed attacks on refugees to the Security Council, invoking Article 99 of the Charter of the United Nations. The Security Council may then take the necessary action, including calling upon states to assist asylum countries to strengthen the security of refugee camps and settlements within their territories.

Conclusion

All members of the United Nations have pledged themselves to take joint and separate action, in co-operation with the organization, for the achievement of universal respect for, and observance of, human rights and fundamental freedoms (Articles 55 and 56 of the United Nations Charter). States parties to the 1949 Geneva Conventions have undertaken to *respect and ensure respect* for the Conventions in all circumstances (Common Article 1), and the parties to the 1951 Refugee Conventions have undertaken to co-operate with the UNHCR in the exercise of its functions, which include the international protection of refugees (Article 35 (1)). There is therefore a collective legal obligation for members of the

[107] See above, n. 4.
[108] See above, n. 106.

international community to take the measures necessary to find a solution to the problem of violation of the rights of refugees to life and safety. Furthermore, when so many innocent people are the victims of man's brutality, the principles of humanity on which the whole concept of asylum is based and the dictates of public conscience must compel the international community to act.

In the final analysis, the question is as moral as it is legal. It is a humanitarian problem requiring a humanitarian approach. It is a matter that threatens international stability, peace, and security among nations and endangers respect for the cardinal principle of refugee law, the principle of *non-refoulement*. The question should therefore be 'What approach conforms better with the humanitarian ideals on which the whole question of asylum is based?' No humanitarian instrument develops without a full commitment to humanitarian ideals and the spirit of selflessness in the service of humanity. The major powers whose influence is crucial in every major international effort have therefore a moral obligation to play a leading role. The international community has the duty to promote international interest and generate the necessary political will for an agreement that is so vital to the life, safety, and well-being of refugees in all parts of the world.

It is recommended that, in order to clarify and consolidate the relevant legal principles, the point of departure must be agreement on a set of principles concerning the prohibition of military attacks on refugees to be negotiated through the Executive Committee of the UNHCR and submitted for adoption as a solemn declaration of the UN General Assembly. I have suggested an outline of possible principles and recommendations. I recognize, however, that just as the obstacles to an agreement are based on political rather than legal considerations, so progress can be achieved only with increased political will and an enhanced desire to strengthen international solidarity. The sentiment of human solidarity would in the long run generate world-wide international interest in this grave problem, and, more important, contribute to the improvement of the safety and well-being of refugees in all parts of the world.

Postscript

As this paper was being completed, the UNHCR Executive Committee adopted a Conclusion on a set of principles on Military and Armed Attacks on Refugee Camps and Settlements (Doc. A/AC.96/702, of 12 October 1987). The Conclusion declares that military or armed attacks on refugees are indiscriminate in nature, unlawful, and deserve condemnation in the strongest terms. It goes on to condemn all violations of the rights and safety of refugees and asylum-seekers, and in particular military or armed attacks on refugee camps and settlements, stating that such attacks violate the principles of international law and cannot be justified. States and international organizations are called upon to assist victims of attacks if ever they occur. It recommends that the states of refuge should do all within their power to ensure that the civilian character of refugee camps and settlements is maintained, and that other states and international organizations be asked to assist in that regard. It further recommends that states should co-operate in granting the High Commissioner access to camps and settlements of concern to him, particularly when he cannot effectively accomplish his functions without such access.

My main criticism of this Conclusion is that it is predicated on the assumption that refugee camps and settlements are exclusively civilian and humanitarian. Few camps and settlements around the world correspond to this precise definition, and even if these did exist the precise language used could be twisted to provide a pretext for reprisals or other politically motivated attacks. The language used falls short of the absolute prohibition of attacks on refugee camps and settlements demanded by countries of refuge and envisaged in the principles recommended above. Furthermore, there was no decision to submit the agreed set of principles to the United Nations General Assembly for adoption as a solemn declaration, as was proposed by Ambassador Felix Schnyder in 1982. It is submitted, therefore, that the result of the deliberations in the UNHCR Executive Committee has been unsatisfactory, and hence the pursuit of specific action at the United Nations General Assembly should continue. The ultimate goal of a solemn declaration and an international legal instrument on the physical security of refugees remains a pressing necessity.

5. The Origins and Effects of 'Humane Deterrence' Policies in South-east Asia

DENNIS McNAMARA

IN the last decade, as governments have devised various methods to reduce the number of uninvited foreigners, including refugees, entering their countries, deterrence measures have increasingly become part of the established armoury of many potential host states. Such measures are, of course, not new and have usually coincided with periods of economic decline or political isolation, or have been prompted by strong domestic resistance to immigration programmes in general. The recent efforts that have been aimed at asylum-seekers and have been presented as part of 'humane deterrence' policies may be traced directly to responses to the Indo-Chinese influx which were formulated in South-east Asia in the early 1980s, and the terminology is misleading.

There is a present danger that these restrictive practices may come to be regarded as part of an acceptable international response to unwelcome population movements across frontiers. In reality, the term 'humane deterrence' should be used only advisedly, to denote the restrictive treatment of newcomers by receiving governments in order to deter further potential asylum-seekers. Used in this sense, the phrase contains an obvious contradiction, as potential refugees are unlikely to be deterred by treatment which can objectively be designated 'humane'. In fact there is little historical evidence to support the contention that the majority of refugees are deterred even by the threat of inhumane treatment on arrival—which they have too often received—when the need to leave their own country has been compelling.

Dennis McNamara is with the UNHCR. The views expressed in this article are entirely his own and do not necessarily reflect the views or position of the UNHCR.

Deterrent measures have traditionally been resorted to by states anxious to control population movements across their borders, and have ranged from the military sealing-off of borders and the forcible return of all arrivals, to more sophisticated procedures involving visa requirements prior to departure, and the return of arrivals to countries of temporary transit. The more recent formulation of 'humane deterrence' has developed a special meaning in this context and it is necessary to look at its historical roots in order to assess its full implications.

The concept which was formulated in South-east Asia during the height of the exodus from the countries of Indo-China into neighbouring states, particularly Thailand, arose from a movement which began in a relatively small way, following the fall of Phnom Penh and then Saigon in April 1975. After the initial American evacuation of some 130,000 Indo-Chinese, mainly from Vietnam, subsequent influxes into the region did not cause undue concern until the end of 1977. The important exception was Thailand which, during the same period, received more than 100,000 Laotians, as well as some Cambodians and Vietnamese.[1] One response to this movement was an attempt to screen arrivals from Laos to determine those who should properly be considered to be refugees, a process which had been formally agreed upon by the government of Thailand and by UNHCR in August 1977. It was, however, strongly opposed by the major Western countries, which objected to the prospect of forcible return to Laos of those who were excluded, as reports increased of new arrivals being expelled at the Thai border before being processed. The screening, which in fact had not markedly affected arrival rates, was officially abandoned in March 1978.[2]

Within a short time increased Sino-Vietnamese tensions, coupled with a series of new economic measures within Vietnam, were to change dramatically the entire refugee dimension of the region. By the end of the year 86,000 boat people had arrived in countries throughout the region, in a movement which also included the first organized charter ships carrying several thousand

[1] There were some 21,000 boat arrivals in the region and 30,000 Cambodian arrivals in Thailand during this period. At the same time, between 100,000 and 200,000 Cambodians reportedly crossed into Vietnam.

[2] In practice, it was subsequently used spasmodically and remained official Thai policy, endorsed by a Cabinet decision in August 1977.

fare-paying Vietnamese. As the influx doubled during 1979, the regional reaction was hostile and harsh. Malaysia put its 'push-off' policy into full effect, rejecting more than 50,000 Vietnamese who attempted to land, and threatening to send away 70,000 more who were already in camps, while all five ASEAN states officially announced that no further Vietnamese would be admitted.[3]

Vietnam's invasion of Cambodia at the end of 1978 had been the main cause of heightened regional tensions and was to result in a further 140,000 Cambodians entering Thailand in early 1979.[4] Arrivals from Laos had also doubled during 1978, to reach almost 60,000, and Thailand was soon receiving more than 17,000 Indo-Chinese a month from all three countries. In the words of Thai Premier Kriangsak, the country was not being flooded by refugees, it was being drowned.

The UN-sponsored meeting of governments in Geneva in July 1979 in response to this crisis—the first of its kind—was attended by sixty-five states, including China, the United States, and the Soviet Union. The outcome, in brief, was a pledge by Vietnam to take steps to control the exodus, and offers by the industrialized states to take more than a quarter of a million Indo-Chinese from camps in the region for permanent settlement. The meeting, which had been prompted by the widespread regional resistance to the dramatic influx by boat from Vietnam, devoted little attention to land cases—much to Thailand's dismay. In the short term it was highly successful for the former group: within a few months boat arrivals had dropped to minimal levels[5] and a massive third-country resettlement operation had reduced the population of the Vietnamese camps in South-east Asia by almost two-thirds. The Thai authorities were determined that arrivals by land should be similarly controlled. In August 1979 Thailand and Laos formally agreed on the repatriation (with UNHCR assistance) of Laotian illegal immigrants who wished to return home, and early the following year the Thai–Cambodian border was officially closed to all new arrivals.

The Geneva meeting had given unequivocal endorsement to the ASEAN states' demand that all Indo-Chinese who had been

[3] At the ASEAN Ministerial meeting in Bali, June 1979.

[4] In addition to more than 200,000 others who remained along the border in temporary settlements.

[5] Some 2,700 only by Dec. 1979.

granted sanctuary in the region should promptly be accepted by third countries. Thailand strongly shared the ASEAN preoccupation with substantially reducing camp populations and was also concerned that many of the new arrivals, particularly those coming from Laos, were largely motivated by the prospect of a better life in the West. The newcomers were seen as common economic adventurers rather than people fleeing danger, attracted by camps in Thailand, such as Nong Khai, which were clearly visible from the Laotian side and which provided relatively secure and comfortable conditions in which to await selection by third countries. The large ethnic Lao population in north-eastern Thailand, estimated to be up to four times that of Laos itself, provided an added incentive for many Laotians to attempt to escape the economic hardships they were enduring, and effective control of the border proved almost impossible.

After 1980 the Thai authorities instituted stricter measures to return Laotians apprehended at border crossings, but the policy continued to be applied spasmodically and to have little noticeable effect on arrival rates. By this time many UNHCR officials also were convinced that Laotians were being enticed to cross into Thailand by the easily accessible camps and by prospects of resettlement, particularly in the United States. The UNHCR Office in Bangkok had previously indicated that this could be countered only by the implementation of a comprehensive screening procedure, along the lines tried unsuccessfully in 1977, to determine which arrivals should properly be admitted to camps. Mindful of the consequences of earlier attempts, UNHCR headquarters was unwilling to support this suggestion and in its place UNHCR officials in Bangkok suggested to the authorities that as a deterrent measure the camp in Nong Khai should be closed to all new arrivals, who would instead be held in a centre away from the border where—at least initially—they would not be eligible for resettlement processing. At the same time the activities of international voluntary agencies in the camps, which were largely geared to resettlement, would be severely restricted.

The Thai government was quick to seize on this 'humane deterrent' proposal and to apply it, with some variations, as part of a major new approach to attempt to control the seemingly unending refugee influx into the country. As subsequently adopted by the government, the policy had three main facets: the imposition of austere camp conditions; the denial of resettlement processing to new arrivals and, at least implicitly, renewed efforts to apprehend and expel arrivals at the border. There was of course a fundamental dilemma underlying the new approach since, although resettlement prospects were widely viewed as an incentive to further arrivals, the denial of resettlement in the absence of alternative long-term responses would inevitably lead to increased and static camp populations which Thailand, like its ASEAN neighbours, was determined to resist. Consequently the policy was presented to local officials as a temporary expedient aimed primarily at dissuading those contemplating leaving their country. Third country resettlement would then again be made available at a later stage to take care of a hopefully reduced caseload. This stop-go approach was not, in the end, to meet Thai hopes of substantially reducing the number of refugees in camps.

Officially the new policy was put into effect in Thailand in January 1981 with the announcement that all lowland Lao arrivals would henceforth be held in a new 'austere' camp at Ban Napho which would not be open to resettlement delegations or to international voluntary agency personnel. All outside communication with the camp population would be strictly controlled. In September the policy was extended to the Vietnamese camps in Thailand and the following April to all hill-tribe arrivals from Laos, who were to be held in a similarly restricted northern camp at Chiang Kham. Vietnamese would be housed in a detention centre at Sikhui, rather than in the more open coastal camps at Laemsing and Songkhla. The implementation of these new measures was undertaken in conjunction with a camp consolidation programme undertaken by the Thai Ministry of the Interior, which resulted in the systematic closure of a number of former camps, in some cases leading to acute overcrowding in the remaining centres, especially those housing Vietnamese.[6]

The clear intention of the new approach was to let it be known that arrivals *en route* for third countries should not expect the automatic granting of comfortable transit in Thailand and, as such, it received the implicit and sometimes explicit endorsement of major resettlement countries. The United States was particularly

[6] This programme was announced by the Thai National Security Council in July 1981 and foresaw one main camp being available for each of the different ethnic groups of refugees. By 1983 it had been largely accomplished.

supportive, as was made clear in testimony given before the House of Representatives' Committee on Foreign Affairs on 22 October 1981 by Deputy Assistant Secretary of State Sheppard Lowman, who confirmed that 'In spite of difficulties, we have encouraged the Thai in this initiative [of humane deterrence].'

In terms of arrival rates, the policy initially seemed to achieve its objective. By the end of 1981 total arrivals from Laos had dropped to less than half those for 1980, and then fell by a further 75 per cent in the course of 1982. Boat arrivals in Thailand also dropped sharply, from more than 21,000 in 1980 to some 6,000 in 1982. Lack of resettlement prospects seemed to act as a disincentive, particularly to Vietnamese and lowland Laotians, although increased expulsions of arrivals during this period undoubtedly contributed to the reduction in numbers.[7] Stringent screening as to the refugee status of applicants by INS[8] officers in the region under the new US Refugee Act also meant that large numbers of Laotians already in camps no longer qualified for acceptance. It was notable that, with this drop in resettlement departures, voluntary repatriation movements to Laos reached a peak of more than a thousand during 1982. With the resumption of resettlement processing after 1983 there were again very few candidates for return.

In June 1982 Hong Kong, with a total case-load of less than 15,000, decided to adopt similar deterrent measures. Despite the relatively small numbers involved, two aspects of the influx particularly bothered the Hong Kong authorities: first, arrivals comprised mainly unqualified Vietnamese from the northern and central regions of the country, for whom resettlement was almost impossible, and second, there were increased domestic protests that Vietnamese entering Hong Kong received better treatment than the many thousands of Chinese from the mainland who had been forcibly refused permission to join relatives in the colony. Hong Kong officials specifically referred to the US call for deterrent measures in announcing the policy, under which resettlement was not denied, but closed camps were established for all arrivals, to 'discourage refugees from leaving Vietnam'.[9]

[7] There was also a region-wide reduction of almost 50% in boat arrivals during this period, mainly as a result of various developments within Vietnam.

[8] US Immigration and Naturalization Service.

[9] Statement by Hong Kong Secretary of Security Davies, reported by *Agence Presse Française*, Bangkok, 18 June 1982.

Many within UNHCR were also prepared to support efforts to reduce the Indo-Chinese case-load, and noticeably the Office did not formally protest against the new measures. They soon led, however, to serious limitations in the ability of UNHCR and others to attempt to safeguard the basic rights of the camp inhabitants. Badly overcrowded conditions and prison-like restrictions, particularly in the Vietnamese camps, soon prompted international criticism, but did not prevent the new policies from being officially maintained in both countries throughout the rest of the decade. Most importantly, tacit acceptance by governments and refugee agencies of the deterrent approach as an acceptable means of dealing with an unwanted influx made effective resistance to the increased rejections of new arrivals along the Thai border almost impossible. Formal UNHCR protests at these actions reached a peak during 1982 and were largely ineffective.

Many of those who were able to enter Thailand had close relatives in third countries, where domestic pressures mounted for these and similar cases to be released for processing. Partly as a result of these pressures, the Thai authorities finally agreed in July 1983 to permit the phased release for departure of various special groups within these categories. Although the government had requested that the lifting of the resettlement embargo be given minimum publicity, word soon spread among the camp populations and contributed, in the view of many observers, to the immediate increase in arrivals from Laos which followed. By 1984 the arrival rate for lowland Laotians was almost five times as high as it had been in 1982, although clearly there were push as well as pull factors which contributed to this increase.[10]

'Humane deterrence' was to remain the official policy of the Royal Thai government in dealing with all arrivals from Laos and Vietnam, although, in practice, increased releases of different categories for resettlement processing gradually undermined one of its main objectives. Hong Kong also maintained its closed camp regime, only slightly modifying some of its more extreme restrictions in response to widespread criticism. Both approaches represented an indirect attempt to deal with the causes of the continuing exodus, based on the assumption that those motivated primarily by economic or other personal reasons would be deterred

[10] Such as new economic and other measures within the country.

from leaving their countries.[11] From the point of view of refugee protection, the policy was inherently contentious in its endorsement of the principle that those seeking refuge could be subjected to harsh treatment in order to discourage further departures, an approach which opened the door in many instances to the mistreatment of arrivals, particularly those coming from Vietnam. The denial of automatic resettlement prospects for all arrivals reaching Thailand was perhaps its least objectionable aspect, although in practice it remained a poor substitute for a properly instituted screening process to determine who should be considered for this option. As the Thai government acknowledged in 1983, a blanket denial of resettlement could not be maintained if the objective was eventually to resolve the problem of refugees who could neither stay in camps indefinitely nor return home. Resettlement countries and UNHCR, equally concerned to see an end to the influx, had similar difficulty in supporting the prolonged denial of third country resettlement for those groups such as split families and other special cases for whom it was the obvious and apparently only humane alternative.

In its application in South-east Asia, humane deterrence was largely a reactive response by regional states frustrated by an apparently endless flow of refugees whose status and motivation they seriously questioned. It arose principally as a consequence of the political constraints faced by states in dealing more directly with the underlying causes of this influx and was an attempt to minimize the incentives inherent in the international response to it which had been demanded by the region. The formulation of the policy and its broad acceptance by the international community, however, made a serious inroad into the basic principles underpinning international refugee protection structures. It ran directly counter to the minimum standards of treatment for asylum-seekers in large-scale influxes, which were endorsed by the General Assembly in 1981,[12] as well as to the precept of fundamental protection that individuals should not be punished merely for seeking asylum. In the South-east Asian context the policy formalized some of the more negative

[11] For the Vietnamese in particular there was little historical support for this view, as arrivals had shown no sign of diminishing in number, even during the height of the Malaysian 'push-off' policy in 1978–9.

[12] UNGA resolution 36/125 which endorsed Conclusion 22 of UNHCR's thirty-second Executive Committee meeting in 1981.

aspects of the regional response to arrivals since 1975, particularly in the case of the Vietnamese. Official endorsement of this approach by Western states, which had been among the principal architects of the mandate of UNHCR and the subsequent international protection structures, held serious implications for the protection of refugees generally.

To a considerable degree humane deterrence was also an inevitable consequence of the nature of the international response to the Indo-Chinese exodus. The unchallenged acceptance at the Geneva meeting of third country resettlement as the only substantial solution to the problem, and the subsequent infusion of massive international aid for those in camps until this option was available, was clearly a two-edged sword. Well-provided and relatively secure camps close to the border of Laos, one of the world's poorest countries, were inevitably a compelling attraction for impoverished Laotians, just as the chance to move to the United States strongly appealed to many dispossessed Chinese traders in southern Vietnam.

At least in theory, there would have been scope for alternative responses to the Indo-Chinese influx, had geopolitical considerations not excluded them. A formal screening procedure for all arrivals from Laos, with a view to identifying those who had left for primarily personal reasons and who could safely return, would be likely to have substantial impact on this movement, as it did when it was eventually introduced in 1985. The fact that earlier attempts at screening had been accompanied by increased expulsions at the border meant, however, that there was little government support for this option. The majority of donor governments were also reluctant to endorse any action which formally acknowledged that a substantial proportion of those leaving Indo-China might not meet refugee criteria.

The location of camps and the level of services available in them were also seen as an important factor in enticing Laotians to cross into Thailand. Camp inhabitants were known to send encouraging messages back to families and friends in Laos, sometimes by telephone, and on occasion even in person, about the relatively comfortable and secure conditions in the camps. The massive injection of international aid for refugees in South-east Asia following the 1979 meeting in Geneva meant, of course, that the level of economic assistance in such camps remained high. Many of the educational and medical facilities in particular which were available in refugee camps in Thailand during this period were far better than those available in the neighbouring countries of origin. For both political as well as humanitarian reasons, donor governments and non-governmental agencies were generally unwilling to reduce these aid levels, and UNHCR similarly made little headway in trying to do so. At the same time, proposals for locating camps further away from the border were seen in some quarters as an impediment to possible early repatriation, while for others it represented an unnecessary restriction on cross-border resistance activities.

One factor which outweighed these various incentives for Laotians to enter Thailand, which humane deterrence was intended to reduce, was the attraction of readily available resettlement quotas. The basic dilemma of the ASEAN states between wanting to empty camps as quickly as possible on the one hand, and not wanting to attract further arrivals on the other, was compounded by the 265,000 resettlement places for Indo-Chinese which were announced or confirmed at the 1979 meeting. Laotians were more vulnerable to the pull factor of resettlement than were any other group because of the ease of communications between the camps and Laos. In some instances arrivals confirmed that their departure had been precipitated by news of renewed quotas, or even by the visits of selection teams to camps in Thailand. The absence of any screening procedure to determine who should properly be eligible for subsequent resettlement processing meant that there was little that could be done to reduce this incentive. This dilemma fundamentally affected the international response to the entire Indo-Chinese exodus and was to become even more acute in the following years, as receiving governments sought to impose increasingly stringent selection criteria.

Another fundamental element which contributed to the creation of the deterrence regimes in South-east Asia was the absence of any unified approach to the Indo-Chinese exodus by the international community. For a variety of national, geopolitical, and even global political reasons, there was little international effort made either by governments or by the agencies concerned to address the underlying causes of the exodus, including the economic ones. For similar reasons, there were few sustained initiatives to promote realistic alternatives to open-ended resettlement for arrivals from

Indo-China, including Laotians. The countries of origin, and particularly Vietnam after its invasion of Cambodia, remained diplomatically and economically isolated by most of the Western group to a degree that largely precluded such initiatives. Inevitably, as the complexities of the geopolitical constraints on the humanitarian options available intensified, particularly after 1979, host governments looked for more pragmatic ways to stem a seemingly unending influx. Humane deterrence measures in South-east Asia to a large extent epitomized a response which grew out of this frustration.

6. The Detention of Refugees and Asylum-Seekers

A Misguided Threat to Refugee Protection

ARTHUR C. HELTON

ASYLUM-SEEKERS are being detained in significant numbers around the world. A 1984 survey of just twenty-three countries showed that some form of detention was practised in a significant number of countries.[1] Over 150,000 Indo-Chinese (principally Cambodians, Laotians, and Vietnamese) waiting for resettlement in third countries were confined to camps in Hong Kong, Indonesia, Malaysia, the Philippines, Singapore, and Thailand.[2] Some, such as the 5,761 Vietnamese in Hong Kong, lived in closed camps from which release is not permitted pending resettlement.[3] In other countries, the numbers of aliens in administrative detention are relatively small. Detention generally ranges from ten days to three months, although prolonged or indefinite confinement is not unusual in India, Sudan, Tanzania, and Zambia.[4] Over a thousand asylum-seekers are currently incarcerated in immigration gaols in the United States; many have already been held for unreasonable lengths of time.[5]

[1] The countries surveyed were Austria, Belgium, Cameroon, Canada, Federal Republic of Germany, Hong Kong, India, Indonesia, Kenya, Laos, Malaysia, the Netherlands, Nicaragua, the Philippines, Portugal, Singapore, Somalia, Sudan, Tanzania, Thailand, the United States, Zambia, and Zimbabwe (hereinafter cited as 'Survey'). Cited in Guy Goodwin-Gill, 'International Law and the Detention of Refugees and Asylum Seekers', *International Migration Review*, 20 (1986), 193, 202–5.

[2] Survey, see above, n. 1. The largest number (127,209) are in camps in Thailand. See also *New York Times*, 23 June 1985, sect. i, p. 7, col. 1.

[3] Survey, see above, n. 1. See also Philippe Grandjean, 'The Boat People's Alcatraz', *Refugees* (May 1985), 30–1; W. Shawcross, *The Quality of Mercy: Cambodia, the Holocaust and the Modern Conscience* (New York: Simon and Schuster) 1984, 405–6.

[4] Survey, see above, n. 1.

[5] Arthur C. Helton, 'The Legality of Detaining Refugees in the United States', *New York Review of Law and Social Change*, 14 (1986), 353, 363–6.

The reasons for detention vary, but a principal justification is deterrence. States use detention to try to encourage aliens to leave their territories or to discourage others from ever coming to them in the first place. The policy implications of this so-called humane deterrence approach to immigration control are far-reaching.

This chapter examines the phenomenon of alien detention in terms of the nature and the rationale for the practice. The policy consequences of an alien detention programme are assessed in terms of the impact on refugee protection. Deterrent measures are not only questionable under international law but are also inappropriate as a response to current patterns of refugee flows.

The first question to pose is what is meant by the term 'detention'? Construed broadly, the concept might include restriction of movement or travel within a territory in which an alien finds him or herself. An example of such controls can be found in the Federal Republic of Germany, which prohibits the employment of asylum-seekers for five years. They are, in turn, effectively required to stay in so-called collective accommodation and are subject to travel restrictions.[6] Detention can take many forms. The kind of confinement which this chapter discusses involves aggravated restraints on personal liberty, whether they be in the form of closed camps, such as those in which Indo-Chinese are held in Hong Kong, or gaols, such as those in which aliens are held in the United States.

The next question, then, is what is the policy rationale for the detention of asylum-seekers? Traditionally, administrative detention has been used to promote immigration control, either by facilitating expulsion, or by ensuring that the aliens subject to immigration proceedings do not abscond. Aliens are held, pending investigations into their true identity, when they arrive with false travel documents. Detention is also used to protect the public, as when aliens are forcibly quarantined where there are indications that they are infected with a dangerous, contagious disease. Occasionally, aliens have been held as a threat to security or danger to public safety, but such preventive detention measures raise troubling questions as to whether it is possible to predict dangerousness, and whether the procedures used to make that

[6] See Alex Aleinikoff, 'Political Asylum in the Federal Republic of Germany and the Republic of France: Lessons for the United States', *University of Michigan Journal of Law Reform*, 17 (1984), 183, 198, 201–3.

assessment are fair and reliable. Detention therefore has been used extensively in the past as part of general immigration control.

More recently asylum-seekers have been detained in furtherance of a policy of deterrence. The rationale is that those in detention will be encouraged by their treatment (or rather mistreatment) to leave and, more generally, others will be discouraged from coming to the territory where detention is practised. For the refugees themselves this could mean being persuaded to return to areas where they face persecution or to remain in situations where they face threats to their lives or freedom. The specific intention of the authorities, however, may simply be to deflect the arrival of so-called spontaneous refugees who may move across borders in an irregular fashion, and to make them go elsewhere, perhaps to another state of asylum. One example of this policy is the recent Canadian proposal to detain those asylum-seekers who are deemed returnable to safe third countries.[7] Such an approach parallels the development of the first asylum principle in Europe, where countries seek to limit access to the asylum procedures for those refugees who have travelled through other countries where they presumably could have sought asylum.[8] This approach is one which precludes the possibility of asylum for those refugees who move beyond the first country they enter in flight from their homeland.

Detention for purposes of deterrence is a form of punishment, in that it deprives a person of their liberty for no other reason than their having been forced into exile. It is a practice that is legally questionable under Articles 31 and 33 of the United Nations Convention and Protocols Relating to the Status of Refugees, which prohibit the imposition of penalties and restrictions on movement, as well as *refoulement*.[9] Moreover, detention is a bad policy because it does nothing to further any possible solution to the increasing problems of refugees.

The present legal regime and institutional framework for the provision of protection and assistance to refugees was instituted under the auspices of the League of Nations after World War I. A treaty made in 1921 made provision for Russian refugees, followed

[7] The *Christian Science Monitor* (28 Apr. 1987). p. 3, col. 3.

[8] See Goran Melander, 'Responsibility for Examining an Asylum Request, *Asylum Seekers* vs. *Quota Refugees*', *International Migration Review*, 20 (1986), 220–9.

[9] See Goodwin-Gill, *International Law and the Detention of Refugees*, pp. 193–219, and Helton, *The Legality of Detaining Refugees*.

in 1924 by a treaty concerning Armenian refugees.[10] These *ad hoc* measures were typical of the approach to refugees until, in an effort to deal with the massive displacement of humanity occasioned by World War II, the United Nations sought through the 1951 Refugee Convention to provide a systematic regime of protection for refugees.[11] A refugee was defined as one who had a well-founded fear of persecution on account of race, religion, nationality, political opinion, or membership of a particular social group. However, the definition was limited to Europe and related specifically to events that occurred prior to 1951. In 1967 a Protocol to the Convention removed the geographical and dateline limitations and provided a truly universal definition of refugee.[12] The Office of the United Nations High Commissioner for Refugees (UNHCR), which was established to supervise the application of the Convention, has subsequently extended its protection mandate through *ad hoc* resolutions of the General Assembly and its 'good offices' jurisdiction to protect individuals who do not meet the technical definition of refugee, but who find themselves in similar situations.[13] In Africa, the Organization of African Unity (OAU) has specifically provided protection for those who have fled civil strife,[14] a concept of refugee discussed increasingly in relation to Latin America. In many countries constitutional and statutory instruments provide for a right of asylum to individuals who find themselves within the territorial jurisdiction of the respective states. Such protection frequently goes beyond the international refugee regime, to include programmes of non-return and tolerated stay—sometimes called 'B' status.[15] The trend is patently clear and irreversible: an international refugee concept and regime is evolving which necessarily impinges on sovereignty and which is animated by humanitarian necessity. Policies that do not recognize this inescapable fact are destined to fail and are likely to cause arbitrary hardship to those to whom they are applied.

Refugees and displaced persons are created by a wide variety of

[10] I. A. Grahl-Madsen, *The Status of Refugees in International Law*, 2 vols. (Leiden: A. W. Sijthoff, 1966, 1972), 12–13.

[11] 189 United Nations Treaty Series (UNTS) 137.

[12] 606 UNTS 267.

[13] See Guy Goodwin-Gill, *The Refugee in International Law* (Oxford: Clarendon Press, 1983), 6–12.

[14] UNTS No. 14, 691.

[15] See Goodwin-Gill, *The Refugee in International Law*, 165–211.

factors that range from natural disasters, such as earthquakes or volcanic eruption, to civil war and persecution. Individuals sometimes migrate because of crushing poverty or a desire to reunite with family members abroad. Unauthorized movements of persons across borders occur both on an individual and on a mass basis. Many of those who cross borders have mixed motives and are both pushed and pulled by circumstances in their home countries and abroad.

Receiving countries have a few very predictable choices. They can grant asylum on a temporary basis and hope for eventual repatriation or resettlement elsewhere. Receiving countries may also grant permanent asylum and give individuals a durable new source of protection and an opportunity to assimilate into the nation's political life. The possible solutions are indeed few, but they are not conceptually difficult. Prevention is obviously the preferred solution. The root causes of movement of people across borders can be dealt with by wise political and economic development strategies. Fewer refugees would be created if there were more respect for human rights and humanitarian principles. The early and efficient provision of assistance and relief can ameliorate the consequences of a disaster, whether it be of natural or man-made origin. What the theoretician sees as conceptually obvious, however, frequently founders as being politically unfeasible. Refugee flight and migration are chronic phenomena.

A policy of arbitrarily or indiscriminately detaining asylum-seekers inflicts suffering on people who come for a variety of reasons, ranging from well-founded fear of persecution, to the desire for basic economic betterment. Not only does this mistreatment of individuals indicate an anti-humanitarian approach, but it is a policy that simply will not work. Deterrent measures such as detention are rarely related to the complex variety of reasons for movement across borders, and result in the seemingly capricious infliction of harm. They do not stop the movement of people across borders; at most, they tend to divert flows elsewhere, and are likely to inspire defensive action in return among other states wishing to avoid refugee influxes. A policy of detention is wholly antagonistic to the development of international solidarity. Rather, it tends to maximize hostility and unilateral behaviour among nations, with helpless individuals arbitrarily victimized by governments competing to initiate deterrent measures.

Furthermore, a policy of detaining asylum-seekers is completely unrelated to the reality of refugee movements. In 1985 the United Nations High Commissioner for Refugees counted 11,613,300 refugees, 82 per cent of whom had found asylum in developing countries.[16] Frequently, refugees are forced to cross borders secretly and in an irregular manner.[17] It is cruel in the extreme to incarcerate asylum-seekers for something which is simply inherent in their situation. Rather, collective discussion and action are required with a view to burden-sharing among affected nations. A system of international review and response could better distribute the burden, allocating adequate resources to meet the various needs, and thereby alleviating the pressures that lead to the incarceration of refugees. A comprehensive system such as this would promote a constructive refugee policy which addressed social reality. Detention policies are fundamentally inconsistent with the universal approach needed to achieve any kind of solution, and threaten to retard development of the international refugee regime and impose arbitrary abuse on large numbers of individuals. While perhaps attractive to the authorities of the country as an expedient, short-term diversion of the problem, detention is both destructive over the long term, as a way of dealing with refugees, and unworthy as an anti-humanitarian measure.

[16] Report of the Thirty-Seventh Session of the Executive Committee of the High Commissioner's Programme, A/AC, 96/688, 15 Oct. 1986, annex, p. 2.

[17] UNHCR, *Handbook on Procedures and Criteria for Determining Refugee Status* (Geneva, 1979), para. 196.

7. Refugee Women

The Forgotten Majority

GENEVIÈVE CAMUS-JACQUES

Introduction

'I DID not see any women', declared the High Commissioner for Refugees, following a recent visit to Afghan refugee camps in Pakistan. He recognized that women and girls outnumber male refugees by far in these camps and also that cultural patterns oblige women to remain 'invisible' to foreign male eyes. Thus, being a woman gave me the advantage of being allowed to cross the thresholds of their huts or tents to talk to them. In other camps in Honduras, Mexico, Jordan, South-east Asia, and Papua New Guinea, it was also easier for me to see those refugee women rendered invisible to most visitors, kept in the back yards of their shelters, overburdened with household tasks. Through talking to them and to field workers, by visiting programmes for refugee women run by YWCAs in various parts of the world, by attending conferences, and reading reports on refugees, I came to realize that the invisibility of refugee women was a much deeper issue than a simple question of custom. Other refugee workers and researchers—albeit only a few—had come to the same conclusion, even before I did.

The Decade for Women, which officially ended in 1985, will have helped to point out a paradox which can be summarized briefly: that refugee women are a forgotten majority. Although basic statistical data are not well documented even at the international level, it is nevertheless commonly accepted that women and girls make up the majority of the world's refugee population. Earlier extrapolations of local observations in areas where the majority of refugees are concentrated (Horn of Africa, Pakistan) had led to this assumption but, until now, there have been no reliable statistics to provide a gender-specific picture of populations in exile.

There exists not only a real difficulty in obtaining data on refugees in general, but there also appears to be little interest in such information. For more than ten years the need for collecting statistical and sociological data and for encouraging research on refugee women has been repeatedly expressed but, to date, no comprehensive global information or analysis has been made available. In the past refugee policy-makers believed that it made no difference whether one was male or female once one was a refugee. However, the trend observed over the last decade towards a 'feminization of global migrations', with its consequent economic and human components, is starting to change earlier perceptions. It is now opportune to examine the social and economic consequences of the increase in women in contemporary migratory flows.

Overlooked in data collection, refugee women are forgotten in other areas as well. Until recently policy-makers, refugee workers, donors, and researchers had badly neglected both the specific problems and the specific resources of refugee women. A clear illustration of this lack of attention is the very limited research on refugee women and the relative scarcity of literature specifically about women compared to the extensive publications dealing with refugee questions in general.

The *Selected and Annotated Bibliography on Refugee Women* published by the UNHCR Refugee Documentation Centre in 1985 provides ample material for reflection. Out of the 139 titles listed, less than twenty are based on scientific research, and even these do not give anything like a balanced view of the refugee women's situation. Six studies deal with integration problems in the United States, four with income-generating and integration programmes in Africa, and four with the problems of violence against Vietnamese boat people.

The variety of issues pertinent to refugee women's protection and assistance problems which I shall discuss here should offer a direction for the new investigation and research that is badly needed at the moment. After briefly describing the general framework within which the plight of refugee women is placed, I shall attempt to identify the major *specific*—and largely unmet—*needs* of the women in terms of protection and assistance, as well as their *specific*—and largely unused—*resources*. Finally, I shall offer some suggestions for a positive and affirmative approach which calls for new policies and new research.

In my many years of work with refugees I have witnessed enough sorrow and anxiety in refugee women's eyes and have seen enough examples of their resilience and courage to wish that their specific needs were better known and their specific strengths better encouraged and supported. Specialist agencies, field workers, and scientific researchers must now collaborate to give refugee women justice and more visibility.

The global context

Traditionally there has been no gender attached to the term 'refugee'. When describing refugee populations, distinctions were made for assistance purposes between adults and children, but rarely has any mention been made of women as a separate category deserving special attention. Over the past ten years, however, most of the large-scale influxes of refugees have been predominantly of women and children. In response to this today a growing number of people are searching for ways to respond to the plight of this forgotten majority within a global framework. At several international meetings, resolutions have been passed calling on governments, international agencies, The United Nations High Commissioner for Refugees (UNHCR), and non-governmental organizations to give recognition to the specific needs of refugee women and to take appropriate measures to ensure their protection and equal access to material assistance.[1] In 1985, however, at the conference in Nairobi which marked the end of the UN Decade for Women, and at the NGO Forum held simultaneously, it was made clear that much more still needs to be done.

The plight of refugee women cannot be understood without first examining the political, social, and economic reasons which have forced all refugees—women, children, and men—by the million, on the road to exile. It is not the purpose of this presentation to analyse the root causes of the refugee tragedy of the twentieth century, but a few realities need to be recalled if we are to understand why so many human beings have been obliged to take the harsh path of exile.

When we use the term refugee we refer to the generic name given to people uprooted by force. On arriving in another country all

[1] World Council of Churches, *Refugees*, 56E (Jan. 1984), 1.

kinds of labels—refugees, displaced persons, exiles, asylum-seekers, illegal aliens—are put on people driven by fear or hunger from their homeland. Indeed, the particular label that is attached to them can be crucial in determining their fate. Yet the basic problem is not one of labels, it is the result of international conflict, global injustice, and inequality.

News of tragedies pours in at such a speed and in such profusion that we tend to forget that behind the news there are people whose suffering lasts longer than the short-lived attention given them by the mass media. In the West we are accustomed to talking about the post-war period, even though continuous wars and armed conflicts have ravaged the world since 1945, taking at least 21 million lives and banishing millions of others to exile.

The world refugee map tallies almost perfectly with the world conflicts map, and illustrates the fact that the overwhelming majority of refugees come from and move between Third World countries. Out of the 12.5 million refugees officially registered by UNHCR and UNRWA in 1985, 83 per cent have found sanctuary in the Third World.[2]

The international economic disorder which prevails in the world today is responsible, among other things, for the mass displacement of people. While billions of dollars are spent on armaments, entire populations can barely survive in their own countries. Economic repression and threats to survival force people to leave their homes. Fewer people flee today as a result of individual persecution. For millions of men and women it is not one single dramatic event which makes them leave, but an accumulation of setbacks which, little by little, kills their hopes. It is becoming increasingly difficult to distinguish clearly between those fleeing individual persecution and those fleeing conditions of violence and economic deprivation. Is hunger coercion less dramatic than political coercion? The problem cannot be easily evaded.

In Europe and in other industrialized areas economic recession and large-scale migrations from south to north have exacerbated xenophobic and racist attitudes. The result has been an alarming tendency by governments to use restrictive policies towards asylum-seekers and other incomers.

[2] 'World Refugee Populations', in *The Stranger Within Your Gates*, André Jacques, app. I (Geneva: World Council of Churches, 1986).

It is hard for anyone to find themselves a refugee, but it is even harder for a woman in those societies where equal rights and opportunities for both sexes are far from a reality. During their time in exile, refugee women face specific hardships precisely because they are women, yet this fact remains largely unacknowledged. It is ironic to find that a theoretical understanding of equality has led to discriminatory practices towards refugee women. A case in point was the 1985 UNHCR Executive Committee meeting, where a debate followed the introduction given by the Director of International Protection on the theme 'Refugee Women and International Protection'.[3] While some delegates argued that the international refugee instruments apply equally to men and women, and are therefore not discriminatory, others pointed out that simply *because* they were applied indiscriminately of sex, they failed to take account of the special problems with which refugee women are confronted.

Special problems of refugee women

Refugee women encounter specific problems regarding protection, assistance, and participation in decision-making. The following remarks are unfortunately not based on statistical data, for the simple reason that such data on refugee women do not exist. In spite of the recognition that women and girls constitute most of the world's refugee population, policy-makers and field-workers still do not have the proper information which would enable them to implement adequate protection and assistance for refugee women or to allow them a greater voice in decisions regarding their own lives.

Refugees today are in need of better protection. Men and women share the same needs for physical protection, but women refugees, because of their sex, are frequently subject to the additional physical and emotional risk of sexual abuse. The most serious and fairly well-documented example of ongoing physical violence against women is in the Gulf of Thailand, where pirate attacks on Vietnamese boat people involve the almost inevitable rape and abduction of women. In spite of the Anti-Piracy Programme launched in 1982 at the instigation of UNHCR, these crimes

[3] Executive Committee of UNHCR, Thirty-sixth session, A/AC.96/671, 1985.

continue to occur. A short notice in the press on 7 November 1986[4] reported that a boat had been rescued recently by Malaysian fishermen; four Vietnamese women were missing, abducted by pirates—one more incident, among thousands, in this distressing tragedy that no one seems able to control. According to UNHCR, at least 2,400 women were raped by pirates between 1980 and 1984, and some thousand were abducted. Only 43 per cent of the women abducted since 1982 are known to have survived. In their desire to humiliate the whole group, Thai pirates generally violate these women in front of their families and other boat companions. Women of all ages are raped. In 1983, for example, the ages of the victims ranged from 9 to 67 years. The physical and psychological effects are often disastrous and can lead to complete mental breakdown.

Unfortunately these are not the only examples of refugee women being raped by unscrupulous men who take advantage of their loneliness and distress. In a presentation to the Women and International Development seminar on refugees,[5] Roberta Aitchison addressed the issue of sexual violence against refugee women who cross the Djibouti border: 'Since refugees are routinely detained and separated by sex, guards have easy targets.' But, as she pointed out, these women are reluctant witneses, and most sexual abuse remains undocumented because women fear speaking out. In some refugee camps women without the support of husbands or male relatives have been subjected to sexual violence in exchange for food rations or relief items. Outside the camps, in urban areas in the country of first asylum or in the resettlement country, it has become distressingly common to find young refugee women falling prey to extortion and sexual abuse, if not being directly involved in prostitution networks.

This whole question of physical and sexual violence against refugee women has to be placed in the larger context of violence, breakdown of social and cultural norms, and dislocation of the family unit, which characterizes most of the situations refugees encounter during the first phase of their exile. It has taken almost five years for the international community and UNHCR to take into account the specific needs of South-east Asian women who are

[4] *Le Monde* (7 Nov. 1986).

[5] Women and International Development, Joint Harvard/MIT Group Synopsis of seminars on 'Women Refugees as a Factor in Development', Mar. 1984.

victims of violence and to implement a counselling programme staffed by Vietnamese-speaking professionals. (Since 1984, the World YWCA has seconded five Vietnamese-speaking counsellors to UNHCR in four camps in Thailand and Malaysia.) The experience in South-east Asia should serve as an example to encourage those involved to deal more promptly with the problems of violence that refugee women encounter in other parts of the world today. But this again would require more information about the real situation, which is too often hidden by shame and fear. It would also require more sensitivity from field-workers and the appropriate authorities in identifying abuses and taking appropriate measures to punish the criminals and help the victims.

In addition to this problem, a new issue related to the protection of women has emerged into the international arena: the need to recognize as refugees those who suffer persecution in their own country because of their sexual status. In many parts of the world women who do not live up to the moral or ethical standards imposed on them by their societies can suffer cruel or inhuman treatment. For example, refusing arranged marriages, having sexual relations outside marriage, providing unsatisfactory dowries, or even wearing certain dress can result in physical persecution, if not death. Because of social constraints, relatively few of these women manage to flee to other countries for protection.

Such cases, however, have been numerous enough during recent years to provoke a public debate on the interpretation of Article 1 of the Geneva Convention, which defines those who qualify for refugee status. In 1983 the Conference of International Socialist Women called on 'all governments and member parties to amend the Geneva Convention . . . to include the victims of oppression and discrimination on the basis of sex as well as race and religion'. A year later the European Parliament adopted a resolution calling upon states to consider women who have been victims of such situations as belonging to a 'particular social group', within the definition of the 1951 Geneva Convention, and therefore as people qualifying for refugee status[6]. Many NGOs actively support such resolutions, which unfortunately have not yet been translated into policy decisions by the Executive Committee of the UNHCR

[6] Resolution on the application of the 1951 Convention relating to the status of refugees, adopted by the European Parliament on 13 Apr. 1984.

which, in its thirty-sixth session in 1985,[7] stated only that '[The Executive Committee] recognised that States, in the exercise of their sovereignty are free to adopt the interpretation that women asylum seekers who face harsh or inhuman treatment due to their having transgressed the social mores of the society in which they live may be considered as a particular social group.'

Any inequities faced by women in their home countries are generally exacerbated in their life as refugees, where they are often at a disadvantage in receiving assistance because of their lower social status. Individual situations differ considerably, according to the conditions in the country of origin and in the receiving country. Some common problems have, nevertheless, been identified as key issues for refugee women living in camps in Third World countries and for those who have found asylum in industrialized countries.

One social worker in a refugee camp reported that: 'Third World refugee women are in every sense refugees at the end of the charity line where they endlessly wait for food, for water, for medicines, for whatever basic needs have to be met. The female refugee head of family is even worse off.'[8] Discriminatory patterns of food distribution observed in various camps have led to serious malnutrition problems for women, even when food supplies were adequate at camp level. This vividly demonstrates how refugee policies for the administration of material assistance are insufficient when such biased practices against women are allowed to develop and to persist.

Health services are often inadequate for women in camps. Poor sanitation in overcrowded refugee camp housing affects women the most, because it is they who have to cope with frequent pregnancies and with children's illness. Gynaecological problems and mental stress are key female refugee health issues, requiring not only qualified, but also understanding and culturally acceptable medical staff. In spite of UNHCR's efforts to deal with this particular need, much more needs to be done, particularly in the training of refugee women in primary health care. The issue of refugee women's health is of particular importance because, when a woman becomes ill or incapacitated, or dies, the whole family structure is likely to collapse.

[7] Report of the thirty-sixth session of the Executive Committee of the High Commissioner's programme, A/AC.96./673, Oct. 1985.

[8] World Council of Churches, *Refugees*, 56E (Jan. 1984), 1.

Discrimination—in practice if not on purpose—also appears in education and skill-training programmes. Arriving in the host country with less education and fewer marketable skills than men, most refugee women have little chance of improving their situation, for two main reasons: first, overburdened with household tasks, women find it difficult to free themselves to attend regular training courses. And, second, most of the training opportunities have a predominantly male focus. Because of the traditional assumption that heads of families are men, skill-training programmes and income-generating activities have been directed primarily at them. Once again, the lack of proper data on the gender and sociological profile of the refugee population has contributed to aid agencies overlooking the fact that women must frequently be the sole support of their families—be they widows, single mothers, or married women whose husbands are in gaol, are involved in fighting, or have deserted the family.

When refugee women are resettled in industrialized countries, their problems take on completely different dimensions. It is not, then, either their overwhelming numbers or their basic material needs that call for special help, but their difficulties in adjusting and coping with a completely new environment. Confronted with drastic changes, for which very few of them have been prepared, women in resettlement countries remain the most invisible of the refugees and their specific needs go largely unrecognized. Torn between their traditional role of maintaining and reproducing the social patterns of their society of origin, and yet confronted with the need to adapt to the host society, they are, more than men, subject to traumatic pressures. The often low level of their formal education makes it difficult for refugee women to learn a new language quickly, and this hampers their social integration through community participation or work. Refugee women can rarely afford to attend regular language or training courses if child care is not provided. Isolation, loss of a frame of reference in the absence of traditional support systems, and frequent family breakdowns aggravate the physical and emotional stress of being uprooted: 'Little by little, silence has settled into my life. It has appropriated my will-power, leaving me paralysed. Fear and guilt have always haunted me', wrote a Chilean woman in exile.[9] Unable to meet her

[9] Ana Rosa Oriate '*La réappropriation de mon histoire ou l'histoire de ma réappropriation*' (1984) (in author's files).

own needs, the refugee woman becomes increasingly dependent not only upon her husband but on her children too, to accomplish even the routine tasks of daily life. The consequent feeling of depression and hopelessness is damaging not only to the woman herself, but to the stability and integration of the family as a whole. Despite these problems, the question of the specific needs of refugee women in resettlement countries does not seem to have attracted much attention among government agencies and voluntary organizations. A survey conducted in 1985 by the US Committee for Refugees revealed 'both a lack of funding for services which benefit refugee women and a low priority assigned to such services'.[10]

It would be impossible to conclude these remarks on the specific problems encountered by refugee women, both in terms of protection and assistance, without mentioning another, distinctly related, issue which needs to be discussed: women are excluded from decision-making at almost every stage of their lives as refugees. They have little opportunity to participate in the major decisions that affect their lives. Many women become refugees as a result of the political choices of their husbands or fathers. This is not always the case of course and an increasing minority of women have to pay for their own involvement in political activities with a life in exile. Once in exile, typically, they become subject to decisions taken exclusively by males: male refugee policy-makers, male camp authorities, male refugee leaders, male heads of family—with the predictable resulting bias.

When talking about improving needs assessment within the assistance system, Lance Clark from the Refugee Policy Group in Washington, DC stressed a crucial point:

> There is a widespread tendency for expatriates to feel that simply by talking to those whom they understand to be 'traditional leaders' they have heard the accurate statement of refugee needs. This often leads to an over-representation of the picture as seen by older men, to the detriment of other sub-groups. For example, older men seldom see the problems of fuelwood collection, or the difficulties in participating in income generating activities when one is taking care of small children, with quite the clarity that women do.[11]

[10] *Refugee Reports* (New York: American Council for Nationalities Service), 6/5 (May 1985).

[11] Lance Clarke, 'The Refugee Dependency Syndrome: Physician, Heal Thyself!', (Refugee Policy Group, Washington, July 1985).

The failure to include women in the decision-making process has long been identified as a major obstacle to the successful implementation of any refugee aid programme. In 1982 the International Committee for Migration Seminar introduced their recommendations by stating: 'The following recommendations assume as general principles that refugee women should be included in the design, management and implementation of assistance programmes . . .'[12] These recommendations are obviously not yet 'assumed' in most parts of the world today. The active participation of refugee women needs to be stressed at every level of the planning and implementation of programmes and must become a criterion for any refugee aid policy.

The potential of refugee women

Refugee women are indeed victims of accumulated disadvantages, but, increasingly, they are beginning to assert that they are not just victims of circumstances beyond their control but creative and dynamic actors in their own histories:

> Refugee women are not merely vulnerable and needy. Throughout the years, UNHCR [and many NGOs working with refugees have] . . . witnessed their moral and psychological strength, their ability to innovate, create and adjust; their energy to struggle to give a new meaning to life, their capacity to lead the family and to overcome the difficulties that come with family separation or breakdown. (High Commissioner for Refugees' Introduction to the Round Table on Refugee Women.)[13]

The pivotal role played by refugee women, not only in the welfare of their own families, but in the entire refugee community, has been documented in various mini-studies in different parts of the world and reported by many field-workers. The women are the ones who ultimately keep the family together when the men are absent or no longer able to cope. The women are the ones who manage to 'make do with nothing', to secure as much as they can to meet the basic needs of their families. The women are the ones who find the inner strength to assume new roles, despite overwhelming personal tragedy.

When recognized and encouraged to develop their potential, refugee women have proved to be essential elements in the solutions

[12] World Council of Churches, *Refugees*, 56E (Jan. 1984), 1.
[13] 'Refugee Women', A Round Table organized by UNHCR, Geneva, 1985.

to their own problems and the problems of the refugee community at large. In the refugee camps in Thailand and Malaysia, where the counselling programme for victims of violence at sea has been implemented, counsellors have encouraged women to set up women's associations and community self-help groups. The purpose of the groups is to restore the self-confidence of women by giving them responsibility for the care and social well-being of the camp community. In refugee camps in Africa, Central America, and South-east Asia the training of refugee women health workers has systematically improved refugee women's access to health programmes and has been an important element in primary health care programmes. Very few examples of women's involvement in camp management have been documented, but in the case of the Solumuna camp for Eritrean refugees,[14] and in the Tendelti camp in Sudan for Chadean refugees, women 'have proved themselves more than competent in taking over administrative work generally reserved for men'.[15] By giving them the opportunity to use their skills and acquire new ones, refugee policy-makers should realize that it is true that refugee groups which are in control of their own affairs seem to achieve much more.

The strength required to assume new roles and responsibilities does not come easily, nor does the courage to overcome personal distress in the face of an uncertain future. For some, it might never come. But, paradoxically, this tremendous challenge can be a source of liberation and positive change for many women refugees. 'Once attitudinal changes occur and new skills are acquired, changes are there to stay', relates Masako Hoshino from her ten years' experience working with refugees in South-east Asia and Somalia[16]. It is time to realize that, while there is no development process without women's participation, there is also no solution to refugee problems without women's full contribution.

Towards a positive and affirmative approach

For too long planners—blind to the fact that refugee women's needs are simply not the same as men's—have failed to recognize

[14] 'Shaming the World: The Needs of Refugee Women' (London: Change–World University Service, 1985).

[15] Helen Calloway, 'Women Refugees in Developing Countries' (Refugee Studies Programme, Queen Elizabeth House, Oxford, Dec. 1985).

[16] 'Refugee Women'.

the necessity for relating protection and assistance policy to women's specific requirements, not only to ensure equal access to facilities but also to increase participation in community-level organizations. The objectives pursued should not merely be anti-discriminatory; rather, a positive and affirmative approach to meeting refugee women's needs should be implemented. This new affirmative approach to refugee women's needs and potential should apply at all levels of policy-making and field implementation—from UNHCR and government ministries, to local authorities, camp administration, and refugee organizations.

Incorporating this approach into the wide diversity of programmes concerned with the lives of refugees will take time. It will also meet either with passive resistance—because it shakes the routine and the comfortable assumption of stereotypes—or active opposition—because it ultimately challenges traditional male/female roles. Given that it will be a long and probably uneasy process, several practical stages can be identified which are neither mutually exclusive nor sequential:

1. Making refugee women visible in data collection. In an environment largely hostile to incorporating gender as a concern in refugee aid planning, it is of primary importance to collect solid data reflecting the demographic profiles of refugee populations by age, sex, household composition (including gender of head of household), education, skills, and gender-specific health status. Such information, essential to the development of effective programmes and policies, requires a system for collection, analysis, and dissemination and a gender-consultative process with the refugees. Because the source of diagnosis of the specific problems women encounter must be the refugee women themselves, their contribution forms a critical component of any refugee planning process.

2. Improving provision for the physical safety of refugee women in flight, in camps and in urban areas. Sexual abuse and violence against women needs to be confronted more openly. Shame and fear should be directed towards the aggressors, not the victims. This requires the mobilization of public opinion, prompt investigation by appropriate authorities to find and punish the criminals, and the sensitivity of UNHCR and other agencies to identify and denounce such abuses.

Experience has proved that psychological counselling is indispensable in helping victims of violence regain their confidence and self-respect. Current programmes undertaken by UNHCR in South-east Asia should be strengthened and developed. The wealth of knowledge and experience accumulated there should be extended to other places and shared among the NGOs' partners.

3. Enlarging the interpretation of the Geneva Convention definition on refugees to include the victims of oppression and discrimination on the basis of their sexual status. Although some people think this an inappropriate time to call for a revision or amendment of the Geneva Convention, the broad interpretation of 'particular social group' within the meaning of Article 1 of the Convention should provide a legal basis for the recognition of women being threatened and persecuted because they have broken or have refused to accept the social mores of their society.

4. Ensuring equal access to material assistance. In some cases positive discriminatory measures should be taken to redress those practices heavily biased against women. Furthermore, international agencies and non-governmental organizations administering assistance programmes to refugees should make sure that women are involved in both needs assessment and the distribution of food and materials.

5. Implementing educational and training programmes that are available to and affordable by refugee women. Education to enable refugee women to become self-reliant can play a pivotal role in both first asylum and resettlement countries. Planners of education programmes should take into account the constraints that women experience in balancing their roles as housekeepers and productive workers. Courses are sometimes poorly attended simply because they are scheduled at a time when women are involved in productive work or because they have nowhere to leave their children. Appropriate time schedules, as well as provision for child care, should be arranged to ensure the attendance of women in educational and training programmes.

6. Encouraging a community-based approach to health problems. Experience has proved that refugee women who are trained health workers can considerably improve women's access to health centres and women's participation in primary health care programmes. The policies of specialized agencies in charge of health programmes should emphasize the need to train refugee women health workers, thus enabling them to help themselves—in a way that might also be more effective.

7. Ensuring refugee women's participation in decision-making. The active participation of women is not only desirable as a means of achieving refugee aid objectives, but as an end in itself. The remarks made by Caroline Moser and Coreen Levy on women's participation in the development process apply equally to refugee women: 'The experience of popular mobilisation and participation of women organized mainly around their domestic role indicates the importance of participation as an end in itself. Through such experience women's consciousness and the ability to exert control over their own lives can be dramatically influenced.'[17] Once again, affirmative action should be taken to ensure that such recommendations are implemented, if not enforced, through specific criteria for funding.

8. Assisting and supporting refugee women in organizing themselves. Refugee women need less of our compassion and more of our solidarity and support. Unless considered *partners*, they will remain dependent, mere recipients of charity. Establishing true partnership means recognizing and respecting their identity and their abilities. It means helping refugee women to help themselves whenever possible, often by assisting them with the formation of organizations of their own, where they can better identify their priorities and find solutions to their problems.

9. Encouraging the self-expression of refugee women. A few of these women have been able to express publicly through books, interview, or films what they really feel and think as women confronted by these situations: Domilila Chungarra's testimony '*Si me dan la palabra*' ('If you allow me to speak') illustrates well the impact on world opinion of a grass-roots voice, able to address issues that are common to thousands of women like her. It helps to give a human content to cold reports, it helps to restore the dignity of human beings too easily classified as powerless victims. This kind of expression should be actively encouraged in the future.

Conclusion

The heightened vigilance of the UN Decade for Women has helped unveil some of the most blatant problems that refugee women have to face, merely because they are women—increased risk of violence,

[17] C. Moser and C. Levy, *A Theory and Methodology of Gender Planning: Meeting Women's Practical and Strategic Needs* (Development Planning Unit, Bartlett School of Architecture and Planning, University College, London, 1986).

unequal access to assistance, exclusion from decision-making bodies—but these past ten years have also witnessed many examples of refugee women standing up and successfully assuming new responsibilities within their families and communities. Despite the fact that some changes have begun to occur, and a greater sensitivity to a gender-specific approach to refugee questions has become noticeable, much more still needs to be done to identify precisely and to analyse key refugee women's issues and to propose adequate responses. To date research on refugee women has been extremely limited. In order for fresh directions in policy and practice to develop, refugee women need to become a focus of refugee studies.

TABLE 1. *World refugee populations*

		Number	%
Europe		677,000	17
Canada		353,000	
United States		1,000,000	
Australia/New Zealand		93,000	
Middle East		2,100,000	83
Africa*		2,939,200	
Horn of Africa	1,471,800		
East Africa	643,300		
Southern Africa	260,500		
West Africa	386,800		
North Africa	167,800		
Pakistan/Iran		4,400,000	
South Asia		286,900	
China		179,800	
Papua New Guinea		10,900	
Central America		332,200	
Caribbean		8,000	
South America		22,000	
Other countries (in Asia, Africa, Latin America)		109,900	
Total refugee population		12,503,400	100

Sources: UNHCR, UNRWA, 1985.

* Not including persons assisted under the UNHCR special appeal for emergency needs in Africa.

TABLE 2. *The refugee burden in 1984–1985*

Country	No. Ref. 110 000 h	GNP/inhabitant in US $
Jordan	2,149	1,182
Somalia	1,375	250
Lebanon	887	?
Djibouti	657	480
Burundi	580	203
Iran	447	2,455
Sudan	348	400
Pakistan	333	325
Syria	202	1,680
Zambia	165	413
Canada	139	13,258
Angola	130	?
Swaziland	115	959
Australia	57	11,129
Sweden	52	11,365
Switzerland	50	13,874
United States	43	15,481
France	29	9,049
Federal Republic of Germany	19	10,012

Sources: UNHCR, UNRWA, 1984–5; *L'État du Monde 1985*, Ed. La Découverte, Paris.

8. The Churches, Refugees, and Politics

ELIZABETH G. FERRIS

IMPORTANT changes are occurring in the ways in which Churches and Church-related agencies approach their work with refugees. Today, as many of these agencies are becoming increasingly aware of the political dimensions of their work, they are adopting more overtly political strategies. This chapter analyses this trend in terms of the causes of this politicization, the obstacles to greater political action by the Churches, and the consequences of a more politicized role. It is true that many of these trends are also evident in the secular NGO community, but generalizations are more difficult to make here because of the heterogeneity of the hundreds of non-governmental organizations (NGOs) currently engaged in some form of refugee service.[1]

Non-governmental organizations have always played an important role in refugee matters, from encouraging governments to adopt more liberal admissions policies, to providing material assistance in refugee settlements around the world and facilitating the resettlement of refugees in third countries. NGOs have many human and material resources which they bring to this work. They

[1] In his opening speech to the 1986 Executive Committee of the UNHCR, the new High Commissioner referred to the contributions of NGOs in providing essential services to refugees, while noting the 'astonishing proliferation' of NGOs working with refugees (UNHCR, 1986). Indeed he noted that, while UNHCR presently works closely with some 250 NGOs, there are in fact over a thousand NGOs with which UNHCR is in direct contact. This growth in number of NGOs involved in refugee work reflects growing interest and concern with refugees on the part of the international NGO community, as the International Council of Voluntary Agencies (ICVA) noted in its statement at the 1986 UNHCR Executive Committee meeting (ICVA, 1986). As Gorman points out, voluntary agencies differ in terms of their resources, orientations, expertise, and geographic areas of concern. They also increasingly differ in terms of their political orientation, with growing numbers of conservative NGOs becoming involved in politically sensitive areas of refugee concentrations. See Robert F. Gorman, 'Private Voluntary Organizations in Refugee Relief', in Elizabeth G. Ferris, ed. *Refugees and World Politics*, (New York: Praeger, 1986), 82–104.

frequently have access to information which is inaccessible to governments and international organizations. Moreover, NGOs have constituencies which can be mobilized to affect public opinion and government policies. While their contributions have long been recognized by governments and by the United Nations High Commissioner for Refugees (UNHCR), there is an appalling lack of scholarly analyses of their role in the international refugee policy arena.[2] Yet, politically significant changes in the orientation of non-governmental organizations in general and of Church-related NGOs in particular are taking place. Church-related agencies share many characteristics with their secular counterparts. They range from a few volunteers operating out of a church office to huge national and international agencies working with multi-million dollar budgets. Some Church-related agencies in the industrialized countries direct huge emergency and development programmes for refugees, while many others are involved in resettlement and local integration of refugees. Some provide a wide range of services—from counselling to advocacy—while others administer small scholarship programmes or provide pastoral care. Some are operational partners of UNHCR, while many others work with

[2] A number of studies have analysed the role of voluntary agencies in development. See e.g. Judith Tendler, *Turning Voluntary Organizations into Development Agencies: Questions for Evaluation* (Washington, DC: Agency for International Development, 1982); Robert F. Gorman, *Private Voluntary Organizations as Agents of Development* (Boulder: Westview Press, 1984); Landrum Bolling and Craig Smith, *Private Foreign Aid: US Philanthropy for Relief and Development* (Boulder: Westview Press, 1982); Jane Blewitt, Peter Henriot, and Elizabeth Schmidt, *Religious Private Organizations and the Question of Government Funding* (Mary Knoll, NY: Orbis Books, 1981); and Wynta Boynes, ed., *US Non-profit Organizations in Development Abroad* (New York: Technical Assistance Clearing House, 1983). Bolling and Smith 1982; Blewitt *et al.*, 1981, and Boynes 1983. A smaller number of studies have analysed the role of NGOs in refugee assistance (see e.g. Robert F. Gorman, 'Coping with the African Refugee Problem: Reflections on the Role of Private Voluntary Organization Assistance', *Issue, A Journal of Africanist Opinion*, 12 (Spring–Summer 1982), 35–40; and 'Beyond ICARA II: Implementing Refugee-Related Development Assistance', *International Migration Review*, 20/2 (1986), 283–98; Leon Gordenker, 'Organizational Expansion and Limits in International Services for Refugees', *International Migration Review*, 15 (Spring 1981), 74–87, and 'Refugees in Developing Countries and Transnational Organizations', *Annals of the American Academy of Political and Social Science*, 467 (May 1983), 62–77; and Peter I Rose, 'The Business of Caring: Refugee Workers and Voluntary Agencies', *Refugee Reports*, 4 (1981), 1–6. In addition, several of the principal studies of refugee situations discuss the pivotal role of NGOs, albeit somewhat anecdotally (e.g. William Shawcross, *The Quality of Mercy: Cambodia, the Holocaust and Modern Conscience* (New York: Simon Schuster, 1984); B. E. Harrell-Bond, *Imposing Aid: Emergency Assistance to Refugees* (Oxford University Press, 1985); Gil Loescher and John A. Scanlan, *Calculated Kindness: Refugees and America's Half-Open Door, 1945 to the Present* (New York: The Free Press, 1986)).

refugees who are not officially recognized as such either by UNHCR or by governments.[3]

However, Church-related agencies have two characteristics which set them apart from their secular counterparts. First, they are motivated by Christian compassion, although their beliefs/ideas/views on how to interpret the Gospel in refugee ministry take many different forms. This means that there is a certain unity of purpose which serves to connect Church-related refugee agencies around the world—at least in a general moral sense. Although virtually all of them work with secular agencies, there is none the less a certain bond between Church people—a bond which, it will be argued later, has the potential for sustaining a politically effective network of these agencies around the world.

The second major difference between Church-related and secular agencies lies in the nature of their constituencies. Most fundamentally, the religious agencies are supported by their Church members and congregations, even when financially supported by Church agencies outside the region. Thus, for example, a Church refugee agency in Africa may count both on outside financial assistance and on the active support of local congregations. This broad-based constituency gives the religious agencies a potentially powerful role when engaging in advocacy *vis-à-vis* governments. These agencies, especially when acting in concert, have the potential for mobilizing public opinion on a wide scale—at least in those countries professing to be Christian. Moreover, Churches, as corporate bodies, have a certain degree of protection from recrimination. Whereas in many cases, for example, governments have not hesitated to publish the names of individuals working on behalf of refugees, Churches, because of their wider constituency support, have been less susceptible to the same kinds of pressure. Of course, in countries where Christians are in a minority, the Churches do not have this immunity, but they may enjoy a certain degree of protection precisely because of their connections with churches in other powerful countries.

[3] The refugee work of Churches and Church-related agencies is described in a number of regular publications, including the *Refugees* newsletter of the World Council of Churches, and *Monday*, of the Church World Service. In addition many Church agencies have their own newsletters, e.g. *CIMADE Informations* (a publication of CIMADE, Paris); *Drame de l'espoir* (Centre Social Protestant, Belgium); *Moving* (Inter-Church Commission for Immigration and Refugee Resettlement, New Zealand). A list of these publications is available from WCC's Refugee Service.

Clearly there are many differences among Church-related agencies. On the one hand, the traditional agencies affiliated with the World Council of Churches have generally held a fairly progressive view of their service to refugees, as have many of those affiliated with the Roman Catholic Church. On the other hand, conservative agencies, often linked to fundamentalist Churches and/or right-wing political groups, are becoming increasingly active in many parts of the world. With often substantial financial resources, they have been accused of proselytizing and of using their resources and position to support the foreign-policy objectives of outside governments. In eastern Honduras, for example, a number of conservative agencies, some with ties to US religious groups, have in the past complicated the already difficult situation of Nicaraguan refugees. By providing aid along the Honduras–Nicaragua border, in areas dominated by rebel activity, they drew some refugees out of the relative protection of the UNHCR camps and made it possible for them to join the military forces of the *contras*.

Although the trend of increasing politicization is evident among all of these groups, the focus of this paper is on the long-established, refugee-serving Church agencies, which have generally seen their work as non-partisan.

The development of political awareness

Throughout recorded history Churches have ministered to refugees. The biblical injunction to care for 'the stranger in your midst' has often inspired Christians to welcome and assist refugees. But it was only during and after World War II that Churches organized specific agencies to serve refugees. Indeed, it was the experience of co-operation among Churches working with refugees and displaced persons in the aftermath of World War II that stimulated the ecumenical movement, leading to the creation of the World Council of Churches (WCC) in 1948. From the beginning most of these agencies saw themselves as humanitarian, non-partisan organizations. Some were involved primarily in the resettlement of refugees, some with direct relief, but virtually all of them saw themselves as essentially non-political.

In many cases this was a direct response to the politically charged atmosphere of the post-war period. In order to serve the millions of desperately needy refugees and displaced persons in Europe, many Churches and Church-related agencies consciously emphasized their humanitarian and non-political nature. As the years went by, most Churches and Church-related agencies maintained this non-political orientation, although, by doing so, some agencies were making a political statement, while eschewing overt political involvement. Not to question or to challenge government policies is to give tacit support and even legitimacy to these policies.

Within the past decade Churches and related refugee agencies have been forced to change or to reassess their traditional role of not becoming involved in overt political activities. The reason for this shift stems both from the changing nature of refugee situations around the world and from changes occurring within the agencies and Churches.

Organizations created in the immediate post-war period initially saw their work as essentially temporary. However, with the increase in refugee migrations in the 1960s and 1970s, Church-related agencies, like intergovernmental organizations, began to understand the permanent nature of the refugee problem and the need for different kinds of responses. In the contemporary world, providing emergency assistance or processing resettlement applications requires technical expertise; grappling with development issues and protection problems requires much more attention to larger political and economic issues. As refugees have become a permanent phenomenon in many countries, traditional solutions are no longer adequate. Wars, frequently supported by outside intervention, last longer, and voluntary repatriation seems a distant possibility for most refugees today. As governments in countries of first asylum experience economic decline and political turmoil, local integration becomes more difficult. Finally, resettlement opportunities for the refugees are more limited and can meet the needs of only a small percentage of the world's 10–15 million refugees.

With the growth in information and communication among refugee-serving agencies and UNHCR, refugee service agencies are more aware than ever of what is happening in countries far from those in which they work. The publication of periodicals such as UNHCR's *Refugees*, and the growth of refugee documentation centres, have made it more likely that Churches and related agencies will be able to see the connections between their own situations and other, more distant ones. As agencies come to see these connections—say, for example, between repatriation in Djibouti, closed camps in Hong Kong and Honduras, and the imposition of visa requirements in the Netherlands—it becomes more difficult to ignore the needs of refugees and asylum-seekers and the root causes that provoke their flight.

Difficulties in providing protection to refugees are becoming both more widespread and more widely known as a result of improved communication. Traditionally, UNHCR was charged with protecting refugees, and voluntary agencies with providing material assistance; but the distinction between protection and assistance is breaking down. The UNHCR can no longer adequately protect refugees in certain situations, e.g. armed attacks on settlements, and, in urban areas particularly, refugee-serving agencies are coming to the realization that without adequate material assistance there can be no physical or legal protection. For example, when Chilean refugees in Argentina have been unable to survive economically there, they have returned home to Chile, where they have often faced even more serious security problems than when they originally left the country.

In many different parts of the world Churches are playing an increasingly important protective role, particularly for those refugees not officially recognized as such by UNHCR or by their governments. Historically, Christians and church congregations have offered protection to refugees directly, by hiding them in their homes or sheltering them within their church communities. In all countries the potential costs of such efforts are high. In South Africa the South African Council of Churches is the principal organization working with the thousands of Mozambicans who are not recognized as refugees.[4] In Europe dozens of churches have sheltered asylum-seekers who were facing deportation.[5] For example, by 1986 it was estimated that some two thousand Swiss Christians were hiding refugees in their homes. Most commonly, these have been asylum-seekers whose applications for asylum have been rejected and who faced deportation.

This involvement in protection issues perhaps inevitably draws Churches and related agencies into more overt political activity.

[4] World Council of Churches, *Ecumenical Consultation on Asylum and Protection* (Geneva, Apr. 1986).

[5] World Council of Churches, *Refugees Today and Tomorrow*, Report of WCC Consultation on Refugee Resettlement (New York: Church World Service, Sept. 1986).

Thus, in northern Mexico, the Centro de Investigacíon y Estudíos in Tijuana has secured the release of hundreds of Central American refugees imprisoned by the Mexican authorities.[6] In its efforts to protect the refugees, CIEM has turned to both advocacy and public awareness-building efforts. Similarly, in the United States, Churches and ecumenical agencies are in the forefront of providing legal services to refugees in an attempt to allow them to live in safety. Church World Service (CWS), which is the service arm of the National Council of Churches of Christ in the USA, provides counselling for refugees in more than fifty CWS-related refugee projects throughout the United States. When the Immigration Control and Reform Act came into effect in May 1987 CWS established a special Immigrant Service Project to respond to the immediate needs for information, counselling, and processing of those immigrants affected by the new immigration law.

For refugee agencies working in Western countries, the arrival of refugees in large numbers from the developing countries, and the restrictive policies of their governments, have led to the dramatic politicization of agencies. European Churches, for example, which ten years ago focused most of their energies on providing social services to officially registered refugees, now find themselves confronting their governments' exclusionary policies. For example, in Belgium and Switzerland the Churches traditionally worked with their governments in providing the necessary services to refugees resettled in those countries. But, as governments of both countries have adopted much more restrictive policies which have led to the deportation of many refugees, the Churches have begun openly and vocally to oppose their governments' decisions. This has been a difficult change in orientation for many European Churches, which have traditionally seen themselves as supportive of their governments. Given present trends, it is likely that Church–state tension will increase in both Europe and North America.

The awareness of human rights violations in the late 1970s, and the subsequent development of a broad-scale, effective human rights network, have further challenged the refugee-serving agencies to become more involved with large political issues,

[6] Perez Canchola, José Luiz, 'Refugiados Centro-Americanos en Méxicσ: La Frontera del Norte', WCC, *Refugees*, 81S (Nov. 1986).

particularly questions concerning the root causes of refugee flows. Initially, agencies resisted getting involved in questions of root causes; given UNHCR's reluctance to deal with these issues and the agencies' own self-perceptions as being non-partisan, root causes were considered by voluntary agencies only with difficulty. But as human rights groups became more active in publicizing the horrific violations of human rights, and as it became politically acceptable in Western countries to talk about human rights abuses occurring in Third World countries (albeit while human rights situations at home were often ignored), refugee-serving agencies began to make the connection with their own work.

Since World War II the nature of refugee migrations has changed. Most asylum-seekers in industrialized nations today come from the Third World, and the majority of these people are not Christian. This has drawn Churches and related agencies into closer contact with other faiths, and this alone has challenged and enriched the Churches themselves. But it has also raised questions about the relationship of Christian service agencies to non-Christian aid recipients. Most of the Churches and agencies described here have rigorously defended the cultural integrity and religious traditions of the refugees. They see their ministry to refugees as rooted in their Christian commitment to help those in need, regardless of their religious beliefs. However, there are other groups that have not drawn such a distinction between evangelizing and service. Fears of proselytizing by Christian agencies have been expressed by Governments and by refugees themselves. In the past, for example, there have been charges that some religious agencies in Central America and South-east Asia have given preferential treatment to those refugees who attended their church services.

These external changes in the global refugee situation produced an impetus for politicization of refugee issues, but were not in themselves sufficient to change the orientation. Changes in the nature of the organizations themselves created a receptivity to these external conditions, which made it possible for the agencies to come to see themselves as political entities.

Within the Churches, over the last two decades, the humanitarian/political dichotomy has begun to break down. Progressive elements within the Churches began to talk about solidarity with the poor, the need for just and participatory societies, and the preferential option for the poor. With the growth of liberation theology, an important element within the Churches began to argue that the Churches could not and should not be politically neutral. The Gospel imperative is clear, they say: the Churches must opt to be on the side of the poor and oppressed. It soon became clear that, if Churches were to be on the side of poor and marginalized populations, they would come into conflict with the powers supporting the status quo. The emphasis on the need for structural change in society also meant a change in the methods and orientations of the refugee-serving agencies—from assistance to advocacy, from a goal of working *for* to one of working *with* refugees.

Once Christians in developed countries began listening to refugees, and began to be challenged by refugee demands, they inevitably became politicized. As refugees themselves slowly began to be incorporated into decision-making structures within the Churches, the conception that refugee work could be politically neutral was further eroded, and agencies began to assume a more overtly political stance. It is notable that refugee participation in meetings about refugees often leads to a change in emphasis. At the 1986 Ecumenical consultation on Asylum and Protection held in Zurich, the refugees present made a forceful and articulate demand for the Churches to do much more to tackle the root causes of refugee flows. This trend was paralleled outside the organizations by the growth of political exile and solidarity groups in the West, which also pushed the agencies to become more political.

These trends have combined to produce pressure on Churches and Church-related agencies to adopt more openly political strategies in their service to refugees, although the transition from non-partisan to politically active roles is fraught with difficulty. Perhaps most fundamentally, the transition is impeded by the self-perceptions of Christians and agency personnel. The consequences of overt political involvement by Churches can be at best unsettling and at worst personally dangerous. The political culture of a country determines in large part the extent to which politicization of Churches is viewed as acceptable. In fact, the legal status of Church-related agencies may be jeopardized by overt political activity. The tax-exempt status of Church-related agencies in some North American and Western European countries, for example, precludes lobbying of government officials although, in practice, of course, it is difficult to draw the line between public education efforts and political pressure. Moreover, in many countries, the acceptance of government funds by Church agencies may result in an unconscious effort on the part of the agencies to avoid criticizing government policies.

Political involvement is particularly difficult in some Third World countries, where refugee agencies are already viewed with suspicion by their governments. Unfortunately, because refugees frequently find asylum in countries in which human rights abuses are widespread and where freedom of expression is limited, Church agencies must weigh the consequences of overt political action. In general we can say that the more repressive the government—and thus the higher the cost of political involvement—the less local agencies will be able to tackle political issues. This reality makes it imperative that such local agencies work in conjunction with Churches and agencies outside the country which may enjoy greater protection from the consequences of their political involvement. Church-related agencies in the industrialized world have found it easier to become politically active and many—though not the majority—have begun to make the connections between the needs of the refugees they serve and the role of their own governments in contributing to the violence which forces refugees to flee their homes. This has been most clearly the case with US-based agencies working with Central American refugees either in the United States, Mexico, or in Central America. For example, a local US Church may begin by helping an individual Central American refugee family as a humanitarian act. But, as the members of the Church learn more about the reasons for the refugees' flight, they begin to raise questions about the role of the United States in Central America. Similarly, contact with South African exiles has led many to see the connections between their own government's support of apartheid and the human suffering it causes.

The kind of political involvement engaged in by NGOs takes many forms. Most commonly perhaps, Church-related agencies engage in advocacy work *vis-à-vis* their own governments for better treatment of refugees and asylum-seekers. To a lesser extent, they advocate particular issues to UNHCR and express solidarity with other like-minded NGOs, particularly those working in Third World countries. They are beginning to address themselves to root causes of refugee flows.[7] And, perhaps most significantly, they are beginning to co-ordinate their political efforts with other agencies, both religious-based and secular, at the national, regional, and international levels.

While Churches recognize the importance of increasing such co-operation, this has in fact proved very difficult to achieve. Even among Church-related agencies, who have more in common with each other than do secular agencies, there are differences in orientation and priorities. Different constituency pressures make it difficult to co-ordinate political strategies, particularly in the absence of many successful models of inter-agency collaboration.[8]

Among local organizations working in the developing countries, suspicion and sometimes competition with each other for UNHCR contracts or funds from outside donors limit co-operation. The realities of aid flows from North to South may mean that a particular local agency will be more tied to its donors than to other local agencies, which are also dependent on other foreign donors. Different political philosophies, ethnic conflicts, and personal disputes may also make local agencies reluctant to co-operate with each other in activities as sensitive as political advocacy.

Among large Church-related agencies in the industrialized world, a different set of pressures works against co-ordination of political and assistance activities. Voluntary agencies mounting fund-raising campaigns seek to assuage public fears that funds are not reaching the most needy, by ensuring the presence of their own staff in the assisted region. This 'our man in the field' syndrome has led to appalling duplication of personnel, programmes, and unco-ordinated assistance. Some agency representatives recognize this,

[7] WCC, *Refugees*, 81S (Nov. 1986).

[8] The International Council of Voluntary Agencies (ICVA) is one model of inter-agency co-operation which brings together secular and religious agencies. Through ICVA's sub-group on refugees, agencies share information and co-operate in producing a statement to the annual Executive Committee meeting of the UNHCR. Over the past few years, these ICVA statements have become both more specific and more critical of UNHCR, while affirming the agencies' desires to maintain close working relationships with UNHCR (see ICVA Statement to the 37th Session of the Executive Committee of the High Commissioner's Programme, 1986). Another example of successful inter-agency co-operation is the League of Red Cross/voluntary agency group on disasters. This group meets monthly in Geneva to share information on disasters, including refugee emergencies. Representatives of UN and voluntary agencies discuss particular situations, with the object of co-ordinating the response of the international community. Church-related agencies are active participants in both of these forums.

but explain that they would otherwise be unable to raise the necessary funds for the programmes. Another unfortunate consequence of this phenomenon is its impact on indigenous NGOs. While local NGOs undoubtedly have a better understanding of local needs and will be better able to follow programmes through, there is a reluctance on the part of international agencies to rely on local groups rather then fielding their own staff. The limits of such policies are clearly seen in the present situation in southern Sudan. When the violence there reached alarming proportions, most international NGOs were forced to withdraw their expatriate staff. The staff of the two principal Sudanese agencies, the Sudan Council of Churches and Sudan Aid (a Sudanese Catholic organization), remained behind.

Many Churches and Church-related agencies, in both North and South, are currently struggling to make their relationship more egalitarian and more open, in order to overcome the negative consequences of donor-recipient relations. Thus, in the Sudan Round Table, representatives of large agencies work in close co-operation with the Sudan Council of Churches to assess and fund large-scale refugee programmes throughout the country.[9] At a recent WCC Consultation in Cyprus, participants from all over the world committed themselves to improving relationships with each other.[10] As Churches strengthen their relationships with each other in refugee service, co-operation in other areas—such as addressing root causes—becomes more likely.

In spite of the obstacles, Churches and related agencies are increasingly seeing the need for more political involvement on behalf of refugees and for co-ordination of their actions. Two examples of the ways in which such politicization is occurring are the US sanctuary movement and global ecumenical co-operation on protection and asylum issues.

Sanctuary and the Central American refugees

The sanctuary movement in the United States offers a challenging response to the plight of refugees. Over three hundred

[9] WCC *References* (Oct. 1985).

[10] Larnaca Declaration: *The Alms Race: The Impact of American Voluntary Aid Abroad* (New York: Random House, 1986).

Protestant congregations, Catholic parishes, and Jewish synagogues across the country have declared themselves to be public sanctuaries, offering shelter and hospitality to Central American refugees fleeing the violence of their homelands. In declaring themselves to be places of sanctuary, congregations place themselves in opposition to current US policy and risk fines and imprisonment for their actions. The refugees themselves are also well aware of the risk they face in choosing to speak out publicly on behalf of their countrymen, but both they and the Churches feel the issue to be too important to allow considerations of personal safety to take precedence.

Sanctuary for Central Americans began on 24 March 1982, when the Southside Presbyterian Church of Tucson, Arizona, informed the US authorities that it was sheltering Salvadorean refugees who had fled to the United States in fear for their lives. For the members of the Southside congregation, the decision to extend sanctuary was the product of a long period of prayer and discussion about the best way to help the Central Americans coming to the US in search of a safe haven. Prayers for the refugees were followed by efforts to raise bail funds. But the members of the church wanted to do more. They wanted to take action which would respond both directly and personally to the needs of the Central Americans and which would tackle the larger political issues in the Central American conflict.

The decision to declare sanctuary is made by the whole congregation, usually through a consensus that takes weeks or months of deliberations to achieve. Around each such congregation there are many other groups and individuals who support the sanctuary church. Local church councils frequently serve as avenues for co-operation. As a grass-roots movement, sanctuary takes many forms. Congregations decide to become involved in different ways and to varying degrees. Some congregations support the sanctuary movement by becoming a stop on the 'underground railroad', giving temporary protection to individuals *en route* to places of sanctuary, or to refugees being transported out of the country.

The political consequences of the sanctuary movement are many. By making the connection between US foreign policy and the treatment of refugees, the sanctuary movement seeks to reach and educate American citizens, who would otherwise not have been aware of this link. While the sanctuary movement remains a grass-roots phenomenon and lacks any kind of national organization or co-ordination, at least one faction sees itself as part of a larger movement of resistance to the US government. Moreover, the sanctuary movement—by virtue of its size and rapid growth—is challenging traditional Church structures and other voluntary agencies to become more politically involved. Although the sanctuary movement has received substantial support from national and international Church organizations, it remains largely outside those agencies. This unfortunately, may become typical of the politicization of refugee issues, with such initiatives largely taking place outside traditional structures and forcing the Churches to respond only by virtue of their widespread public support. When large numbers of local congregations are involved in sanctuary, significant pressure is exerted on national Church structures to take a more activist stand on the asylum issue.

Another consequence of the US sanctuary movement has been its effect on Churches in other parts of the world. Many Christians and Churches in Europe, for example, have been challenged by the US example to consider their own response to asylum-seekers. By adapting principles of sanctuary to their own national contexts, many Europeans have taken similar action. Churches in Great Britain, Norway, the Netherlands, Switzerland, Italy, and the Federal Republic of Germany have all been involved in some form of sanctuary, by offering protection to asylum-seekers. As the movement develops, sanctuary activists feel the need to link up with similar movements in other countries in order to learn from and support each other.[11] The development of such a network parallels ecumenical co-operation on asylum and protection issues.

[11] There is a burgeoning literature on the sanctuary movement, including many articles and publications by US ecumenical groups. Ronny Golden and Michael McConnell, in *Sanctuary: The New Underground Railroad* (Mary Knoll, NY: Orbis Books, 1986), provide an excellent overview of the sanctuary movement. Ignatius Bau, in *This Ground is Holy: Church Sanctuary and Central American Refugees* (Mahwah, NJ: Paulist Press, 1985), focuses on the theological bases of the sanctuary movement, while Gardy MacEoin, in *Sanctuary: A Resource Guide for Understanding the Participating in the Central American Refugee Struggle* (New York: Harper and Row, 1985), provides a collection of reports of different experiences with sanctuary. *Basta!*, the regular publication of the Chicago Religious Task Force on Central America, is particularly helpful for news of current developments. An annotated bibliography of materials dealing with sanctuary has been compiled by Anne Meyer Byler, *Annotated Bibliography on Sanctuary* (Champaign, Ill.: Urbana Ecumenical Committee on Sanctuary, 1986). Finally, WCC's *Refugees* produced a special edition on sanctuary in Sept. 1986.

Ecumenical co-operation on asylum and protection issues

As early as 1981 Churches and related agencies in North America and Europe recognized the need for closer co-operation on asylum and protection. Meeting in Stoney Point, New York, they began a process of consultation which has grown steadily over the past five years. Most recently, in May 1986 an Ecumenical Consultation on Asylum and Protection held in Zurich brought together one hundred participants from countries of asylum and countries of origin.[12] As Western governments intensify their co-ordination of exclusionary refugee policies, the Churches realize that their only hope of arresting this trend is by fuller co-operation with each other. Participants at the Zurich meeting identified several areas for joint action, including:

1. the establishment of a systematic means of sharing information on root causes of refugee flows, governmental policies towards refugees, and church refugee programmes;
2. the establishment of mechanisms for joint advocacy *vis-à-vis* UNHCR and governments;
3. the express commitment to work more closely with other NGOs on questions of asylum and protection;
4. the establishment of a mechanism for co-ordinating and disseminating studies of root causes;
5. and probably most importantly, the creation of an ongoing consultative committee to follow up and implement these recommendations. The lack of a systematic follow-up mechanism had hampered previous efforts to co-ordinate ecumenical strategies.

What does this mean in practice? Although it is still early to judge the results of the Zurich recommendations, Churches and Church-related agencies have met to begin identifying their priorities for ecumenical advocacy *vis-à-vis* the UNHCR. In a few specific instances they have approached UNHCR on protection cases and expressed their concern. For example, they have repeatedly expressed their concern about protection issues in Central America, and have raised general questions, such as the need for more UNHCR attention to the special concerns of refugee

[12] WCC, *Refugees* (Sept. 1986).

women. The committee to follow up the consultation has met to begin the process of co-ordinating regional advocacy and studies of root causes. Efforts are under way to link up Church refugee networks with other NGOs working with refugees and related areas of human rights, development, and justice. In several cases where refugees have been deported to their countries of origin, contacts have been established between Churches in the countries of origin and arrival. Sometimes Churches in the country of origin are able to provide information on human rights to their counterparts in countries of asylum—information which can be used to advocate a stay on deportation orders. In some cases Churches in the countries of origin have been able to contact individuals deported by Western countries and to report back about their fate. Churches and related agencies in Chile, for example, have been able to provide services and information to Chilean exiles who return, either voluntarily or involuntarily. Much more needs to be done to strengthen this network, but it is encouraging to see the initial steps being taken in this direction.

Consequences

As Churches and related agencies become more politically active in refugee issues, the potential increases for Church–state conflict, and for conflicts with other international organizations. Furthermore, this trend towards greater politicization of Churches is paralleled in the secular community. As agencies from many different orientations become more politically active, it is likely that refugee issues will become even more politicized in the future.

Churches which have become more politically active have found difficulties with their own constituencies and with their governments. In a climate of fear and xenophobia in Europe, for example, Church agencies risk losing the support of their Churches when they work too vigorously and too publicly on behalf of asylum-seekers. Similarly, they find themselves in conflict with their governments—a fact which, given government funding of many of their programmes, could jeopardize their continued existence. In the United States, Church–state tension over the sanctuary movement has resulted in government surveillance of church workers and infiltration of church Bible study classes. It also has resulted in a ground swell of popular support for the sanctuary movement, greater public awareness of the plight of Central American refugees, and more Churches challenging the law by declaring themselves public sanctuaries. In some Third World countries governments have reacted harshly to NGOs' politicization of refugee and displaced persons issues. The case of the expulsion of Médecins sans Frontières from Ethiopia is well known. Less well known are the cases of indigenous Church groups who have been quietly but firmly warned not to get involved in sensitive areas.

When NGOs get involved in refugee protection issues, they may find themselves at odds with UNHCR which, because of its mandate and history, must respond to a different set of political pressures than NGOs. This has consistently been the case in Honduras, where NGOs vigorously and vocally opposed the relocation of the camp for Salvadorean refugees at Colomoncagua, away from the militarized Honduran–Salvadorean border area. In supporting this relocation, provided that it was done in a humane fashion, UNHCR affirmed the right of the Honduran government to determine the location of the refugee settlements. The NGOs, listening to the voices of the refugees, opposed the move on both practical and political grounds. Finally, as international publicity increased, the Honduran government quietly dropped the plan; but relations between the government and the agencies continue to be tense. In the case of Honduras, relations between the agencies and UNHCR have also remained somewhat antagonistic, with neither side completely trusting the motivation of the other.

The NGOs not only have different priorities from governments, but also possess certain strengths which challenge the hegemony of governments. They control funds and human resources which governments may need. They have access to information which may contradict government sources. They may have constituencies capable of mobilizing public opinion at home or abroad. In this respect, as mentioned earlier, the Churches stand out from other NGOs since they possess not only large numbers of adherents but also a certain moral authority which may be used to sway public opinion.

There have been many cases, of course, where NGOs' politicization of issues, even where it has affected public opinion, has not had the desired effect for refugees. In spite of the growth of the sanctuary movement and the large amount of publicity surrounding it, the US has continued to deport thousands of Salvadoreans back to El Salvador. Despite the efforts of NGOs to dramatically publicize and vigorously lobby the British government to increase the numbers resettled from Hong Kong, the closed camps remain intact in Hong Kong. In Honduras in 1981, and in Mexico three years later, both governments relocated refugees against the strenuous objections of NGOs working with the refugees. Despite NGOs and other entities strenuously protesting against South African attacks on refugee camps in neighbouring countries, the attacks have continued.

In spite of these failures, it is important that voluntary agencies continue to expand their political activities. Given the present realities of ever-more restrictive asylum policies in Western countries, the declining independence of international organizations, and the increasing violence which forces people to become refugees, refugee-serving agencies must become more politically aware and active in order to meet the needs of refugees.[13]

At the same time, however, the Churches must never lose sight of their fundamental, humanitarian concern for individual refugees. In the long term perhaps only political action offers hope for the resolution of those conflicts which produce refugees, and for open and humane government policies towards refugees. Meanwhile, there is still a need for service to those who are refugees today and in need of assistance. Increasing political awareness and involvement must be coupled with expressions of concern and support to those in need. This is admittedly a difficult balance to achieve: between ministering to refugees through material assistance and counselling, and seeking to change the policies of governments and other actors. Yet it is essential that Churches work at both levels in their service to refugees.

As Churches and related agencies develop political expertise and as they co-ordinate their actions with other NGOs, the effect on the international system will be considerable. The NGOs, and Church-related agencies in particular, have access to information collected at the grass-roots level which can be used to challenge restrictive government policies in both the industrialized world and in developing countries.[14] This is precisely what is happening in the

[13] WCC, Ecumenical Consultation, 1986.

[14] Elizabeth G. Ferris, 'Refugees Today and Tomorrow', paper presented at WCC Consultation on Refugee Resettlement, Miami, USA, Sept. 1986.

case of US policies towards Central American refugees—although during the Reagan administration it did not result in changes in that policy. The ability to mobilize public opinion to put pressure on governments is an NGO resource, the potential of which has hardly been tapped. The Churches have a particular role to play in reconciliation efforts to bring some conflicts to an end. In this respect co-operation over refugee issues may lead to co-operation in resolving the conflicts which produce refugees. In sum, the politicization of voluntary agencies in refugee issues is a trend which has the potential to challenge governments, to reverse present dangerous developments, and to move towards conflict resolution. As such it should be encouraged and carefully nurtured, as the lives of many refugees—both now and in the future—will depend on how effectively agencies can become politically active.

9. Co-ordination of Refugee Policy in Europe

ROY McDOWALL

IN order to evaluate both present and future aspects of the co-ordination of refugee policy in Europe it is first necessary to consider the extent of such co-ordination in the past. The high point of European co-ordination was the period of the preparatory work for the 1951 Refugee Convention. Since that instrument focused primarily on the post-war situation in Europe, all Western European states acceded to the central norms of the new international refugee system.

Over time it became clear that the problem of refugees was not uniquely European and not necessarily directly related to the immediate post-1945 situation. Work had begun on the drafting of the 1967 Protocol which lifted both the geographical and the time limits from the 1951 Convention. At the same time it became evident that the harmony in refugee policy in Western Europe had been eroded. Two major European states, Italy and Turkey, withheld accession to the 1967 Protocol, and continue to this day to withhold agreement to the lifting of the geographical limitation.

Further evidence of a breakdown in European co-ordination in refugee policy occurred in 1977 when the Geneva Conference of Plenipotentiaries considered the formulation of a Convention on Territorial Asylum. European governments failed to produce a comprehensive and sustainable text (although the Conference did compose three or four draft articles, which have since been used as the basis for detailed discussion by Western European groups of experts and elsewhere). The failure of the Conference led to the formation of an *ad hoc* committee of experts on asylum and refugee law and practice (CAHAR), under the aegis of the Council of Europe. CAHAR was, to all intents and purposes, a continuation of the pre-Conference European working group on territorial asylum and had as its primary objective the formulation of a regional instrument on the lines of the global draft convention on territorial asylum. The fact that CAHAR has been in existence since 1977 and has not so far broached the subject may be taken as a clear indication that the climate is not yet right—not a good omen for European co-ordination of refugee policy.

There have been nevertheless some indications of progress towards a unified outlook and practice within Europe. The establishment in 1975 of the Sub-Committee of the Whole on International Protection by UNHCR's Executive Committee resulted in a series of Recommendations of the Executive Committee which were both generally sponsored and wholeheartedly supported by the Western European Group. Some of their recommendations were later reconsidered in CAHAR and became regional instruments endorsed by the Council of Europe.

In the period from 1951 to the present day there have been many instances where European refugee policy has been seen to be co-ordinated. Some of these have been regional problems in which other areas of the world have played a generous part, such as the resettlement of Hungarians and Czechs following the events of 1956 and 1968 respectively and, more recently, the acceptance of Polish nationals following the declaration of martial law in 1979. Others have been of extra-regional origin, such as the reception of refugees from Latin America and, still continuing, the South-east Asian resettlement programme.

European states invariably respond generously and in co-operation with other regions to programmes initiated by a burden-sharing appeal launched by UNHCR. European states are much less likely to co-ordinate policies in regard to the treatment of individual asylum-seekers and, more particularly, where the individuals appear in such numbers as to impose severe strains on local infrastructures and reception facilities. Despite the recommendations of UNHCR's Executive Committee and the requirements of regional instruments, European states sometimes have difficulty in dealing in a humanitarian and expeditious way with much smaller case-loads of refugees and asylum-seekers.

The corner-stone of co-ordination of refugee policy within Europe must be the 1951 Convention; all Western European states are parties to it, and its basic element—the protection from *refoulement*—can be seen to date back to historical concepts of asylum and sanctuary. But there are essential differences between the modern concept of refugee status and the earlier one of asylum. First, the refugee definition seeks to ensure a universality which will allow for extra-territorial effectiveness, whereas each state may have its own concept of the need for asylum granted or ordered under its sovereignty. Second, the Convention contains a clear prescription of what a refugee is, what his duty to the host state is, and what that state's obligations are to him. On the other hand, there is no international obligation upon states to prescribe which persons may expect asylum and, if granted, what benefits and protection they might then receive. Some European states, e.g. Italy and the Federal Republic of Germany, do offer a subjective right to asylum, or else define the circumstances in which a person may so qualify, but there is no clear co-ordination between states in this respect. Nevertheless, Western Europe demonstrates a variety of administrative provisions for that group which, while not qualifying for (or, in some cases, unwilling to be endowed with) refugee status, are deserving of some lesser status involving elements of protection.

Efforts at harmonization within Europe of so-called *de facto* refugees have not really produced a co-ordinated standard. In recent years, UNHCR has to some extent filled the lacuna by pronouncing on situations to which they consider return to be unsafe; individuals covered by this safeguard are described as being 'of interest or concern to UNHCR'. Return may be considered unsafe for a variety of reasons, such as civil strife, factional warfare or, in some instances, the liability of certain groups to particularly rigorous forms of military service. For example, UNHCR considers it unsafe for Tamils to be returned to Sri Lanka under present circumstances. Some European states disagree with UNHCR's interpretation of particular situations. This should not be surprising: states, even in these days of Communities, Councils, and other alliances, both commercial and political, still jealously guard their sovereignty and do not welcome external interpretations of their domestic obligations. States are also concerned about losing control of their borders, and being overwhelmed by large numbers of refugees, not all of them with genuine claims to asylum. It is sad that, over thirty-five years after the publication of the 1951 Refugee Convention, the co-ordination most clearly seen in Europe today is that of seeking to ensure that flows of asylum-seekers from other regions are controlled or restricted.

All the indications are that the major concerns of Western European states, together with North America, are that co-ordination be directed principally towards measures which will serve to regularize the movement of asylum-seekers. These measures are fairly simply identified as visa regimes and carrier sanctions, with the subordinate effort of seeking to identify and isolate those unscrupulous people—sometimes fellow-nationals—who exploit clients who seek to leave their country or region of origin for a better life elsewhere. We are now experiencing in the developed countries what was last seen in the immigration rackets of the 1950s, which produced the illegal movement of, for example, unskilled southern Italian and Sicilian labour to northern Europe, including the United Kingdom. But there is a difference: whereas in the 1950s the movement was uniquely generated by economic deprivation, there are now the additional elements of civil unrest, including factional warfare, elemental hardship such as drought or crop failure, and, to a lesser extent, political, religious, and sectarian oppression.

But can visa regimes or carrier sanctions solve the problem of refugees for Western governments? Experience to date would seem to indicate that while, from an individual state's point of view, they might appear to do so, the sole effect is that of deflection rather than solution. For example, in March and April 1985 the Netherlands government, in the face of an increasing influx of Sri Lankan Tamil asylum-seekers, decided to apply more restrictive measures (with the widely rumoured possibility of enforced repatriation for those who failed to achieve refugee recognition) to deter further arrivals. This situation resulted in the dispersal of Tamils from the Netherlands, a major part of which directly affected the United Kingdom in late April and early May 1985: The government, faced with the mass arrival of some thousands of refugees over a period of two or three weeks, imposed a visa regime for Sri Lankan passport-holders at forty-eight hours' notice, and the flow stopped. Or, rather, it was deflected for another friendly state to cope with. Since May 1985, arrivals of Sri Lankan Tamils in the United Kingdom have shown signs of a gradual increase, not from neighbouring European states but from as far afield as Kuala Lumpur and Bangkok. Our obligations to them, because of the terms of various Executive Committee Recommendations, require the United Kingdom authorities to enter such arrivals into the established asylum procedure, whether or not the asylum-seeker has fulfilled the visa requirement and, indeed, whether or not he/she holds proper travel documents at all. The United Kingdom is not unique in its obligations: these apply, and are generally applied, throughout Western Europe. It might therefore be deduced that, while the imposition of visa regimes, whether piecemeal by individual states, or as a co-ordinated policy of a group of states—the European Community or the Council of Europe—may have an apparent, temporary effect, it has not so far been shown in itself to be a remedy to the inter-regional movement of asylum-seekers. Nevertheless, forces other than the irregular movement of asylum-seekers will clearly necessitate the extension of visa regimes in Europe.

It is the aim of the European Commission to create a 'common travel area' of the states of the Community by the early 1990s, and it has been accepted that in order to achieve this objective it will be necessary to harmonize the frontier procedures and the visa regimes of the member states. Although I will leave aside the question of frontier procedures since it involves extremely complex considerations outside the scope of my subject, the harmonization of visa restrictions is highly relevant, particularly in the light of the frequent exhortations of successive UN High Commissioners for Refugees that states should not resort to restrictive practices in order to stem the flow of asylum-seekers. Visa regimes—and abolition agreements—have varying bases: colonial ties, the stemming of potential immigration flows, perceived national security needs, and reciprocity. It is hard to envisage those states that have visa regimes for certain nationalities—for any of the reasons listed above—agreeing to their abolition, but it is clearly less hard to anticipate that states that have had no previous visa requirement will accede to a harmonization of regimes when this can be defended in the light of the concept of the People's Europe. It would therefore seem to follow that a direct result of the Commission achieving free travel within the Community will be a stronger outer perimeter because of an increase in visa requirements for non-member states. Nor, one might suggest, can matters rest there: the obvious outer perimeter is incomplete without the inclusion of certain crucial non-member states, such as Norway, Sweden, Austria, and Switzerland, and it seems likely that any effective zoning must involve a further harmonization with them.

The concept of the European Common Travel Area implies

other considerations, such as unifying the functions of aliens police. Of particular significance in the context of the co-ordination of refugee policy in Europe is the fact that aliens law generally, and asylum procedures in particular, will need to be co-ordinated. Although it might be accepted that social benefits may differ from state to state (while it might be anticipated that harmonization in this field, too, will be sought), asylum procedures, including appeal rights, cannot be allowed to vary excessively. More significantly, it would not seem unreasonable to suggest that, since the Community would have free internal movement, rejection of entry or stay on purely immigration policy grounds in one state would apply in the rest of Europe. It would accordingly follow that the rejection of an asylum claim in one state would need to have an equal extra-territorial effect. Nor might it be unreasonable to suggest that the argument which might apply to visa regimes of neighbouring non-EC states could also apply to the extra-territorial effect of negative decisions in asylum. This topic has long been on the agenda of CAHAR, and no doubt the European Community initiative on free internal travel will give it added impetus. It is also questionable whether, in the event of the establishment of a common travel area within the Community, the maintenance of the geographical limitation by one state, Italy, can continue: proper harmonization would seem to require either that Italy lift the limitation or that the remainder of European states re-impose it!

The past few years have seen an increase in sub-groups—comprised primarily of certain European states, but with the addition of the United States, Canada, and Australia—to discuss the phenomenon of irregular movements of asylum-seekers and the possibility of co-ordinating action to combat these. Originally, states most affected by such arrivals, and national airlines which realized that failure to find a solution could result in an increase in carrier sanctions, met to seek solutions. These early meetings gave little consideration to protection aspects of the problem and UNHCR was not even invited to observe the meetings. Perhaps predictably, when the carriers realized that commercial considerations were not paramount, the meetings came to an end. But the irregular movement problem was no nearer a solution and it is much to the High Commissioner's credit that, under his Office's auspices, a new series of consultations was initiated to resolve the problem. Mr Gilbert Jaeger, former head of UNHCR's Protection

Division, was commissioned to prepare a paper on the subject. He analysed both the historical basis of asylum and protection and sought to define the causes of the flow of asylum-seekers and to find possible solutions for the receiving states.[1] More recently Jonas Widgren has written on the movement of peoples from the Third World to developed countries (see Chapter 2) and has suggested that it is a combination of adverse factors, such as internal instability and climatic extremes, with a rapidly increasing work force, which is contributing to the south–north movement. Given this background, and the continuing recession in the developed world, it is hardly surprising that the quality of asylum-seekers has markedly deteriorated and the resistance of developed states to what they see as abuses of their asylum procedures has increased.

What, then, is the direction for the future? There are two essential elements for European co-ordination. First, the humanitarian motives demonstrated by the countries of Western Europe in the formulation of the 1951 Convention must be maintained, both for regulated large-scale movements of identifiable Convention refugees and for individual arrivals with well-founded cases. With present-day ease of travel between the less developed and the developed regions of the world, it is naive to argue for sharing proportions of the refugee load equally between Western Europe and, for example, Africa or South-east Asia. Western systems, by comparison with the Third World, are more sophisticated and therefore more susceptible to breakdown if overloaded. Once pressure is applied to European systems or, worse, if breakdown is imminent, the genuine asylum-seeker is likely to suffer together with the abusers of the procedure. The solution to present refugee problems seems to lie in a direction which is presently being actively pursued by UNHCR, namely the linking of development aid with regional resettlement. It is to the long-term advantage of the major donor states—which are also the prime receivers of today's irregular movements—to share UNHCR's view since funds which are now used to support extra-regional arrivals in a developed state can be put to far wider use within a developing or Third World region. As has frequently been stated in recent years, funds can only be used once, and it is beyond question that local

[1] Gilbert Jaeger, *Irregular Movements of Asylum-Seekers and Refugees* (Geneva: Subcommittee on International Protection, Executive Committee, UNHCR, 30 Sept. 1985).

resettlement, as well as being less expensive, has the added advantage of making voluntary repatriation much more simple than from distant countries of resettlement.

The second element in European co-ordination is less easy either to define or to resolve. Essentially there exists a problem of what to do with asylum-seekers who fail to qualify for refugee recognition. States argue that those who fail to qualify for refugee or some other form of tolerated status should be returned either to the country from which they embarked (in the case of applications made at a frontier) or, in the case of post-arrival applications, to the country of origin or normal domicile. Over the past few years, UNHCR has increasingly invoked the formula that particular individuals or groups, whom they accept do not qualify for recognition, are of concern to their office. This practice is perceived by some states as the assumption by an international agency of the sovereign state's function of deciding whether or not asylum outside the Convention should be granted. States argue that such action by UNHCR inhibits the normal (and proper) functions of immigration control and *de facto* enlarges the effective limitation of the refugee definition in the 1951 Convention. States maintain that the solution to this problem is to hold them to their obligations under the 1951 Convention and, where applicable, to the 1967 Protocol. In addition, states believe that, where asylum is not justified, they themselves should decide how those 'selected out' should be treated—whether by indulgence outside domestic aliens law or by rejection or expulsion. It is unlikely that states would agree to increase their overseas development aid and, at the same time, tolerate within their boundaries those whose case for asylum is perceived to be marginal, at least within the terms of the 1951 Convention.

The factors are beyond dispute; the solutions are open to much further discussion. Under the aegis of UNHCR, a start has been made, and I would therefore hazard the prediction that, sooner rather than later, positive steps will be taken to ensure a better option both for the genuine asylum-seeker, and for the irregular though often involuntary migrant. Forces outside the scope of the refugee field will dictate that visa regimes not only harmonize but inevitably increase in Europe. These same forces will also lead European states to the position where negative, as well as positive, asylum decisions will have extra-territorial recognition.

10. Responses of European States to *de facto* Refugees

JOHAN CELS

In Europe today three categories of asylum-seekers can be distinguished: those who fulfil the criteria laid down in the 1951 Refugee Convention; those who move to Europe to find employment, or for other reasons of personal advantage; and those who are *de facto* refugees, that is those persons who are refugees in a broader sense than that allowed for by the Refugee Convention, but who cannot be returned to their countries of origin for humanitarian reasons. This paper examines the third category, which has in recent years provided the largest number of asylum-seekers in Europe.

The current refugee debate in Western Europe has concentrated largely on the search for appropriate solutions to the problems of this category of asylum-seekers. The High Commissioner Jean-Pierre Hocké, in his contribution to this volume, has pointed out the inadequacy of the 1951 Convention in dealing with the problem of 'extra-Convention' refugees, and the need for humanitarian solutions.[1] This chapter discusses the problem of *de facto* refugees in Europe, first by analysing briefly the legal provisions and practices of states, and then by examining alternative solutions to the problem of *de facto* refugees, as perceived by European governments.

A first draft of this paper was presented in January 1987 at the Refugee Studies Programme at Queen Elizabeth House, University of Oxford. The final draft was completed in August 1987 and the developments in policies towards *de facto* refugees were included at that date. This paper has benefited greatly from discussions with visiting fellows, staff, and visitors at the Refugee Studies Programme and from the editorial assistance of Gil Loescher and Laila Monahan. But the responsibility for the contents of the paper lies, of course, with the author.

[1] Jean-Pierre Hocké, 'Beyond Humanitarianism: The Need for Political Will to Resolve Today's Refugee Problem', Joyce Pearce Memorial Lecture, delivered at Oxford University on 19 Oct. 1986.

As described above *de facto* refugees is a general term applied to persons who are not granted Convention status but who are in need of protection. These might be refugees who fulfil the criteria in the refugee definition but who have not received the status for technical and/or administrative reasons, or refugees who have not applied for Convention status, fearing retaliation against relatives who remain in their country of origin. However, the largest number of *de facto* refugees, and those causing the most concern for European governments, are persons fleeing for other reasons than those specified in the narrow refugee definition: reasons such as 'external aggression, occupation, foreign domination or events seriously disturbing public order in either part or the whole of his country of origin', which are dramatically apparent in Iran, Iraq, Turkey, Lebanon, parts of Africa, and Sri Lanka.[2]

The level of protection given to *de facto* refugees varies, but in nearly all European countries they may be granted a humanitarian status which protects them against *refoulement* and provides for minimal material assistance. This exceptional form of protection for non-Convention refugees arose in the 1970s in response to the changing character of refugee movements, in particular as increasing numbers of asylum-seekers arrived in Europe from Third World countries. However, since the beginning of the 1980s, the refugee problem in Europe has taken on new dimensions. Whereas in the 1970s the majority of asylum-seekers arrived in an orderly manner and met the criteria in the refugee definition, the opposite is now true. The changing character of and increase in the refugee flow, together with a worsening economic climate, increasing xenophobia, and the re-emergence of nationalist politics have resulted in the adoption of restrictive and deterrent measures to prevent both the admission of *de facto* refugees and access to the refugee determination procedures of European states. In addition, measures have been taken to return rejected asylum-seekers to their countries of origin or first asylum.

The problem of *de facto* refugees in Europe

The 1951 Refugee Convention was the outcome of extensive negotiations among the major Western states to respond to the large

[2] Article 1.2 of the Organization of African Unity Convention governing the specific aspects of refugee problems in Africa, 10 Sept. 1969.

number of displaced people in post-war Europe and the continuous flow of refugees from Eastern Europe. This Convention defines a refugee as a person who fears persecution for reasons of race, religion, or political opinion. Initially the definition was intended to apply to persons fleeing the totalitarian political regimes of Eastern Europe. Although the drafters of the Convention were aware of the refugee crises in the Middle East, China, and the Indian subcontinent, they feared that a general refugee definition would imply too many obligations on the resettlement states. Therefore the 1951 Convention limited the term refugees to those who had fled persecution in Europe prior to 1951.

Immediately after the Convention came into force and the Office of the High Commissioner was established, it became clear that the large groups of refugees in need of protection in non-European regions of the world who fell beyond the geographical and time limitations of the Convention could not be ignored. Through subsequent General Assembly resolutions enlarging the mandate of UNHCR, United Nations member states allowed the Office to use its good offices to provide humanitarian assistance and protection to those refugees and displaced persons who did not specifically come under the Convention definition.

In Europe the interpretation of the refugee definition caused little political controversy until the late 1960s and early 1970s since the large majority of refugees were Eastern European and were therefore granted Convention status, even on often quite dubious grounds. The 1956 Hugarian uprising served as a test case for the interpretation of the time limitation in the refugee definition. To overcome the obvious difficulties presented by this crisis, it was decided that the events in Hungary were a direct outcome of World War II, and therefore the time limitation in the Convention definition did not apply. During the entire post-war period the preferential treatment of Eastern European asylum-seekers has been apparent in the refugee policies of all Western countries.[3] For example, in 1966 the German *Länder* declared that no Eastern European would be returned to his country of origin, but would be given a special legal status regardless of whether or not the criteria in the Convention definition were fulfilled.[4] In later years this

[3] Gil Loescher and John A. Scanlan, *Calculated Kindness, Refugees and America's Half-open Door, 1945–present* (New York: The Free Press, 1986).

[4] Beschluss der Innenminister Konferenz der Länder, 26 Aug. 1966.

resulted in large numbers of Eastern Europeans, especially Poles, travelling to West Germany to obtain employment.[5] By the late 1960s, however, it was evident that the majority of refugee crises were occurring not in Europe but in the Third World.

The growing awareness of the world-wide refugee problem and the inability of the convention to provide an effective framework to deal with non-European refugees resulted in negotiations leading to the signing of the 1967 Protocol which removed the time and geographical limitations from the refugee definition. An important further development was the adoption of the 1969 Refugee Convention by the Organization of African Unity, which took the specific causes of refugee movements on the African continent into consideration by extending the refugee definition to include persons fleeing war or warlike conditions, occupation by a foreign or colonial power, or events seriously disturbing public order. These changes in the international legal framework for refugees affected the way in which European states responded to *de facto* refugees.

The problem of *de facto* refugees came home to Europe when increasing numbers of asylum-seekers arrived from closely aligned Western countries. During the 1960s significant numbers of draft evaders and deserters from the United States, Greece, and Portugal flocked to Western Europe.[6] European governments were reluctant to grant full refugee status to these groups of asylum-seekers lest it might lead to a deterioration in political and economic relations with the countries of origin. Nevertheless, certain countries, especially in Scandinavia, thought it unacceptable to return asylum-seekers to countries fighting wars considered unjust by the international community, or to military regimes violating human rights. In response, European governments created a special humanitarian status for persons in 'refugee-like situations'.

Once again, in the 1980s, the character of refugee movements has changed. During the 1970s the large majority of refugees arrived in an orderly manner through the quota programmes adopted for

[5] 'Die Spreu vom Weizen trennen', Serie über Asylanten und Scheinasylanten in der Bundesrepublik (IV): Polen, *Der Spiegel*, 38 (1986).

[6] Anne Paludan, *The New Refugees in Europe* (Geneva: International Exchange Fund, 1974). A 1974 study on the problem of *de facto* refugees examined in detail the nature and legal problems of *de facto* refugees and provided the best available definition yet. See also Paul Weis, *The Legal Aspects of the Problems of De Facto Refugees* (Geneva: International Exchange Fund, 1974).

Latin American and Indo-Chinese refugees. Humanitarian considerations superseded the strict application and interpretation of the refugee definition and resulted in the granting of Convention status on a prima-facie basis, on the assumption that members of a specific group feared persecution. In recent years, however, the majority of asylum-seekers have arrived haphazardly, fleeing civil war, the consequences of natural disasters, economic decline, and external aggression. The nature of their arrival, by air and either without travel documents or with false ones, has complicated the application of the Convention and has resulted in irregular movements and in refugees being 'in orbit'. Economic stagnation has led to the adoption of stringent immigration laws which in turn have caused economic migrants to apply for refugee status in the hope of obtaining residence and work permits. In addition, intolerance towards aliens has increased with the resurgence of right-wing political parties and the increase in terrorist activity.

Further, the deterioration in the socio-economic and political climate in Europe has resulted in the undermining, through various restrictive and deterrent measures, of the protection offered to refugees. Access to Western countries has been made difficult by the imposition of visa and transit visa requirements, the fining of airline carriers for transporting persons without the required documents, and the concluding of agreements with East Germany limiting the transfer of persons to those who hold valid visas for Western European countries. These measures have effectively closed off several escape routes to asylum-seekers and have resulted in a drop in the number of arrivals. Protection has been further undermined by the *refoulement* of asylum-seekers to their countries of origin without the validity of their claims to protection having been examined by the relevant authorities.[7] In other instances asylum applicants have been returned to countries where they faced severe violation of their basic human rights. In addition, all European governments have reduced the material assistance given to asylum-seekers, and certain countries, such as Germany and the Netherlands, have established restricted housing quarters to deter further arrivals. European governments have introduced special procedures to deal with manifestly unfounded applications, to limit

[7] *Der Spiegel*, 13 (1983); Deutscher Bundestag, Kleine Anfrage: Auskünfte des Auswärtigen Amtes in Asylverfahren—Auslieferungsverkehr mit der Türkei, 10. Wahlperiode, *Drucksache* 10/140, 8 June 1983.

appeal procedures, and to allow for the stricter interpretation of the international refugee instruments.

Under these circumstances, all asylum-seekers, but particularly those who do not meet the Convention definition, are threatened. Governments have argued that *de facto* refugees do not fall within the provisions of the Convention, but are rather fleeing civil wars or seeking economic betterment. The UNHCR, Amnesty International, and other non-governmental agencies do not agree with governments on this issue, and argue that the problem of *de facto* refugees can be solved through a liberal interpretation of the Convention.[8]

The following section briefly examines the humanitarian status granted to *de facto* refugees in the major European countries. Special attention is given to government responses to the arrival of Tamil asylum-seekers. During the mid-1980s, thousands of Tamils fleeing civil war in Sri Lanka arrived in Europe, seeking political asylum. Responses to the Tamils have varied considerably between European countries: some countries have viewed them as *de facto* refugees, others have regarded them as illegal migrants. The debate about the status of Tamil asylum-seekers lies at the core of the problem of *de facto* refugees in Europe and illustrates the search by European states for appropriate solutions to the world refugee problem.

Humanitarian status granted to *de facto* refugees

In national legislation *de facto* refugees are referred to as B- or F-status refugees, who are permitted to stay for humanitarian, special, political, or other reasons.[9] Their legal and material protection varies considerably between countries. They are protected against *refoulement* and receive basic material assistance, but are not allowed to work or receive educational benefits in all countries. The major disadvantage of this lesser status is the lack of a Convention Travel Document. Residence permits are granted to *de facto* refugees for a limited period, ranging from six months to several

[8] Johan Cels, 'A Liberal and Humane Policy for Refugees and Asylum Seekers: Still a Realistic Policy Option?' Report prepared for the European Consultation on Refugees and Exiles, London, Dec. 1986.

[9] European Consultation on Refugees and Exiles, *Asylum in Europe: A Handbook for Agencies assisting Refugees* (Amsterdam: European Consultation on Refugees and Exiles, 1983), 15.

years, after which their status is reviewed in the light of political developments in their country of origin. If they have resided in a country for a long time they will often be granted residence permits of unlimited duration since, for humanitarian reasons, they cannot be returned.

B-status has proved to be an important development in governments' responses to the changing character of refugee flows to Europe. It has allowed governments to assist refugees from allied countries without damaging bilateral relations. B-status has also given authorities greater flexibility in responding to sudden refugee crises, e.g. immediately after the imposition of martial law in Poland, when many European governments offered residence permits to Poles without their having to apply for refugee status.[10] In recent years governments have granted B-status to groups of refugees on a prima-facie basis, assuming that members of a group face a similar threat of persecution. An additional advantage has been to prevent any group of asylum-seekers from entering and thus blocking refugee determination procedures.

Critics of government policies have argued that the B-status has undermined the Convention status. Politically sensitive cases have often been granted this lesser status to avoid a deterioration in political and economic relations. Furthermore, considerable economic savings have been made as a consequence of the lower level of material and legal assistance provided to *de facto* refugees. In the Netherlands this has resulted in the large majority of asylum-seekers being granted B-status and on average less than 5 per cent Convention status.[11]

Swedish aliens legislation states that a residence permit cannot be refused, except for special reasons, to a person who is not a Convention refugee but who is unwilling to return to his country on account of the political situation there (Article 6). A unique article allows deserters and war resisters to seek protection if there is a fear of imminent war service (Article 5).[12] In practice the special reasons clause has been evoked when a group has applied for refugee status, e.g. the Turkish Christians. The number of asylum-seekers accepted under either the Convention or B-status has depended on

[10] Mary Spillane, *Flight to Uncertainty: Poles outside Poland* (New York: US Committee for Refugees, 1982).

[11] J. A. Hoeksma, *Tussen Vrees en Vervolging* (Assen: Van Gorcum, 1982).

[12] Swedish Aliens Act of 1980, No. 376.

the employment situation and the resources available at national and local levels.[13] A recent study analysing the percentage of asylum-seekers granted Convention versus B-status in Sweden concluded that approximately 50 per cent are given B and 50 per cent Convention status.[14]

In 1983 Danish aliens legislation calls for the issuing of residence permits to those aliens who, 'for reasons similar to those listed in the Convention or "for weighty reasons", ought not to be required to return to their home country'.[15] In practice the large majority of Poles, Iranians, Iraqis, and Tamils who arrive spontaneously are granted F-status.

The initial use of B-status in Europe occurred in the Netherlands in 1974 as a result of a Council of State decision dealing with the case of an American military deserter.[16] B-status has subsequently been granted to large groups of asylum-seekers such as Poles and Surinamians. Persons who have been granted neither Convention nor B-status have been given temporary residence permits if there are exceptional humanitarian reasons for doing so.

In Germany asylum-seekers who are not granted asylum under Article 16.2.2. of the West German constitution or the Geneva Convention and who cannot be returned for political or humanitarian reasons receive a temporary residence permit (tolerated status).[17] Those who have been granted tolerated status can receive a residence permit of limited validity after two or three years. The latter status is granted to all East European asylum-seekers, as agreed by the 1966 *Länder* understanding, if they do not obtain Convention status. In 1978 the German Bundestag examined the extent to which refugees from collective persecution or from war zones could be given protection within the provisions of the aliens legislation.[18] As a consequence, residence permits without formal

[13] Delbetänkande av Invandrarpolitiska Kommitten, *Invandringspolitiken: Forslag* (Stockholm: SOU, 1983), 302.

[14] Ann-Christine Gullesjö, 'Bevilade Uppehallstillstand P G A Flyktingeller Flyktlinglik-nande skäl ar 1985 fördeling mellan paragraferna 3, 5 och 6 i utlänningslangen, Arbetsmarknadsdepartementet', Stockholm, Apr. 1986.

[15] Hans Gammeltoft-Hansen, *The Status of Refugees in Denmark* (San Remo: International Institute of Humanitarian Law, 1985), 22–8.

[16] See above, n. 11.

[17] Law on the Asylum Procedure of 16 July 1982.

[18] Christoph Gusy, 'B-Status—Eine Alternative für Härtefälle?', in Otto Benecke Stiftung (Hrsg.), *Asylpolitik der Bundesrepublik Deutschland* (Baden-Baden: Nomos Verlagsgesellschaft, 1983).

asylum have been granted to, among others, Tamils, Palestinians, Christian Turks, and Afghans. The status protects them against *refoulement*, but the duration of the permit and the extent of material assistance depends upon the individual *Land*. In the past, Berlin and Bavaria have decided to return Lebanese, Turks, and Iranians, or have granted them residence permits for a very short period of time, whereas other *Länder* have allowed them to stay for longer periods. The Federal government has called for improved co-ordination among *Länder* to prevent large discrepancies in practice and to allow for the development of a national policy towards certain groups.

In Great Britain the Home Office has granted individuals and groups of asylum-seekers exceptional, temporary leave to remain if they are not granted refugee status.[19] This practice originated in response to the Greeks who fled the Turkish invasion of Cyprus in 1974, and this permission has since been granted to Ugandan Asians, Iranians, Poles, and Tamils as a group, on the basis of a policy decision. In addition, nationals of Afghanistan, Iran, and Lebanon have been granted exceptional leave to remain on an individual basis. The Home Office reviews their status annually, taking into account political developments in the countries of origin. After four years an individual can apply for indefinite leave to remain, a status which cannot be repealed by the Home Office in other than exceptional circumstances. However, persons granted exceptional leave to remain as part of a group decision are not granted indefinite leave after a period of time, unless a special policy decision is made. When indefinite leave is granted, the protection offered is extensive and includes the right to work. Critics and non-government agencies have, however, criticized government decisions as being unfair and lacking clear-cut criteria for granting the status.[20] Political preferences have played a significant role. For example, Polish citizens were given this option within twenty-four hours after the imposition of martial law in Poland, whereas the legal situation of Tamils remained unclear for several months, despite the violent conditions in Sri Lanka.

Both Italy and Austria are countries of first asylum because of their geographical location. In Austria approximately 90 per cent of

[19] House of Commons, Home Affairs Committee, Race Relations and Immigration Sub-Committee, Session 1984–5, minutes of evidence.

[20] Ibid.

asylum-seekers arrive from Eastern Europe, the large majority of whom are resettled. Italy too has adopted a generous policy towards Eastern Europeans, who are allowed to remain, often without having to apply for refugee status, until the opportunity for emigration arises. But refugees from outside Europe are considered foreigners since Italy still enforces the geographical limitation of the Convention definition, although in the past exceptions have been made for Chilean and Indo-Chinese refugees entering the country under a quota programme.[21] Originally, UNHCR recognized non-European refugees under its mandate only in so far as it provided material assistance until resettlement countries could be found. In recent years the Office has broadened its role by extending the protection under its mandate to those *de facto* refugees who wish to emigrate because the Italian authorities have been unwilling to provide either work permits or social assistance. As a consequence, many *de facto* refugees have resided illegally in Italy and have worked unofficially for a subsistence wage.

Before 1982 the majority of asylum-seekers in Europe were Turks, Poles, Afghans, and Ghanaians. Since 1983 Tamils and Iranians have dominated the statistics, followed by Poles, Ethiopians, Turks, Ghanaians, Lebanese, Pakistanis, and Indians. The distribution of asylum-seekers among European countries has varied considerably because of colonial links, accessibility of countries, and degree of protection offered. Tamils have gone to West Germany, Denmark, France, Switzerland, the United Kingdom, and the Netherlands, whereas few have travelled to Sweden and Belgium. Iranians are concentrated in Switzerland, the United Kingdom, Sweden, Denmark, West Germany, and the Netherlands. The adoption of deterrent policies has deflected refugee movement from one country to another. After the Dutch government imposed its controversial 'bed-bath-breakfast' policy in 1985, obliging Tamils to live in communal housing, with all their needs catered for by the government instead of receiving financial aid, more than two thousand Tamils arrived in Britain in a matter of weeks.[22]

[21] 'The Difficult Situation of Non-European Asylum-Seekers in Italy', in *Refugees*, Jan. 1984; Office of the United Nations High Commissioner for Refugees, *Note on the Integration of Refugees in Italy*, 1983 Seminar on the integration of refugees in Europe, Geneva, 12–15 Sept. 1983.

[22] Home Office, Statistical Bulletin, *Refugee Statistics United Kingdom 1985*, 1 May 1986.

But then, when the British imposed visa restrictions, the flow was deflected to Switzerland.[23]

Government policies towards Tamils have aroused considerable controversy in the media and have led to critical exchanges between governments, non-governmental agencies, and UNHCR officials. The hitherto little-known struggle of the Tamil minority in Sri Lanka for an independent homeland, and against discrimination by the Sinhalese majority, came to the fore in the European media as large numbers of Tamils sought protection. Amnesty International reports have painted the harsh realities of indiscriminate killings, disappearances, arbitrary arrest, ill-treatment, and torture of prisoners.[24] UNHCR has argued on several occasions that many Tamil asylum-seekers are refugees under the Convention—especially young males between 18 and 30 years old—so that grounds exist for recognizing group persecution; and that, given the political situation in Sri Lanka, no Tamil should be returned to Sri Lanka after receiving a negative refugee decision.[25]

Tamils have comprised the largest group of asylum-seekers in West Germany since 1983, the majority of whom arrived via Berlin.[26] The city is governed under a four-power agreement, and West Germany has not imposed official border controls, for political reasons. Initially, the refugee recognition rate by the Federal Agency for the Recognition of Foreign Refugees was high since young male Tamils were considered to be targeted for persecution by government soldiers and opposition forces. The lower courts of appeal supported this view and treated sympathetically the issue of group persecution in their explanatory statements. However, the government disagreed and thus in 1985 the Federal Commissioner for Asylum Affairs asked for a reopening of all positive decisions. A

[23] Roy McDowall, Home Office, Refugee Unit, United Kingdom on 'Co-ordination of Refugee Policy in Europe', at Refugee Studies Programme, Queen Elizabeth House, Oxford, 4 Feb. 1987.

[24] Amnesty International, *Sri Lanka: Reports of Recent Violations of Human Rights and Amnesty International's Opposition to* Refoulement *of the Tamil Community to Sri Lanka* (ASA 37/01/85); *Sri Lanka: Updated Statement of Amnesty International's Position on* Refoulement *of Tamils to Sri Lanka* (ASA 37/09/85), May 1985; *Sri Lanka: Amnesty International Reaffirms its Continued Opposition to* Refoulement *of Tamils to Sri Lanka* (ASA 37/02/86), Apr. 1986.

[25] Patricia Hyndman, 'The 1951 Convention Definition of Refugee: An Appraisal with Particular Reference to the Case of Sri Lankan Tamil Applicants', *Human Rights Quarterly*, 9 (1987), 49–73.

[26] Deutscher Bundestag, *Drucksache* 10/3346. The number of applicants for 1983 was: 2,645; for 1984, 8,063; for 1985, 6,074.

Federal Administrative court (Bundesverwaltungsgericht) decision in 1985 stated that there was no group persecution and that therefore all cases should be referred back to the lower courts to determine whether there was individual fear of persecution.[27]

This reopening of cases and the increase in numbers of new applicants have put considerable strain on the refugee determination procedure and have put pressure on the Federal government to search for ways of dealing speedily with asylum applications. On 15 July 1985 an agreement was concluded with East Germany to limit the transfer of Tamils to those with valid documents. The outcome of this agreement was dramatic. Whereas in 1985 14,885 Sri Lankans entered West Germany via East Germany, the number for 1986 was drastically reduced.[28]

Denmark, sharing Germany's view that a large percentage of Tamils fear individual persecution and should not be returned to Sri Lanka, granted the humanitarian F-status to more than 90 per cent of Tamil asylum-seekers. An additional motive for this exceptionally generous policy was to prevent Tamils from flooding the country and blocking the refugee determination procedures.

German and Danish policies towards Tamils contrasted sharply with those of the Dutch, Swiss, and British. In 1986 Britain received 2,500 Tamils, the majority of them within a short space of time. Fearing a similar flow to that in West Germany, the British government decided to impose visa requirements. Only after several months of heated discussions between the Home Office and non-government agencies were the Tamils granted exceptional leave to remain.[29]

The Dutch authorities took a firm stand on the Tamil refugees by arguing that the large majority were not Convention refugees but had fled civil war and had come to the Netherlands to seek economic betterment. This view was reflected by the exceptionally small number of Tamils who were granted any status at all. To support its view, the Dutch government sent a special fact-finding mission to Sri Lanka in 1985 to examine the nature of the conflict. The mission

[27] Bundesverwaltungsgericht (Federal Administrative Court), BVerwG. 9 C 33.85, 3 Dec. 1985.

[28] Antwort der Bundesrigierung auf die Kleine Anfrage Einreise von Asylbewerbern über die DDR bzw. Berlin (Ost), Deutscher Bundestag 10. Wahlperiode, *Drucksache* 10/5557, 28 May 1986.

[29] Letter from W. R. Fittall, Home Office, to Martin Barber, British Refugee Council, 11 June 1986; *The Times* (17 Feb. 1987).

came to the controversial conclusion that, whereas the north and east of the country were unsafe, an alternative internal flight to the south of the country existed. This led to the official view that Tamils could be returned to the south of Sri Lanka. Dutch non-governmental agencies and UNHCR strongly rejected the conclusions of the mission. The subsequent media furore pressured parliament to force the Dutch authorities concerned to seek UNHCR's advice on each individual negative decision before a Tamil could be returned.

Switzerland, taking a similar view to that of the Netherlands, threatened on several occasions to return Tamils. Initially the government allowed rejected Tamils to remain in Switzerland by postponing the delivery of the order to leave the country after a negative refugee decision. In early 1986 this policy was reversed and the Swiss authorities stated that the order to leave the country would be delivered after six weeks. It was hoped that during this period a large number of Tamils would voluntarily move to neighbouring countries. The imposition of the return policy coincided with the announcement of the conclusions of a Swiss fact-finding mission to Sri Lanka. However, the government suppressed the report because, as fragments leaked to the press indicated, the mission deemed it unsafe to return Tamils.[30] Subsequent pressure by non-governmental agencies and the mobilization of public opinion in early 1987 forced the Swiss government to change its plan to return rejected Tamils. But on several occasions the government reaffirmed its intention to return rejected Tamils once conditions in Sri Lanka permitted.

What is apparent from the above discussion is the divergent treatment of *de facto* refugees among European countries. Although nearly all European countries have created specific provisions for asylum-seekers in refugee-like situations, the application of the provisions has varied considerably. Explanations for this divergence are the varying interpretations of the refugee definition,

[30] A similar mission was organized in 1984 to examine the situation in Sri Lanka after the non-governmental agencies pressured the Ministry of Justice not to return rejected Tamils. The report concluded that the root of the problem went back to the British colonial period. It recognized that the Sri Lankan government responses to the separatist struggle were out of proportion. But the report continued to argue that the authorities were making continuous efforts to improve their human rights record. (Département Fédéral de Justice et de Police, Office Fédéral de la Police, 'Rapport sur les investigations effectuées au Sri Lanka du 11 au 20 août 1984', Bern, 29 Aug. 1984.)

foreign policy, and domestic interests. The provisions of the humanitarian status developed in the 1970s in response to the increasing number of refugees from Third World countries have become inadequate in recent years now that the large majority of asylum-seekers belong to this category.

The search for solutions to the problem of *de facto* refugees

Recognizing the weaknesses in the status of *de facto* refugees, European states since the 1970s have sought for ways to strengthen the provisions. Two distinct approaches can be distinguished: until the early 1980s, when the number of *de facto* refugees was small, states sought to negotiate a European agreement resolving the question of country of first asylum, and to create a consistent status for *de facto* refugees within the framework of the Council of Europe. But since the early 1980s, when the majority of asylum seekers have been *de facto* refugees, the attempts to reach legal agreements have failed as states have been unwilling to commit themselves to additional agreements. Instead European countries have sought solutions through political consultations directed towards negative measures aiming to limit the number of asylum-seekers reaching Europe. This section outlines both approaches, and discusses their shortcomings as possible solutions to the problem of *de facto* refugees.

The Parliamentary Assembly of the Council of Europe responded favourably to the conclusions reached by the 1974 studies on the 'New Refugees in Europe' and the 'Legal Aspects of the Problems of *De Facto* Refugees' by adopting Recommendation 773 on the situation of *de facto* refugees.[31] This recommendation called for the preparation of an appropriate instrument for *de facto* refugees covering the granting of residence and working permits, the application of as many articles in the Convention as possible,[32]

[31] Anne Paludan, *The New Refugees*; Paul Weis, *The Legal Aspects of the Problems*; Council of Europe, Parliamentary Assembly, Recommendation 773 on the situation of *de facto* refugees, 1976.

[32] Recommendation 773 refers to the following articles in the refugee Convention: 'Especially those relating to wage earning employment (Article 17), public relief (Article 23), labor legislation and social security (Article 24) as well as the provisions concerning refugees unlawfully in the country of refuge (Article 31), expulsion (Article 32) and, especially, prohibition of expulsion or return (Article 33);' (Recommendation 773, para. 5.I.b.)

and the issuing of travel documents. As indicated earlier, the majority of European countries did adopt a humanitarian status in accordance with Recommendation 773. The primary objective of Recommendation 773 has, however, not been achieved. The political complexities, the varying interests among countries of first and second asylum, and the unwillingness of states to commit themselves to additional international obligations, the consequences of which cannot be foreseen, have made agreement on an appropriate instrument for *de facto* refugees impossible.

In addition, the Council of Europe adopted Recommendation No. R (84)1 on the protection of persons satisfying the criteria in the Geneva Convention who are not formally recognized as refugees.[33] The recommendation calls for the scrupulous application of the *non-refoulement* clause so that no 'person should be subjected to refusal of admission at the frontier, rejection, expulsion or any other measure which would have the result of compelling him to return to, or remain in, a territory where he has a well-founded fear of persecution . . .'.[34] The recommendation refers to various categories of *de facto* refugees: persons who have not applied for refugee status for personal reasons, for fear of their own safety, or for lack of information; refugees in countries where there is no proper refugee determination procedure, or whose claims have been rejected for procedural or administrative reasons; and asylum-seekers who are awaiting the outcome of a refugee determination procedure. Reference is made to Article 3 of the European Human Rights Convention which states that the expulsion or extradition of an alien to a country where he faces a serious threat of violation of his basic human rights constitutes inhuman and degrading treatment.

Within the Council of Europe, the *Ad Hoc* Committee on the Legal Aspects of Territorial Asylum and Refugees (CAHAR), a group of government experts from the member states, has been active in the preparation of legal documents on territorial asylum and related issues. They have been working on a draft declaration on the protection of persons not satisfying the criteria set forth in the Geneva Convention.[35] The central provision of the draft declaration states that:

[33] Council of Europe, Committee of Ministers, Recommendation no. R(84)1 on the Protection of Persons satisfying the Criteria in the Geneva Convention who are not formally recognized as Refugees, 25 Jan. 1984.

[34] Ibid.

[35] CAHAR (85)6, restricted doc.

whenever a decision is envisaged involving the return of a person to his country of origin they [member states] take into consideration whether, in the light of the political conditions prevailing in that country, the person concerned would be exposed to a serious risk either to life or limb or of arbitrary measures of unjustifiable detention.[36]

The draft declaration refers to persons who have a reasonable belief that they will be hindered in the exercise of their human rights, as proclaimed in the European Convention of Human Rights, and discriminated against for reasons of race, religion, ethnic origin, membership of a particular social group, political opinion, or because they do not conform to the moral imperatives in force in the society to which they belong.[37] Originally CAHAR aimed to prepare a recommendation, but certain European countries feared that this would entail an additional obligation and constraint on their policies. The form of the draft was downgraded to a declaration to include reference to the liberal and humanitarian principles already applied towards *de facto* refugees in the majority of European countries. The fate of the draft declaration is unclear as it is still under consideration by the various national administrations.

Both the Recommendation and the draft declaration reflect a limited consensus among European governments. States are only called upon to 'make use of their rights' not to send back or expel anyone. This phrasing implies the explicit recognition of states' sovereignty over the entry and residence of aliens. Both documents deal only with *refoulement* and exclude any reference to the material protection of *de facto* refugees.[38]

The failure to develop legal instruments regulating state behaviour towards *de facto* refugees has been a consequence of the unwillingness of states to agree to additional obligations, the

[36] CAHAR (85)6, restricted doc.

[37] The expressions 'prejudiced' and 'discriminated' go beyond the Convention expression of 'well-founded fear', and refer to the general political situation in the country of origin, but exclude economic motivations.

[38] Various documents cover the minimal material protection which should be granted to *de facto* refugees: Conclusion 22 (XXXII) on the Protection of Asylum Seekers in Situations of Large-Scale Influx, Executive Committee of the UNHCR Programme, sec. II; Council of Europe, Parliamentary Assembly, Recommendation 773 on the situation of *de facto* refugees, 1976; Office of the United Nations High Commissioner for Refugees, *The Integration of Refugees in Europe,* 1983 Seminar on the integration of refugees in Europe, Geneva, 12–15 Sept. 1983.

conflicting interests among states, and the absence of political commitment. The rapid undermining of refugee protection by European states and the resulting tensions between governments and UNHCR led the then High Commissioner Poul Hartling to arrange for consultations in Geneva between governments, non-governmental agencies, and UNHCR in May 1985. This initiative has been followed by various political consultations and working groups between governments and UNHCR to try to agree on a common practice towards *de facto* refugees in accordance with minimal humanitarian standards.

In 1984 and early 1985 the Swiss and Dutch governments had arranged secret meetings, from which UNHCR was excluded, to develop common policies towards Tamils and other groups. To prevent further restrictive policies on the part of governments, UNHCR convened a meeting under its own auspices. It strongly criticized government policies towards Palestinians, Iranians, and Tamils, and argued that in cases of large-scale influxes of asylum-seekers it might 'be necessary to find an intermediate solution for the group as a whole, e.g. by regularizing the situation of the group on a temporary basis until individual screening can be carried out, or by resorting from the outset to a so-called *prima facie* group determination of refugee status'.[39]

Governments responded by criticizing UNHCR for showing a lack of understanding of the 'political ramifications of the maintenance of traditional refugee policies, which implies that the advice of the Office should not be of such a nature that it leads to confrontations between the Office and individual governments when judging whether a particular ethnic or religious group, as a group, could be considered at risk of persecution'.[40] Government frustration with UNHCR's attitude follows from its claim that these persons are of concern to the Office, as reflected in the various

[39] Executive Committee of the High Commissioner's Programme, Sub-Committee of the Whole on International Protection, Follow-up on earlier Conclusions of the Sub-Committee—The Determination of Refugee Status, *inter alia*, with reference to the Role of the UNHCR in National Refugee Status Determination Procedures, 1982, restricted doc. High Commissioner Hocké in his contribution to this volume points to a similar direction by proposing the option of temporary asylum as a possible strategy for *de facto* refugees.

[40] Statement by Jonas Widgren, Under-Secretary of State, Swedish Ministry of Labor, Raoul Wallenberg Institute of Human Rights and Humanitarian Law, *Responsibility for Examining an Asylum Request*, Report of seminar held in Lund, Sweden, 24–6 April 1985 (Lund: Raoul Wallenberg Institute, 1986), 28.

General Assembly resolutions. But states have viewed this practice as 'the international agency taking over the Sovereign State's function of deciding whether or not asylum outside the Convention should be granted and the general effect is twofold, namely that the normal (and proper) functions of immigration control are inhibited and the effective limitation of the refugee definition in the 1951 Convention is *de facto*, enlarged'.[41]

In preparation of the May Consultation, the High Commissioner distributed a note which analysed the protection problems and pointed out alternative solutions.[42] The meeting was a mixed success. The discussion was restrained because of the presence of non-governmental agencies and Third World countries. The Thai representative criticized European governments for making such a fuss about so few refugees compared with the burden that developing countries had to carry. Non-governmental agencies were frustrated by the request from governments to hold the important discussions in closed session. In his final remarks the High Commissioner reported that 'there was general agreement that such persons should be treated humanely and, in particular, should not be returned to areas where they may be exposed to danger'.[43] Subsequent treatment of Tamils proved this conclusion to be premature, as indicated above.

The May Consultation laid the foundations for subsequent informal and *ad hoc* consultative arrangements, called on the initiative of UNHCR and governments. A two-stage approach was envisaged. At the first stage European governments were to consult to develop common policies and co-ordinate their execution. At the second stage countries of origin and transit and the relevant international organizations were to be consulted to regulate the refugee flow between the various regions to and from Europe. The inability of the European countries to develop common policies on key issues stalled the political consultations at the first stage.

Late in 1985 the Swedish government arranged a second European Consultation in Stockholm. Only those countries which

[41] See above, n. 23.

[42] Office of the United Nations High Commissioner for Refugees, *Note by the High Commissioner*, Consultations on the arrivals of asylum-seekers and refugees in Europe, 29 Apr. 1985, restricted doc.

[43] Office of the United Nations High Commissioner for Refugees, *Summing-Up by the United Nations High Commissioner for Refugees*, Consultations on the arrivals of asylum seekers and refugees in Europe, 29 Apr. 1985.

faced large-scale influxes of refugees and irregular movements and held similar views on how to deal with them were invited to attend.[44] However, the outcome of the meeting was limited since key countries were sceptical about the need for consultations. West Germany in particular refrained from the beginning from actively participating in the consultations for domestic and foreign policy reasons. Because the domestic debate about the constitutional right to asylum became an issue in the early 1987 elections, Germany was unwilling to agree to any additional commitments as part of a regional resolution to the refugee problem. In addition, the other European countries showed little sympathy for the recent large increase in asylum-seekers in Germany. Thus the rhetoric for improved co-ordination has so far had little appeal. No suggestions for burden-sharing on a European level have been discussed, and no major country has been willing to take the political initiative or assume leadership during the early consultations.

A third meeting was held in the Hague in early 1986.[45] Little is known about the proceedings but, according to observers, four principal elements were agreed upon: the establishment of working groups, the clarification of the role of UNHCR in countries of first asylum, an examination of resettlement opportunities, and recognition of the need for collection of data. Despite government claims that they are being flooded with *de facto* refugees and manifestly unfounded applications, no sound statistical data are available to substantiate these claims. It is impossible to provide and to compare statistical data on *de facto* refugees since the collection and presentation of data vary considerably between countries. To alleviate this problem UNHCR has begun to develop guidelines for the collection and interpretation of statistics.

To prevent the occurrence of irregular movements governments have put pressure on UNHCR to play a more important role in countries of first arrival. Governments consider it unacceptable that

[44] The invited countries were: Sweden, France, Britain, West Germany, Denmark, The Netherlands, and Switzerland. Absent were Austria, Italy, and Belgium. Previous experiences, during the negotiations on an agreement on the country responsible for examining asylum requests in CAHAR, brought forward the conflicting interests between countries of first asylum, Austria and Italy, and the countries of second asylum. *Herald Tribune*, (26 Nov. 1985); *The Times*, (25 Nov. 1985).

[45] The meeting was held on 15 Apr. 1986 and was called by the Dutch government. In addition to the countries present in Stockholm, Belgium attended, and Norway and Canada were invited as observers.

asylum-seekers bypass both European embassies and UNHCR offices in countries of first arrival and travel on to other countries to seek asylum.[46] What a number of governments would like to see is:

> a system by which the UNHCR field office in the first country of asylum undertakes a first screening of those asylum seekers who want to continue elsewhere. Results would be channeled to headquarters in Geneva where resettlement should be sought in order of urgency. The arrival would then not depend solely on the personal resources and preferences of the individual, but also on considerations by the UNHCR as well as by potential recipient countries.[47]

As a consequence, UNHCR has strengthened its offices in certain countries of first arrival, e.g. Turkey and Pakistan. In addition, co-operation among UNHCR branch offices has been improved so that inconsistencies in policy can be overcome. In the past the recognition rate of Iranians by UNHCR's field office in Pakistan has been lower than the recognition rate by its office in Turkey. As a result, Iranians not recognized in Karachi have travelled on to Turkey and India to seek protection. Better co-ordination among UNHCR branch offices should prevent these problems from occurring.

The effectiveness of UNHCR's role in countries of first arrival will partially depend upon the creation of a speedy resettlement programme in Europe for urgent cases. In recent years, European countries have objected to the unscheduled arrivals and irregular movements of asylum-seekers which complicate the application of the refugee instruments and overload the refugee determination procedures. To relieve the pressure, governments have expressed their preference for scheduled arrivals through planned quota programmes. The advantage of such programmes is the greater control over both the numbers and quality of persons entering the country as asylum-seekers. In the past, European countries have gained extensive experience with quota programmes for Chilean and Indo-Chinese refugees. During the May 1985 Consultations the High Commissioner raised the issue of strengthening resettlement programmes, but Sweden has criticized the resettlement

[46] Statement of the Dutch representative, UNHCR Consultations, see above, n. 43, restricted doc.

[47] Statement by Jonas Widgren, Under-Secretary of State, Swedish Ministry of Labour, UNHCR Consultations, see above n. 43, restricted doc.

approach as being inappropriate and unrealistic since few European countries have quota programmes of any size, and it is unlikely that other European countries will adopt quota programmes in the near future.[48]

Since early 1986, in addition to the political consultations, working groups of government experts have been created to examine common approaches towards Tamils and Iranians. Meetings have been arranged to examine and compare national policies, the level of protection upon return to the countries of origin and first arrival, the role of embassies and UNHCR, and the possibility of regional solutions.

The working group on Tamils has had limited success. After reports from UNHCR and Swiss fact-finding missions to Sri Lanka, governments agreed that the political situation in Sri Lanka did not permit a safe return for Tamils. The initial agreement was made possible by the steep decline in arrivals of Tamils in Europe after the conclusion of an understanding between West and East Germany on the transfer of Tamils through Berlin.[49] The effectiveness of the agreement was, however, undermined by unilateral decisions by Britain and Switzerland to return Tamils after an increase in arrivals of Tamils in late 1986 was observed in these countries.[50]

The political developments in Sri Lanka and the conclusion of a peace agreement in July 1987 between the Tamil guerrillas and the Sri Lankan government will have a considerable impact on European governments' policies. Depending upon the effective execution of the agreement and the restoration of public order, the return of Tamil asylum-seekers will be made possible since they will not face threats to their safety. Within the framework of the Tamil working groups, European governments agreed at the beginning of August to adopt a wait-and-see policy in order to take into account the implications of the peace agreement.[51] It is

[48] Statement by Jonas Widgren, at Council of Europe, The law of asylum and refugees—present tendencies and future perspectives, 16th Colloquy on European Law, Lund, 15–17 Sept. 1986.

[49] The agreement came about after strong pressure had been exerted on East Germany by European governments not to transport asylum-seekers to the West for profit. Reports indicated that the United States had asked the Soviet Union to intervene with its East German ally to stop the flow.

[50] *The Times* (18–19 Feb. 1987).

[51] *Neue Zürcher Zeitung* (9 and 11 Aug. 1987).

expected therefore that governments and courts will postpone status decisions on Tamil asylum-seekers, depending upon political and security developments in Sri Lanka.[52]

The meetings of the working group on Iranians have been even less fruitful. Whereas some agreement existed about political conditions in Sri Lanka, European governments have disagreed about conditions in Iran and countries of first arrival. They have argued that refugees could be returned to Iran, Turkey, or Iraq because many young Iranian males have sought asylum in Europe to escape the draft, which is, strictly speaking, no ground for refugee status, except in specific cases such as South African deserters. An UNHCR fact-finding mission, however, concluded that the war conditions permit few Iranians to return safely, especially war evaders and draft resisters, who are sent to the front upon return. Most European countries grant humanitarian status to Iranian war resisters, members of ethnic minorities, and religious groups. But the question remains as to whether Pakistan and Turkey provide sufficient protection for Iranian returnees.

While little progress has been made during the working group meetings, the political consultations between governments and UNHCR have stalled. It took more than six months after The Hague before another meeting was organized in Geneva by UNHCR. The results of this meeting were limited and the debate acrimonious. National interests dominated policy formulation, despite the realization that the refugee problem could only be effectively solved by co-ordinating policies among countries. Incentives to co-operate were limited because a series of unilateral measures had brought temporary relief to the asylum crisis in Europe, e.g. the border agreements with East Germany, and neither UNHCR nor any government was willing to take further initiatives in what was a deteriorating situation.

Switzerland was host to the third inter-governmental Consultation in February 1987. The meeting continued the discussions held during the previous consultations and reiterated the need for protection of asylum-seekers who do not fulfil the conditions in the refugee definition but who cannot be returned to their countries of origin. In addition, the need to control the flow of asylum-seekers by means of stringent checks on airline passengers from Third

[52] *Frankfurter Allgemeine* (14 Aug. 1987).

World countries and by preventing the destruction or intentional loss of documents was stressed. But a new working group was created to study the minimum criteria for the safe return of rejected asylum-seekers to their countries of origin and first asylum.

Although states agree on the basic premiss that certain persons cannot be returned, for humanitarian reasons, they disagree on what exactly these reasons are. A comparative analysis of European policies towards Tamils illustrates the divergent opinions among states as to whether the security situation in Sri Lanka is such as to permit the return of rejected asylum applicants. Lack of agreement on this issue hampers co-operation among states and causes tensions with UNHCR. The core question to be addressed is: under what conditions should rejected asylum-seekers receive protection for humanitarian reasons, or when does return to their country of origin imply a violation of the principle of *non-refoulement*.

As the discussions at the February 1987 meeting indicated, the interpretation of 'safe return' varies considerably between countries. The Swiss delegate is reported to have argued for the return of all rejected asylum-seekers 'if their situation in their country of origin would not be worse than that of people already there'.[53] During a conference of the German Ministers of the Interior, agreement was expressed that all *de facto* refugees could be returned to crisis areas, without specifying what was meant by the latter.[54] During the meeting UNHCR expressed its willingness to extend its mandate and to become more involved in discussions to determine when and how rejected asylum-seekers could be returned, and to intervene with countries of origin and transit.

The discussions on a safe return imply a shift from determining whether certain groups are *de facto* refugees and require protection, towards the question of whether a safe return can be guaranteed. But the views adopted by Switzerland and Germany indicate a very broad interpretation of 'safe' return, potentially violating Article 3 of the European Human Rights Convention—to which nearly all European states must abide—forbidding the subjection of anyone to torture, or inhuman or degrading treatment.

[53] European Consultation on Refugees and Exiles, meeting report, 10 Mar. 1987, restricted doc.

[54] Standige Konferenz der Innernminister und Senatoren, Pressemitteilung 7186, 3 Oct. 1986.

Both the legal and the political approaches to the problem of *de facto* refugees have yet to produce effective humanitarian action, although the prospects for the latter are more hopeful because of the inherent flexibility in the negotiation process and the *ad hoc* policy decisions permitting states to change tactics, depending on the character and number of asylum-seekers, without being constrained by international agreements. Lack of success to date has partly been determined by developments in related fields which have forced the consultations into different directions from those intended, and have undermined the consensus-building measures. For instance, the wave of terrorist attacks in France during the summer of 1986 led the French government to take the unilateral step of imposing visa requirements on all persons except those from European Community member states, Sweden, and Switzerland.

A consequence of the increase in terrorism has been the establishment of the Trevi group, consisting of the ministers of justice and the interior of the European Community member states. This group, created to allow a co-operative effort against terrorism and international crime, involving international police co-operation, has a sub-group—an *ad hoc* committee on immigration and asylum. Although the outcome of the meetings is confidential, press reports have indicated that various measures have been supported which aim to restrict the arrival of asylum-seekers: airlines transporting persons without valid documentation should be penalized; European Community officials should be allowed to check passengers boarding flights in third countries; asylum procedures should be simplified in order to facilitate the return of asylum-seekers to their countries of origin and first asylum; and measures should be taken to prevent asylum-seekers from making multiple requests in various countries.[55] The implicit link here between asylum and the fight against terrorism and illegal immigration is deplorable since the extent of the link is unproven; it creates further distrust towards refugees, and it goes against the spirit of the refugee Convention. The impact of the conclusions of the Trevi group upon the political consultations is considerable since the conclusions endorse the negative and restrictive trends in present asylum policies and do not encourage the search for positive solutions.

[55] *De Standaard* (29 Apr. 1987); *The Times* (29 Apr. 1987).

The role of the Trevi group in improving co-ordination among European countries must be seen within the context of the planned creation of a true common market in 1992, which would mean the creation of an internal market with common external borders. The Commission of the European Council has committed itself in a White Paper to issue a directive by 1988 on the co-ordination of provisions governing the right of asylum and refugee status.[56] The implications for the European asylum and admission policies are far-reaching since common external borders assume harmonized admission, country of first asylum, and expulsion policies. In addition, the interpretation of the refugee definition and the procedures for determining refugee status must be harmonized to prevent asylum-seekers from submitting multiple applications or travelling to a neighbouring country after receiving a negative asylum decision.

To smooth the transition to the 1992 Common Market, the Agreement of Schengen was negotiated in 1985 among the Benelux countries, France, and Germany to gradually abolish border controls and establish working groups to discuss areas of tension.[57] Whether the ultimate objectives of the creation of a common market will be reached in 1992 is open to question. The differences among European countries regarding the admission of aliens and the granting of nationality, not to speak of the economic aspects of the problem, are considerable. A common market implies a significant limitation of national sovereignty in favour of transnational determination. But the development of the political consultations seems to indicate that the interests of European countries do not coincide on all issues, and states have preferred to retain their independence through the adoption of unilateral actions which circumvent the understandings reached during the consultations.

A potentially more difficult problem to overcome is the co-ordination of the approaches and outcomes of the various consultation forums. A core problem is that certain states do not participate in the different forums. The Scandinavian countries play a leading role in the political consultations but are excluded

[56] Com (85) 310 final.

[57] Akkoord tussen het Koningrijk der Nederlanden, het Koningrijk Belgie, de Bondsrepubliek Duitsland, de Franse Republiek en het Groothertogdom Luxemburg betreffende de geleidelijke afschaffing van de controle aan de gemeenschappelijke grenzen: Schengen, 14 June 1985. Tractatenblad van het Koningrijk der Nederlanden, 1985, nr. 102.

from the meetings of the Trevi group and the preparatory meetings for the 1992 Common Market. Given the ease of travel in Europe, it is thus necessary for neighbouring states of the European Community to adopt similar policies so as not to be confronted with asylum-seekers who have failed to gain access to the European Community. More importantly, Italy and Turkey—both countries of first asylum—have not taken part in the political consultations because they favour generous admission policies and maintain the geographical limitations in the refugee definition. Any effective European asylum and refugee policy will require the full participation of these countries.

But the search for solutions to the problem of *de facto* refugees cannot be limited to European measures which transfer the problem to neighbouring states and countries of first asylum. The political consultations have recognized the need for co-operation with the countries of first asylum, but they have not yet participated in the discussions, as of early 1987. Their agreement to the return of those asylum-seekers declared inadmissible and to an orderly departure policy to countries of resettlement is necessary. On a bilateral basis, and to a limited extent within the framework of the Council of Europe, understandings have been concluded concerning the return of refugees to countries of first asylum, often in return for assistance in helping to deal with the refugees. West Germany has played a leading role by exerting diplomatic and political pressure on countries of first asylum, in particularly Turkey.[58]

In the face of the changing character of refugee movements and of restrictive policies, governments and UNHCR have argued that the best available solutions are voluntary repatriation and, where this is impossible, reception and resettlement within the region.[59] In 1985 the German Bundesrat decided to encourage regional solutions to the world refugee problem by stressing the following: the good neighbour principle of states bordering refugee-generating countries; the easier reception of refugees in a culturally-related environment; and the fact that it is cheaper to maintain asylum-seekers and refugees in the Third World than in Europe. In order to effect this approach, it would be necessary to give the countries in

[58] 'Zusammenfassung der Ergebnisse des Berichts der Interministeriellen Kommission Asyl, Teil II', in Arbeiterwohlfahrt, *Materialen zum Info-Dienst-Flüchtlinge*, 22 Sept. 1986.

[59] The humanitarian need must be addressed before all others, *Refugees* (Nov. 1986), 5.

the region financial and organizational help, to strengthen the role of UNHCR, and create the conditions for successful repatriation. In situations where repatriation or regionalization is impossible, it will be necessary to find resettlement opportunities in the West.[60]

The link between refugee problems and political/economic development has attracted considerable attention.[61] In 1980 West Germany launched an initiative in the United Nations General Assembly to avert new flows of refugees.[62] Its objective was to develop international principles to stress the responsibilities of those states causing a large-scale exodus of their population.[63] The results have been limited, however. Initially it was recommended that a code of conduct for states be drafted, a set of practical measures be developed, and an *ad hoc* political body established. The only outcome so far has been the establishment of a Group of Governmental Experts on International Co-operation to Avert New Flows of Refugees, which has produced a set of general recommendations reiterating the need for co-operation and solidarity among states.[64]

A second major development has been the pressure upon states by the international community and advocacy groups not merely to pay lip service to severe human rights violations in refugee-generating countries, but to develop an effective policy to counter such violations. The High Commissioner Jean-Pierre Hocké has exhorted governments to tackle the root causes of refugee movements and has stressed the link between humanitarian

[60] Bundesrat, Entschliessung, *Drucksache* 100/85, 14 Juni 1985.

[61] Independent Commission on International Humanitarian Issues, *Refugees: Dynamics of Displacement* (London: Zed Books, 1986); Gudrun Lachenmann and Uwe Otzen, *The World Refugee Problem—A Challenge to Development Policy* (Berlin, German Development Institute, 1981); European Parliament, Committee on Development and Cooperation, Report on Aid to Refugees and Displaced Persons in Developing Countries, draft report, 6 June 1986.

[62] David A. Martin, 'Large-Scale Migrations of Asylum Seekers', *American Journal of International Law*, 76 (1982).

[63] Leon Gordenker, 'International Initiatives on Refugees: A Comment', in Lydia F. Tomasi, *In Defense of the Alien: Immigration and Refugee Policy*, vi (New York: Center for Migration Studies, 1984); Hans-Dietrich Genscher, 'Internationale Zusammenarbeit zur Vermeidung neuer Flüchtlingsströme', *ZAR-Abhandelungen*, 4 (1981); Peter J. Opitz, 'Flüchtlingspolitik und Deutsche VN-Initiative', *Aussenpolitik*, 36 3 (1985).

[64] Group of Governmental Experts on International Co-operation to Avert New Flows of Refugees, Working paper submitted by the Chairman pertaining to the substantive considerations of the programme of work, Sixth Session, A/AC.213/1985/WP.5; UN General Assembly, International Co-operation to Avert new Flows of Refugees, Forty-first session, 13 May 1986, A/41/324.

activities and political bargaining.[65] But whether this is a realistic policy option is debatable, given the foreign policy interests of states and their limited concern for the fate of refugees.

Conclusion

Given the character and number of *de facto* refugees, solutions cannot be limited to national measures. Two distinct national approaches can be distinguished. During the 1970s positive steps were taken to strengthen the protection of *de facto* refugees through the adoption of humanitarian status. But the increase in the number of applicants during the 1980s has led governments to introduce negative measures to limit the number of beneficiaries and to reduce what governments perceive to be abuse of the asylum system. The recognition that appropriate solutions must be sought at the European level, given the costly effects of unilateral policies upon neighbouring countries, has led to positive steps in areas of co-operation towards certain refugee groups in recent years.

The failure to negotiate European legal agreements regulating the activities of the country of first asylum and providing for a status for *de facto* refugees was the result of the lack of attention being paid by the drafters to the political willingness of states to accede to additional agreements limiting states' sovereignty over immigration and asylum policies. To date the consultation process has provided a framework for negotiating positions among European countries, stressing the need for closer co-operation on refugee policies. But the stress being laid upon negative measures threatens to undermine the norms of the Refugee Convention and the role of UNHCR in Europe, and to circumvent the problem that many asylum-seekers have a well-founded need for either long-term or temporary protection.

Solutions for *de facto* refugees must encompass all European states and not be limited to a few key countries or to the European Community, as this would imply shifting the burden on to neighbouring states of countries of first asylum. The challenge facing European states is to negotiate understandings with countries of first asylum, regulating the flow of asylum-seekers to

[65] Jean-Pierre Hocké, 'Beyond Humanitarianism'; 'Humanitarian activities versus political bargaining', *Refugees* (June 1986).

and from Europe by taking into account the problems with which these countries are confronted without closing the borders to those asylum-seekers who arrive directly or are in need of protection.

But the prospects for humanitarian solutions to the problem of *de facto* refugees, and for the protection of refugees in general, are dim. Other contributors to this volume have pointed out the difficulties involved in developing a co-ordinated European policy and the consequences of restrictive policies. The core problem is still that the needs of individuals are subjected to the perceived political interests of states aiming to retain their sovereignty and further their prestige abroad.

III

The Search for Appropriate Responses to the Refugee Problem

11. Refugees

Development or Relief?

JACQUES CUÉNOD

Introduction

Once the emergency phase of a refugee crisis is over, the question of whether to respond to a refugee situation with continued relief or with development aid would seem to be self-evident. It would appear incontrovertible that extended relief operations result in dependency among refugees. Nevertheless, UNHCR spends more than half of its nearly $400 million annual budget on care and maintenance. Moreover, over two million Palestinian refugees are still registered with UNWRA, which spends more than US$200 million per year on relief, forty years after this problem first arose. Despite the abundance of examples of relief programmes prolonging dependency among refugees, the international community continues to be hampered by this approach, although it may in fact prefer one which aims at long-term development programmes for refugees.

There must therefore be variables or forces at work which prevent relief operations from evolving towards long-term solutions within a development context. This chapter will consider these variables, how they interrelate, and how they influence refugee problems. It also will examine alternative solutions to refugee problems and investigate past attempts to avoid extended relief and to promote development. There is no doubt that more could be done to tap the vast human resources of refugees, in order to foster sustained development activities, to the advantage of all concerned.

The Five Variables

The following five variables can influence the solution to a refugee problem:

(i) the attitude of the refugees themselves;
(ii) the attitude and policy of the country of first asylum;
(iii) the attitude and policy of resettlement countries;
(iv) the attitude and policy of the country of origin;
(v) the 'hidden' forces.

The refugees

Refugees are people who have been uprooted. They have lost their homes and livelihoods and find themselves in a foreign environment. Their attitudes are difficult to analyse, often unpredictable, and sometimes work against their own interests because the refugees are not aware of all the relevant factors in the situations in which they find themselves. One historical example of this occurred during the exceptionally cold winter of 1949–50 in the Middle East. Palestinian refugees in many camps refused to have their tents waterproofed because they believed that this would signify their acceptance of permanent settlement in the countries of first asylum and thereby rule out a return to their homeland. As a result many refugees died of cold that winter.

Refugees' attitudes are also difficult to assess because the social structure of a refugee community is often disrupted as a result of an exodus. Politically active members may try to supplant traditional leaders, with the likely consequence that once homogeneous communities will split into several groups, each with different attitudes towards their long-term goal. This pattern is clearly evident among the Afghan refugees in Pakistan who have now divided into several movements.

A refugee group also may be divided on goals where individuals have differing reasons for leaving their home country: in a situation of internal conflict some people may flee for political reasons; others may be looking for a safe haven, although they are not directly involved in the strife; whereas a few may seize the opportunity to try their luck abroad for very personal reasons. This situation makes it difficult to take one single approach to the whole group. The Sri Lankan Tamils in Europe illustrate this situation in that some are certainly bona fide refugees while others are taking advantage of the crisis to try to emigrate for economic reasons.

Yet the attitude of the refugees, difficult though it may be to assess, is the most important variable in dealing with their problems, for without their participation there can be no lasting solutions. It is therefore important to train refugees to work as community development workers, living among their fellow refugees and discussing the various options available to them, in order to elicit from them their choice of solution. It is also important that social anthropologists should assess the attitudes of the various factions within a refugee community. This should be repeated periodically, since the attitudes of a refugee group are likely to alter, particularly when one or more of the above variables change.

It is worth noting here that an uprooted community will often be more receptive to new development inputs than a national community which may encounter difficulties in breaking with traditions that resist the introduction of new technologies. This receptiveness should not only facilitate a development approach but, in favourable conditions, allow a refugee area to become a focus for development of the whole area, for the benefit of refugees and nationals alike. A good example of this happened in the Karagwe district in Tanzania, where it proved to be easier to introduce animal traction first among a community of Rwandese refugees, and subsequently among the local farmers who were less receptive to this new development.

Countries of first asylum

Attitudes and policies of countries of first asylum cover a wide spectrum: from countries trying to prevent asylum-seekers from entering, or sending back those who succeed (*refoulement*), to countries granting full citizenship to bona fide refugees. Within the last decade countries of first asylum have devised measures (often referred to as humane deterrence) to discourage potential refugees from seeking asylum. This practice started on a large scale in South-east Asia with the Indo-Chinese (see McNamara, Chapter 5 in this volume) and is now being followed by European countries with respect to other groups.

The two most common responses among countries of first asylum are:

- (i) either to allow asylum-seekers to come in and stay temporarily, until they decide to return to their home countries, or until they are accepted for resettlement in third countries (e.g. the Inco-Chinese refugees in Thailand);
- (ii) or to let asylum-seekers come in and settle either temporarily or permanently (e.g. Ethiopian refugees in the Sudan).

The first approach may lead to an indefinite care and maintenance programme, depending on the willingness of the resettlement countries to open their doors to refugees, and on the willingness of the latter to choose this option. The second approach generally leads to a local settlement programme, again depending on the attitude of the refugees. In low-income countries this option will usually require a development approach.

Countries of resettlement

It is part of the policy of several countries, notably the United States, Canada, and Australia, whose populations comprise a very significant proportion of immigrants, to accept a number of foreigners, including refugees, every year. Other more homogeneous industrialized countries, recognizing how unjust it is that, merely because of their geographical location, some countries receive all the refugees from a given outflow while others receive none, accept refugees for resettlement in the spirit of burden-sharing. A good example of this burden-sharing was the international response to the influx of Hungarian refugees into Austria and Yugoslavia after 1956. Countries all over the world accepted large numbers of Hungarians for resettlement.

Some countries, like France with the Indo-Chinese, receive refugees because of special historical or political ties with a region; others, such as Denmark, accept handicapped refugees for humanitarian reasons. Generally speaking, however, the economic situation in industrialized countries is a major determinant of policy regarding the admission of refugees for resettlement. With current high rates of unemployment, Western European countries provide a sad illustration of the consequences of this policy.

The attitudes of countries of resettlement may change, as indeed may the other variables. Having initially opened wide their doors, the main resettlement countries adopted a restrictive policy towards Indo-Chinese refugees after 1981–2. This policy had a direct impact on the countries of first asylum in South-east Asia, which, seeing the increasing numbers of refugees in camps, were moved to adopt measures of humane deterrence. In turn, the refugees who had been temporarily admitted to the countries of first asylum, pending their admission into third countries, had to review their position. These deterrent measures have also had an effect on the numbers of asylum-seekers. Many governments, and also some public opinion, have concluded that many people who had previously been recognized as refugees had in fact no real fear of persecution but were by and large economic migrants. Whereas this is true for a proportion of cases, one should not underestimate the impact of deterrent measures on people in a country of origin who do have a justifiable fear of persecution. These potential refugees may nevertheless decide to risk staying in their home countries, in the hope that their fears of persecution will remain groundless, rather than opting to go to a country where they will be subject to harsh treatment.

The UNHCR must constantly monitor each refugee situation. When resettlement in industrialized countries is no longer a solution, UNHCR should ensure that other options become available to refugees. This will require a change in one of the other variables. It could be that the country of origin might accept the voluntary return of refugees, or that the country of first asylum might now allow refugees to settle, at least temporarily. It could also mean that a country which has never before accepted refugees for resettlement would agree to do so under certain conditions. If it were a Third World country these conditions might well entail a refugee group being resettled within the context of a development programme.

This approach was used in 1964 when Tanzania agreed to take 10,000 Rwandese refugees and resettle them in Mwesi, an area east of Lake Tanganyika, already earmarked for development by the government. Eventually only 3,000 refugees were transported from the Kivu province of Zaïre to Tanzania. Unfortunately this group was too small to become an economically viable community and consequently, in 1970, the Tanzanian government transferred some 10,000 of their own citizens from the overpopulated Kilimanjaro region to Mwesi. The government simultaneously initiated a development programme and introduced new farming methods, cash crops, and cattle raising.

Another example of the adoption of this approach was when a group of 6,850 Indo-Chinese Muslim refugees from Kampuchea who sought asylum in Thailand were subsequently accepted for resettlement in Malaysia during the period 1975–85.

One also should mention as an example of a regional solution the situation of almost half a million people, mostly Biharis, who found themselves stranded in Bangladesh when this territory (formerly East Pakistan) became an independent state. Many of these people wished to resettle in what was West Pakistan, and indeed 170,000 of them did so under an agreement signed in 1973 between the three states of the subcontinent. Ten years later the Pakistan government showed signs of being willing to accept another 250,000 Biharis, on the condition that the international community financed their resettlement. Unfortunately it seems today that the chances of this second group finding a regional solution involving the development of a large area have vanished, at least for the time being.

Resettlement within a region has the great advantage of minimizing the negative impact of refugees being resettled in a new environment. However, this regional approach can only succeed if, as a result of the wide participation of the international community, the acceptance of refugees for resettlement is perceived by receiving countries as a new form of development co-operation and not as an additional economic and social burden.

Countries of origin

The international image of a country is tarnished when its nationals flee to seek refuge in other countries. This signals to the international community that at least part of the population no longer enjoys full human rights. It is therefore normal to see the government of a country of origin endeavouring to prove that the fears of persecution that drive people to leave are unfounded. The sincerity of these efforts to encourage refugees to return home can be judged by the measures taken by the government of origin to remove the causes which provoked the exodus. It is extremely difficult to assess whether human rights violations no longer exist and whether conditions are safe for return.

The UNHCR is the international agency charged with the protection of refugees and the Office should be sensitive to political developments which might provoke refugee influxes. However, UNHCR is not supposed to be concerned with the reasons why people leave their countries and therefore is not supposed to concern itself with the measures to be taken to resolve these causes. In the absence of a United Nations High Commissioner for Human Rights, only the UN Secretary-General can, in spite of the constraints inherent in his function, partly tackle the root causes of refugee problems. A good example of positive action is the mission undertaken by the UN Secretary-General to conduct proximity talks with the parties involved in the civil war in Afghanistan. These talks have continued over the past few years. If they eventually succeed, they will have contributed to the possible repatriation of Afghan refugees from Pakistan and Iran but, meanwhile, they serve to keep open the channels of communications.

Once the governments of the countries of asylum and of origin have agreed at the political level on voluntary repatriation, it is up to the refugees to decide whether or not to go back. There exists a possible source of conflict between the attitude of the country of asylum, on the one hand, withdrawing refugee status on the grounds that the fear of persecution is no longer justified, and the claim of the refugees, on the other, that the causes of their exodus have not been sufficiently eliminated to justify a safe return home. In such a situation UNHCR should give the benefit of the doubt to the refugees—even if their status is withdrawn by the country of first asylum—and ensure that they are not repatriated against their will.

The UNHCR can also play an important role in ensuring that there are no circumstances in the countries of asylum which would unduly 'encourage' refugees to repatriate. Measures such as administrative harassment, as was the case with Eritrean refugees in Djibouti, frequent relocation of camps, as with the Burmese refugees in Bangladesh, and reductions in the amount of food aid, as with the Guatemalan refugees in Mexico, have on occasion been adopted by countries of first asylum, sometimes with the possible tacit or secret agreement of the country of origin.

The classic examples of successful voluntary repatriation have occurred when a change in the political regime has taken place in the country of origin. When this happens it is important that UNHCR should reassess the attitude of the refugees and ascertain whether or not they would be prepared to go home. A recent case in point was the situation of the Ugandan refugees in southern Sudan. A change of political regime took place in early 1986 when Museveni constituted a new government in Uganda. Six months later, when the security situation and the supply of food became precarious in southern Sudan, the refugees decided to return to Uganda, a move which indicated that they no longer considered themselves refugees. A close monitoring of the refugees' attitude in southern Sudan might have revealed this shift in attitude sooner, which would have given UNHCR time to plan an organized repatriation under better conditions than the operation that was improvised at short notice, when refugees started to repatriate spontaneously.

There are exceptions to the classic scenario of refugees voting with their feet following the access to independence of their country of origin or a change of political regime. One of these occurred in Algeria. In 1962, when the Evian agreement was signed between France and the authorities representing Algeria, it was agreed that UNHCR would endeavour to return voluntarily those Algerian refugees who had sought asylum in Tunisia and Morocco, *before* the referendum which marked the independence of Algeria, i.e. when the country was still under French administration. This case is also relevant to the present study in that for the first time the UN General Assembly requested UNHCR to assist the new Algerian government in the reintegration of the former refugees into their home country. The assistance was not limited to relief but included development infrastructure such as the construction of primary schools.

Another exception to the classic scenario was the voluntary return of some 200,000 Burmese refugees from the Arakan state, who sought asylum in Bangladesh in 1978. Although there was no change of regime in Burma the refugees agreed to return once a political understanding had been reached between the two governments concerned. The UNHCR was responsible for providing logistical support and for verifying the voluntary nature of the refugees' decisions at the border crossings. All returned home, with the exception of one thousand politically active refugees, who remained in Bangladesh. As in Algeria, UNHCR helped the Burmese government in the reintegration of the returnees.

'Hidden' forces

What are the hidden forces that influence policy on refugees—either towards an extended relief operation or the integration of refugees into a larger development programme? There are many government and non-government actors who are in a position to influence policy-making. They may do so for various reasons and by various means:

(i) Public opinion may exert pressure on governments, as was the case in several resettlement countries after 1975, to admit large numbers of Indo-Chinese refugees and, six years later, to adopt restrictive admissions policies towards these refugees.

(ii) Governments may earmark a percentage of their contributions to UNHCR for specific refugee situations, at the cost of other groups equally deserving of international aid.

(iii) Governments may reach agreements on outstanding political issues which may incidentally provide an avenue towards the resolution of refugee situations.

(iv) Influential governments may encourage the government of the country of origin, of first asylum, or of resettlement to change its approach to the solution of a given refugee problem to that favoured by the influential government.

Here are some illustrations of how these factors influence refugee policy. When Afghan refugees sought asylum in Pakistan the US government was reluctant for UNHCR to provide assistance to the Pakistani government because the US Embassy in Islamabad had been burned down in November 1979 and the negotiations on possible compensation had not yet been concluded. As a result little assistance was initially provided for this refugee group. However, when Soviet troops entered Afghanistan in December 1979 the US government, reversing its position, urged UNHCR to provide massive assistance for the Pakistani government to help the Afghan refugees, and even provided the means for it to do so.

Another example was the pressure exerted on the US government and on American public opinion by groups of citizens who had relatives or friends among those US soldiers who were missing in action (MIA) during the Vietnam War. Together with other factors, this pressure resulted in the decision of the US Government not to provide reconstruction aid to Vietnam after 1975. The situation of the Indo-Chinese refugees might be quite different today if substantial aid had been provided for Vietnam, Laos, and then Cambodia soon after the end of the war.

The solutions

The variables discussed above combined will direct a refugee situation towards one of the following four solutions: voluntary repatriation, settlement in the country of first asylum (whether temporary settlement, socio-economic integration, or full assimilation), resettlement in another country, or the 'no solution' solution—indefinite care and maintenance in the country of first asylum.

An analysis of the interplay among the variables should point to the way a refugee problem is moving. But, because the variables are not static, they must be constantly monitored to detect change. When a change does occur, a new analysis should be made of the interplay in order to see whether the possible solution to a given refugee problem has changed. Before analysing how a development approach can assist positive solutions to a refugee problem it may be of interest to study some past experiments in this area.

Lessons from some past experiments

A lesson from UNDP

When the centre of gravity of the world's refugee problems shifted from Europe to the developing countries of Africa in the early 1960s, UNHCR realized that direct assistance to refugees would be insufficient to allow large refugee groups to become self-supporting. As a rule, refugees were allowed to settle in remote and marginally fertile land, where public services were at best sparse. Hence it became necessary to develop these rural areas to enable them to absorb a large and sudden increase in population.

At that time UNHCR policy was to bring the standard of living of refugees to a level comparable to that of the surrounding nationals. After achieving this level with direct assistance to refugees, UNHCR would hand over the problem to the host government which, with the help of development agencies such as the United Nations Development Programme (UNDP), would ensure that the infrastructure of an area was developed and that the refugees became economically and socially viable communities within a region.

Two attempts were made by UNDP between 1967 and 1972 to apply this policy to existing situations. One, in Burundi, involved Rwandese refugees and the other, in the Central African Republic, refugees from southern Sudan. The UNDP entrusted the first project to ILO and the second to FAO. The aim of both projects was to achieve long-term development in refugee-affected areas. The project in the Central African Republic ended with the return of the refugees to the Sudan in 1972, following the Addis Ababa agreement which put an end to seventeen years of strife in the southern part of the country. Unfortunately, to the best of my knowledge, no report of any evaluation mission was published by the UN agencies concerned with these two projects, and it is therefore not possible to draw comprehensive conclusions from these experiments.

It is important to note, however, that UNDP was able to support the two projects from its own resources since they occurred when the allocations of funds to developing countries were made on the initiative of UNDP headquarters. Whereas at that time UNHCR was able to ask UNDP to earmark funds for these projects, today it would be extremely difficult for UNDP to fund such projects because developing countries currently have a decisive role in allocating UNDP resources. It would be highly improbable that a government of a low-income country would agree to earmark part of the limited UNDP funds to a development project required as a result of the presence of refugees while its own nationals faced so many problems. In the eyes of many less-developed countries of asylum, UNHCR remains the sole instrument of the donor community within the UN system for dealing with refugees until their full integration or their voluntary repatriation can be effected.

A lesson from Pakistan

An interesting experiment has been taking place in Pakistan since 1983. The UNHCR asked the World Bank to identify, design, negotiate, and supervise the implementation of some development projects, the aims of which are to create temporary employment, mainly for refugees. These projects involve afforestation, irrigation, and road building which reflect the real economic needs of Pakistan.

Whereas the projects are generally referred to in UNHCR documents as 'income-generating', 'income-earning' would better reflect the nature of the scheme. Although at least 70 per cent of the labour-force must be refugees, the refugees have to return to their camps when their work is completed because the projects have not been created to generate sustained employment opportunities for refugees. During their period of employment, food aid is not suspended to working refugees, even though they are earning normal wages. Had this dual assistance been avoided, it would have provided an interesting alternative to the old 'food for work' formula, the disadvantages of which have been analysed in other forums.

In spite of these drawbacks, the World Bank/UNHCR experiment in Pakistan is interesting from more than one point of view. First, it generates pure development projects which are in line with the overall objectives of the government plan. Second, the projects are connected in various degrees to the presence of refugees and are implemented in or near refugee-affected areas. Third, the identification, formulation, and negotiations related to these projects take place between the World Bank and the Pakistani central planning authorities and technical ministries concerned. The UNHCR and government officials responsible for refugee affairs are not directly involved. Fourth, since the World Bank will not invest any of its own resources, UNHCR has collected the required funds (US$20 million) from various governments as special contributions. Fifth, the international funding of these projects is contributed in the form of grants, not even as interest-free loans. Finally, Pakistani participation has been kept to a bare minimum, and does not involve the use of scarce hard currencies.

In brief, this is a development project connected with the presence of refugees, the programming of which is done by development bodies, and which has been funded from additional contributions collected by UNHCR on the most favourable terms, with a token counterpart contribution from the host government.

The lesson from ICARA II

The first International Conference on Assistance to Refugees in Africa, held in 1981 in Geneva, was a disappointment to many African governments. They perceived it as an exercise to finance UNHCR projects, whereas what they needed was additional resources, particularly for the development of their infrastructures. Having drawn lessons from ICARA I, the African governments were prepared for the Second International Conference on Assistance to Refugees in Africa (ICARA II), which was held in Geneva in July 1984. The projects they consequently presented at ICARA II were divided into two groups: projects of direct assistance to refugees, and infrastructure projects related to the presence of refugees in the country of asylum. The Conference concentrated on the second group. ICARA II recognized the fact that direct refugee aid provided by the international community to developing countries of first asylum was insufficient, that another type of assistance was required: projects of a development nature, aiming at restoring the damage caused by refugees to the environment, and developing the infrastructure in those areas affected by refugee work or by the presence of refugees (transport, water, health, education, etc.). Some 163 projects of this type, requiring approximately US$430 million of external aid, and to be implemented in nineteen African countries, were presented at or after ICARA II.[1]

Unfortunately the results achieved so far by funding these projects have been disappointing. The concept of linking refugee aid to increased development co-operation is relatively new and has not yet been generally accepted by the donor community. The structure of the UN system and of most governments of industrialized countries is such that humanitarian issues are dealt with separately from development co-operation: an integrated approach is a new process which will take time to be accepted. An additional factor has been that a number of industrialized countries have already used the funds they had earmarked for ICARA II projects to assist African governments to respond to the widespread drought which has affected the continent in the mid-1980s.

Nevertheless, useful lessons can be drawn from ICARA II. First, low-income countries of asylum need both humanitarian aid directed specifically towards refugees and also support for infrastructure/development projects linked to the presence of large refugee groups. Second, refugee projects should be developed by UNHCR, whereas infrastructure/development projects require the involvement of development agencies. The funding of both kinds of project should be the responsibility of the donor community.

On the question of funding development projects directly linked to the presence of refugees or returnees, ICARA II offers a further interesting lesson. At the Conference, the UK government announced a contribution of £5 million to finance ICARA II, or other similar projects. The projects had to be developmental, benefiting both refugees/returnees and nationals, and implemented by voluntary development agencies based in the United Kingdom. The fund of £5 million is administered by the Overseas

[1] UN General Assembly Doc. A/Conf.125/2 of 23 Mar. 1987 and Addendum no. 1 of 8 Nov. 1984, 'Detailed description of needs, project outlines and background information on the refugee situation'.

Development Administration (ODA), which worked out a special simplified procedure for processing funding requests submitted by NGOs, and for the NGOs to report on use made of the aid. This fund has proved invaluable in financing development projects in areas affected by refugees or returnees, for instance in Chad, the Republic of Guinea, and the Sudan, projects which could never have been financed from regular UNHCR or UNDP resources, for reasons explained earlier.

A similar scheme has been set up by UNDP. At the ICARA II Conference governments were informed that, if they preferred not to tie up their contributions to specific projects or countries, they could transfer them to a central fund administered by UNDP. A dozen governments availed themselves of this opportunity and some US$7.8 million was credited to this fund. At present it supports fifteen projects submitted by governments of asylum countries or development NGOs. These projects are in addition to those included in the UNDP country programmes although in several instances they are complementary to each other in order to maximize their impact on refugee and national communities. To simplify the procedure NGOs are treated as subcontractors of the Office for Project Execution (OPE). Here again this fund allows for those situations where there are refugees/returnees to be approached from a development angle, and finances projects in Rwanda and Angola, for instance, which would otherwise have received no direct support from UNDP or UNHCR.

Attempts by UNHCR to help

During the second half of the 1970s hundreds of thousands of refugees sought asylum in countries which allowed them to stay only temporarily. Since resettlement to third countries either could not keep pace with the influx or was not a feasible solution, provision for care and maintenance became the most important part of the UNHCR budget, which swelled to US$500 million in 1980.

Poul Hartling, the then United Nations High Commissioner for Refugees, took the initiative to convene a meeting of experts in August 1983 to study whether or how a development approach to refugee situations could remedy this situation and contribute to the solution of the problem.[2] The conclusions of the group of experts

[2] UN General Assembly Doc. A/AC.96/627 of 12 Sept. 1983, 'Refugee Aid and Development'.

were then discussed at a meeting of non-governmental organizations in November 1983[3] and at a meeting of intergovernmental organizations in December of the same year.[4]

From the conclusions of the experts, the two consultations mentioned above and the views of the High Commissioner, a number of 'Principles for Action in Developing Countries' were drawn up in August 1984 and endorsed by the UNHCR Executive Committee in October 1984.[5] These Principles, which represent the UNHCR terms of reference in the area of refugee aid and development, are reproduced below:

Principles of action in developing countries

Durable solutions[6]

(a) Refugee problems demand durable solutions. A genuinely durable solution means integration of the refugees into a society: either reintegration in the country of origin, after voluntary repatriation, or integration in the country of asylum or country of resettlement.

(b) Resettlement in third countries, which is a necessary solution in certain circumstances, is the least desirable and most costly solution, so that for refugees in most countries a durable solution should be sought, through repatriation to their country of origin, which is the best option wherever it is voluntarily accepted by the refugees, or through settlement in the country of asylum.

(c) In either case, the solution will be lasting only if it allows the refugees or returnees to support themselves and participate in the social and economic life of the community on an equal footing with the surrounding population, and this should therefore be the ultimate aim of assistance to refugees.

Temporary measures pending a durable solution

(d) Where voluntary return is not immediately feasible, conditions should be created in the country of asylum for temporary settlement of the refugees and their participation in the social and economic life of the community, so that they can contribute to its

[3] UN General Assembly Doc. A/AC.96/635 of 21 Dec. 1983, 'Refugee Aid and Development', annex III.

[4] UN General Assembly Doc. A/AC.96/635 of 21 Sept. 1983, 'Refugee Aid and Development', annex V.

[5] UN General Assembly Doc. A/AC.96/645 of 28 Aug. 1984, 'Refugee Aid and Development', annex I, corrigendum i.

[6] 'Development Approaches to Refugee Situations', UNHCR informal report by M. L. Zollner, 2 Jan. 1986.

development. For the refugees it is essential to free themselves from dependence on relief, and reach a situation where they can take care of themselves, as soon as possible.

(e) From the outset, therefore, their productivity should be encouraged through self-help activities, engagement in food or other agricultural production, participation in local works to improve economic and social infrastructure, or skills-training projects.

(f) In low-income areas, the needs of the local people should also be taken into account; in such areas initiatives may therefore be needed which would permit both refugees and local people to engage in economically productive activities to ensure them a decent livelihood. Such initiatives do not necessarily imply a commitment to one or another longer-term solution.

Settlement in country of asylum

(g) Initiatives of this kind will be necessary in low-income areas where significant numbers of refugees (by comparison with the local population) need income-earning opportunities; in these areas development-oriented projects are required that will generate work opportunities and—where local integration of the refugees is feasible—long-term livelihoods for refugees and local people in a comparable situation, through activities which create assets of a continuing economic value with a good rate of return, so that they contribute to the overall development of the area.

(h) The projects should be consistent with existing and planned development schemes for the area; wherever possible, these schemes should be extended as appropriate to include refugees. Such projects or extensions should be additional to, and not at the expense of, the country's ongoing development programmes.

Roles of the partners involved

(i) UNHCR, while being the focal point of durable solutions, should not assume the role of a development agency, and where developmental initiatives are needed to help refugees support themselves, the High Commissioner's role should be essentially that of a catalyst and coordinator; he should initiate suitable projects, promote their development by a competent organization and the host government, and then promote their financing and monitor the results for the refugees.

(j) missing in original document

(k) Under its normal programmes UNHCR should continue, in close cooperation with other organizations of the UN system, governmental organizations and NGOs, to seek durable solutions through projects planned specifically for the refugees, even though local people may eventually benefit from some of them.

(l) Where the need is for developmental projects conceived for the benefit of both refugees and substantial numbers of local people with similar needs, UNHCR should, in consultation with the host government, invite a developmental organization—intergovernmental, governmental or non-governmental—to provide its services for the formulation, appraisal, negotiation, and supervision of appropriate projects. These would normally be implemented by, or under the responsibility of, the host government, where necessary with the assistance of suitable executing organizations which might be non-governmental; such organizations should be brought in as early as possible. UNHCR could provide its good offices for the financing of such projects, and would need to follow them to ensure that the refugees benefit as planned.

(m) Development projects aimed essentially at repairing or improving a host country's economic or social infrastructure to help it cope with the presence of refugees, but which do not directly benefit significant numbers of refugees, should as a rule be handled by UNDP and/or other developmental organizations including NGOs. Where such projects provide durable income-earning opportunities for refugees, UNHCR could contribute to their financing in proportion to the number of refugees among the beneficiaries.

(n) Where successful reintegration of voluntary returnees in a low-income country requires developmental investments beyond UNHCR's programmes, for the benefit of the returnees as well as their compatriots in the areas concerned, UNDP and/or other relevant developmental organizations and NGOs should be involved as soon as possible in the planning and implementation of further appropriate rehabilitation assistance.

(o) In all phases of a refugee problem it is important that the beneficiaries of projects be involved in their planning, management, and implementation as much and as soon as possible.

Coordination measures

(p) Governing bodies of development agencies should consider the presence in a country of substantial numbers of refugees or returnees as one of the relevant factors in their programme planning.

(q) The complementarity between refugee aid and development assistance, i.e. the close relationship between what refugees need to help them support themselves and what the disadvantaged local people need, should be reflected in the structures and/or coordination procedures for addressing these issues at the national level, both in the host countries and in the assisting countries, as well as within and between the international organizations concerned.

(r) Proper coordination of refugee-related development projects with other development projects, in the context of the host country's development strategy, should take place on a country basis, through existing consultative mechanisms such as Consultative Group or Consortium meetings or Round Table conferences where they exist; where a country has received substantial numbers of refugees so that their presence affects its development, refugee-related development assistance would be reviewed as a regular part of these consultative processes.

At the General Conference of ICVA held in Dakar in May 1985 it was proposed to hold a joint UNHCR/NGOs workshop on Development Approaches to Refugee Situations. The UNHCR having agreed to the suggestion, the workshop took place at Crêt Bérard at Puidoux near Lausanne (Switzerland) from 1–4 December 1986. The recommendations and suggestions made at the workshop are reproduced below:

Recommendations and suggestions made at ICVA/UNHCR Workshop on Development Approaches to Refugee Situations held at Puidoux 1–4 December 1985[7]

1. Emergency Relief and the dependency syndrome; how to put newly arrived refugees to productive work at a very early stage so as to avoid a dependency syndrome developing; transition from emergency to development

   (a) *Siting and logistics of camp*
   avoid organized camps;
   refugees should be encouraged to settle in small groups on a permanent site, if possible close to agricultural or other work possibilities;
   if camps are unavoidable, they should be small and dispersed;
   food distribution should be decentralized—there should be as many distribution points as possible;
   where possible, refugee camps/settlements should be sited within a reasonable distance of job opportunities;

[7] Recommendations and Suggestions, drafted by Anna Cleary, UNHCR Liaison Unit with NGOs, 8 Aug. 1986.

(b) *Avoiding the dependency syndrome*

refugees should be employed early on in camp construction and other infrastructural building activities;

refugees should be allowed to build their own huts with local materials which should be provided by UNHCR and NGOs when required.

(c) *Transition from emergency to development*

a series of indicators should be used in order to recognize when the emergency phase is over, in order to switch from purely care and maintenance assistance to development oriented activities;

a completely separate team should be sent out, early in the relief phase, with expertise in self-reliance activities to suggest activities which would lead to at least partial self-sufficiency;

there should be a joint assessment of the situation involving UNHCR and capable and interested NGOs;

UNHCR and NGOs should work with and reinforce the local support systems;

refugees (and local population where applicable) should be informed about assistance and protection systems by means of written material in the refugees' languages, training sessions, etc.

projects should include needs assessments in which refugees play a central role—they should be given as much say in the project as possible—it was suggested that the question of assessment of refugee needs and refugee participation should be written into the UNHCR/NGO agreement for each assistance project.

(d) *Development activities*

developmental activities should start as soon as possible and involve as much refugee participation as can be achieved right from the beginning;

income-generating measures should be identified—but before starting any new initiatives an assessment should be made of available tools and skills, what the local people are producing and how they are doing it;

use female agriculturalists to explain farming techniques to refugee women;

it was suggested that the fact that emergency funds are only available for relief items and that there are none available for development activities should be rectified;

it was proposed to have revolving funds or ensure that refugees can obtain loans locally through banks or other credit institutions—it was suggested that a clause should be added, wherever possible, to the agreement, to the effect that loans should be available to refugees from local banks, with the possibility of using their crops as collaterial.

2. Practical opportunities to integrate existing refugees in small scale schemes so as to facilitate the maximum involvement of both refugees and nationals

improve local infrastructure;

ensure long-term assistance schemes are incorporated in the national development plans of the host country—in this way local resentment can be minimized;

durable solutions should be linked with the existing commercial and social relationships;

local materials and the skills of the local population should be used whenever possible;

increased flexibility to disburse funds at field level.

3. Practical arrangements to improve cooperation of NGOs and UNHCR in planning, financing, management, and execution of activities discussed in the Workshop

All organizations involved in refugee activities (particularly NGOs and UNHCR) should:

work on the establishment of an effective prevention and preparedness policy. Refugee prone countries should be identified. It was suggested that UNHCR Assistance Division, ICVA, and the NGO Liaison Unit should review the current global refugee situation and select three countries, one in Africa, one in Asia, and one in Latin America as a representative cross section. During 1986 UNHCR, UNDP, NGOs and relevant government officials could jointly sponsor meetings of UNHCR and NGO field staff in each of these countries in order to identify suitable projects and discuss them. Interested NGOs and local UNHCR officials would be invited to make exploratory visits to existing or potential sites;

NGOs should be directly involved at the needs assessment stage of a project as well as in the implementation process—it was suggested that a clause stipulating this should be included, wherever possible, in UNHCR/NGO agreements;

once the evaluation is made, identify all resources available before the assistance situation in the receiving country reaches the crisis point;

have a multi-faceted approach since refugees are from numerous different backgrounds;

strengthen the status of the relief coordinating body, particularly as regards representations to donors that cash resources are needed instead of goods in kind;

for expatriate staff and local staff considerations are that they should:

be suitably trained and experienced, and remain long enough to ensure continuity;

have required political awareness of the situation.

regarding refugee participation, it was proposed that UNHCR should include within its programme contracts with NGOs a requirement for NGOs to demonstrate the following:

evidence that the refugees feel that the project goals are important, and that they have been integrally involved in the needs assessment process;

evidence that the refugees feel that the project's approach has merit;

how refugees will be involved in the design, implementation, monitoring, and evaluation of the project.

importance of coordination between all parties involved;

it was suggested that when drafting a project description, clear mention should be made of refugees' training, i.e.:

each specific skill required by the project and covered through the hiring of expatriate experts, ought to correspond to allocations and activities for the training of refugees in each particular field;

refugees with particular skills should be identified and then trained in order to allow them to participate in the running of a project;

training should also be geared to preparing refugees for leadership functions.

develop ways, means, and mechanisms to identify specific urban areas where UNHCR and NGOs could or should become operative;

NGOs with a sound track record in the field of self-employment and employment in urban areas need to be identified and encouraged to cooperate with UNHCR;

institutionalize information sharing;

it was suggested that there should be regular coordinating meetings between governments, UNHCR, and NGOs at the field level;

an attempt should be made to simplify UNHCR/NGO agreements;

promote joint fund-raising campaigns;

explore more systematically ways and means to contribute towards national development programmes which could benefit refugees;

a computer-based information network should be established to keep feed-back from the NGOs up-to-date;

a suggestion was made to set up a centre to disseminate information in the form of a small booklet published a few times a year;

> the idea of exchanging staff members between NGOs and UNHCR on a temporary secondment basis was proposed.

The two texts quoted are complementary. The second indicates in concrete terms how the Principles of Action could be translated into action. Unfortunately, little progress has been made, as of mid-1987. This is partly the result of the change of High Commissioner on 1 January 1986 and the extensive reorganization of the UNHCR management structure which followed.

The development approach

Care and maintenance

At present many refugees find themselves in the 'no solution' situation. This is the situation of large refugee groups stuck in countries of first asylum and benefiting from extended relief operations, as for instance with the 130,000 Indo-Chinese refugees in Thailand. Either no country is prepared to accept them under conditions which will allow them to earn their living, or the refugees themselves refuse the opportunities available.

These seemingly hopeless situations arise in different ways. Some countries of first asylum put refugees behind barbed wire, preventing them from carrying out any kind of productive activity, as is the case with Salvadorean refugees living in camps in Honduras, or the Vietnamese refugees in the closed camps of Hong Kong. The situation is different in other countries of asylum which do not officially allow refugees to settle. In some of them refugees are allowed to work unofficially, to pursue income-generating activities, and to practise or improve their skills in organized workshops. Many agencies promote measures aimed at making refugees partly self-sufficient. These positive moves deserve encouragement, but in most countries of first asylum where refugees have not been allowed to settle, the number of refugees who succeed in sustaining a means of livelihood remains small. Moreover, the per capita cost of the measures needed to make them even partly self-supporting is high, while the overall cost of the care and maintenance programme does not seem to decrease as a result of the expenditure incurred by UNHCR in funding what are classified as self-sufficiency activities.

The most likely way of moving a refugee situation out of such a deadlock is to approach it from an economic perspective. Industrialized countries should offer additional economic aid to those developing countries which have accepted large refugee groups. This aid should support projects aimed at providing sustained means of livelihood for a substantial number of people. Some of the beneficiaries should be nationals, some refugees. In other words, development co-operation between a low-income country of asylum and an industrialized state should be increased as a result of the former accepting that refugees benefit together with nationals from development activities financed from the additional external sources. Thus, the problem should be moved from the humanitarian to the economic level. But this approach may have strong political connotations. One can be cynical and consider it as buying the goodwill of a country of asylum with increased economic aid; one can also consider that refugees offer an economic potential which, if properly tapped, would contribute to the development of the country of asylum. The negative attitude of countries of asylum towards allowing refugees to settle is a normal reaction aimed at protecting their nationals. This initial reaction may change if the direct and indirect costs of granting asylum to foreigners are more than offset by the benefits derived by nationals from additional development projects.

The problem is how to approach the country of asylum. The UNHCR must be careful to maintain a low profile, for if the High Commissioner's Office is perceived by the country of asylum to be playing a major role or to be pushing for local settlement, the government of that country will suspect that refugees may become the main beneficiaries of the scheme. As the 'consul' of the refugees, the UNHCR is the victim of its mandate in such a situation, and any action taken by the Office may be counter-productive. The UNDP is not in any better position to advocate development assistance to refugees because the use of its resources is determined jointly by the government of the developing country (country of first asylum in this instance) and by UNDP. Governments ensure that UNDP's limited resources are used for the benefit of their own nationals before that of foreigners, particularly those refugees whose presence was not solicited, or probably not even welcome in the first place.

The role of convincing a host country to allow refugees to settle, even temporarily, within the context of additional development projects benefiting nationals as well, could best be played by one or more industrialized countries. Let us take a hypothetical example to illustrate this approach. Among the Laotian refugees who sought asylum in Thailand were hill tribes, the largest of which were the Hmong, who fought on the side of the French Army in the battle of Dien Bien Phu, and later on the side of the Americans in the Plaine des Jarres. People of the same tribe live in Thailand, north-east of Chiang Mai, near or in the 'golden triangle'. When the Hmongs from Laos sought refuge in Thailand in 1975, there were several rural development programmes for Thai Hmong, one of which was financed by a fund administered by the King of Thailand. The official objective was to eradicate the opium poppy and promote alternative crops. The resources of the fund under the King's administration were too limited to fulfil the objectives of the programme, which embraced too small an area with too limited a population. This programme would have provided an opportunity for one or more governments of industrialized countries, particularly the United States, to offer substantial additional contributions to Thailand to widen the scope of the programme, on the condition that a number of Hmong refugees from Laos who were living in camps in Thailand were allowed to settle in the programme area. For such an approach to have a chance of succeeding, however, required the use of channels other than those employed by UNHCR. In this instance, it might have been possible to obtain the support of the Thai Ministry of Defence, which would have seen the advantage of having Hmong communities—known for their anti-communist feeling and their fierce fighting—settled in an area adjacent to Laos and Burma and close to Vietnam and China.

Voluntary repatriation

Voluntary repatriation is considered the best solution to the problem of refugees. Indeed, what could be better for people who have had to abandon their homes and seek refuge abroad, than to be able to go back home? One precondition of course is that the cause of the exodus must have ceased to exist. If the refugees flee because of the violation of human rights, their voluntary return will usually take place after a change of political regime, a change which often provokes strife. If the refugees flee because their lives are in danger as a result of serious disturbances, as laid down in the OAU Convention, they will repatriate voluntarily once the internal conflict is over. In both cases, the area of origin of the refugees may have been disrupted or destroyed, and this will consequently need to be rehabilitated. Another problem which can face returnees is the hostility of their compatriots who stayed at home. Care has to be taken not to give returnees preferential treatment which might provoke resistance in those who stayed to welcome back those who left. The best way to tackle these two problems is to avoid launching a programme of assistance aimed mainly at returnees and instead to provide development aid to a returnee-affected area.

What should the role of UNHCR and possibly other international agencies be in such an approach? Legally speaking, once refugees have returned home they are no longer under the mandate of UNHCR, since they have decided to put themselves under the protection of the government of their country of origin once again. However, the Statute of the Office[8] invites the High Commissioner to promote voluntary repatriation, and one resolution of the UN General Assembly[9] authorizes him to provide 'assistance in rehabilitation of returnees'. Although UNHCR can thus assist former refugees under these conditions, the practice has been to limit this aid both in scope and in time. The UNHCR participation is normally restricted to direct assistance to returnees for one year, or, in some instances, two.

So far UNHCR contributions to the rehabilitation of returnees have been dependent on the High Commissioner receiving contributions specifically earmarked for such operations. These are treated as special trust funds to be administered outside the UNHCR Annual Programme. As a rule, the High Commissioner's Office has not met with too many difficulties in securing additional sources of funding, principally among governments willing to support a new political regime or wishing to participate in the reconstruction of an area which has been badly affected by civil war. This has not always been the case, however, For example, in 1979 when the present government came to power in Nicaragua, many Nicaraguans who had sought refuge from the Somoza regime in neighbouring countries returned home. To help the new government cope with this, the High Commissioner launched a special

[8] UN General Assembly Res. no. 428 (v) of 14 Dec. 1950, 'Statute of the Office of the United Nations High Commissioner for Refugees'.

[9] UN General Assembly Res. no. 31/35 of 30 Nov. 1976, 'Report of the United Nations High Commissioner for Refugees'.

appeal to assist in the rehabilitation of these returnees—an appeal to which, for political reasons, only a limited number of governments responded.

In order to prevent such problems arising in the future, it would be preferable if UNHCR participation in the rehabilitation of returnees were financed from its annual programme rather than from *ad hoc* contributions. Indeed there already exists the legal basis for these changes to be initiated.[10] Even more preferable would be the identification of funding sources other than UNHCR to finance the development of returnee areas. This problem is discussed in the funding section of this chapter.

Local settlement

After voluntary repatriation, settlement in the country of first asylum is considered the second-best solution since it enables refugees to remain within a region generally familiar to them. The fact that there are hundreds of thousands of refugees living in these countries today, still dependent on care and maintenance, can be considered a failure on the part of the international community. This would not necessarily be the case if the international community accepted the following guidelines.

The international community should adopt a development approach in providing further support to low-income countries of first asylum as soon as the emergency phase of the refugee influx is over. This economic aid in the form of development programmes benefiting a large proportion of nationals would have to be generous enough to convince the host government of the clear advantages for its country of letting the refugees settle. Financial support to such programmes should be additional to the development co-operation already agreed and should take the form of grants. The contribution from the country of asylum should be clearly below the usual level for similar development programmes benefiting nationals only, the difference reflecting the will of the international community to share the burden effectively, each country contributing according to its means, and recognizing that the most valuable contribution to the refugee is the granting of asylum. These days developing countries, in spite of all their problems, often practise a more generous policy of asylum than many industrialized countries,

[10] UN General Assembly Res. no. 31/35 of 30 Nov. 1976, 'Report of the United Nations High Commissioner for Refugees'.

which are increasingly trying to close their doors to asylum-seekers. Over 90 per cent of the world's refugees are located in the developing countries. Under these circumstances, the least the industrialized countries can do is to provide the means to those developing countries of asylum to continue to keep their doors open.

The present policy of UNHCR is to respond quickly to new refugee situations with emergency relief operations, and then study the various lasting solutions, giving the highest priority to voluntary repatriation. If repatriation is not possible but local settlement in the country of first asylum appears possible, UNHCR policy currently focuses on bringing the standard of living of the refugees to a level comparable to that of the nationals living in the same area. After completion of this phase of the response further measures required to ensure that the refugees constitute a sustainable community integrated into the national context should be transferred, within the UN system, from UNHCR to UN development agencies since such measures are clearly of a developmental nature.

There are several shortcomings in the current UNHCR approach to refugee situations. 'The Lessons of ICARA II' and repeated experiences demonstrate that a group of refugees who reach the living standard of nearby nationals rarely become a sustainable community unless the whole area is part of a development process. The UNHCR cannot dissociate itself from what is required beyond the stage of 'standard of living equal to nationals'. Although development work falls outside UNHCR's mandate, other international development agencies, such as UNDP, cannot easily fill the void because governments of developing countries give priority to their own nationals over refugees. Since refugees remain under UNHCR mandate, the Office must ensure lasting solutions for them. The UNHCR therefore should play a role in ensuring that development activities required to integrate such refugee communities into the country of asylum are implemented. In promoting this development approach to local settlement, UNHCR's role should be that of a catalyst and co-ordinator, as outlined in the Principles for Action in Developing Countries endorsed by the Executive Committee of the High Commissioner's Programme in October 1984.

Resettlement

The donor community does not involve itself when refugees are resettled from the country of asylum to an industrialized state. All costs are covered by the adoptive country, even though they may be very high, particularly when refugees have to learn the language, improve their skills, or when they belong to a vulnerable group requiring social assistance. Resettlement is not limited, however, to industrialized countries. The OAU tried to promote such a solution within Africa, in the spirit of burden-sharing. In the section on 'countries of resettlement', I gave three examples of this regional solution—the resettlement of refugees from one developing country to another.

There may be a case for more actively promoting this solution. To achieve this objective, the cost to a low-income country of accepting and integrating a refugee group would have to be more fully covered by the donor community, i.e. the developing country would have to find some compensation for admitting refugees. Here again, the compensation might be the development of an area where refugees were resettled, but the development scheme would equally benefit the nationals living in that area. Such a programme would have to be in line with the overall development plan of the country and be financed from external contributions, in addition to planned bilateral or multilateral programmes.

International fund for refugee-related development projects

Sustainable solutions to refugee problems will require the creation of programmes attractive enough to encourage a country of first asylum to allow refugees to settle through the provision of additional development co-operation, programmes to develop returnee areas in the case of voluntary repatriation, programmes to integrate refugee settlements into a development scheme embracing national communities as well, programmes to promote the resettlement of refugees within the region through refugee-related development projects. Obviously, all these development approaches require large amounts of money. Crucial questions about financing remain unanswered. Who will be the contributors? Who will administer the funds? Who will ensure the implementation of these development projects? What will be the mechanism of co-ordination among the actors?

The establishment of an international fund for refugee-related development projects is necessary to enact the recommendations adopted in several meetings for a development approach to refugee situations. This is not a new idea. In 1979 the Carter administration envisaged the creation of a fund for durable solutions. At that time an original figure of US$200 million was mentioned. The aim of the fund was to promote the resettlement of refugees from low-income countries of first asylum to other low-income countries by financing development projects which would enable this additional population to be absorbed. The hidden agenda was to put an end to the massive resettlement of Indo-Chinese refugees in the United States. The idea was abandoned as the result of a change of US administration. The idea has not vanished completely, however.

As described in the section 'The Lesson from ICARA II', the UK government established a fund for refugee-related development projects, and UNDP has created a similar fund, outside its regular programme. Although these moves are in the right direction, what is required is the creation of an independent fund on an international basis.

Such a fund would require a carefully planned framework to ensure its optimum use and its good administration. Three main principles should be followed to determine which bodies should form part of the framework: first, because the organization must be relevant to the refugee situations in the developing countries, part of it should be based in these countries or regions. Second, as one of the aims of the new structure is to obtain a more equitable sharing of the refugee burden by facilitating the transfer of funds from the North to the South, it should be partly based in the industrialized countries. Third, the creation of a heavy new structure must be avoided. Based on these principles, one possible structure would include a board of trustees, three project review committees (one in each region: Africa, Asia, and Latin America), and a task force in each of the countries concerned, in addition to a small secretariat.

Country task forces

A development-orientated refugee task force would be put together in each low-income country that hosts large groups of refugees. This task force would include representatives of the government of the country concerned (preferably represented by the development planning authorities), of UNHCR, the UN development system (by the UNDP representative in his/her capacity as the UN resident co-ordinator), other governments likely to support a development approach to refugee problems, international development NGOs, local structures from the areas to be developed (local institutions, indigenous groups, etc.), and representatives of the refugee communities or the refugee-based organizations concerned.

The composition of the task force would vary from country to country, depending on the organizations likely to participate in a given refugee situation. For instance, the representation of the UN development system would include the World Bank, the International Fund for Agricultural Development (IFAD), and the other UN programmes or specialized agencies, depending on their interest in and relevance to a given refugee situation. Similarly, the European Economic Commission (EEC) would also be a member of the task force, where appropriate.

The UNHCR should play a crucial role in promoting the creation of a task force where a low-income country accepts refugees in large numbers. Although it would not deal with the emergency phase of a given refugee situation, the task force should be in place, during which time it would act in an advisory capacity to ensure that whatever action was taken during the relief phase facilitated the subsequent development activities required to ensure a sustainable settlement of the refugee communities. The early involvement of refugees, NGOs, the UN development system, bilateral aid, and the host country would also facilitate their subsequent participation in such a development approach and the phasing out of UNHCR material assistance.

In the proposed decentralized structure, the country-based task force would have as its primary responsibilities: assessment of development needs, formulation of projects, implementation, monitoring, reporting, and finally evaluation. The task force would entrust some of these responsibilities to one or a group of organizations. For large infrastructure projects, most of these six programming stages would be entrusted to the UN development system; for projects requiring a community-based approach to development, local institutions and international NGOs would be in a better position to carry out these functions. The procedure would be flexible enough to make use of the most appropriate resources—not excluding research institutions and private firms—particularly resources available locally. As a rule, the assessment of needs, project formulation and implementation, as well as reporting would be carried out by one agency (or a group of organizations) designated by the task force. The monitoring would be done jointly by the government, UNHCR, and the representatives of the UN development system. The evaluation would include the members of the task force (including the representatives of the national and refugee communities concerned) and representatives of donor governments with the possible participation of research institutes.

Regional project review committees

The project proposals would be appraised by a project review committee (PRC). Such a committee would be composed of well-known specialists either from development or refugee fields (practitioners and academics). They would either come from or be very familiar with the regions involved. For this reason it would be essential to have three PRCs: one in Africa, one in Asia, and one in Latin America.

For each PRC, a panel of experts would be drawn up, some being specialists in a given part of the region, others in a particular field (food, security, women in development, income-generating activities, etc.). The composition of a PRC would vary from one meeting to the next, depending on the kinds of project proposed for appraisal, and their location. Each proposal received from the task force would be delegated to the most appropriate specialist, who would undertake a thorough study and present the proposed project to the PRC. The PRC would undertake the technical scrutiny of the project proposals against a set of criteria and priorities and within an agreed general policy.

The board of trustees

The board of trustees would be responsible for the administration of the monies deposited in the international fund for refugee-related development projects. It would develop policy governing the fund and approve the projects proposed by the PRCs. Its tasks also would include the nomination of specialists for the PRC panels and the appointment of the head of the secretariat.

The board would be composed of representatives of the

industrialized countries contributing to the fund and of countries of asylum. The UNHCR and UNDP would be ex officio members of the board. International NGOs might be represented through their federations, e.g. International Council of Voluntary Agencies (ICVA), American Council for Voluntary International Action (InterAction), Australian Council For Overseas Aid (ACOA), and Canadian Council for International Co-operation (CCIC).

The board would meet at different venues, alternately in countries of asylum and in industrialized countries. The mandate of the members of the board would be limited in time to enable other countries, IGOs, and NGOs to serve on the board on a rotation basis.

The secretariat

A small secretariat would be established, preferably in Geneva where UNHCR has its headquarters. The secretariat would serve the board and the PRCs, and make the link with task forces at country level. The secretariat would be responsible for soliciting contributions to the fund and for forwarding reports and financial reviews to the donors. The secretariat would not be directly involved in the project work as the programming process would be decentralized at regional and country levels.

The fund

The international fund for refugee-related development projects would be located in the same place as the secretariat. The UNHCR and UNDP would agree to launch a joint appeal to promote the initial contributions, possibly with the participation of IVCA and other NGO federations. A joint UNHCR/UNDP document would be submitted by the two heads of these organizations to their respective governing bodies. The document would underline the participation of NGOs.

There are good reasons why governments of industrialized countries should contribute to the fund. First, the scheme would fill a gap in the UN structure where development falls outside the UNHCR mandate and where the resources of the UN development system are concentrated on nationals. Second, it would enable industrialized countries to better share the refugee burden with the countries of asylum by participating in the development of refugee areas, in the rehabilitation of areas damaged by the presence of large refugee groups, and where necessary in the development of the infrastructure needed to cope with the consequences of a refugee influx. Third, it would provide a more humane solution by preventing refugees from spending years in non-productive camp life. Fourth, in the long run, it would be less costly to the international community to support development projects to settle refugee groups than to finance extended care and maintenance operations. Finally, it would promote durable solutions within the region where refugees sought asylum, thus avoiding resettlement in an unknown and often hostile environment. The industrialized states which are at present adopting restrictive policies of asylum should at least give generous support to the low-income countries which continue to keep their doors open to asylum-seekers.

It is estimated that the resettlement of one refugee in Europe costs at least US$25,000 to the country of asylum. At the thirty-eighth session of the Executive Committee held in Geneva in October 1987 the Danish Delegation stated that 'the [Danish] commitments to alleviating the plight of those asylum-seekers who are received in Denmark have now reached, on a yearly basis, around US$300 million'. The Swedish Delegation stated that some $400 million are spent each year on reception and integration programmes for those refugees who are permitted to stay in Sweden. To my knowledge, no survey has been undertaken to estimate the total direct and indirect costs of settling one refugee in a developing country, and to assess the share of the country of asylum. We know, however, that the international community contributes an average of less than US$900 for each refugee settled in Tanzania, a country where many refugees have found a new home.

These figures, approximate and incomplete as they are, clearly show how the refugee burden is not shared fairly between developing and industrialized countries and that, for regional solutions to become a reality, a new approach is required and new mechanisms will have to be put in place.

Conclusions

The scheme briefly outlined above is only a sketch of a possible scenario. Many questions still require exploration: what changes should be made to such a structure in order for them to apply not only to refugees but also to returnees? Could the same structure be used when dealing with displaced persons who are not refugees, whether they remain in their own countries or cross international borders? Could the structure outlined above apply, regardless of political considerations, to groups of Palestinian refugees in the Middle East, with UNRWA replacing UNHCR in the scheme? Could the board and the project review committees be combined into one single body comprised of persons of international repute who would give sufficient credibility to the scheme? Should the proposed scheme be limited during the initial phase to community-based development projects implemented by NGOs, or should it include from the outset large infrastructure projects, to be implemented by other agencies?

This development approach could also possibly be applied to countries where it is likely that a large-scale movement of population might take place, in order to prevent a mass exodus. The concept of a development approach to refugee problems has been discussed in various forums for several years without much progress. This is probably largely because of the gap which exists in the system, at both international and country level, where responsibilities for humanitarian aid and development co-operation belong to different agencies and where resources are made available from different budgets. The proposed approach necessarily falls between the two.

What is required is the will to proceed. The NGOs could play a key role in launching the scheme since their mandate—to support disadvantaged communities—applies to both refugees and nationals, and since they have expertise in both humanitarian aid and development co-operation. What they need to initiate the scheme is the support of a few governments and the co-operation of UNHCR and the UN development system.

Oppressive economic, social, and political systems, liberation wars, wars of hegemony, natural disasters, and poverty all combine to create a population in forced exile. Displaced persons and refugees are the inevitable and tragic casualties of our age and some solution must be found for them. The development approach I have suggested could, if implemented, provide a glimmer of hope in the form of genuinely sustainable solutions in which all nations of goodwill, both rich and poor, could work together to their mutual benefit to resolve the problem of the refugee. Through a development approach to which, in effect, the industrialized nations contribute both their money and their expertise, and the poorer countries their hospitality and their available expertise, this urgent problem of helping the poorer countries to develop their resources and the refugees to create a home for themselves can be solved.

12. Voluntary Repatriation

Legal and Policy Issues

GUY GOODWIN-GILL

Introduction

Refugees, as understood by international law, are those who have fled their country of origin because they have a well-founded fear of persecution for reasons of race, religion, nationality, membership of a particular social group, or political opinion; or those who, since they no longer enjoy the protection of their government, are compelled to flee to escape the violence of armed conflict or widespread violations of human rights.[1] No analysis of the refugee in international law is complete, however, without reference to the ultimate objective of the relevant rules and principles: a permanent or durable solution to the problem. This can take the form of voluntary repatriation, or assimilation into new national communities, with the latter encompassing either integration into the country of first refuge or resettlement in a third state.

The availability of durable solutions clearly depends on political factors, among them the conditions which gave rise to the refugee's flight. The situation of the refugee remains a situation of exception, and re-establishment of an effective relationship between citizen and state has long been considered the most appropriate answer. The return of refugees, however, raises problematic questions relating to the termination of refugee status, the entitlement to return as an incident of nationality, and the enjoyment of fundamental human rights after return. Return itself must be

The views expressed in this paper are the personal views of the author and do not necessarily reflect the views of the United Nations or UNHCR.

[1] See generally Guy Goodwin-Gill, *The Refugee in International Law* (Oxford: Clarendon Press, 1983), Chs. 1, 2.

analysed in the light of the legal relations existing between the countries of origin and refuge, and of the juridical interest of the international community.

Refugee problems and their causes vary, and there may be a substantive difference between the individual refugee who flees from, for example, personal persecution on account of his/her political opinions, and the individual member of a group numbering perhaps hundreds or thousands, who flees the daily impact of a struggle for national liberation, the breakdown of law and order, or localized and sometimes centrally directed discrimination and persecution on racial, ethnic, or religious grounds. In a purely practical sense, the chances of an improvement in circumstances will clearly vary from case to case.

Paragraph 6 of the Statute of UNHCR and Article 1C of the 1951 Convention relating to the Status of Refugees provide in similar terms for the cessation of refugee status.[2] Broadly speaking, this can result from voluntary return to the protection of the country of origin; voluntary reacquisition of nationality; acquisition of a new nationality and protection under that; voluntary re-establishment in the country of origin; and a change in the circumstances which gave rise to the claim to be a refugee. Termination of refugee status may thus make redundant the question of voluntary repatriation: the former refugee will either now be a local citizen or be subject to the general regime of immigration and aliens law.[3] As a matter of policy, however, these former refugees are often assisted in repatriation by the appropriate international agency.

It is frequently difficult, and even impossible, to determine whether circumstances have changed to such a degree as to warrant the formal termination of refugee status, even supposing that it was ever formally recognized. Assessment of change commonly involves subjective elements of appreciation; the fact of repatriation may be the sufficient *and* necessary condition, bringing the situation or status of refugee to an end. Moreover, in the uncertain and fluid dynamics which characterize mass exodus, the fact of return can itself be an element in the change of circumstances, contributing to the re-emergence of stability and to national reconciliation. The

[2] Texts in Goodwin-Gill, *The Refugee*, annexes III, IV; see also ch. 3.

[3] On acquired rights in the immigration context, see Guy Goodwin-Gill, *International Law and the Movement of Persons between States* (Oxford: Clarendon Press, 1978), 178–9, 255–61.

voluntary character of repatriation can thus be seen as the necessary correlative to the subjective fear which gave rise to flight; willingness to return negates that fear. The act of will is also essential as evidence of abandonment or conscious surrender of the particular legal interest which the status of refugee and its concomitant rights and benefits comprises; this act of will is crucial where there is no significant evidence of a change of circumstances. For a durable solution to satisfy the interest of the international community, however, it must generally be accompanied by well-founded changes in the material circumstances which originally caused the exodus. These verifiable changes are all the more important where, as in situations of mass influx, the subjective element is less central, or even absent, from the process of characterizing the cross-border movement as a refugee flow.

In practice, voluntary repatriation has often been left to the individual refugee. Now, however, the increasing number of refugees, as well as world-wide economic factors, have highlighted the limitations of local integration and the scarcity of resettlement places. In the search for some composite formula covering every manifestation of the refugee phenomenon, the promotion of voluntary repatriation is increasingly discussed, though easy generalizations often result.

The great variety of causes and circumstances has to be recognized, as does the fact that irreconcilable differences frequently dictate one solution over another.[4] Voluntary repatriation may be preferred; the question is, whether inherent personal and political factors can be substantially influenced or structured. This chapter offers a short analysis of some of the legal and policy issues, followed by a narrative review of the 1983–4 repatriation plan for Ethiopian refugees in Djibouti, and some comment on developments in 1986–7. Next, consideration is given to how appropriate mechanisms may be developed within existing international organizations, competent to pursue and to oversee the attainment of the desired objective. Finally, certain basic principles are briefly examined in the light of various recent problems.

[4] Under a 1974 Chilean law, for example, the government may, and does, prohibit the return of those Chileans considered to be a danger to the state; many other states have also shown themselves reluctant to readmit their nationals.

Legal relationships in the pre-repatriation period

(a) The country of origin and the refugee

Although it is the subject of resolution and debate, voluntary repatriation has not hitherto figured to any great extent in international instruments.[5] The UNHCR Statute calls upon the High Commissioner, *inter alia*, to seek 'permanent solutions for the problems of refugees by assisting Governments . . . to facilitate the voluntary repatriation of refugees, and to provide for the protection of refugees by 'assisting governmental and private efforts to promote voluntary repatriation . . .'. General Assembly Resolution 428(V), adopting the Statute, also calls upon governments to assist 'the High Commissioner in his efforts *to promote . . . voluntary repatriation*',[6] and these calls have been voiced consistently ever since, often including formal acknowledgement of the 'right to return'. Resolutions on the situation of the Palestinian people, for example, have recognized both the inherently political dimension of that problem, and the inalienable right to return.[7] The Palestinian question is of course inextricably bound up with the issue of self-determination, but at a general level also the United Nations has expressly recognized 'the right of refugees to return to their homes in their homelands . . .'.[8]

The putative human right to return to, or not to be arbitrarily deprived of, the right to return to one's own country must not be ignored. It is implied in Article 9 of the Universal Declaration of Human Rights ('No one shall be subjected to arbitrary arrest, detention or exile'),[9] and is expressly recognized in Article 13(2): 'Everyone has the right to leave any country, including his own, and

[5] One exception is Article 5 of the 1969 OAU convention; see annex I.

[6] See also UNHCR Statute, para. 9.

[7] See e.g. General Assembly Res. 37/120 E, 16 Dec. 1982, expressing the view that measures to resettle Palestinian refugees away from their homes and property in the Gaza strip constituted a violation of their inalienable right to return.

[8] General Assembly Res. 36/148, 16 Dec. 1981, on international co-operation to avert new flows of refugees. See also Report of the Group of Government Experts (set up under this resolution), UN doc. A/41/324, 13 May 1986, para. 66 (f).

[9] See UN doc. E/CN.4/826/ Rev.1 (1964), 'Study of the Right of Everyone to be Free from Arbitrary Arrest, Detention and Exile'. The study's conclusion (para. 8/16) that 'exile has virtually disappeared' is belied by the dimensions of recent refugee problems. The study interpreted exile 'to denote expulsion or exclusion from one's own country', which *de facto* if not *de jure* describes the situation of many refugees.

to return to his country.'[10] A similar provision is found in other universal and regional instruments, such as the 1965 Convention on the Elimination of All Forms of Racial Discrimination, the 1966 Covenant on Civil and Political Rights, the Fourth Protocol to the 1950 European Convention on Human Rights, and the 1969 American Convention on Human Rights.[11] Whether such an individual right has established itself apart from the treaty context is debatable, however, and traditional analysis identifies the duty to admit nationals as an obligation between *states*, being the corollary of the right to expel foreign nationals.[12]

Whatever the precise legal status of the right to leave and to return, or the right to be free from arbitrary exile, certain other legally relevant rules are undeniable. Thus, in its judgment in the *Nottebohm* case, the International Court of Justice referred to the necessity, from the point of view of international law, for nationality to be based upon 'a social fact of attachment, a genuine connection of existence, interests and sentiments, together with the existence of reciprocal rights and duties'.[13] Both the Court and leading jurists have recognized the fundamental importance of the relationship between people and territory, and the implications which that has both for sovereignty and for the responsibility of the state.[14] In his separate opinion in the *Western Sahara* case, Judge Ammoun contrasted to its disadvantage the materialistic concept of *terra nullius* with 'a spiritual notion: the ancestral tie between the land . . . and the man who was born therefrom, remains attached thereto, and must one day return thither to be united with his ancestors. This link is the basis of the ownership of the soil . . .'.[15] Essentially

[10] José Inglés, 'Study of discrimination in respect of the right of everyone to leave any country, including his own, and to return to his country', UN doc. E/CN.4/ Sub. 2/229/ Rev.1 (1964); Rosalyn Higgins, 'The Right in International Law of an Individual to Enter, Stay in and Leave a Country', *International Affairs*, 49 (1973), 341–57; Richard Plender, *International Migration Law* (Leiden; Sijthoff, 1972), 74.

[11] Convention on the Elimination of All Forms of Racial Discrimination, art. 5 (0), 1965; Covenant on Civil and Political Rights, Art. 12, 1966; European Convention on Human Rights, Arts. 2, 3, Fourth Protocol, 1950; American Convention on Human Rights, Art. 22, 1969.

[12] Goodwin-Gill, *Movement of Persons*, pp. 20–1, 44–6, 136–7.

[13] ICJ Report (1955), 23.

[14] Cf. *Namibia* (Advisory Opinion), ICJ Report (1971), 16, 54, 56.

[15] *Western Sahara* (Advisory Opinion), ICJ Report (1975), 12, 59 (para. 137), 64 (para. 152); Ammoun, sep. op., 85–6.

similar views have been expressed in other contexts, for example with regard to state succession and statehood.[16]

A state is duty-bound to admit its nationals who have been expelled from other states; although international law permits denationalization in certain circumstances, that competence may not be misused in order to avoid international obligations. The concept of nationality does not just represent the municipal relationship between individual and state but it is also a legally relevant fact which has consequences in international law.[17] A state of refuge may be bound by obligations with regard to refugees, but the obligations of the state of origin, deriving from the internationally relevant fact of attachment, are not extinguished. That state cannot oblige any other state to admit or keep its nationals by virtue of any formal or informal measure of denationalization.[18]

(b) The country of refuge and the refugee

Whether by virtue of the express provisions of Article 33 of the 1951 Convention relating to the Status of Refugees, or of the equivalent rule in general international law, states are bound by the principle of *non-refoulement*. Save in certain limited and exceptional cases, refugees must not be returned in any manner whatsoever to territories in which their lives or freedom may be endangered, for reasons of race, religion, nationality, social group, or political opinion. The rule thus prohibits both rejection at the frontier and expulsion after entry. *Non-refoulement* through time, the rule in its dynamic sense, forms the basis moreover of temporary refuge, the minimum content of *asylum* which is required by general international law.[19]

Pending a durable solution, whether voluntary repatriation, local integration, or resettlement, the state of refuge is obliged to treat refugees according to certain minimum standards, deriving in particular from the rules and principles which enjoin respect and

[16] Ian Brownlie, *Principles of Public International Law* (Oxford: Oxford University Press, 3rd edn., 1979), 554–60; James Crawford, *The Creation of States in International Law* (Oxford: Oxford University Press, 1984), 40–1.

[17] The deprivation of state citizenship does not *per se* justify the subsequent application of international explusion: Goodwin-Gill, *Movement of Persons*, p. 202.

[18] Both the right to seek and to enjoy asylum and the right of expatriation (Arts. 14, 15, Universal Declaration of Human Rights) must therefore be considered incomplete, in the absence of any correlative or approximate duty.

[19] Goodwin-Gill, *The Refugee*, pp. 114–21.

protection of fundamental human rights.[20] The state of refuge has further obligations to the international community, deriving from general international law, from elementary considerations of humanity, and founded on the international community's interest in and concern for refugees. The UNHCR, in the exercise of its functional protection role, represents the (legal) interest of the international community. It is that Office which has the standing to protect refugees and to ensure that international obligations are observed.

(c) The country of refuge and the country of origin

In the normal situation of controlled entry a legal relationship comes into existence whenever one state admits the national of another. Again, this normally encompasses, *inter alia*, the right of the admitting state to expel the foreign national and the duty of the state of origin to receive back its citizen; the right of that state to exercise diplomatic protection, and the duty of the admitting state to accord the foreign national a certain standard of treatment.[21]

The admission of refugees evidently introduces other considerations, but the bases of a similar legal relationship remain. In particular, the legally relevant fact of nationality continues, considered apart from municipal law and in the sense of the genuine connection, the social fact of attachment, even if ruptured for the moment. On the other hand, the legally relevant fact of the refugee's presence in the state of refuge is itself sufficient both for jurisdictional purposes and as a basis for the attribution of responsibility.[22]

The state of origin may choose to ignore the link of nationality and to 'write off' those who have fled, but this potentially involves a breach of obligation to the state of refuge and perhaps also to the international community. This is the case, even though, given the conditions prevailing in the country of origin, the actual return of

[20] Ibid. 136–48.

[21] See *Nottebohm* case, ICJ Report (1955), 4; per Judge Read, dissenting, pp. 47–8; Brownlie, *Principles*, pp. 504–34; Goodwin-Gill, *Movement of Persons*, pp. 58, 87.

[22] In the *Namibia* case, ICJ Report (1971), pp. 16, 54 (para. 118), 56 (para. 127), the International Court observed: 'Physical control of a territory, and not sovereignty or legitimacy of title is the basis of State liability for acts affecting other States . . . The injured entity is a people which must look to the international community for assistance in its progress towards the goals for which the sacred trust was instituted.' The situation of refugees is analogous, for they too must look to the international community for protection and assistance.

refugees may be barred by that complex of duties *ergo omnes* which derives from the principle of *non-refoulement*. A refugee movement necessarily has an international dimension, but neither general international law nor treaty law obliges any state to provide durable solutions. Indeed, such a development may not be desirable. As the Australian government observed in 1981, when commenting on the German Federal Republic's initiative regarding international co-operation to avert new flows of refugees, such a rule or principle,[23]

> would effectively relieve the country of origin of its serious responsibility to take whatever measures are possible and necessary to enable people who have fled its territory to return. It would also undermine the right of people who have had to flee their homeland to seek the support of the international community in obtaining the conditions which will make possible their voluntary return, and it would institutionalize exile at the expense of the fundamental right of the individual to return to his country and enjoy his basic human rights.

Similar sentiments were expressed by other countries which favoured voluntary repatriation,[24] although the particular emphasis did vary according to each state's perception of the initiative.[25]

At base, a state of origin retains obligations in regard to its nationals, while a state of refuge retains obligations in regard to foreign nationals, including refugees. If a dispute exists between them it must be solved in accordance with the relevant principles of international law. No deductive process will produce, from the principles set out in the 1970 United Nations Declaration concerning Friendly Relations and Co-operation,[26] a formula that is right for all time and all circumstances. Those principles do indicate, however, related objectives and a manner of proceeding, and the following are thus relevant to the problem under discussion:

> The principle that states shall settle their international disputes by peaceful means in such a manner that international peace and security and justice are not endangered.

[23] 'Report of Secretary-General', UN doc. A/36/582, 23 Oct. 1981, p. 5.

[24] Ibid. 9 (Belgium), 15 (Egypt), 36 (Qatar).

[25] e.g. the German Federal Republic's proposed guidelines not only sought to maintain the 'right to return', but also the 'right to leave' and the 'right not to be compelled to leave'. Italy hoped that preventive measures would not restrict free movement or impose limits upon the principle of asylum, ibid. 21–7, 30.

[26] Text in Ian Brownlie, *Basic Documents in International Law* (3rd edn., 1983), 35.

The principle concerning the duty not to intervene in matters within the domestic jurisdiction of any state, in accordance with the Charter.

The duty of states to co-operate with one another in accordance with the Charter.

The principle that states shall fulfil in good faith the obligations assumed by them in accordance with the Charter.

Where refugees are concerned, the international community, besides the states directly involved, has a legal interest both in protection and in the attainment of an appropriate, lasting solution. This interest is evident in the role entrusted to UNHCR and has been consistently emphasized in international instruments and General Assembly resolutions.

The facilitation of voluntary repatriation

The necessary involvement in voluntary repatriation of both country of refuge and country of origin is expressly acknowledged in Article V of the 1969 OAU convention, the only multilateral treaty provision so far concluded on the subject (see Annex I). This article stresses the essentially voluntary character of repatriation, the importance of collaboration by country of origin and country of asylum, of amnesties and non-penalization, as well as assistance to those returning. The subject was considered further at the 1979 Arusha Conference on the situation of Refugees in Africa, when it was recommended that appeals for repatriation and related guarantees should be made known by every possible means.[27]

In the Executive Committee of the High Commissioner's Programme, voluntary repatriation was first examined in detail in 1980, and the conclusions then adopted (see Annex II) are closely modelled on the provisions of the OAU Convention.[28] In the Sub-Committee of the Whole on International Protection, a number of representatives commented on the functions considered appropriate for UNHCR to undertake. Accurate information on the numbers and identity of the refugees was required, as was

[27] UN doc. A/AC.96/ INF.158, paras. 3, 4. The importance of adequate information was also recognized in the 1946 Constitution of the International Refugee Organization; see annex I: 'Definitions', pt. i, sect. C, para. 1, text in Goodwin-Gill, *The Refugee*, pp. 235–9.

[28] See 'Note on Voluntary Repatriation', UN doc. EC/SCP/13, 27 Aug. 1980; see also Report of the Sub-Committee, UN doc. A/AC.96/586, 8 Oct. 1980, paras. 17–29.

information on whether the causes of flight still existed. Voluntary repatriation should be promoted in consultation with both the country of origin and the international community, should take place under public scrutiny, and with an international agency such as UNHCR entrusted with an audit function. The conditions favouring repatriation might need to be created, but it was essential to avoid the appearance of preferring one regime to another. One representative called attention to the distinction between the return of refugees to countries which have attained independence from colonial rule, and return to countries whose governments themselves were responsible for the exodus; the distinction had a bearing on the kind of arrangements which might be made.

The need for access to all relevant information was repeatedly stressed, both with regard to the situation prevailing in the country of origin, the guarantees provided and, presumably, the type and duration of assistance available for reintegration.[29] The Executive Committee recognized that voluntary repatriation is generally the most appropriate solution for refugee problems, particularly when a country accedes to independence. It stressed that the essentially voluntary character of repatriation should always be respected, and that appropriate arrangements should be made to establish this, both in individual cases and in large-scale repatriation movements; UNHCR should be involved 'whenever necessary'. Other conclusions noted the joint responsibilities of country of origin and country of asylum, and the importance of refugees being provided with the necessary information regarding existing conditions. Visits by individual refugees or refugee representatives to the country of origin to inform themselves of the situation there could also be of assistance. Formal guarantees for the safety of returning refugees were called for, together with arrangements in countries of asylum to ensure that the terms of such guarantees and other relevant information regarding conditions prevailing there were duly communicated to refugees. The Executive Committee considered that 'UNHCR could appropriately be called upon—with the

[29] 'Report of the Sub-Committee', UN doc. A/AC.96/586, paras. 23–4. The General Assembly, in a series of resolutions dating back to 1961, has approved and required UNHCR assistance in rehabilitation following return. See e.g. UNGA Res. 1672 (XVI), 18 Dec. 1961 (Algerians returning from Tunisia and Morocco); 3143 (XXVII) of 14 Dec. 1973 (assistance with rehabilitation generally). Such an extended mandate is in line with para. 9 of the UNHCR Statute and is now a regular part of annual General Assembly resolutions; see e.g. UNGA Res. 41/124, 4 Dec. 1986, para. 9.

agreement of the parties concerned—to monitor the situation of returning refugees with particular regard to any guarantees provided by the governments of countries of origin.' The governments concerned were requested to provide the necessary travel documents and transport facilities and to arrange for the reacquisition of nationality where it had been lost. Finally, it was recognized that reception arrangements and reintegration projects might be necessary.

Both the OAU provisions and the Executive Committee conclusions are oriented towards the facilitation, rather than the promotion, of returning refugees; the latter aspect was examined more thoroughly in 1985, and is now considered below.

The voluntary repatriation of Ethiopian refugees from Djibouti in 1983

Events in Ethiopia during the 1970s led to massive movements of people into the surrounding neighbouring countries, with some 30,000 present in Djibouti on 30 June 1983. Djibouti itself became independent in 1977, with refugees already forming a significant percentage of its population, but nevertheless proceeded to accede to the 1951 Convention/1967 Protocol. The first general programme for the assistance and rehabilitation of Ethiopian returnees was initiated in 1978, but prevailing conditions did not then permit the repatriation of significant numbers. A special appeal was subsequently launched by UNHCR for assistance to returnees, particularly those returning to Hararghe and Eritrea.

Preliminary consultations took place in Geneva, between the governments of Djibouti and Ethiopia, during the 1982 meeting of the Executive Committee of the High Commissioner's Programme. These led to the formation of a Tripartite Commission, Djibouti–Ethiopia–UNHCR, which met in January and April 1983 to work out a scheme to promote and facilitate repatriation. At the opening session, the Ethiopian representative referred to the promulgation in June 1980 of Proclamation No. 183 on the subject of repatriation, which provided for an amnesty, exempting from prosecution any Ethiopian refugee in Djibouti for any crime committed for political purposes before he or she left Ethiopia, or prior to the date of return to Ethiopia. The amnesty was subsequently renewed and extended.[30]

In its decisions and recommendations, the Tripartite Commission expressed its satisfaction with the firm desire of both governments to effect voluntary repatriation, and with their assessment that the conditions leading to the exodus were no longer present. The Commission agreed on the need to define an assistance programme, and for UNHCR to provide the Ethiopian government with full technical and promotional assistance. The UNHCR also was called upon to do its utmost to mobilize any necessary additional resources, and to work jointly with the two governments to organize refugee movements. Djibouti, for its part, was to inform refugees of the measures to be taken for their reception and rehabilitation, and to make available to the Commission the necessary information on numbers and places of origin. Both governments, finally, were to facilitate travel by UNHCR and voluntary agency staff, who were to be allowed free access to sites and movement between the two countries.

A second meeting of the Tripartite Commission was held in Addis Ababa from 15 to 16 April 1983. The UNHCR representative reiterated the importance of maintaining the voluntary character of repatriation, and it was noted that the success of the operation depended on measures taken in the country of origin. Some were political and legal, such as amnesties; others were material and practical, affecting the well-being, reception and reintegration of those returning. The Commission concluded with a number of specific recommendations on information and registration of refugees; assistance; practical implementing measures, including education of local officials; travel, telecommunications, and customs, immigration and health procedures.

In a press release issued on 16 April 1983 the Commission reiterated the strictly humanitarian and non-political character of assistance to refugees. It noted with satisfaction that both UNHCR and non-governmental organizations had free access to the returnees and their settlements; it noted the further assurances given regarding the safety of refugees upon their return, reaffirmed its conviction that close co-operation between the country of asylum, the country of origin and UNHCR was imperative in the

[30] The amnesty was renewed under Proclamation No. 231 of 1982, extended to 31 Dec. 1983 by an amending Proclamation of 15 Dec. 1983, and later extended further.

promotion of voluntary repatriation, and appealed to the international community to ensure that the humanitarian and non-political character of assistance to refugees was respected.

A major feature of the repatriation scheme was indeed the project for assistance to those returning. The objectives, stated in the outline submitted to UNHCR, were to facilitate the initial social and economic reintegration of those expected to return to their places of origin in Harargghe and Wollo provinces, and to promote self-sufficiency for returnees through the provision of housing construction materials, support for farmers and pastoralists, and support for small-scale cottage industry activities.

The project, with 29,869 potential beneficiaries (13,637 adults, 16,232 children up to 17 years), was divided into sub-projects according to type and locality. The principal types of assistance were: food aid and immediate relief assistance; town and village reintegration support; rehabilitation of agri-pastoralists and pastoralists; and rehabilitation of agricultural workers. As every refugee phenomenon differs, so too will the details of any proposed scheme for return. A summary of the Djibouti–Ethiopia project, however, is helpful for its indication of the very practical measures which may be required, in addition to formal legal or political initiatives.

The first type of assistance, food aid and immediate relief, was thus intended to be available at specified transit and destination points, where infrastructure support in terms of shelter, water, storage, health workers, and communications would also be provided. A basic food basket would be issued (one month's supply to be carried ex-Djibouti, two months' to be transferred in bulk), to include grain, cereal, edible oil, tinned meat, dried skim milk, and salt. Basic domestic needs would be covered by the issue of soap, blankets, clothing material and kitchen utensils. Other measures included the provision of tents for temporary shelter, water trailers to supplement existing supplies, sanitation units at tent sites, the use of existing and the construction of new warehousing, transportation by rail, bus and truck, or by air for family groups containing aged, sick, or handicapped members; and the extension of the relief and rehabilitation communications network.

To ensure proper identification of the beneficiaries of the scheme, forms developed in Ethiopia would be processed by the Djibouti government and UNHCR, and completed on a beneficiary group basis, subject to the written declaration of voluntary repatriation by the head of the family. The records would be transferred in turn to the Relief and Rehabilitation Commission, on the arrival of the returnees in Ethiopia. Prior to departure, each repatriate would also be issued with a laminated photo-identity card, to be used to establish eligibility for assistance in transit or on arrival at the final destination.

The scheme for town and village reintegration contemplated the reconstruction of permanent accommodation and, to this end, the provision of materials as appropriate either for *chika* dwellings (packed mud, straw and thatch, wooden frames); or stone housing (cement wall supports, foundations, etc.). Materials were issued on the basis of standard specifications. The scheme aimed further at the development of water storage facilities, strengthening health centres, clinics, and primary education opportunities. The promotion of small-scale cottage industry included support for weaving, metalwork, woodwork, and tailoring, the construction of small workshops, and the provision of essential equipment, tools, and initial stocks of raw materials.

The programme for the rehabilitation of pastoralists and agri-pastoralists acknowledged the trend to a less nomadic life-style, motivated by loss and hardship, drought, and conflict, together with often lengthy periods in camps, dependent on external assistance. Mixed agri-pastoral packages were therefore proposed for those intending to resume, in part at least, their former way of life. These packages would include seeds, fertilizer, handtools, one ox, and additional livestock (sheep, cows, or goats) according to the returnee's choice, to the value of $US176 per family (the choice also being subject to rangeland limitations). Self-sufficiency packages for pastoralists, again subject to rangeland and grazing limitations, envisioned a free choice of livestock, to the value of $US345.

Finally, the assistance project aimed at the rehabilitation of agriculturalists in Shinille and Harawa. Two sites were identified by the Relief and Rehabilitation Commission and the UN Food and Agricultural Organization as sites for large-scale irrigated agriculture, the joint potential amounting to some 37,000 hectares. At each site the project aimed at the initial improvement of up to 300 hectares for small-scale irrigated agriculture, to benefit 300 returning families (1,500 persons). Land clearing would be undertaken, and the construction of main and secondary canals, office, and residential accommodation for administrative staff, and shelters for a co-operative workshop, equipment and machinery storage and warehousing. Existing water sources would be augmented with hand-dug wells, and farm machinery—including tractors, ploughs and harrows, seeds, fertilizers, pesticides and handtools—would be provided. Classroom equipment to extend existing primary education facilities was also contemplated.

The project proposal was initially intended to cover a twelve-month period, commencing in August 1983, and was costed at US$8,200,000. By then, large numbers of refugees in Djibouti wanted to return home, the governments concerned were keen to promote the movement, and the international community, through UNHCR, was willing to contribute the necessary material assistance to facilitate return. No formal provision was made for supervision of the amnesty proclaimed by the government of Ethiopia—always a sensitive issue falling prima facie within the reserved domain of domestic jurisdiction. The government's undertaking in this case to allow and facilitate site access by UNHCR and voluntary agency personnel can be considered significant in any overall evaluation of the project, although future operations may call for more sophisticated mechanisms. On this occasion, none of the participating agencies or personnel reported any threat to the security of returnees.

In addition to organized movements, many refugees returned spontaneously, usually to their places of origin, but not necessarily registering at focal points. A report dated April 1984, based on visits to villages and discussions with elders and others, estimates such spontaneous returns at 10,000. The numbers grew in the succeeding months, and a total of 26,993 repatriates was recorded on 31 August 1984 (9,792 organized returns, 7,342 spontaneous returns along the railway, and 9,859 outside the line). Distribution of grain, dried skim milk, edible oil, and canned fish had gone ahead, but there were some delays with housing construction because of a shortage of poles and water. Health was being monitored by voluntary agencies, and refurbishing of schools was scheduled, but the implementation of cottage industry projects had not been particularly successful. There were also some problems with the self-sufficiency plans for agri-pastoralists and agricultural workers, owing to land and water shortages, but a considerable number of livestock had already been distributed. However, the climatic situation gave cause for serious concern: the project area had had no rain after May. By October the situation had worsened. Persistent drought was affecting Hararghe and Wollo, and the victims were moving towards Djibouti, where the government was providing food. At the end of the month nomads and returnees were reported to be severely affected by lack of pasture, water, and resulting livestock losses. The assistance programmes required thereafter for the whole spectrum of victims are too well known to need repeating.

The development of appropriate institutional arrangements to promote voluntary repatriation

The OAU Convention and the first conclusions of the UNHCR Executive Committee take for granted the existence of the necessary political will on both sides; the objective is to oil the wheels once moving, not to get them to turn. The question is whether these very practical suggestions cannot also be incorporated into a broader scheme, designed overall to create or galvanize that political will. The legal context remains clear. Return is the objective to which international law aspires; it derives from the conception of nationality in international law, being coterminous with the notions of attachment and belonging; and is supported by the concept of fundamental human rights, now including the positive legal implications of the right to development.

Effective protection of those returning, measures to ensure the voluntary character of repatriation, and guarantees against victimization are themselves dictated by elementary considerations of humanity. The promotion of the dual objectives of return and protection is the natural consequence of the well-established principles concerning friendly relations and co-operation, international solidarity, and burden-sharing.

No single answer will solve every refugee problem. Similarly, one should beware of the temptation to set up new bodies or procedures, in the expectation that they will be able to work successfully in what is frequently a highly political and politicized arena. Recent initiatives on mass exodus and measures to avert new flows of refugees have revealed a continuing belief in the potential of United Nations machinery to produce solutions to humanitarian problems. In some cases, new posts are suggested (such as that by

Sadruddin Aga Khan[31] for a Special Representative for Humanitarian Questions), but an overall reliance on established mechanisms is preferred. Experience shows, however, that these may not yet be appropriate to resolve all the delicate issues raised by refugee problems.

Article 14 of the United Nations Charter specifically empowers the General Assembly to recommend measures for the peaceful adjustment of any situation, regardless of origin, which it deems likely to impair the general welfare or friendly relations between states.[32] This would allow action on the occasion of any refugee exodus, but General Assembly involvement has tended to be both indirect and *ex post facto*. Thus, it has repeatedly stressed the necessity for states to uphold relevant legal and humanitarian principles and to provide solutions to refugee problems. It has also occasionally approved UNHCR action on specific issues, but has otherwise refrained from participation in the resolution of situations. Politicization can affect any dispute between states and, given voting patterns in the General Assembly, is more likely to lead to stalemate than to effective solutions.[33]

Like the General Assembly, the Security Council is empowered to establish the subsidiary organs it deems necessary for the performance of its functions,[34] but there is little to suggest that its efforts are any more likely to meet with success. The potential of *ad hoc* arrangements, for example, under the authority of the Secretary-General, may be somewhat greater, however, and has been highlighted in the recent report of the Group of Governmental Experts on international co-operation to avert new flows of refugees.[35]

More attention can still be given to the scope for action by the

[31] 'Human Rights and Massive Exoduses', UN doc. E/CN.4/1503, 31 Dec. 1981, paras. 133–5.

[32] Article 14 was specifically invoked, e.g. in General Assembly Res. 1542 (xv), 14 Dec. 1960, calling on Portugal to submit information regarding its non self-governing territories. See Nissim Bar-Yaacov, *The Handling of International Disputes by Means of Inquiry* (1974), 313–14.

[33] Bar-Yaacov, *International Disputes*, pp. 247 ff.

[34] See Article 29, United Nations Charter. Article 24 confers primary responsibility of the Security Council for the maintenance of international peace and security. Article 34 empowers the Security Council to 'investigate any dispute, or any situation which might lead to international friction or give rise to a dispute, in order to determine whether the continuance of the dispute or situation is likely to endanger the maintenance of international peace and security'.

[35] See UN doc. A/41/324, paras. 67–72; also UNGA Res. 41/70, 11 Dec. 1986.

Office of the United Nations High Commissioner for Refugees. To this subsidiary organ of the General Assembly are expressly ascribed the functions of providing international protection and seeking permanent solutions for the problems of refugees. Its role in voluntary repatriation encompasses both promotion and facilitation, but other provisions of the Statute have sometimes led the Office to play a lesser role than might have been expected. Thus, Paragraph 2 prescribes that the work of the Office shall be 'of an entirely non-political character [and] shall be humanitarian and social'. To what extent any work on behalf of refugees can ever be truly non-political (particularly where it involves protection) is debatable, but the provision has been understandably invoked in circumstances in which UNHCR's credibility with governments might be threatened. In 1981, for example, the Office formally declined to provide any information about the German Federal Republic's initiative on international co-operation to avert new flows of refugees. The non-political and purely humanitarian nature of its work means that, while it assists in the solution of refugee problems, 'it cannot concern itself with the circumstances which have brought them into existence'.[36]

While abstention in such cases may be politic, it is not necessarily dictated by the 'non-political' directive. In so far as the latter is a jurisdictional restriction on the competence of the Office (as opposed to a judgement on the ideal quality of its efforts), it must be subsidiary to the two fundamental objectives, protection and solutions. Protection, in the sense of determination of refugee status, cannot avoid the consideration of causes. Similarly, UNHCR would hardly be justified in promoting or facilitating repatriation where it had express knowledge that the conditions which had produced the initial exodus still persisted. The word 'non-political' therefore requires careful, if not hesitant, application; the phrase may imply no more than that UNHCR should not prefer one group of refugees over another, where both meet the criteria of the Statute and/or the Convention and Protocol, on political grounds. Even this otherwise unexceptional injunction may be overridden by express policy directives of the General Assembly or the Economic and Social Council.[37]

The above views are not necessarily reflected in the daily work of

[36] 'Report of the Secretary-General', UN doc. A/36/582, p. 43.

[37] See UNHCR Statute, para. 3.

UNHCR which, for obvious reasons, has often tended to await the initiatives of governments or political bodies before embarking upon the unpredictable waters of the most desirable of solutions. Whether UNHCR should be expected or required to shoulder more than the technical, logistical responsibilities accompanying a programme of voluntary repatriation is a debatable point; it is nevertheless clear that some attention must be given to the feasibility of any such programme before commitments are made on the promotion of other durable solutions.

The UNHCR Executive Committee re-examined the subject of voluntary repatriation at its 1985 session. As usual, preliminary debate took place in the Sub-Committee of the Whole on International Protection, which had before it the report of a Round Table held earlier in the year.[38] The right of the individual to return was accepted as a fundamental premiss, but linked to the principle of the free, voluntary and individual nature of all repatriation movements. The UNHCR's mandate was considered broad enough to enable the Office to take all appropriate initiatives, including those which might promote favourable conditions. Some, indeed, considered that UNHCR had a responsibility to begin the dialogue, while others cautioned against entanglement in political issues. The UNHCR involvement with returnees was recognized as a legitimate concern, particularly where return takes place under amnesty or similar guarantee, but legal difficulties might arise with the government of the country of origin. One suggestion was made that UNHCR should seek a special mandate through the General Assembly.

Opinions were divided on the value of *ad hoc* informal consultative groups in the context of promotion; reservations centred particularly on potential political problems and on the advisability of dealing with possibly unrecognized 'entities'. The Round Table had proposed endorsing freedom to deal with any such entity if 'concern for the basic well-being of the individuals' so required, but the Sub-Committee held back.[39]

Many states commented on the voluntary repatriation issue in

[38] See 'Voluntary Repatriation', UN doc. EC/SCP/41, 1 Aug. 1985.

[39] See 'Report of the Sub-Committee', UN doc. A/AC.96/671, 9 Oct. 1985, paras. 48–51. On occasion UNHCR has been criticized for limiting its assistance to repatriation, which follows the legal and administrative procedures of established governments. The difficulties for a UN agency in assisting repatriation to liberated areas in time of civil conflict should not be underestimated, but this may not exclude an *ad hoc* response to spontaneous movements.

debate in plenary, both with respect to specific problems, such as Indo-China, and to general principles. The United Kingdom, for example, acknowledged the role of states, but stressed that the primary responsibility for initiatives lay with UNHCR as the 'recognized and apolitical international agency'. Morocco considered that UNHCR could be even more actively involved, by facilitating communication between governments and promoting dialogue in cases of deadlock. Canada said that UNHCR should not be inhibited from working with all groups concerned, whatever their status, in seeking to overcome problems preventing voluntary repatriation. The ICVA observer struck a more cautious note: some of the proposed conclusions could be supported, but on occasion promotion could be viewed as coercion, especially where the circumstances leading to the original exodus had not changed. It also was essential to involve refugee representatives in any discussions or tripartite commission meetings.

The Executive Committee adopted the Conclusions unaltered from those recommended by the Sub-Committee (see Annex III).[40] In brief, these Conclusions reaffirm the right of refugees to return, conditional upon their freely expressed wish; stress the voluntary and individual character of repatriation and the necessity for it to be carried out in conditions of safety, preferably to the refugee's former place of residence. They also emphasize the inseparability of causes and solutions, and the primary responsibility of states to create conditions conducive to return. Of particular importance is the recognition given to the view that the UNHCR mandate is broad enough to allow the promotion of voluntary repatriation by taking initiatives to this end. These include promoting dialogue, acting as intermediary, and facilitating communication, but also the active pursuit of return where prevailing circumstances are appropriate. The UNHCR should be involved from the outset in assessing feasibility, planning, and implementation. Reintegration assistance should be available where appropriate and, it is emphasized, UNHCR should have direct and unhindered access to returnees, in order 'to monitor fulfilment of the amnesties, guarantees or assurances on the basis of which the refugees have returned'. Recommendations on the provision of guarantees and on

[40] See 'Report of the Executive Committee', UN doc. A/AC.96/673, 22 Oct. 1985, paras. 100–6; and for the summary records of debate see UN docs. A/AC.96/ SR.385–400.

the necessity for refugees to receive relevant information were also included in the 1980 Conclusions.

Practical and political problems

Repatriation movements during late 1986 and throughout 1987 have given rise to controversial debate, highlighting a variety of critical issues. These have included the question of information as to conditions in the country of origin; the use of coercion or active encouragement in the process of promoting repatriation; the cessation or revocation of refugee status; and the ways and means of ensuring the security of refugees once they have returned. These issues are not only interlinked, but also invite assessments and judgements in areas where precise evidence is lacking; given the interplay of deep humanitarian concern and differing political inclinations (for or against, or neutral, in respect to particular regimes), it is perhaps not surprising that discourse on return arouses such polarized opinions.

(a) Conditions in the country of origin

The return of Chadian refugees from west Sudan provides one illustration of this.[41] The refugees left their country during a period of drought and guerrilla war in 1984–5; many went into the Sudan and many thousands of others to Cameroon, the Central African Republic, and Nigeria. Those who fled to the Sudan went in search of protection and, in particular, to escape discrimination and ill-treatment at the hands of troops in Ouaddai, their province of origin.[42] During 1985 the Chadians and displaced Sudanese in the region totalled some 300,000 and, given the drought and famine, they had to be supplied with food in an emergency operation using aircraft, rubber boats, and four-wheel-drive vehicles.

During and after the period of crisis many of the refugees settled into a regular way of life, renting and cultivating land, establishing Koranic schools and dispute settlement mechanisms within their

[41] See UN doc. A/AC.96/677 (pt. ii), paras. 2.12.4, 2.12.10 (1986); UN doc. A/AC.96/693 (pt i) (1987). I am grateful to Nicholas Morris, Deputy Head, UNHCR Regional Bureau for Africa, for advice and comment regarding Chadians in the Sudan, and Ethiopians in Djibouti, but I remain responsible for comment and conclusions, as well as any errors.

[42] See H. Ruiz, *When Refugees won't go home: The Dilemma of Chadians in Sudan*, (Washington, D.C.: United States Committee for Refugees, 1987), 11–13.

communities.[43] Local integration plans were also initiated in 1986 by UNHCR, in collaboration with COR (the office of the Sudanese government's Commissioner for Refugees) and voluntary agencies. According to one report, however, within a few months the emphasis turned to the promotion of voluntary repatriation, notwithstanding the opposition of the refugees themselves.[44]

The core issue was whether conditions in Ouaddai had so changed as to allow refugees to return in safety. On the one hand, it was argued that discipline had been restored among the troops, and that overall stability had come from the central government's success in the north; refugee leaders, by contrast, were reported as saying that conditions were not yet secure enough. Some suggested that the leaders themselves might not be representing the views of all refugees, being more anxious to maintain their authority in the camps.[45] An easier life in the settlements was possibly a factor, for Chadians in other countries, as well as those spontaneously settled in the Sudan. Nevertheless, the apparent uncertainty of conditions in the country of origin and a perception that repatriation was being encouraged by methods designed to make continued stay more difficult led to criticism of UNHCR's policy.[46]

The criticism was fundamentally neither exceptional nor controversial, but focused precisely on conditions in the country of origin.[47] It was suggested, rightly, that UNHCR should thoroughly investigate the situation at first hand and report back to the refugees and others concerned; any doubts should be resolved in favour of the refugees, but if the position was clear, UNHCR should invoke the cessation clause. In fact, UNHCR was already back in Chad; its staff were visiting Ouaddai, where its operational partner, German

[43] Ruiz, *When Refugees won't go home*, 20.

[44] Ibid. 22.

[45] Ibid. 25. Refugee leaders are likely to be equally suspect when they favour return.

[46] Ibid. 30–2. The UNHCR was criticized in particular for introducing Food for Work programmes late in 1986 which were interpreted as 'part of a plan to make life in the camps more inhospitable'. The UNHCR said that this was done to reduce refugees' dependency, as part of a policy of trying to 'ensure that an imbalance in levels of assistance on return [to the home country] and in the country of asylum does not provide an economic incentive not to repatriate', ibid. 21–2.

[47] The opposing view itself was hardly persuasive on the final count: 'We are not in a position to know if it is safe for these refugees to return to Chad. We are sure, however, that UNHCR has not, to date, proven to the refugees that this is the case.', ibid. 30–1. A reasonable doubt nevertheless suffices in the context of protection.

Agro-Action, was participating in the returnees' programme.[48] Apart from isolated incidents, there was no evidence of theft or physical abuse by government soldiers, and no reports of new arrivals seeking asylum in west Sudan.

The situation of Chadians in the Sudan is a useful illustration of the problem of obtaining adequate information and making accurate assessments about conditions in the country of origin. The experience correctly emphasizes the necessity to maintain a bias in favour of refugees where any doubt persists. At the same time the ideal of return in 'absolute' safety, notwithstanding its inclusion in Executive Committee Conclusion no. 40 (Annex III), is unattainable in the real world. For similar reasons, formal application of the cessation clause may not be appropriate in the often fluid circumstances of a mass movement; over time the very fact of returns may form part of the dynamic which re-establishes stability.

(b) 'Coercion' and 'encouragement'

The issue of coercion and pressure on refugees to return calls for close monitoring. It was also central, with somewhat greater initial justification, to the controversy which surrounded the second phase of repatriation from Djibouti to Ethiopia in 1986 and 1987.[49]

On 29 July 1986 the government of Djibouti issued a circular to all refugees in the Republic. It declared that the majority had left their country of origin for reasons which had now ceased to exist, and that the time had come to return. The circular referred to an amnesty law enacted by the Ethiopian government, and to official statements appealing to refugees to return home, where they would again enjoy full citizenship. The circular further declared that

[48] In 1986, 106 individuals repatriated under UNHCR auspices. By the end of June 1987 a further 1,535 had returned home, with considerable numbers going back spontaneously during that month. Two factors in the spontaneous movement appear to have been the continuing uncertainty regarding stability, and the fact that livestock could not be repatriated by truck. Others were reported to have delayed return because early rains in West Sudan both made travel difficult and encouraged local planting.

[49] See N. Van Pragg, 'Spontaneous Return to Ethiopia', *Refugees*, 19 (July 1985), 9; M. Hutchinson, 'A Bridge Back Home', *Refugees*, 37 (Jan. 1987), 8; H. Hudson, 'The Train to Shinille', *Refugees*, 37 (Jan. 1987), 9; C. Braeckman, 'Returning to the Ogaden', *Refugees*, 40 (April. 1987), 31; P. Brooks, 'Repatriation to Ethiopia: A Journalist Reports', *Refugees*, 42 (June 1987), 30; J. Crisp, 'Voluntary Repatriation: The Hope for Thousands of African Refugees', *Refugees*, 43 (July 1987), 21–30; 'Voluntary Repatriation of Refugees', Editorial, *Refugees*, 44 (Aug. 1987), 5.

UNHCR would ensure that security was guaranteed and would facilitate reintegration, within the means available. The succeeding paragraphs were more ominous. All those who did not accept repatriation voluntarily would have to request continuation of their refugee status. A specially created committee would examine these requests, and decide rapidly, giving no chance of appeal. Those who lost their refugee status, it was said, would have to leave Djibouti but would 'not receive any assistance of any kind as opposed to those who repatriated voluntarily'. Provision was made for the cancellation of old refugee cards, with effect from 1 January 1987, and for the registration of those who elected to return. In the meantime all third country resettlement programmes were suspended.

Not surprisingly, the circular created a furore, among refugees, their advocates, and concerned organizations. Its juridical foundation was questionable on several grounds; first, it made no distinction between those refugees recognized under the 1951 Convention/1967 Protocol by the Djibouti authorities on an individual case-by-case basis, and others, particularly those who had fled the civil war in the Ogaden and been accorded *de facto* refugee status, in the spirit of the OAU Convention.[50] Second, it confused the issues of cessation and cancellation of status, an error compounded by the limitations placed on due process. Third, there was little doubt that the combination of factors amounted to a coercive process, which entirely negated the essential element of free choice. It was also clear, however, that one of the causes of the flight to Djibouti—war in Hararghe—had indeed come to an end, and this was relevant to the situation of some of the refugees, for the most part those of rural origin.[51]

The UNHCR prepared to assist those who had elected to return[52] and also sent a senior delegation to Djibouti to ensure that the rights of refugees were effectively protected. As a result the Djibouti government agreed to drop the re-determination of

[50] Article I (2); Djibouti is not in fact a party to this Convention.

[51] Many refugees had in fact returned voluntarily, sometimes more than once, to their regions of origin. Rural settlement in Djibouti is quite impractical, given the soil and climate; employment prospects are also scarce and resettlement has only helped a few individuals.

[52] See Executive Committee, 37th Session, 1986, UN doc. A/AC.96/ SR.404, paras. 80–4 (Observer Djibouti); SR.408, paras. 37–9 (Head, UNHCR Regional Bureau for Africa). As with the earlier operation, assistance included the provision of food, health care, and water, as well as rehabilitation assistance in regard to housing construction and livestock distribution.

refugee status of those already recognized by the Eligibility Committee or issued with Convention travel documents. This concession principally benefited the 'political' refugees, many of them of urban origin, for whom there had been no substantial change of circumstances in their country of origin. The government also undertook to continue to grant asylum to those who met the Convention criteria, but called for assistance from the international community for those who wished to stay.

By the end of November 1986 over a thousand refugees had registered for voluntary repatriation. The first train was scheduled to leave on 8 December and reception facilities had been completed at three transit centres along the Djibouti–Ethiopia railway line (Adigala, Shinille, and Erer). The train duly departed,[53] accompanied by UNHCR officials, and was followed by other such trains; by 30 August 1987 over 3,360 Ethiopian refugees had been repatriated to Hararghe, and several hundred more had registered to return.

The controversy continued, however, and was fuelled by a separate incident, on 20 December 1986, when five Ethiopians died of suffocation in a train returning some 125 illegal immigrants. This was not a UNHCR voluntary repatriation train, and the nominal list disclosed that none of those being returned was registered as a refugee or asylum-seeker.[54] None the less, the incident added to the feeling of many observers that the nature of the exercise left much to be desired.[55] What was less widely known was that UNHCR officials were checking the voluntary character of registration for repatriation, and following up the process at successive stages (relief distribution, transfer to the railway station, travel across the border, and subsequent assistance with reintegration). Even when

[53] UNHCR Press Release REF/1593 (9 Dec. 1986); H. Hudson, 'The Train to Shinille', *Refugees*, 37 (Jan. 1987), 9. Cf. 'Reluctant Refugees Return to Ethiopia', *Guardian* (9 Dec. 1986).

[54] In the circumstances of admission and protection prevailing in Djibouti, such a nominal list might not be conclusive. The Eligibility Committee suspended its operations on 1 Sept. 1986 (since resumed at the end of Mar. 1987), and new arrivals were not registered. Protection and assistance were provided at Dikhil Camp, however—the only authorized residence. Those who remained outside Dikhil or who failed to report there ran the risk of being arrested as illegal immigrants and deported.

[55] The 20 Dec. 1986 continues to surface; see 'Deaths in a Boxcar; Who cares about Ethiopian Refugees?', *Wall Street Journal* (10 Aug. 1987).

these activites became known, they were sometimes ignored,[56] even when UNHCR actions were perceived to be in the best interests of the refugees.

The line between permissible encouragement and outright coercion will always be difficult to draw, and is likely to move according to one's perspective. Monitoring the element of voluntariness is critical, and should involve not only officials from international organizations, but also representatives of non-governmental implementing agencies and of groups concerned with the human rights of refugees.

(c) Cessation or cancellation of refugee status

Cessation and cancellation were controversial factors in the Djibouti scene, and the former also was invoked by critics of Chadian repatriation.[57] Cancellation of refugee status, however, is a relatively rare phenomenon.

In the present context, cessation depends on the evolution of events in the country of origin, and is based on the view that international protection may no longer be called for or justified if the reasons for a person becoming a refugee have ceased to exist. There is a strong presumption in favour of the continuation of refugee status, however; this is in turn justified in the light of generally prevailing standards of proof, and of the recognized need to contribute to the security of the refugee by letting it be known that status will not be subject to continual review as a result of temporary or insubstantial changes.

While the 1951 Convention and the UNHCR Statute both

[56] See 'UN Body Accused of Failing Refugees', *The Times* (3 Feb. 1987), referring to an anonymous report criticizing UNHCR's policy in Djibouti and the apparent lack of protection, and doubting the voluntary character of the operation. This report was considered the same day by the Africa Committee of the British Refugee Council, attended by the UNHCR representative in London and a UNHCR official who, coincidentally, had travelled with the first repatriation train. As a result of information and comment supplied by UNHCR on that occasion, and at a later meeting on 12 Feb., the British Refugee Council accepted that the anonymous report gave an often misleading and factually inaccurate report of the operation in Djibouti and of UNHCR's role, while noting nevertheless that the situation of refugees in Djibouti remained a potential cause of concern. Notwithstanding these developments and the continuation of repatriation without significant problems, other commentators rehashed the same story, leaving aside facts and explanations. See *Refuge* (Canada's periodical on refugees) 6/4 (May 1987); the preface to the report in question contains other inaccuracies and fails to mention the British Refugee Council/UNHCR discussions mentioned above. Cf. *Refuge*, 6/5 (Aug. 1987).

[57] See above, n. 47 and following. On cessation in the general context of repatriation, see above, n. 2 and following.

provide for cessation, neither makes any mention of cancellation of refugee status. General principles of law would justify such action in some circumstances, for example when new evidence emerges indicating that refugee status has been wrongly granted, or obtained by fraud or wilful misrepresentation of material facts.

In the case of Djibouti, it may have been felt that refugee status had been accorded too liberally. But positive determinations, while declaring status, also constitute rights. Those determined to be refugees plan and live their lives on the basis of their status, benefiting as appropriate from the provisions of municipal law and international convention. The principle of acquired rights begins to work in their favour, and the mere fact that the initial decision may have been wrong does not thereby entitle the determining authority to retreat from its original position. Cancellation of refugee status is thus limited to the exceptional circumstances described above; moreover, the onus is on the authority which would reverse the earlier decision to prove its case, fully conforming in procedure with due process of law.

(d) The security of returnees

In each of the situations described the question arises of how to protect the security of returning refugees. This breaks down into three subsidiary issues: who, or what body, should be responsible for protection? What form should such protection take (e.g. reporting to the international community, interventions with national authorities in regard to individual cases or particular situations, moderating advice to other prospective returnees, adjusting locations for return, etc.); and for how long should responsibility for such protection continue?[58]

Both the Executive Committee Conclusions on voluntary repatriation (No. 18(XXXI) and No. 40(XXXVI)—see Annexes II and III respectively) recognize the potential role for UNHCR in regard to the fate of returning refugees. Both cite the instance of return inspired by government amnesty or other guarantee. Conclusion No. 40, in particular, stresses the High Commissioner's 'legitimate concern for the consequences of return', especially where assisted by the Office; direct and unhindered access to

[58] The present section benefits from an analysis of and conclusions drawn from the return of Guatemalans from Mexico, by UNHCR colleagues Anders Johnsson and Maria Siemens. Any errors in summation and application remain my own.

returnees for monitoring purposes is called for, and should be considered inherent in the mandate.

Notwithstanding the competing claims of national sovereignty, on a number of occasions states have invited UNHCR to adopt a supervisory role in the context of repatriation. Zaïre asked UNHCR to monitor its amnesty provisions in 1978, Ethiopia allowed the overseeing of return and integration phases in both 1984–5 and 1986–7, and Guatemala similarly in 1987.[59]

The UNHCR may indeed be the appropriate body to monitor the security of returning refugees, for it has a duty to protect those repatriating, wherever it is involved in the process of return. What is less certain is the manner in which its protection function can or should be exercised. Particular amnesty or guarantee arrangements may make this clear, but the Office's traditional concern with the human rights of refugees will broadly define the scope of its interest. Where those rights are violated in the country of origin, interventions with national authorities would be justified. If that proves ineffective, UNHCR would be obliged to report either to the Executive Committee, to the Economic and Social Council, or to the General Assembly, given the underlying legal interest of the international community.[60]

The time limit for such monitoring functions cannot be prescribed in advance, but must depend upon individual circumstances. Where UNHCR is financing reintegration programmes, the duration of those endeavours, with their target of self-sufficiency, may be the appropriate time span. In other situations, e.g. where UNHCR is assisting refugees to return at their own request, and where no significant change has taken place in the country of origin, there may be no time limit to the responsibility to monitor, intervene, and report.

Some preliminary conclusions

Repatriation will always be a sensitive issue, particularly when considered in the context of promotion by an outside body, rather

[59] See statement by President Vinicio Cerezo Arevalo of Guatemala, on the occasion of the visit of Mexican President De la Madrid, reiterating his government's decision to organize the reintegration of refugees into Guatemalan society 'under the permanent vigilance of the UN High Commissioner for Refugees in order to ensure respect for their fundamental rights', *La Jornada* (Mexico) (9 Apr. 1987).

[60] Resort to regional human rights machinery also may be appropriate.

than as an individual decision taken independently of outside pressures. There will always be scope for assistance to particular cases, even though experience here sometimes goes contrary to expectations: voluntary repatriation to Chile, for example, continues steadily, notwithstanding the absence of any fundamental change of regime.

The one self-evident fact seems to be that no two refugees and no two refugee situations will ever be the same. General categories are available, such as flight from war or civil strife, or from varying degrees of racial or religious persecution, but these will not necessarily permit ready conclusions regarding the viability of repatriation.

Promotion and facilitation retain their potential, provided certain fundamental objectives and guidelines are adopted. The following tentative and non-exhaustive suggestions, directed largely towards the resolution of large-scale refugee problems, take their cue from Executive Committee considerations and from practical experience. They are also based on the belief that there is an important qualitative distinction between promoting the necessary political will in the inter-state context, and determining the individual will of refugees.

(a) Objectives

The principle objective in the promotion of voluntary repatriation is the *interest of the refugee*. This implies the continuing exercise of protection to secure the rights, the security, and the welfare of refugees. It entails recognition of the refugee's right to return to the country of his or her origin, and to the restoration of the severed link between citizen and state. It also entails recognition of the acquired rights of refugees, which may prevail even where the status of refugee has come to an end. Recognition of the interest of the refugee also requires respect for the essentially voluntary character of repatriation; coercion or compulsion in the context of return are therefore unacceptable.

(b) Guidelines

Information regarding both the advisability and the feasibility of return are critical elements in the decision-making process, both for organizations such as UNHCR or prospective implementing agencies, and for refugees themselves. The best available information regarding conditions in the country of origin must therefore be obtained. This should include an analysis of the causes which gave rise to the refugee flow, and of their modification over time in the light of policy changes and the emergence of stability. An assessment of security considerations should be made, taking account of amnesties and other guarantees in context. Practical methods, analogous to those which govern fact-finding in the human rights field, must be developed to evaluate changes in circumstance.

Experience shows that multi-party commissions can contribute to securing and maintaining the necessary level of agreement and commitment among states. Their existence and performance, subject to the scrutiny of the international community, can thus prove important elements in the resolution of differences by peaceful means, in the reaffirmation of the principle of non-intervention, and in the promotion of co-operation and the fulfilment of obligations. They also have a very practical function in planning (including the modalities of transport, feeding, assistance, and rehabilitation), implementation, and monitoring. Again, it will be necessary to ensure that such commissions are kept fully informed; formal representation by the refugees themselves could also offer distinct advantages.[61]

Beyond the commitment of states and the planning stage, practical methods must be developed to evaluate and confirm the voluntary character of the decision to repatriate. The free exercise of will is essential to the termination of refugee status; it is equally relevant in the less clearly defined situation of change of circumstances, where a commitment is required of those who will return, involving the loss or abandonment of valued refugee status. In individual cases, where no inducement, promise, or reward, let alone duress, is involved, the simple signature of a voluntary repatriation form will usually suffice; however, even in cases such as these, counselling may still be called for.

In large-scale situations, the individual approach may be impractical or even inappropriate, particularly where community decision-making structures are centred elsewhere than on the

[61] Cf. the caution expressed by the Netherlands, at the 37th Session of the Executive Committee (1986), against too much haste, 'for instance by entering into tripartite repatriation arrangements with the Governments concerned without due consultation with the refugees themselves', UN doc. A/AC.96/ SR.407, para. 67.

individual. In principle there is no reason why voluntary repatriation should not be decided by chiefs or elders; the problem is to ensure that they are indeed representative and that the decision-making is fully informed and free from coercion. Often only a fine line divides encouragement from duress, particularly where rehabilitation programmes in the country of origin are contrasted with what is available in the country of refuge. Pressure and inducement are not unknown; but these are functional problems that it is possible to avoid in the design and implementation of programmes which maintain the interest of the refugee in a durable solution as the ultimate objective.

Closely related to the principle of safeguarding the interests of refugees, and often essential to the success of repatriation as a solution, stands the need to develop practical and effective methods of monitoring the security of those returning. This includes not only overseeing the application of amnesty laws and other formal guarantees, but also contributing to successful reintegration into the national community. There may thus be developmental aspects to this activity, extending beyond the fate of returnees, to the receiving society at large. At another level, practical measures will often be required to train administrators and to open up channels of communication and redress. Regional political and human rights mechanisms may here make an effective contribution, and thereby assist UNHCR to maintain its humanitarian and non-political mandate, while actively ensuring the protection of fundamental human rights.

ANNEX I

1969 OAU Convention on Refugee Problems in Africa

Article V
Voluntary Repatriation

1. The essentially voluntary character of repatriation shall be respected in all cases and no refugee shall be repatriated against his will.

2. The country of asylum, in collaboration with the country of origin, shall make adequate arrangements for the safe return of refugees who request repatriation.

3. The country of origin, on receiving back refugees, shall facilitate their resettlement and grant them the full rights and privileges of nationals of the country, and subject them to the same obligations.

4. Refugees who voluntarily return to their country shall in no way be penalized for having left for any of the reasons giving rise to refugee situations. Whenever necessary, an appeal shall be made through national information media and through the Administrative Secretary General of the OAU, inviting refugees to return home and giving assurance that the new circumstances prevailing in their country of origin will enable them to return without risk and to take up a normal and peaceful life without fear of being disturbed or punished, and that the text of such appeal should be given to refugees and clearly explained to them by their country of asylum.

5. Refugees who freely decide to return to their homeland, as a result of such assurances or on their own initiative, shall be given every possible assistance by the country of asylum, the country of origin, voluntary agencies and international and intergovernmental organisations, to facilitate their return.

ANNEX II

1980 (Executive Committee—31st Session)
No. 18 (XXXI) VOLUNTARY REPATRIATION*

The Executive Committee,

(a) *Recognized* that voluntary repatriation constitutes generally, and in

*Conclusion endorsed by the Executive Committee of the High Commissioner's programme upon the recommendation of the Sub-committee of the Whole on International Protection of Refugees.

particular when a country accedes to indepdence, the most appropriate solution for refugee problems;

(b) *Stressed* that the essentially voluntary character of repatriation should always be respected;

(c) *Recognized* the desirability of appropriate arrangements to establish the voluntary character of repatriation, both as regards the repatriation of individual refugees and in the case of large-scale repatriation movements, and for UNHCR, whenever necessary, to be associated with such arrangements;

(d) *Considered* that when refugees express the wish to repatriate, both the government of their country of origin and the government of their country of asylum should, within the framework of their national legislation and, whenever necessary, in co-operation with UNHCR take all requisite steps to assist them to do so;

(e) *Recognized* the importance of refugees being provided with the necessary information regarding conditions in their country of origin in order to facilitate their decision to repatriate: recognized further that visits by individual refugees or refugee representatives to their country of origin to inform themselves of the situation there—without such visits automatically involving loss of refugee status—could also be of assistance in this regard;

(f) *Called* upon governments of countries of origin to provide formal guarantees for the safety of returning refugees and stressed the importance of such guarantees being fully respected and of returning refugees not being penalized for having left their country of origin for reasons giving rise to refugee situations;

(g) *Recommended* that arrangements be adopted in countries of asylum for ensuring that the terms of guarantees provided by countries of origin and relevant information regarding conditions prevailing there are duly communicated to refugees, that such arrangements could be facilitated by the authorities of countries of asylum and that UNHCR should as appropriate be associated with such arrangements;

(h) *Considered* that UNHCR could appropriately be called upon—with the agreement of the parties concerned—to monitor the situation of returning refugees with particular regard to any guarantees provided by the governments of the countries of origin;

(i) *Called* upon the governments concerned to provide repatriating refugees with the necessary travel documents, visas, entry permits and transportation facilities and, if refugees have lost their nationality, to arrange for such nationality to be restored in accordance with national legislation;

(j) *Recognized* that it may be necessary in certain situations to make appropriate arrangements in co-operation with UNHCR for the reception of returning refugees and/or to establish projects for their reintegration in their country of origin.

ANNEX III

1985 (Executive Committee—36th Session)

No. 40 (XXXVI) VOLUNTARY REPATRIATION*

The Executive Committee,

Reaffirming the significance of its 1980 conclusion on voluntary repatriation as reflecting basic principles of international law and practice, adopted the following further conclusions on this matter:

(a) The basic rights of persons to return voluntarily to the country of origin is reaffirmed and it is urged that international co-operation be aimed at achieving this solution and should be further developed;

(b) The repatriation of refugees should only take place at their freely expressed wish; the voluntary and individual character of repatriation of refugees and the need for it to be carried out under conditions of absolute safety, preferably to the place of residence of the refugee in his country of origin, should always be respected;

(c) The aspect of causes is critical to the issue of solution and international efforts should also be directed to the removal of the causes of refugee movements. Further attention should be given to the causes and prevention of such movements, including the co-ordination of efforts currently being pursued by the international community and in particular within the United Nations. An essential condition for the prevention of refugee flows is sufficient political will by the States directly concerned to address the causes which are at the origin of refugee movements;

(d) The responsibilities of States towards their nationals and the obligations of other States to promote voluntary repatriation must be upheld by the international community. International action in favour of voluntary repatriation, whether at the universal or regional level, should receive the full support and co-operation of all States directly concerned. Promotion of voluntary repatriation as a solution to refugee problems similarly requires the political will of States directly concerned to create conditions conducive to this solution. This is the primary responsibility of States;

(e) The existing mandate of the High Commissioner is sufficient to allow him to promote voluntary repatriation by taking initiatives to this

*Conclusion endorsed by the Executive Committee of the High Commissioner's programme upon the recommendation of the Sub-committee of the Whole on International Protection of Refugees.

end, promoting dialogue between all the main parties, facilitating communication between them, and by acting as an intermediary or channel of communication. It is important that he establishes, whenever possible, contact with all the main parties and acquaints himself with their points of view. From the outset of a refugee situation, the High Commissioner should at all times keep the possibility of voluntary repatriation for all or for part of a group under active review and the High Commissioner, whenever he deems that the prevailing circumstances are appropriate, should actively pursue the promotion of this solution;

(f) The humanitarian concerns of the High Commissioner should be recognized and respected by all parties and he should receive full support in his efforts to carry out his humanitarian mandate in providing international protection to refugees and in seeking a solution to refugee problems;

(g) On all occasions the High Commissioner should be fully involved from the outset in assessing the feasibility and, thereafter, in both the planning and implementation stages of repatriation;

(h) The importance of spontaneous return to the country of origin is recognized and it is considered that action to promote organized voluntary repatriation should not create obstacles to the spontaneous return of refugees. Interested States should make all efforts, including the provision of assistance, in the country of origin, to encourage this movement whenever it is deemed to be in the interests of the refugees concerned;

(i) When, in the opinion of the High Commissioner, a serious problem exists in the promotion of voluntary repatriation of a particular refugee group, he may consider for that particular problem the establishment of an informal *ad hoc* consultative group which would be appointed by him in consultation with the Chairman and the other members of the Bureau of his Executive Committee. Such a group may, if necessary, include States which are not members of the Executive Committee and should in principle include the countries directly concerned. The High Commissioner may also consider invoking the assistance of other competent United Nations organs;

(j) The practice of establishing tripartite commissions is well adapted to facilitate voluntary repatriation. The tripartite commission, which should consist of the countries of origin and of asylum and UNHCR, could concern itself with both the joint planning and the implementation of a repatriation programme. It is also an effective means of securing consultations between the main parties concerned on any problems that might subsequently arise;

(k) International action to promote voluntary repatriation requires consideration of the situation within the country of origin as well as within the receiving country. Assistance for the reintegration of returnees provided by the international community in the country of origin is recognized as an important factor in promoting repatriation. To this end, UNHCR and other United Nations agencies as appropriate, should have funds readily available to assist returnees in the various stages of their integration and rehabilitation in their country of origin;

(l) The High Commissioner should be recognized as having a legitimate concern for the consequences of return, particularly where such return has been brought about as a result of an amnesty or other form of guarantee. The High Commissioner must be regarded as entitled to insist on his legitimate concern over the outcome of any return that he has assisted. Within the framework of close consultations with the State concerned, he should be given direct and unhindered access to returnees so that he is in a position to monitor fulfilment of the amnesties, guarantees or assurances on the basis of which the refugees have returned. This should be considered as inherent in his mandate;

(m) Consideration should be given to the further elaboration of an instrument reflecting all existing principles and guidelines relating to voluntary repatriation for acceptance by the international community as a whole.

13. Prospects for and Promotion of Spontaneous Repatriation

FRED CUNY AND BARRY STEIN

IN the literature on voluntary repatriation the assertion that voluntary repatriation is the 'most desirable' durable solution[1] is often closely followed by pessimistic evaluations of its prospects.

Sir John Hope Simpson, writing in early 1939 about the political, religious, and racial refugees of that time, noted:

> Deliberate repatriation on a large scale is scarcely relevant in a discussion of practical instruments of solution. In predictable circumstances voluntary return of refugees to their home countries will occur on so small a scale as to not affect the refugee problem itself. The possibility of ultimate repatriation belongs to the realm of political prophecy and aspiration, and a programme of action cannot be based on speculation.[2]

More recently the United Nations High Commissioner for Refugees (UNHCR), in his 1985 'Durable Solutions' report, noted that:

> In the last analysis, voluntary repatriation remains—despite many successes—the most difficult of durable solutions to achieve. . . . Even in the best of circumstances, only a proportion may repatriate, and instances such as the return of virtually an entire refugee population from Bangladesh to Burma in the late 1970s or from neighbouring countries to Zimbabwe in the early 1980s are *more often the exception than the rule*.[3]

[1] A durable solution involves the integration of the refugees into a society either by settlement in their land of asylum, resettlement in a third country, or reintegration in their homeland by means of repatriation.

[2] Sir John Hope Simpson, *The Refugee Problem: Report of a Survey* (London: Oxford University Press, 1939).

[3] UNHCR, *Note on International Protection*, Executive Committee, Thirty-sixth Session (A/AC.96/660), July 1985. Emphasis added.

Simpson, in his time, and UNHCR and others today,[4] reflect common misconceptions about voluntary repatriation. Substantial voluntary repatriation frequently occurs but is not clearly perceived. Part of the reason for this is the millions of unrepatriated refugees who are highly visible but who represent a minority of all those who have been refugees. Also, one's conception of the problem depends on the types of refugee movements one is examining. Simpson's pessimistic assessment of repatriation as a solution was basically right when applied to the racial and religious refugees of the inter-war period—Turkish Christians, German Jews—but not to other categories of refugees at other times. As Coles has noted:

> If, however, a broad interpretation is given to embrace all forms of displacement, particularly those as a consequence of armed conflict, serious internal disturbance, or famine or drought, this view is the reverse of the truth. In regard to displacement generally, *return is, on the whole, the rule rather than the exception.*[5]

Although voluntary repatriation is more common than is generally realized, it is by no means easy to achieve. The changing nature of refugee problems brings peaks and valleys in the refugees' prospects for return. For a while during the 1960s and early 1970s many refugees were able to repatriate after the successful conclusion of their struggle for independence and liberation from colonial rule. In recent years the rise of refugee-producing conflicts—nation-building, revolutionary change, and conflicts with neighbours—involving the newly independent states has caused 'the massive arrivals of refugees in low-income countries where often no durable solutions are at hand'.[6] To return refugees to their newly independent homelands, particularly without any change in the regime or in the conditions that caused their flight, will require some new thinking about voluntary repatriation and the ways of promoting it. In this chapter we will examine the contemporary challenge of voluntary repatriation together with some aspects of spontaneous repatriation.

[4] Barry N. Stein, 'Durable Solutions for Developing Country Refugees', *International Migration Review*, 20/2 (summer 1986).

[5] G. J. L. Coles, 'Voluntary Repatriation: Recent Developments', *Yearbook 1985* (San Remo: International Institute of Humanitarian Law, 1985). Emphasis added.

[6] Poul Hartling, 'Opening Statement' to Meeting of Experts on Refugee Aid and Development, Mont Pèlerin, Switzerland, 29 Aug. 1983.

Spontaneous voluntary repatriation

A prominent feature of today's refugee problems is that there are not necessarily more refugees; rather, there are more without solutions, or awaiting solutions. Certain unfortunate refugee groups for whom no durable solution is ever found become a semi-permanent feature of the overall refugee problem. There are still Palestinian refugees from the 1940s; Eritrean and Rwandese refugees from the 1960s; Indo-Chinese, Saharawi, Burundian, Afghan, and Ogaden Somalis from the 1970s. Today three-quarters of the world's ten million or so refugees derive from conflicts that are at least five years old.

> Half a decade ago, the High Commissioner informed the Executive Committee of the presence in the world of some ten million refugees in need of international protection. The overwhelming majority of the refugee situations which had arisen at that time remain because effective durable solutions have so far not been found.
>
> In some refugee situations, flows have now lasted for over a decade.[7]

Although many refugee situations may endure on the political landscape and etch themselves on our consciousness, we should not conclude that progress is impossible. 'The first half of the present decade has continued to see similar movements of return to Argentina, Chad, Ethiopia, The Lao People's Democratic Republic, Uganda, Uruguay, Zaire, Zimbabwe, and elsewhere, in all of which UNHCR has been intimately involved.'[8] However, these successes illustrate some of the contemporary difficulties with voluntary repatriation. In many cases where UNHCR has been intimately involved, only a small proportion of the refugees returned home—e.g. 2,898 Laotian returnees from an estimated total of 89,000 refugees as of mid-1986—and in only a few cases—Chad from the Central African Republic, Uganda from Rwanda and Zaire, and Zimbabwe from neighbouring countries—was the return relatively complete.[9]

[7] UNHCR, *Note on International Protection*, Executive Committee, Thirty-seventh Session (A/AC.96/680), July 1986.

[8] UNHCR, *UNHCR Activities Financed by Voluntary Funds: Report for 1985–86 and Proposed Programmes and Budget for 1987*, pt. i, 'Review of Developments in UNHCR Activities Relating to Assistance, Durable Solutions and Refugee Aid and Development, and Summary of Decisions Required', Executive Committee, Thirty-seventh Session (A/AC.96/677 (pt. i)), 1986. Hereafter cited as UNHCR, *UNHCR Activities*, 1986.

[9] The Chadian (25,000) return and the Ugandan (84,000) return from Rwanda were spontaneous.

Most voluntary repatriation today occurs without, and despite, UNHCR involvement. Each year tens or hundreds of thousands of refugees decide to repatriate spontaneously, without the assistance of international organizations, and outside the framework of protection afforded by international agreements and protective accords. Spontaneous repatriation frequently occurs without any amnesty being promised; without a change of regime or any other decisive event; without a repatriation agreement or programme; without the permission of the authorities in the country of asylum or origin; without international knowledge; without an end to the conflict that caused the exodus. It is based on the decision of countless individual refugees to return home, even in the face of continuing, albeit lesser, risk. It also is influenced by the conditions under which the refugees live in their country of refuge. There are many examples of spontaneous voluntary repatriation:

> Some 400,000 Ethiopian refugees may have returned to Ethiopia from Somalia and Djibouti from 1984 to 1986. Ethiopia in early 1986. . . . some 75,000 Ugandan refugees fled southern Sudan . . . to return with surprising ease to Uganda and to begin the process of reintegration.
>
> When word came that the Obote government had been overthrown in July 1985, the Uganda [Banyarwandan] refugees were jubilant, almost 29,000 refugees returned to Uganda [from Rwanda].[10]

A recent report on voluntary repatriation[11] noted that the vast majority of all repatriation occurs without aid from the international organizations. In some cases where spontaneous and organized repatriation occur simultaneously, the spontaneous flow may be a hundred to two hundred times greater than a UNHCR assisted return.[12] This disparity suggests that a combination of current conditions and UNHCR operating principles is presenting difficulties in giving full assistance to repatriating refugees. Indeed, in some circumstances, such as the return of Tigrayans from Sudan in 1985, UNHCR has been more of a hindrance than a help to repatriation.

To illustrate some of the contemporary problems of repatriation,

[10] US Department of State, *World Refugee Report*, A Report Submitted to the Congress as Part of the Consultations on FY 1987 Refugee Admissions to the United States (Washington, DC: Bureau for Refugee Programs, 1986).

[11] G. J. L. Coles, *Voluntary Repatriation: A Background Study*, for Round Table on Voluntary Repatriation, San Remo, International Institute of Humanitarian Law (Geneva: UNHCR, July 1985).

[12] UNHCR, *UNHCR Activities*, 1986.

it is useful to look at the contrast between an ideal voluntary repatriation and some examples of current repatriation situations.

In ideal circumstances, voluntary repatriation will follow a basic change in the conditions that caused flight, the feared regime will be gone, and the refugees will be welcomed home. Zimbabwe in 1980 comes close to an ideal organized repatriation scenario. As a result of the 1979 Lancaster House agreement the refugees were returning in victory to their liberated homeland. The UNHCR was requested to undertake the overall co-ordination of the international effort to assist the repatriation. The operational arrangements for the refugees in Botswana and Zambia were made through the Lutheran World Federation and, in Mozambique, by government authorities. In several phases, both before and after Zimbabwe's independence, 51,000 refugees returned home through the organized programme, while a larger number, approximately 150,000, returned on their own, but within the framework of the programme.

Over the years UNHCR has established three pre-conditions for its participation in an organized repatriation:

> First and foremost, it must be voluntary. . . . Secondly, there must be clear and unequivocal agreement between the host country and the country of origin both on the modalities of the movement and the conditions of reception; thirdly, it is vitally important that returnees be allowed to return to their places of origin—ideally to their own former homes, their villages, their land.[13]

The UNHCR's overriding concern is the physical safety and socio-economic reintegration of the returnees. It rightly insists on these formal procedures in order to fulfil its protection mandate. However, as the following sketches of recent and current repatriations illustrate, the reality of a situation may mean that these formalities relegate UNHCR to the sidelines.

Five repatriations

Many contemporary repatriations are far from ideal; they are messy and ambiguous, do not fulfil all if any of UNHCR's pre-conditions, and raise serious questions of coercion and protection. The following five refugee situations, which were critical in mid-1987—

[13] UNHCR, *Durable Solutions*, Executive Committee, Thirth-sixth Session (A/AC.96/663), July 1985.

Ethiopia, Cambodia, Mozambique, Uganda, and El Salvador—indicate that efforts to promote or assist voluntary repatriation take place in a context of reluctant, hostile, or unsettled hosts; low-intensity protracted conflicts; repatriation regions controlled by insurgents or by uncertain legal regimes; and pressures on refugees to choose from among unsatisfactory options. New thinking about promoting and assisting repatriation needs to confront the realities that these examples represent.

Tigray

As a result of separate liberation movements in Eritrea and Tigray provinces there have been Ethiopian refugees in Sudan since the 1960s. In 1984 several hundred thousand additional refugees from the war-torn northern provinces poured into Sudan fleeing drought and famine in Ethiopia.

In 1985 after the return of the rains in their home province, some 54,000 Tigrayan refugees left eastern Sudan and returned to Tigray province in Ethiopia, at the height of the drought and famine and during a period of increased military activity. The return was aided by the Relief Society of Tigray (REST) and was 'covered' by the Tigray People's Liberation Front (TPLF). Despite widespread fears that many would die *en route*, either from starvation or bombing, it appears that most arrived home in good health and have done well since their return. Indeed, in 1986 even larger numbers returned, and the spontaneous repatriation continues in 1987. The three phases of return are likely to total almost 200,000 refugees. The UNHCR did not assist the 1985 repatriation; in fact both UNHCR and the United States actively opposed the return. 'In Sudan, far from promoting repatriation, UNHCR and other agencies have found it impossible to dissuade infirm and elderly refugees from setting out on the arduous trek back into Ethiopia!'[14] Only limited assistance was made available, principally by the government of Sudan. Limited international assistance has been given to later returnees.

Cambodia

In 1979, after the Vietnamese invasion overthrew the Khmer Rouge regime, approximately 170,000 Khmer refugees found

[14] Jeff Crisp, 'Refugee Repatriation: New Pressures and Problems', *Migration World*, 14/5 (1987).

safety in camps in Thailand. An additional 250,000 Khmer refugees have been confined to camps on the border since 1979. Thailand has long insisted that all Khmer refugees in Thailand must be resettled in third countries. To demonstrate its resolve regarding resettlement, in June 1979 Thailand forcibly repatriated 44,000 Khmer refugees—with great loss of life. This action led to an international commitment to resettle the refugees. By early 1987 only 20,000 of the original 170,000 Khmer refugees remained in Thai camps. Most of these refugees had already been rejected by the different resettlement countries.

In March 1987 Thailand threatened to force these 20,000 Cambodian refugees to move from the Khao-I-Dang camp to the Thai–Cambodian border camps. Less than one thousand refugees were forced back to the border camps, but the threat remains. These border camps are subjected to attacks from Cambodia and are under the control of various Khmer guerrilla armies, including the Khmer Rouge. The relocated refugees, and the 250,000 other Khmer refugees who have been confined to the border since 1979, are vulnerable to abuse by both the liberation movements and Thai 'protecting' forces. Although UNHCR continues to play a protection role regarding those moved from Khao-I-Dang, it does not have a permanent presence in the border camps.

Mozambique

Mozambique's internal peace has been shattered by the guerrilla activities of the Mozambican National Resistance (RENAMO), which was established in 1977 with the aid of Rhodesia's White minority government, and is currently aided by South Africa. Approximately four million Mozambicans have been internally displaced and, since 1984, 300,000 have fled to South Africa, Swaziland, Zimbabwe, Zambia, and Malawi. The government of Mozambique is trying to arrange for the return of 95,000 of its citizens 'externally displaced' in Malawi in 1986. (Mozambique has 'repeatedly accused Malawi of providing a haven for Mozambican insurgents'.[15]) These refugees have not fled from any action on the part of their government but from a famine caused by civil conflict. Mozambique, when approaching UNHCR for assistance,

[15] Tom Brennan, *Refugees From Mozambique: Shattered Land, Fragile Asylum*, US Committee for Refugees Issue Paper (New York: American Council for Nationalities Service, 1986).

made it clear that it prefers Mozambicans to be displaced in Mozambique than in Malawi and therefore be assisted in their home country (as returnees) than in Malawi (as refugees). . . . The government's strategy is to facilitate the return of refugees [to areas] . . . which may *not be their original homesteads* but are safer as regards security . . . all efforts will be made to guarantee that maximum security prevail in these [returnee] areas. (italics my own)[16]

However, by mid-1987, rather than returning home, the exodus from Mozambique continued and the number of Mozambican refugees in Malawi had increased to 200,000.

Uganda

The initial flow of Ugandan refugees into Sudan began after the fall of Idi Amin in 1979. During 1982 the number of Amin supporters and other refugees in southern Sudan grew to more than 350,000 as civilians fled from abuses and reprisals by the forces of the Uganda National Liberation Army (UNLA). In 1984 and 1985 approximately 100,000 refugees spontaneously repatriated to Uganda. In January 1986 the UNLA forces were defeated by Museveni's National Resistance Army and the prospects for further refugee repatriation improved.

In 1986 there were approximately 250,000 Ugandan refugees in southern Sudan. Although many of the refugees were considering returning home because of 'one of the few periods of genuine peace and security in Uganda in the last decade',[17] their return was hastened by the growing civil war in their host country that had led to a breakdown of authority. In April 1986 after 'armed attacks on Ugandan refugee settlements on the East Bank of the Nile',[18] over 100,000 Ugandan refugees fled southern Sudan and returned to Uganda. The UNHCR and other agencies assisted the returnees with transport and reception facilities. Overall, in recent years the repatriation to Uganda has been a successful one. Fortunately, the timing allowed them a somewhat safer return to their homeland. However, Uganda is still troubled by economic difficulties and political turmoil. One mission noted that 'The relief programme for

[16] UNHCR, 'Mission to Mozambique (12 to 22 Jan. 1987)', first draft, Technical Support Services, TSS Mission Report 87/02, 1987.

[17] US Department of State, *World Refugee Report*.

[18] Ibid.

returnees has not been a success. . . . The [UNHCR] office was crippled by lack of transport and communication.'

El Salvador

Since the early 1980s about 20,000 refugees from the Salvadorean civil war have taken refuge in Honduras. Recently some of the refugees have been returning, both spontaneously and with UNHCR assistance.[19] The Salvadoreans live in closed camps in Honduras and are viewed with hostility. There are 'officially-sponsored campaigns of vilification depicting the Salvadorean refugees and the voluntary agencies which help them as threats to Honduran national security. . . . Violent crimes against the refugees have been committed with apparent impunity.'[20] In 1985 the Salvadorean camp at Colomoncagua was attacked by the Honduran Army and several refugees were killed, wounded, or seized. Not surprisingly, 'a sizeable number of Salvadorean refugees in Honduras have now realized that they cannot reasonably hope for local integration', and that 'repatriation is their only hope of one day returning to a normal way of life'.[21]

After a December 1986 visit by J. P. Hocké, the United Nations High Commissioner for Refugees, approximately 4,500 Salvadorean refugees at the Mesa Grande camp indicated their willingness to return to their homes in El Salvador.

> Another element in El Salvador which is of critical importance to the refugees in Honduras is the process of 'repopulation' which is now going on. . . . After a number of years and even though the war continues in several parts of the country, groups of displaced persons have begun to return to their home communities. . . . many groups of refugees are risking the uncertainty by returning to their home communities.
>
> It is in this context—growing weariness of life in the camps and increasing awareness of the re-population movement in El Salvador—that 4,500 refugees in Mesa Grande submitted a letter to UNHCR and the Honduran and Salvadorean Catholic Churches, outlining their minimum demands for repatriation.[22]

[19] 'Salvadorean Refugees are Taking Their Hearts and Minds Home', *Washington Post* (11 Aug. 1986).

[20] Gil Loescher, 'Humanitarianism and Politics in Central America', *Political Science Quarterly*, 103 (summer 1988).

[21] 'Voluntary Repatriation: What are the Prospects?' *Refugees* (Mar. 1987).

[22] Elizabeth Ferris, 'Voluntary Repatriation: Central America', *Refugees*, 88E (Sept. 1987).

As of mid-1987, however, because of the reluctance on the part of the armed forces in El Salvador to permit a mass return to the refugees' area of origin, only individual repatriations were being arranged by UNHCR. The frustrated refugees at Mesa Grande 'have unilaterally declared that they intend to return to their home areas . . . with or without the cooperation of the Honduran or Salvadorean government',[23] or of UNHCR.

As these sketches indicate, UNHCR's three pre-conditions for participating in an organized repatriation—voluntary return, agreement between the host country and the country of origin, and return to their area of origin in their homeland—are not easily met. In three of these refugee situations, pressures in the countries of asylum—Thailand, Honduras, and Sudan (for the Ugandans)—impelled the refugees to leave and made their return less than wholly voluntary. Indeed, the return of the Khmer refugees to the border was forced by Thailand, and only good timing made the flight from Sudan back to Uganda relatively safe.

Agreement between the host and the country of origin is only likely in the return from Malawi to Mozambique. Indeed, in several of the returns—to Cambodia, Tigray, and El Salvador—the refugees are settling in areas not wholly controlled by the central governments of their homelands. The UNHCR prefers to operate within the framework of a tripartite agreement between itself and the host and home countries, but, in an era of low-intensity conflicts, returns often take place in disputed regions. As part of the United Nations system, UNHCR has to deal through sovereign governments, and is at a disadvantage in the many situations involving liberation fronts and governments which are not represented in the UN. These so-called non-recognized entities play an important role in spontaneous repatriations. Insurgents may control large areas; some even maintain effective civil administrations in their areas. It can be relatively safe for refugees to return to their homes in such areas, and given some assistance many might go home, especially if they see few other options to ending their refugee status.

Oddly, as is made clear in these five sketches, return to the refugees' place of origin is more likely in those situations where governments and UNHCR are not involved. The proposed return

[23] *The Mustard Seed*, newsletter of the Jesuit Refugee Service (Washington, DC, 22 July 1987).

to Mozambique is specifically not to their original homes, and the Cambodian return was to the border areas. In Tigray, El Salvador, and Uganda the refugees were able to go back to their homes.

Failure to satisfy UNHCR's three pre-conditions for return is not necessarily a sign of a flawed return. In the five returns outlined above, only Thailand's forced return of the Cambodians to the border zone appears not to have been in the refugees' best interests. Ironically this forced repatriation has the greatest governmental and international agency involvement. Although the other returns are less than ideal, they do achieve the 'most desirable' goal, of getting the refugees back home.

The nature of contemporary refugee problems

The UNHCR's 1985 *Note on International Protection* indicates that 'the majority of today's refugees are persons who do not fall within the "classic" refugee definition in the UNHCR Statute'. Rather, they are 'persons who have fled their home country due to armed conflicts, internal turmoil, and situations involving gross and systematic violations of human rights'.

'Classic' refugees are caused by government action, and a strong political element is inherent in their situation. Refugees flee because of some controversy between themselves and their government. Because the basic bond between citizen and government has been broken, 'fear has taken the place of trust, and hatred the place of loyalty'.[24] The situations that cause refugees are not trifling ones, and refugees cannot easily pack up and go home until substantial changes occur, or until there is a change in the regime that originally caused them to flee. A continuing controversy over politics, race, or religion may mean that prospects for the refugees' return will remain poor for a considerable length of time.

But today most refugees are externally displaced persons rather than 'classic' refugees. They are not necessarily fleeing a conflict that involves them personally. Often they are simply getting out of harm's way rather than fleeing from persecution. Many who flee a country suffering from a protracted, low-intensity conflict may be fleeing from a proximate cause rather than the conflict itself. Years of conflict lead to adjustments and experience that provide some

[24] Atle Grahl-Madsen, *The Status of Refugees in International Law*, vol. i *Refugee Character* (Leyden: A. W. Sijthoff, 1966).

degree of safety for individual civilians. The final impetus towards a mass exodus is not generally the direct result of the ongoing conflict, but a change of situation which proves to be the last straw, such as a famine, drought, or other natural calamity, or an increase in fighting that gets too close for comfort. These displaced persons may not fear their government, or whoever normally controls their region; they may well be unafraid and willing to return home to an insecure area if the proximate cause has eased, even though the low-intensity conflict persists.

For example, the basic bond between citizen and government has apparently not been broken in the case of the refugees from Mozambique. They are fleeing the atrocities of RENAMO, whose raids have prevented them from farming and have caused famine in a fertile land. The Mozambican proposal[25] to return the refugees from Malawi to areas of Mozambique other than their original homes is thus not contingent on a change of regime or of fundamental conditions. The refugees may fear that the government cannot protect them adequately, but apparently they do not fear the government itself.

Organized and spontaneous repatriation

Both organized and spontaneous repatriation are desirable methods of achieving a durable solution. However, there is a major difference in the effort and resources that are devoted to the two methods, with almost all thought and effort being devoted to organized repatriation. Oddly, the results are strongly inversely related to the resources used; the large majority of refugees return by the spontaneous route.

Because it is a humanitarian, non-political agency, UNHCR takes a mostly passive stance with regard to promoting repatriation. Organized repatriations, with agreements made between the parties must normally await some decisive event. The UNHCR does not have the power to resolve the root cause of a refugee exodus. It does not arrange peace conferences or negotiations; these are the responsibilities of the Secretary-General and other political arms of the United Nations, or of bilateral efforts.

The UNHCR relies heavily on tripartite agreements—between country of origin, host country, and UNHCR—as a method of

[25] UNHCR, 'Mission to Mozambique'.

promoting voluntary repatriation. However, this government-to-government approach with UNHCR in the middle is ponderous, time-consuming, and produces poor results. Without denying the occasional success, such as Djibouti in 1983,[26] the overall record of tripartite commissions does not justify UNHCR's heavy reliance on host government and homeland government agreement as a pre-condition for repatriation. More typical of tripartite commissions is the Uganda–Rwanda–UNHCR commission from 1983 to 1985. It met, talked, processed, detailed, screened—and achieved little. When southern Uganda was liberated by Museveni's advancing forces, the commission temporized. Eventually 30,000 refugees returned spontaneously from Rwanda in late 1985, with little international assistance. The UNHCR's second pre-condition for organized movements—'agreement between the host country and the country of origin on the modalities of the movement and the conditions for reception'—is often irrelevant in contemporary refugee situations involving displaced persons. The time-lag between the onset of improved conditions and the implementation of agreements can be frustrating to refugees.

The difference in scale between parallel spontaneous and organized repatriations can be striking. In many situations UNHCR arranges for the return of dozens or hundreds of refugees while tens of thousands return on their own initiative.

> Spontaneous voluntary repatriation from the Sudan continued on a much larger scale than organized movements. While the repatriation of some 518 Ethiopians was organized in 1985—almost twice as many as in 1984—more than 55,000 Tigrayans returned spontaneously . . . During the same period of 1986 another 65,000 returned to Ethiopia in the same manner.[27]

The difference in scale of more than 100 to 1 between spontaneous and organized repatriations suggests that the refugees and UNHCR hold different standards of safety and perceptions of timing with regard to repatriation.

Voluntary repatriation is a problematical business: people are returning to a place where they once feared or suffered persecution. Not surprisingly, judging from the reactions of voluntary agencies

[26] Some observers feel that the organized repatriation from Djibouti was a forced, or at least a compelled, repatriation. See below, n. 31.

[27] UNHCR, *UNHCR Activities*, 1986.

active in the field, the greatest anxieties accompany organized voluntary repatriations when there has been no change of government in the homeland. Refugees fear that going home through official channels and being 'turned over' to their own government will put them in danger or mark them out as suspect. There is a danger that the country of origin will assume that the returnees have supported an anti-government movement. Additionally, many organized returns are suspect, as being at the convenience of or under pressure from the host government, which is more than happy to be rid of an unwanted burden and is less concerned about questions of protection.

Spontaneous voluntary repatriation may occur in response to certain host pressures or to displeasure at the refugees' continued presence, but in its essentials it represents the refugees' judgement of their predicament and their best interests, and gives the refugees some control over their own fate rather than relying on a tripartite commission or trusting their own government. It is worth noting that spontaneous repatriation restores the refugee's sense of his own effectiveness and importance, while organized repatriation excludes refugees from tripartite commissions and gives them little voice in the modalities and conditions of their return.

Indeed the powerlessness of the refugees when dealing with the international system is sometimes displayed when they choose to go home spontaneously. In 1985, when tens of thousands of Tigrayans decided to return to Ethiopia, attempts were made to block their return. These obstacles were well-intentioned, motivated by a belief that the risks were too great. But this raises a question about the international aid system's obligations to refugees who want to return spontaneously against the advice of the system. The vastly greater numbers of refugees favouring spontaneous return indicate that refugees make their decisions according to criteria other than those of concern to the international community. It is the refugees who must evaluate the risks and make the choice. From border camps they will often have better communications with home and can more effectively evaluate the safety of returning. Once they have evaluated the risk as a tolerable one, the international community has an obligation to assist their return. It is counter-productive and a denial of the 'right . . . to return to his country'[28] to

[28] Universal Declaration of Human Rights, Article 13 (2).

provide aid when they are to remain refugees but not give it when they want to go home.

Issues

Although everyone supports the idea of voluntary repatriation as the ideal and most desirable durable solution, there is little agreement on the means of achieving or promoting it. Coles notes that voluntary repatriation 'has so far not been examined in any depth by experts or scholars. . . . The absence of any adequate treatment of the general question of solution is a striking feature of the traditional approach to the refugee problem.'[29]

In attempting to promote new thinking about voluntary repatriation, the most fruitful avenue of exploration is likely to be spontaneous repatriation. These irregular returns raise major issues regarding the voluntary character of a repatriation, dealing with non-recognized entities, and matters of protection. Because these are issues that have been ignored rather than studied, what follows is more in the form of lines of inquiry than conclusions or recommendations.

Voluntary repatriation

Although many people think of voluntary repatriation as a purely 'voluntary' act reflecting the individual will of the refugee, in practice the decision to return is often initiated from outside—is brought about by outside persuasion, influence, and even pressure. Refugee status is not necessarily permanent; it is dependent on conditions in the homeland. The Cessation clause (Article I.C. (5)) provides that the Convention 'shall cease to apply' if the circumstances causing refugee status have ceased to exist and the refugee cannot refuse to avail himself of the protection of his country. But, as stated earlier, most of those called refugees are really displaced persons fleeing general conflict rather than individual persecution. They therefore do not fit the Convention refugee definition, although they do satisfy the more generous terms of the OAU Convention on refugees. Once conflict has

[29] Coles, *Voluntary Repatriation: A Background Study*. A bibliography—'Voluntary Repatriation for Refugees in Developing Countries: A Bibliographical Survey'—compiled by Jeff Crisp for the United Nations Research Institute for Social Development in early 1987 indicates that Coles's judgement is essentially correct.

subsided in the homeland, either temporarily or permanently, who—UNHCR, the host government, the refugees—decides that refugee status must cease?

Host countries have a definite interest in encouraging the return of refugees. However, non-political factors, such as poor economic conditions at home, may make refugees hesitant about returning. The 1986 overthrow of the Duvalier regime in Haiti opened the door for the potential return of one million exiles. But only a handful have gone back. 'Unwilling to face the uncertainty of a country whose economy remains mired in poverty and despair, most prefer to hang on to whatever opportunities they may have found abroad.'[30]

The 1978–9 return of 200,000 refugees from Bangladesh to Burma had some elements of compulsion; yet it is usually referred to as one of UNHCR's successful operations.

> At the outset of the repatriation there was evidence of marked opposition among the refugees to returning. . . . On the day that the repatriation officially began, only 58 refugees crossed the border. Two and a half months later only 5,300 had returned. . . . the number should have been 50,000. The reluctance to return stemmed from fear of what might await the refugees.
>
> By the end of 1979, however, some 187,000 had suddenly returned to Burma. The return movement seems to have been precipitated towards the end by conditions in the camps and by a curtailment of food rations,[31] designed to encourage an early decision in favour of return.[32]

There is clearly a gap between principle and practice that needs to be explored with regard to 'voluntary' repatriation. The principle as expressed by the 1985 UNHCR Executive Committee is that repatriation 'should only take place at their [the refugees'] freely expressed wish; the voluntary and individual character . . . and conditions of absolute safety . . . should always be respected'. The practice, however, is not to sit back and wait for the refugees to express a desire to go home. A somewhat less individual and less voluntary standard has been accepted and applauded. Evidence of

[30] Tala Skari, 'France: The Dilemma', *Refugees* (Mar. 1987).

[31] There were reports that the rations in the refugee camps in Bangladesh were insufficient and that many excess deaths resulted. See Cato Aall, 'Disastrous International Relief Failure: A Report on Burmese Refugees in Bangladesh from May to December 1978', *Disasters*, 3/4 (1979).

[32] Coles, *Voluntary Repatriation: A Background Study.*

pressure is commonplace, particularly when no other durable solution—settlement or resettlement—is possible. Duress, with its implied lack of free choice by the refugees, is clearly unacceptable, but it is not easy to determine the dividing line between acceptable and unacceptable pressure, encouragement, suggestion, persuasion, and inducement. Crisp, writing about the 1983 return of Ethiopians to Djibouti, notes:

> Even if they still had doubts about returning, the refugees were aware that their future in Djibouti was at best a limited one. After four years of intermittent intimidation, the refugees' morale was low, and the advantages of attempting to remain in Djibouti were difficult to perceive. . . . It seemed preferable to live in proverty and danger in their own country than to remain as unwelcome guests in a foreign country.[33]

Non-recognized entities

There are levels of non-recognized entity, from a government in full but disputed control of its territory but denied international recognition (and a seat in the UN, as in the case of Cambodia); to a guerrilla liberation movement on its way to victory and control—e.g. Museveni controlling southern Uganda, taking the capital, and controlling the north; to a guerrilla force engaged in a long-term struggle that may have control of a variable 'liberated' area, such as in Tigray or Eritrea.

The report of the 1985 meeting on Voluntary Repatriation at the International Institute of Humanitarian Law in San Remo, which was reported to the Executive Committee's Subcommittee of the Whole on International Protection, recommended 'the High Commissioner should not be unduly inhibited by the formal status of any particular entity. . . . he should be prepared, wherever necessary, to deal with non-recognized entities'.[34] This suggestion, however, was objected to in the Subcommittee's deliberations and was not included in the Executive Committee's Conclusions on International Protection.

The Executive Committee's reluctance to grant UNHCR authority to deal with non-recognized entities raises several

[33] J. Crisp, 'Voluntary Repatriation Programs for African Refugees: A Critical Examination', *Refugee Issues*, 1/2 (1985).

[34] UNHCR, *Voluntary Repatriation*, Executive Committee, Subcommittee of the Whole on International Protection, Thirty-sixth Session (EC/SCP/41), Aug. 1985.

questions about protection for those choosing repatriation. What protection can be offered to refugees returned to an area held by a liberation movement or even a *de facto* government? What control or sanctions are available if a non-recognized entity abuses refugees or recruits them for its military units? What protection is there if the opposing force captures the area?

It may well be politically impossible for an international organization such as UNHCR to deal with a non-recognized entity operating on the territory of a sovereign UN member state. One can imagine the Moroccan reaction to UNHCR negotiating with the Polisario Front[35] to return people to Western Sahara. It may, however, be feasible for the International Committee of the Red Cross (ICRC) to deal with non-recognized entities. Its governing instruments and mandate may be more flexible and relevant within the structure of a sovereign state than those of UNHCR. In addition, it is clearly possible for a host government to deal with a non-recognized entity, although whether this is desirable or not is another matter.

Return to heavily contested areas would probably be impossible. However, low-intensity conflict ebbs and flows and has an uneven impact on a wide area. In some cases, as in Tigray, Eritrea, Western Sahara, Namibia, etc., the non-recognized entity is a refugee-based organization. Apart from its political expression as a party, front, or movement, the refugee-based organization will have aid societies, education programmes, and other welfare-based agencies that can play an important role with returnees, as the TPLF and REST have been doing for the returnees in Tigray.

Protection

In suggesting an increased emphasis on spontaneous repatriation, the greatest problem is the issue of adequate protection for the refugees. In particular, in promoting spontaneous repatriation or in dealing with a non-recognized entity, what is the allowable level of risk? Certainly UNHCR must err on the side of caution and not risk the refugees' lives. Moreover, does any other organization have the right to take greater risks? Spontaneous repatriation where the refugees have full knowledge of conditions and risks might be one

[35] The Polisario Front governs the Sahrawi Arab Democratic Republic (SADR) which is recognized by over sixty-six countries and by the Organization of African Unity.

way out of this dilemma. However, it is crucial that spontaneous repatriations be carefully examined for elements of coercion or danger. It is conceivable that spontaneous returnees could be relying on false or self-serving information—perhaps from a liberation movement seeking the return of 'its people'—or be returning in haste without due consideration of the risks involved. Overall, the guiding principle should be respect for the wishes of the refugees, but the responsibility to protect them cannot thus be abdicated.

There are many other issues concerning voluntary repatriation, such as the impact of assistance and the triggers to return, which cannot be covered in this short chapter but which urgently need further study.

Conclusion

Voluntary repatriation is the durable solution least effectively promoted by the international community. Many disputes are too political to allow any humanitarian agency, such as UNHCR, to play a significant role. Often parties use refugees to score political points over a territorial or cold war rival who can thus be cast as a persecutor. Sometimes refugees are used in connection with guerrillas, to prevent a rival from consolidating a victory, as in Nicaragua, Kampuchea, and Afganistan.

Voluntary repatriation normally has to be promoted in a charged political atmosphere of distrust and conflicting interests. Historically, voluntary repatriation has not been easy to arrange, but it is certainly possible.

> While being a refugee should be a *temporary* state of affairs, there is a real danger of refugee situations and the problems of refugees becoming institutionalized and of people remaining refugees forever. The foremost challenge facing the international community today is to reverse this trend.[36]

One glimmer of hope in this situation is the fact that, against great odds, many refugees spontaneously repatriate. Spontaneous repatriation is occurring on a large scale, with little international

[36] UNHCR, *Note on International Protection*, Executive Committee, Thirty-seventh Session (A/AC.96/680), July 1986.

understanding or assistance. It needs to be promoted, assisted, and augmented, without violating the fundamental principles of voluntary and safe return that are present in most organized returns. There is an opportunity here to assist many refugees to find their own durable solutions.

14. Third Country Resettlement

ROBERT L. BACH

> 'England lay before us, not a place, or a people, but a promise and an expectation.'
>
> George Lamming, *The Pleasures of Exile*[1]

Introduction

IF durable solutions are evaluated according to the extent to which they protect human lives, then there is little doubt that resettlement in a third country, usually in the advanced industrialized world, is more valuable than any other option. Resettlement removes refugees from the scene of their greatest hardships and frequently provides the only alternative to their languishing in border camps. Yet, third country resettlement is considered by most international agencies and observers, if not by the refugees themselves, to be the least desirable solution. The further refugees are moved, the less likely they are ever to return home. And to return is the cherished goal.

These contradictory perceptions of safety and desirability reflect a fundamental problem in discussions of durable solutions. Expectations of resettlement and repatriation are full of idealized images of ultimate solutions to the refugees' problems. Repatriation is favoured because it somehow represents a denial of the entire refugee experience. International agencies, as do the refugees themselves, construct idyllic images of 'home', based on conditions that only existed prior to the crises that spawned the outflow. These images typically understate the hardships that once existed in the country of origin and, heightened by the sense of loss, inflate and embellish the security and prosperity of their earlier lives.

The author gratefully ackowledges the support of the Ford Foundation and the Sloan Foundation for research that contributed to this paper. The author, of course, bears sole responsibility for its content.

[1] George Lamming, *The Pleasures of Exile* (New York: Allison and Busby, 1984), 212.

Only recently have international agencies begun to appreciate the realities of repatriation. As observed by other contributors to this volume, international officials are beginning to recognize the need to monitor and assist refugees' integration into their former homelands long after repatriation. The reason is simply that the home that refugees return to is neither that which existed before exile nor that which memories have created. Their homes have changed irrevocably. In dramatic cases, as in war-torn El Salvador, many of the villages from which people have fled no longer exist. They have become battlefield monuments to guerrilla wars. In other instances, family and friends may be gone, and the economic realities may be radically changed. Even their homecoming may be less happy than expected. Experiences with returnees to Argentina, for instance, have demonstrated that even when established communities eagerly await the return of those who fled, refugees stand out as a privileged group, fortunate to have escaped the roughest periods of repression and persecution. Those who were left behind may resent the returnees, who will often encounter both discrimination and intolerance.

As a durable solution, therefore, repatriation involves more than return to a place and a people; it is a process of creating a new home and new conditions which fulfil promises and expectations of a secure and prosperous future. Third country resettlement poses the same problem. Just as simply returning home does not guarantee safety, harmony, and prosperity, resettlement does not provide a durable solution just because refugees have crossed a border into an advanced industrialized country. Recent experiences in the United States, Canada, and Western Europe reveal the complexities of third country resettlement and the hardships that belie claims and perceptions of economic security, cultural toleration, and even personal safety. Like millions of immigrants before them, contemporary refugees resettled in North America and Western Europe learn that the streets are not paved in gold, and that life there can be hard, alienating, and troublesome.

Of course problems faced in third countries may be materially different from those encountered at the borders of countries of first asylum. But regardless of place of settlement, the very nature of refugee situations makes all solutions partial, remedial, and temporary. Durable solutions do not rest on past or promised circumstances, but result from the international community's provision of new conditions, possibilites, and opportunities. Even in the advanced industrialized countries, to which until now international agencies have directed very little attention, refugees need the most important assistance that the international community can offer—protection of individual human rights.

Resettlement

Perhaps the most familiar historical experience of third country resettlement involved the redistribution of hundreds of thousands of European refugees and displaced persons around the globe following World War II. This effort has been matched more recently by the dispersal of refugees from Vietnam, Laos, and Cambodia. Since 1975 roughly two million South-east Asian refugees have left their countries of origin. The vast majority have been settled outside the region, with over 800,000 moving to the United States, over 150,000 each to Canada and Australia, and 100,000 to France. The international response to the boat people tragedy of 1978 and 1979 also included the Federal Republic of Germany, which accepted over 35,000, the United Kingdom, 20,000, Switzerland, 10,000, and Belgium, the Netherlands, Norway, Denmark, Italy, and Sweden, several thousand refugees each. Many of these countries did not have a tradition of accepting large numbers of refugees and even fewer had experiences of resettling refugees from South-east Asia. However, many accepted a share of the outflow that was far greater than indicated by absolute numbers. For instance, the United States has accepted the largest absolute number of refugees, but it ranks behind both Australia and Canada in terms of the ratio of the number of admissions to the size of its own population.

The South-east Asian refugee outflow is a model of third country resettlement because, in addition to humanitarian concern, two basic aims motivated the global effort. First, much of the resettlement occurred immediately after the end of the Vietnam War in 1975, when large numbers of people from Saigon fled the advancing North Vietnamese Army. Governments outside the region quickly offered resettlement opportunities to those refugees who had close connections either with Western government agencies, private companies, or who had been closely associated with Western military advisers. Second, the international community responded to an increasing reluctance among countries of first asylum to accept new arrivals. When the Malaysian government in particular threatened to push boats back out to sea unless other countries agreed to accept significant numbers for resettlement, a direct and critical link between third country resettlement, asylum, and rescue was clearly established.

The importance of that link continues to motivate third country resettlement. A recent review of US policy towards refugees in South-east Asia underscores the concern:

> Above all, the first asylum host governments fear that resettlement country interest is declining. Evidence includes the financial crisis faced by UNHCR, the virtual withdrawal from resettlement by many countries, and decreasing resettlement levels maintained by the major refugee-receiving countries. . . . the threats to first asylum are again increasing and require concerted international efforts to prevent a return to the earlier situation in the region when refugee boats were pushed back into the sea and Lao and Khmer refugees were forcibly repatriated.[2]

As important as concern for first asylum is the competition with other needs and problems. The recent declining interest in resettlement does not necessarily represent a change in the humanitarian commitment or foreign policy interests of the host governments. Rather, it results from increasing concern over the domestic problems of resettlement. In fact the single most important threat to keeping resettlement opportunities open involves the experiences of refugees after they have resettled. Frankly stated, although saving life and humanitarian commitment are the bases of refugee policies, the way in which refugees perform economically and socially after resettlement determines the extent to which host governments pursue their global obligations.

The most visible domestic concerns of host governments are economic, including the perceived high costs of government assistance, and difficulties in education and housing. The most fundamental issue, however, is the kinds of relationships that refugees form with established residents in local communities. The character and quality of these relationships, and the ways in which both refugees and established residents are transformed by them, influence the extent to which refugees are accepted. In turn,

[2] US Department of State, *Report on the Indochinese Refugee Panel* (Washington, DC: Department of State Publication 9476, Bureau of Refugee Programs, April 1986).

acceptance determines the degree of support for or opposition to national policies towards future refugee admissions. In a very real sense, the global commitment to resettlement is realized among the everyday interactions of sponsors, citizens of the host country, and refugees.

Throughout the advanced industrialized countries, interactions among refugees and established residents are generally positive and mutually advantageous; yet they also include difficult encounters, many of which border on, if they do not openly violate, both human and civil rights. Many of these problems are of course not unique to refugees, but many of the responses from citizens and governments target refugees as the source of the problem. Increasingly, refugees are becoming the victims of claims that they are the source of social and economic problems in their countries of resettlement.

Reluctant admissions

Support for large-scale refugee resettlement and acceptance of asylum-seekers has certainly declined from the generous and open reception accorded to South-east Asian refugees in 1979, 1980, and 1981. Government officials frequently allege that 'compassion fatigue' has afflicted the US population, while, in the Federal Republic of Germany, Helmut Kohl has announced the change more boldly: 'We are not a country of immigration'. Even Canada, which *is* a country of immigration and which has held out longer than many others, has recently tightened the interpretation and practice of its regulations. Throughout the countries of resettlement, tighter restrictions have led to finer legal and policy distinctions among different groups of newcomers, preserving refugee status for fewer people and making it more difficult for new sources of refugee influxes to be admitted.

A primary reason for this change in reception policy is the result of the globalization of refugee concerns, especially in contrast to the immediate post-World War II period. Following the war refugees were mainly perceived as a European problem.[3] But decolonization, revolution, and counter-revolution have transformed the refugee phenomenon from a European to a global phenomenon. While

[3] Gil Loescher and John A. Scanlan, *Calculated Kindness: Refugees and America's Half-Open Door, 1945 to the Present* (New York: The Free Press, 1986).

globalization has meant an increase in instances of flight and asylum, and an exacerbation of problems of under-development throughout Africa, Asia, and Latin America, for countries offering permanent resettlement this trend has meant a tremendous increase in the diversity of demand for entry. From the point of view of many host governments, declining interest in third country resettlement is not simply a question of the number of current or potential refugees, but the increasing diversity of their nationality and political or personal motivation.

This increased diversity in the current refugee situation has created problems for host governments of several kinds. They are faced with ethnic and national groups which have virtually no tradition of settlement in the receiving country and, especially, do not have a community organized and waiting to receive them. These groups also may have had less visible or recognized links with the foreign policy of the receiving government. As a result, the new groups must compete for resources in the resettlement countries, where assistance has been mobilized to serve other groups, with long-standing claims on the political loyalties of both established ethnic communities and political leaders. Even when there is a general will to increase assistance, it is politically and socially difficult to transfer the special commitment that provokes public and private help for refugees to new groups. This practical and political difficulty, rather than compassion fatigue, lies at the core of declining interest in settlement.

Diversity among new arrivals has also created problems for resettlement programmes which, although in the abstract may seem trivial, weigh heavily on the capacity to adjust quickly and effectively to new arrivals. For example, increased diversity has required the expansion of resources and the hiring of new personnel to respond to a broader range of linguistic and cultural needs. Personnel with experience of working with the new groups have been less available or, at least, not as well mobilized. In the United States, for example, many of the resettlement agencies are now designed and staffed to serve South-east Asian refugees. Recent increases in the proportion of the US refugee population originating from elsewhere have left these agencies ill-prepared. South-east Asian refugees themselves staff many of these programmes and are now faced with serving Eastern European or Afghan refugees. Cultural and linguistic mismatches re-emerge, government programmes again appear to be in crisis, and the commitment to resettlement becomes strained.

The social composition of new refugee arrivals, especially in contrast to earlier resettled South-east Asian and other groups, has added also to this diversity and to programme difficulties. One of the more familiar examples involves the higher occupational and educational backgrounds of the recent Eastern European refugees to the United States, especially those from Poland and Romania, in comparison with those of South-east Asian refugees. Job service and training programmes geared to the earlier groups have failed to meet the newcomers' needs and have caused friction in the resettlement effort.[4]

The most important problem created by the increasing diversity of refugee flows is that it has pushed aside well-established legal and policy concepts and practices. In their place, governments have established more broadly conceived and universally acceptable criteria for admission and assistance. These changes have certainly expanded the pool of potential claimants, but they also have resulted in less well-defined criteria for making policy, legal, and administrative decisions. The broadening of principles has led to confusion, ambiguity, and conflict over the acceptance of particular groups and, as a result, a general perception of increasing problems in the resettlement of refugees and refugee-like groups.

Some observers have attributed the problems host governments experience in applying existing concepts to increasingly diverse populations to racism, reactionary politics, and blatant insensitivity. All three are certainly involved. Yet each also masks a fundamental crisis in legal and practical policy responses to the diversity of issues. The most dramatic example in the United States resulted from the 1980 influx of Cubans and Haitians. Unable to respond politically and legally to both flows within existing refugee laws, the US administration opted to create an *ad hoc* category of admissions. The 'entrants' category, however, satisfied neither the demand for clarity of admission status nor the need for assistance in resettlement. Seven years later the effects of that ambiguous response continue to haunt domestic resettlement and to portray

[4] Research Management Corporation, *The Economic and Social Adjustment of Non-Southeast Asian Refugees* (Washington, DC: US Department of Health and Human Services, Office of Refugee Resettlement, 1986).

refugees as an overall burden on the US population. Several thousand Cubans who arrived in 1980, but who remain in US prisons awaiting a delayed return to Cuba, recently rioted to publicize their plight and to protest plans to repatriate them without due process of law.

Canada has experienced less dramatic but equally public dilemmas in administering its relatively open refugee admissions policies. Recent cases of Tamils entering Canada under circumstances usually associated with the smuggling of illegal aliens, and cases of religious groups claiming persecution in countries not usually recognized as violating such rights, have put tremendous public pressure on the government to interpret admissions policies more strictly.

The most important current example of the profound conflict involved in responding to the diversity of new influxes is US policy towards Central American refugees, especially those fleeing El Salvador. The political conflict is legend. It has brought mainstream Churches throughout the United States together in a sanctuary movement against US policy and has provoked the UNHCR into a rare disagreement with US resettlement practices. The current US administration considers Salvadoreans as either displaced persons or economic migrants. If they are displaced persons seeking asylum, the argument goes, then they should stop in the first country they reach, Mexico. Because they travel through Mexico to reach the United States, their motivation must be economic. Since few face persecution on their return, the administration argues that Salvadoreans should be deported and returned home.

Critics make the charge that Salvadoreans are seeking political asylum and, at the very least, should be provided with a safe haven and an extension of their period of temporary residence in the United States. They also argue that there will be no long-run domestic cost involved in a safe haven policy since the vast majority of Salvadoreans will return home once conditions have stabilized.

The problem is that most of the Salvadoreans currently resident in the United States are now unlikely to return home, regardless of changes in conditions. In fact many have applied for legal residence under the new US legalization programme, which offers permanent residence to former illegal immigrants. In addition the President of El Salvador José Napoleon Duarte has urged the United States not to send them back because the return flow would cause irreparable damage to the Salvadorean economy.

Situations like these represent a new, derivative form of durable solution. In effect Salvadoreans are engaged in spontaneous third country resettlement. The accepted image of third country resettlement is of course planned, orderly movements conducted under the auspices of the international community to countries of permanent residence. In the case of El Salvador, and perhaps of many of the asylum-seekers in Western Europe, refugees are moving of their own accord in search of a durable solution, which they have been denied at home or in the region of origin. They become irregular refugees, challenging both the laws and the expectations of host governments. In doing so, however, they should not necessarily lose their claim to refugee status. The reality of global migration is that spontaneous movements of groups and individuals are undermining government regulations in a wide range of situations. The force of economic under-development, the lack of political responses to it, and the violence and chaos that accompany these situations are forcing individuals, families, and groups to find their own alternatives, their own durable solutions.

Underlying these and other difficulties created by the globalization of the refugee phenomenon is the link that has emerged between refugee resettlement and immigration in general. From the perspective of the receiving population and government, refugee resettlement cannot be separated from larger immigration issues. In each of the countries where refugees seek resettlement, large numbers of immigrants also have come looking for work. For example, between 1950 and 1975, when major restrictions came into effect, net immigration to Western Europe increased its population by 10 million. In the United States well over 15 million immigrants have entered since the passage of the Immigration and Nationality Act of 1965.

These labour flows also have increased in diversity. In addition to diversity of nationality, however, the most important diversity is that of their legal status. Like refugee groups, it is the proliferation of the different means and status by which newcomers enter that causes the greatest difficulties. In countries such as Canada, Australia, and the United States, legal immigrants have simply followed through their original intention to settle permanently. But others entered the host country under conditions and a legal status designed to make their stay temporary. Throughout Western Europe temporary workers eventually established sufficient connections through jobs and communities in the host country to render their stay unintentionally permanent. Undocumented or irregular immigrants, overstayers on tourist visas, and students working without authorization also have increased in number and are more visible. In fact, if there is any single issue that troubles governments the most, it is the volume of illegal immigration. Unfortunately, concern at these undocumented workers and unanticipated stayers has become mixed up with concern with refugee admissions. A pervasive concern with illegal entry is easily transferred, through impatience and intolerance, to displaced persons seeking asylum under conditions and from areas that do not match the standard, well-defined traditions and experiences of refugee resettlement.

The link between immigration and refugee issues confronts receiving governments with considerable problems in choosing between competing demands for admission. As a result the link has direct implications for the future ability to respond to refugee flows and to fulfil the role that third country resettlement plays in durable solutions throughout the world. Dilemmas caused by these connections, however, also have a direct impact on domestic resettlement experience. A newcomer's legal status, which defines the rights that a person can exercise under his or her new government, strongly influences the extent to which the refugee is able to fulfil the expectations with which he arrives. The differential legal status of these groups is fundamental to the possibility of establishing and maintaining a secure, prosperous, and durable resettlement solution.

Domestic experience

The durability of resettlement depends upon the opportunities there are to establish a new, legitimate relationship to the host government. To accomplish this, refugees must be provided with access to the rights and privileges of citizenship in order to participate fully in their new homelands. In most countries of resettlement, in fact, the largest refugee groups have taken full advantage of this access, with fairly high rates of naturalization.

The effect of refugees' secure legal status on their work and social opportunities contrasts sharply with other groups that are denied refugee status. Groups which receive only a selective asylum classification or 'extended voluntary departure' are hindered by their legal status from fully participating in their host country. Not only do they lack citizenship rights, but, unlike refugees, many cannot even expect to acquire those rights in the future. They also are limited in their opportunities for economic advancement. Most Salvadoreans resettled in the United States, for example, are eligible only for emergency medical care and for education for their children. Despite their other needs, they are barred from participation in the extensive Federally-sponsored refugee resettlement programme.

Newcomers' legal status also limits the ability of voluntary, private organizations to provide basic assistance in finding housing and jobs. In formal refugee situations, private voluntary sponsors are organized to provide considerable financial, material, and personal assistance to newcomers. Sponsors serve as effective bridges to carry refugees into job and housing markets, enrol them in public assistance programmes, and enable them to participate in language and occupational training courses. This aid is so important, in fact, that differences among resources available to sponsors are primary reasons for uneven rates of economic progress among refugees in both the United States and Canada.[5]

The experience of sponsorship differs greatly, however, for those with less than full refugee status. For example, the decision not to grant refugee status to Haitians and Cubans entering the United States in 1980 severely limited the amount and type of aid available for resettlement, and greatly reduced the speed with which these entrants could be moved from their makeshift refugee camps. Legal ambiguities even prevented officials from moving unaccompanied minors from camps in which there was inadequate supervision and protection.

The sharpest contrast, however, once again involves Salvadoreans. In a sense, the sanctuary movement in the United States has tried to serve as sponsor for these spontaneously resettled refugees. Yet, in the absence of a firm legal status for Salvadoreans, the movement has had to rely on a much smaller network of

[5] Robert L. Bach and Rita Carroll Seguin, 'Labor Force Participation, Household Composition, and Sponsorship among Southeast Asian Refugees', *International Migration Review*, 20/2 (1986), 381–404.

contributors and resources. The result is that many Salvadoreans face considerable economic hardships. An unknown but sizeable number have been especially disadvantaged by recent changes in US immigration law. Under the new law, if they entered the United States after 1982, they are now ineligible for permanent legal residence. The new law also prevents them from working and makes them ineligible for public assistance. Anticipating these changes, hundreds again moved spontaneously, this time from the United States to Canada, immediately following the passage of the new legislation.

In Western Europe problems appear even more pronounced. The issue for many parts of Europe is fundamental: will politicians and governments recognize and accept that a process of permanent resettlement is now well advanced? Legal frameworks continue to assume that many newcomers are only temporarily resident in the host country, and governments remain attracted to incentive schemes to entice immigrant groups to return home. There is a recognized need, however, to redirect attention from these incentive schemes, towards an integration framework that offers basic privileges and rights not typically allowed to temporary workers.[6]

The implications of a failure to establish an integrative framework go far beyond policies aimed at guestworkers and their dependants. Such a failure would also reinforce a restrictive collective approach towards asylum-seekers and displaced persons. In the period 1979 to 1981, for instance, the influx of relatively large numbers of refugees into the Federal Republic of Germany prompted media portrayals of refugees from Afghanistan, Eritrea, Argentina, Iran, and Turkey as 'phonies, out to take advantage of social security benefits'.[7] Fearing a domestic financial burden, the government labelled many of these arrivals 'economic refugees', and subsequently restricted their range of assistance and training programmes.[8]

The establishment of such an integrative framework, however,

[6] Ursula Mehrlander, 'Sociological Aspects of Migration Policy: The Case of the Federal Republic of Germany', *International Migration*, 25/1 (March 1987), 87–93.

[7] Stephen Castles, *Here for Good: Western Europe's New Ethnic Minorities* (London: Pluto Press, 1984), 200.

[8] Ibid.

does not necessarily eliminate the resettlement issues that are linked to the differential legal status of refugees, as compared to others in the host population. On resettlement, refugees become part of the general working-class and minority population of the host country. But this integration serves only to augment the visibility of refugees' differential access to public aid programmes. In nearly every resettlement country, refugees benefit from an assistance programme organized at the national level to establish an initial standard of well-being, including the availability of special cash payments, and to promote future economic progress through social and educational services. These programmes are justified politically on the grounds that refugees are a special class of newcomer with a unique set of experiences and needs.

These special aid programmes create problems, however, because this kind of aid contradicts cherished beliefs about the contribution of newcomers to countries with a long tradition of immigration. Immigration in general receives considerable support from host populations for two reasons: a strong belief in reuniting families, and the benefit of immigrants' economic contribution to society. In particular, immigrants comprise a cheap, temporary labour-force which places few demands on social capital. These below average demands made on social expenditure have been especially important during recent periods of budget deficit and efforts at privatization.

The visibility of assistance payments to refugees challenges this image and casts a cloud of uncertainty over the impact of immigration in general. Local governments in particular have protested the financial impact of refugee resettlement and have protested and resisted national immigration and refugee legislation which admits more newcomers without adequate Federal government reimbursement. Anxieties over locally concentrated expenditure have also contributed to one of the most ill-conceived policies of domestic resettlement throughout the world. In the United States, Britain, and Western Europe, the early years of large-scale resettlement involved concerted efforts to disperse the incoming population throughout the country. Strategies were developed to link the geographical placement of refugees with low unemployment and housing occupancy rates. In nearly every case these geographical dispersal schemes failed, both in terms of governments' concerns about local impact and, in particular, of the refugees' expectations and longing to re-establish a supportive and secure community.

Refugees' access to special assistance programmes is, however, not without its own problems. For example, in the United States approximately 60 per cent of the South-east Asian refugee population resettled during the last five years currently live in households that receive public assistance.[9] At the same time approximately 40 per cent of these same households have no members that work: public assistance is their only source of income. Although most evidence suggests that long-term welfare dependency is probably not a problem, the substantial costs represented by these benefits create problems in sustaining the resettlement effort.

The cost of these programmes also serves as a very visible measure of refugees' economic and social progress in the host country, and is a significant source of the government's worries about domestic resettlement. In the United States concerns about 'welfare dependency' among refugees have been a continuous theme of domestic resettlement policies since 1975. The Refugee Act of 1980 provided relatively generous assistance programmes to facilitate rapid progress towards self-sufficiency. This aid included both cash payments and an array of social service and job training programmes. By 1982, however, the duration of cash payments to refugees had been cut in half. Throughout this period there was also an awareness that the surest way of reducing costs was to reduce the number of admissions. The concern has been that the visibility of special assistance to refugees may in time undermine the basic motive for the resettlement programme.

Diversity and minority status

Recent refugees have added considerable racial, ethnic, and cultural diversity to the host populations of North America and Western Europe. Most current refugees form minorities in the countries of resettlement, and, as minorities, they join a wide realignment of working classes throughout the advanced industrialized world. They have been thrust into situations of fundamental change in

[9] Robert L. Bach, *Public Assistance Utilization among Southeast Asian Refugees*, Report to the Office of Refugee Resettlement (US Department of Health and Human Services, 1987).

cultural and ethnic identity that few had ever expected, let alone been prepared for.

As new minorities, their fate has become intertwined with the treatment and conditions of established minority groups. For example, the visibility and significance of larger minority issues has intensified reactions to refugees and to refugee-like groups. According to the World Council of Churches, there has been an escalation of racism throughout Western Europe that has included both immigrants and refugees.[10] One observer gave the following example: 'The campaign against refugees did much to stimulate racism against all foreigners, and its impact may be compared with that of the campaign against the East African Asians in Britain in the mid-seventies.'[11] Racism also has been an important feature of the resettlement experience of the Black Cuban and Haitian refugees of 1980. Throughout the United States and Canada, an increased diversity of language, nationality, and race have all fuelled reactions, ranging from minor abuses and discrimination to full-scale crimes of hate against new immigrants. Violent crimes against newcomers have become much more evident. In Detroit, for instance, an Asian man was beaten to death by an unemployed automobile worker because he was believed to be a newcomer. Only later was it determined that the victim was a native-born US citizen.

Dramatic and very obvious hardships are reinforced by social problems that arise in schools and local communities. Refugees in the United States have encountered a particularly invidious form of discrimination that further isolates and targets them as a special group: South-east Asian refugees have become an integral part of the mythology surrounding the 'Asian success story'. For instance, frequent examples of rapid educational achievements in schools by Hmong children, who often come from households where the parents speak no English, are consistently cited as evidence of successful Americanization and achievement through hard work. As the popular media have become attracted to the large numbers of new ethnic minorities, these exceptional achievements are contrasted with the continued decline and failure of native-born

[10] World Council of Churches (ed.), *Migrant Workers and Racism in Europe* (Geneva: WCC, 1980).

[11] Castles, *Here for Good*, p. 201.

minority groups. And, in response, native-born groups have pointed to the special aid that both governments and private voluntary groups favour refugees with, as opposed to the native-born poor and unemployed.

Refugees have become a minority among already marginalized populations. Most new refugees settle in urban areas in which housing is cheaper and there is a sizeable community of their own ethnic group. In these areas they often have few contacts with the majority population. Instead, many of their relationships are with other refugees, immigrants, and native-born minorities. For example, a recent series of interviews, entitled 'Voices of Exile', aired on National Public Radio in the United States described the hardships faced by Central American refugees in Los Angeles. A Salvadorean reported rampant discrimination, expecially in housing and in the job market. When asked who was discriminating against her, she described the ways in which Mexican–American women acted towards her. Her complaints against her landlord eventually identified him as a Vietnamese refugee. The only contact with the majority population came through employment. Several of these interviewed told of the willingness of a construction company owner to hire them even though none of them had proof of authorization to work in the United States. This participation in the black economy has long been a salient feature of the Central American refugees' and undocumented aliens' lives.

Finally, domestic resettlement problems are sometimes sensationalized in reports of crimes committed by refugees. Although many such reports are simply false, a very few dramatic examples can fuel reactions against all refugees. In the United States the Cubans who entered in 1980 have been connected with a dramatic increase in violent crime in South Florida; the US Department of Justice has launched investigations into roving South-east Asian 'pirate' gangs; and the *Los Angeles Times* has carried a series of front-page stories about South-east Asian youth gangs. In England a small number of Tamil refugees have been connected with a drug trafficking syndicate.

Politicization of resettlement

Problems encountered during resettlement have had a wider impact than on the debate to restrict immigrant and refugee admissions alone. They also challenge governments' original policy and commitment to third country resettlement. For many political leaders, the best way to resolve domestic problems related to immigration is to prevent their occurrence, by 'going to the source'. In many receiving countries, immigration and refugee matters are becoming more politically visible and controversial, in the formulation of foreign policy. There is a growing recognition that migration and refugee flows are as important in bilateral and regional relations as trade and development assistance. In the 1986 Immigration Reform and Control Act, for example, the UN Congress explicitly created a Commission on Western Hemispheric Migration to investigate connections between foreign policy, trade, development assistance, and migration and refugee flows.

A consequence of this new interest is that third country resettlement is becoming more politicized than ever before, both in domestic and foreign policy arenas. This politicization has occurred in at least two ways. First, refugees are becoming a political weapon in foreign relations. Of course, behind some of these efforts lurk alarmist fears exploited by political leaders trying to garner support for foreign policy initiatives. United States policy in Central America, for example, is sometimes explicitly defended by arousing a fear of the domestic burden of resettling a flood of new refugees, should that policy fail. More important, however, is the use of refugees by receiving governments as symbolic political weapons against the regimes producing the outflow. Refugee issues become linked to diplomatic negotiations that have little to do with the actual plight of refugees and the families they have left behind.

Second, refugee communities in the countries of resettlement have become politically active, especially on issues involving relations with their countries of origin. On several occasions they have been able to influence national policy decisions. Their influence, however, is not neutral. The selective character of recent refugee flows has resulted in a clearly conservative orientation in their political activities, especially in terms of promoting antagonistic policies towards the countries that caused their own exile. The problem is that to the extent that these refugee groups organize and act effectively to influence political decisions, they may be exacerbating the difficulties in transforming refugee flows into orderly departure programmes or even into normalized emigration policies.

Conclusion

Refugees resettled in third countries face an array of concerns that, in principle, are no different from those encountered in the countries of first asylum or during repatriation. Resettled refugees must first secure a stable and clear legal status which provides full access to the host country's institutions and guarantees them some future in that country. Accomplishing that, resettled refugees then face the uncertainties of establishing a solid economic base and moving towards self-sufficiency for their entire household.

The hardships they face in accomplishing these goals include not only those which result from their newcomer or refugee status, but also those which arise from their participation in the host population as a minority. Struggle for economic progress under these circumstances may take on the character of a battle against inequality, racism, and discrimination, as well as an attempt to conquer the transition from flight to resettlement, that is unique to refugees.

The very presence of refugees in host countries also transforms the character of the communities in which they live and the population that resides there. Full participation in the host's institutions therefore may require assertion of newcomers' culture, language, and goals within schools and local communities. This need is especially acute because it is at this local, interpersonal level that refugees sometimes feel the most insecure and encounter threats to their personal safety.

The promise that third country resettlement offers refugees is the opportunity to re-establish a secure relationship to a government which provides possibilities for social stability and economic progress. The durability of third country resettlement lies in the ability to overcome the hardships reviewed in this chapter, to secure a legal status, and to participate fully in the host country. Positive resettlement experiences abound throughout the advanced industrialized world, and these allow host governments to continue to maintain a commitment to resettlement. But these positive experiences are not easily won. For each durable solution, and for each refugee and displaced person, success is obtained through continuous assistance and protection. In this sense, resettlement in third countries is exactly the same process as integration in countries of first asylum, or repatriation. As such, there is no reason why the international community should be less involved in protecting human and civil rights in countries of permanent resettlement than it is in other areas of the world.

15. Temporary Safe Haven

The Need for North American–European Responses

DENNIS GALLAGHER, SUSAN FORBES MARTIN, AND PATRICIA WEISS-FAGEN

TODAY the United States and Canada and the nations of Europe are countries of asylum for individuals fleeing from Haiti, El Salvador, Guatemala, Nicaragua, Ethiopia, Afghanistan, Iran, Poland, Sri Lanka, and others. Among these migrants are individuals who meet the definition of a refugee contained in national and international law—that is, they have a well-founded fear of persecution based on religious belief, race, nationality, political opinion, or membership of a social group. Those who meet the definition will generally qualify for political asylum in the industrialized countries.

But among these nationalities are also individuals who are unable to demonstrate a well-founded fear of persecution, even though their motives for leaving may have been politically generated, or their circumstances may be equally life-threatening. The characteristics of these kinds of refugees, as elaborated by Alexander Aleinikoff of the University of Michigan Law School before the House Immigration Subcommittee of the US House of Representatives, are:

(1) Persons from a country experiencing civil war, a general breakdown of public order, or occupation by a foreign power;
(2) Persons likely to suffer substantial infringement of human rights if returned home, where such treatment cannot be considered persecution based on religious belief, race, nationality or membership in a social group;
(3) Persons in this country who do not choose to apply for asylum . . . because they would like to return to their home countries once

conditions change, or are fearful that their applications will not be fairly adjudicated here.

For those who cannot demonstrate refugee bona fides there are few formal mechanisms either in the United States or in other Western nations for admission or protection. Faced with the disparity between the asylum system and the need for a humanitarian response to migrants who cannot prove they are refugees, the industrialized nations have granted safe haven to members of some nationalities—albeit on a discretionary basis. Other refugees have benefited from 'benign neglect', i.e. they have been allowed to remain illegally because governments have neither the capacity nor the will to find and deport them. However, these recurring practices do not amount to coherent, consistent policies. Instead, *ad hoc* mechanisms have been used, which often rely on political, ideological, and foreign policy factors that may or may not take into account the actual circumstances from which those in need of safe haven have fled.

There is a growing perception in the industrialized world that these movements of people cannot be handled adequately through uncoordinated responses on the part of receiving countries. Not only does each of the industrialized countries host asylum-seekers from the same countries, but, in some cases, the same individuals seek refuge in more than one industrialized country.

Several areas lend themselves particularly well to co-operative efforts by industrialized countries. First is the handling of refugees who already have safe haven but choose to move from a developing country to an industrialized country or from one industrialized country to another. Some of the factors generating this movement from one asylum country to another are: (1) asylum-seekers' dissatisfaction with the first country that they enter (because of not feeling safe, lack of permission to work, or other reasons); (2) policies of some countries of first asylum that deny permanent residence to those granted refugee status; and (3) a desire on the part of some refugees to obtain the 'best' asylum they can, in terms of their own or their children's future opportunities.

Until recently most of this kind of movement occurred within a hemisphere, but increasingly refugees are moving across the Atlantic (Sri Lankans moving from India to Germany, to Canada; Ethiopians moving from Ethiopia to Italy, to the United States).

Most of the nations of Europe and North America grant permanent asylum to those who come directly from their countries of origin, but are reluctant to provide asylum to those who cross into other countries from those in which they could have stayed. As signatories to the Refugee Convention, these countries do not return bona fide refugees to their countries of origin, but seek instead to return them to the country of first asylum. Often, the developing country—which may be host to hundreds of thousands of refugees, or even millions, as in the case of Pakistan—refuses to readmit the refugee. This can lead to refugees being held in detention often for extended periods of time while the industrialized country negotiates with a developing country. Or it can lead to the phenomenon of 'refugees in orbit'—where refugees travel from one industrialized nation to another in search of permanent refuge.

Co-operative efforts on the part of the receiving countries can also enhance the potential for return of political exiles to their countries of origin, if conditions there permit. For financial reasons, individuals may be reluctant to return. In order to encourage repatriation and reintegration, several European governments have established funds to provide economic assistance to returnees. These efforts have been very controversial, however, because they have been seen as serving the narrow interests of the industrialized countries, and do not usually include adequate mechanisms to assess whether the returnee will be protected or not.

The refugee and asylum policies of industrialized countries have become increasingly interdependent. There are direct cause-and-effect relationships between the immigration or foreign policies of one country and the asylum situation of another. For example, when the United States passed its new immigration law imposing employer sanctions, many Salvadoreans went to Canada to apply for asylum or safe haven. Should the Canadians restrict access to their asylum system, as there is indication they will, then some movement across the Atlantic may take place. Conversely, tightening of immigration policies in European countries could lead to renewed movements into North America.

The recognition of these interconnections in asylum policies among industrialized countries has led to increased discussions among non-governmental organizations, within governments, and among countries. To date, however, most of the discussions continue to take place within North America or within Europe, but not between North America and Europe, despite the fact that these areas share many characteristics. As the phenomenon of cross-Atlantic movement increases in frequency, interest is growing in broadening a North American–European dialogue. There is also a growing awareness of the significant possibility that situations could occur in countries such as India, South Africa, or Turkey that would send a flood of asylum-seekers into the industrialized countries on both sides of the Atlantic, and that there is a need for mechanisms to prepare for such an eventuality.

The objective of the following pages is to establish a framework for reviewing current safe haven practices and laws in North America and Europe in hope of contributing to an informed policy debate on this issue. The remainder of this chapter discusses international legal precedents for safe haven, as well as existing practices in the United States, Canada, and Western Europe. This discussion provides both a context for evaluating current US policies and practices and models for change. In the concluding section we raise the various issues requiring international policy attention if there are to be improvements in safe haven responses.

International legal bases for providing safe haven

In most nations the granting of safe haven is discretionary. Indeed, the granting of asylum has developed entirely within the context of national sovereignty. International treaties bearing on the rights of refugees and other non-citizens are binding only when ratified and incorporated into national law.

Nevertheless, international law, regional accords, and an understanding of human rights under customary international law have established the normative context in which domestic immigration and refugee laws have developed and are considered. International and regional agreements are essential as well in assisting nations to establish consistent measures for dealing with people whose problems cannot be resolved within the legal system of a single nation. This is certainly the situation of people who flee a country because of repression, persecution, or other forms of violence, from which their governments cannot or will not protect them. Such people become, in effect, wards of the international community.

Taken together, the dozens of international and regional

conventions pertaining to refugees and exiles assure limited protection, but neither the humanitarian nor the refugee conventions adequately address the plight of people who leave their countries because of upheavals, armed conflicts, or violence in general. If such people are part of large-scale influxes, they are all the more vulnerable to expulsion from the countries where they seek refuge. But, precisely because issues related to refugee protection and safe haven require a multinational as well as a national approach, it is essential to understand the potential as well as the limitations of the international system.

Human rights instruments define the obligations of states to respect the rights of persons within their jurisdictions, but do not specifically oblige them to accept jurisdiction over the citizens of other states. Article 14 of the Universal Declaration of Human Rights, the normative document of international human rights, grants to everyone the 'right to seek and to enjoy in other countries asylum from persecution'. There is no corresponding state obligation to receive them. The International Covenant on Civil and Political Rights, binding on ratifying states (this does not include the United States), affirms liberty of movement only for persons 'lawfully within the territory of a state', and freedom to leave and return to one's own country (Article 12).

In the body of refugee law the primary protection for people who seek safety in another country is Article 33 of the United Nations Convention (and Protocol) Relating to the Status of Refugees. It requires that states refrain from the *refoulement* of persons meeting refugee criteria. Article 31 of the Convention further requires that refugees not be penalized for illegal entries *if* they have come directly 'from a territory where their life or freedom was threatened'. The UNHCR regularly exhorts governments to provide adequate opportunities for asylum-seekers to establish their refugee identity. But states party to the Convention/Protocol develop their own methods for deciding who is and who is not eligible for refugee protection, and there is no obligatory role for the UNHCR in this process. There is also no clear definition of who is responsible for the protection of persons who have transited one or more states before requesting asylum.

Outside Africa, states are obliged not to *refoule* individuals meeting the conditions set in the United Nations Convention, providing, of course, the states have ratified the Convention and/or

Protocol. Within the region covered by the Organization of African Unity's Refugee Convention, refugees include 'every person who, owing to external aggression, occupation, foreign domination or events seriously disturbing public order in either part or the whole of his country of origin or nationality, is compelled to . . . seek refuge in another place outside his country of origin or nationality'.

Few international instruments provide for the protection needs of mass first asylum entries when entrants are not recognized as being refugees. The most relevant to *de facto* refugees is the 1949 Geneva Convention Relating to the Protection of Civilian Persons in Time of War, which establishes norms for the protection of civilians in time of war. Common Article Three elaborates the protection and assistance to be accorded to the civilian victims of situations of armed conflict. The Second Protocol Additional, ratified by fifty nations (not including the United States), expands on this protection and assistance by applying them to the broader categories of armed conflict, excluding only simple 'internal disturbances and tensions'.[1]

Safe haven responses and the UNHCR

In large-scale complex movements people do not necessarily have recourse to the international instruments of refugee protection. In practice the United Nations High Commissioner for Refugees (UNHCR) has responded to many such large movements in the Third World with protection and assistance programmes. The UNHCR has established jurisdiction for such situations, first, by means of prima facie group determinations, and second, by an expanded definition of people of concern to the High Commissioner that includes displaced persons in 'refugee-like situations'.

The former concept developed in a context of frequent large-scale refugee movements during the 1950s and 1960s, mainly in Africa, where it was not practicable for UNHCR to screen all members of a group to determine whether they met the refugee criteria. The High Commissioner adopted the technique of defining the group as a whole as prima-facie refugees. The premiss

[1] See the lengthy discussion of international humanitarian law in Deborah Perluss and Joan F. Hartman, 'Temporary Refuge: Emergence of a Customary Norm', *Virginia Journal of International Law* (Spring 1986), 551–626.

of the group determination is that, unless there is evidence to the contrary, all members of the group may be considered prima-facie refugees. This classification has been evoked in many parts of the world where there have been large-scale displacements.

Since the 1960s United Nations resolutions have also permitted the UNHCR to expand its protection and assistance mandate to cover persons considered to be 'displaced persons in refugee-like situations'. These are people who do not have a 'well-founded fear of persecution', as defined in the Convention/Protocol, but who have had to leave their countries, and cannot return to them because of the conditions still prevailing there.[2]

The authority and ability of the UNHCR to assist and protect persons in these categories is obviously contingent on the willingness of governments to admit them in the first place. The mandate of the UNHCR is entirely non-binding in so far as either sending or receiving governments are concerned.

The underlying principle for the UNHCR is that 'In cases of large-scale influx, persons seeking asylum should always receive at least temporary refuge.'[3] In 1981 a group of experts on Temporary Refuge in Situations of Large Scale Influx convened to examine this issue. The general conclusions of this group of experts were subsequently endorsed by the Thirty-second Session of the UNHCR Executive Committee in October 1981. At this session the Committee adopted the following conclusions:

1. In situations of large-scale influx, asylum-seekers should be admitted to the State in which they first seek refuge and if that State is unable to admit them on a durable basis, it should always admit them at least on a temporary basis and provide them with protection . . .
2. In all cases the fundamental principle of *non-refoulement*—including non-rejection at the frontier—must be scrupulously observed.[4]

Although the largest movements of refugees and people in refugee-like situations continue to occur between Third World countries within the same region, increasing numbers of people from these regions now move to the more developed industrialized countries of Europe and North America. Despite their govern-

[2] Michel Moussalli, 'Who is a Refugee?', *Refugee Magazine* (Sept. 1982), 42.

[3] UNHCR, Executive Committee, Thirtieth Session, Oct. 1979.

[4] UN Doc. A/AC.96/601, para. 57 (2) II, Oct. 1981. See Guy Goodwin Gill, *The Refugee in International Law* (Oxford: Clarendon Press, 1985), 118–19.

ments buttressing UNHCR exhortations to Third World governments to accept first asylum entries, they have had no comparable or effective pressures to do the same.

The safe haven issue in industrialized countries

In the past few years the UNHCR has devoted increasing attention to the issue of large-scale influxes into industrialized countries:

> Amongst the spontaneous arrivals of refugee and asylum-seekers . . . there are therefore a large number of persons from developing countries for whom, for various reasons, it has not been possible to provide adequate durable solutions within the regions from which they originate. In comparison with the very large numbers of asylum-seekers accommodated in countries in their regions of origin, the numbers of such arrivals in the countries of Europe are significantly lower. It is, nevertheless, appreciated that the problems Governments faced with arrivals of asylum-seekers within their territories cannot be measured solely in numerical terms. Such arrivals can and do pose particular problems for countries where asylum-seekers are treated on an individual basis and entitled to significant socio-economic benefits; if recognized as refugees, they are generally accepted for integration leading to eventual naturalization.[5]

The UNHCR has approached this problem by urging that all governments, whether in industrialized or developing countries, should adopt humanitarian responses. In his opening statement to the Executive Committee in 1986, the new High Commissioner Jean-Paul Hocké commented that it was no longer sufficient for industrialized countries to make refugee assistance available to developing countries. 'The industrialized countries must also share the burden of accepting those . . . who seek asylum outside their regions.' Further, implicitly criticizing some of the efforts in the industrialized countries to impede illegal entries, the High Commissioner urged governments not to take measures that would adversely affect genuine refugees in the course of controlling illegal economic migrants. 'Refugees and asylum seekers who are the concern of my office should not be the victims of measures taken by Governments against illegal immigration or threats to their national security, however justifiable these may be in themselves'.[6]

[5] UN General Assembly, Executive Committee of the High Commissioner's Programme, Thirty-sixth Session (A/AC.96/ INF.174), 4 July 1985, para. 13.

[6] Opening statement by the High Commissioner for Refugees to the Thirty-Seventh Session of the Executive Committee of the High Commissioner's Programe, 6 Oct. 1986.

Additionally, with respect to large-scale influxes into industrialized countries, the UNHCR annual reports and Executive Committee Notes on Protection express concern about possibly exaggerated allegations of 'abusive asylum requests' and 'manifestly unfounded asylum applications'. They also note with concern the detention of asylum-seekers and the growing phenomenon of 'refugees in orbit'.[7] The refugees in orbit problem occurs when the state in which a person requests asylum refuses to accept jurisdiction for the asylum applicant on the grounds that the latter should have applied in another country, through which he or she previously transited.

The two issues—manifestly unfounded asylum claims and refugees in orbit—have been linked to what the UNHCR and industrialized country governments (mainly in Europe) have characterized as 'irregular movements of asylum seekers'. The term 'irregular movements' is used because the people in these influxes have left countries where, presumably, they might have found safe haven, and have entered the industrialized countries without permission or proper documentation. When they do so, they are accused of having disrupted the regular channels of refugee protection and assistance.[8] Some of the industrialized countries agree that they need not do case-by-case evaluations of refugees claims and/or provide safe haven for the new arrivals if the aliens had—or might have had—safe haven in immediately adjacent countries. Recognizing that some of the migrants cannot return safely to their home countries, the industrial nations seek other alternatives, sometimes including return to the country of first asylum.

In a comprehensive analysis of the irregular movements question, UNHCR consultant Gilbert Jaeger seriously questioned the premiss that the large-scale influxes into the industrialized countries should be considered irregular. He found that the component of genuinely abusive asylum applicants was small and noted that the movements themselves were in large part 'the consequences of deficient legal, economic and social conditions in

[7] Thirty-third Session of the Executive Committee of the High Commissioner's Programme (A/AC.96/613), 12 Oct. 1982, paras. 28–33; and Report of the Subcommittee of the Whole on International Protection (A/AC.96/660), 23 July 1985.

[8] Report of the Subcommittee of the Whole on International Protection, July 1985 and A/AC.96/671, 9 Oct. 1985, paras. 59–70.

countries adjacent to the countries of origin of refugees, chiefly developing countries, as well as in some industrialized countries of arrival'.[9]

Safe haven responses in Western Europe

From the beginning of the twentieth century civil and religious strife, regional upheavals, war, and repression have driven European refugees back and forth across the continent. The safe haven policies and practices developed in Europe, originating and evolving in a different historical context, reflect a different set of expectations than those of North America. Far more than the United States or Canada, Europeans are accustomed to providing asylum for political exiles. Nevertheless, in Western Europe, as in the United States and Canada, treatment of the newly arriving would-be refugees has become controversial.

Since the 1950s the dominant movement of refugees to Europe has been from Eastern Europe. Not only have Eastern Europeans almost always been able to remain in Western European countries of first asylum, but those whose refugee credentials have not been recognized in the country of first asylum may, none the less, be eligible for resettlement in the United States, Canada, Australia, or New Zealand. Among the Eastern Europeans there are numerous or even a preponderance of cases of persons who were not targets of particular persecution at the moment they left their countries, but who risk arrest and other penalties, by virtue of having left without documents, or having abused the terms of their exit permits. People in this situation, more often than not, are given a status other than that of Convention refugee, based on humanitarian grounds.

In the past two decades the movement from east to west that began in the 1950s has coincided with a large-scale immigrant movement essentially from south to north. So-called guestworkers were brought from Southern Europe, as well as from Turkey and Greece, and, in the case of France, from North Africa. Although few guestworkers were imported into Western Europe after the oil-induced recession of 1973, would-be workers continued to arrive, and those already in place often resisted returning home.

Many of the Turks, one of the largest groups of guestworkers,

[9] Gilbert Jaeger, *Study of Irregular Movements of Asylum Seekers and Refugees* (Geneva: Subcommittee of the Whole on International Protection: Executive Committee, UNHCR, 30 Sept. 1985).

refused to return when their work contracts expired in the late 1970s. The Turkish government's human rights record had deteriorated seriously during that period. In addition to the guestworkers who expressed fear of persecution if they returned, other Turks arrived, claiming to be victims of repression rather than guestworkers. Western European governments have acknowledged that claims from Turkish Christians (Assyrians) and from Kurds might be valid, but usually view other Turkish claims unsympathetically.

During the same period other national groups, from the Middle East, South Asia, and Africa, also arrived in substantial numbers, citing repression in their countries of origin: Iranians, Lebanese, Ethiopians, and smaller numbers of Afghans, Ghanaians, Kurds, Zaïrians, Pakistanis, and Latin Americans joined the Eastern European asylum-seekers during the 1980s. These groups, still arriving at the time of writing this, undoubtedly include a large proportion of economic migrants, but their asylum claims are by no means necessarily abusive. At the present time the single most numerous and controversial group in the European asylum pool are the Tamils from Sri Lanka. As noted earlier, in the chapter by Johan Cels, the Tamils pose a dilemma for their European hosts. While the latter are unhappy about the number of entries, they also recognize the Tamils' reasons for flight, more often than not, to be compelling.

Western Europeans complain about the first asylum entries from the Third World countries on grounds of large numbers and perceived problems of integration. Individually, nearly all the governments have imposed visa restrictions on the nationals of countries from which there are large immigrant *or* refugee migrations. The German, Dutch, and Scandinavian governments have negotiated with the German Democratic Republic to convince the latter to adopt measures that will prevent its territory from being used as a transit for illegal entry into the West. Collectively, the governments have attempted through the UNHCR, the Council of Europe, and the European Community to develop a common framework for handling first asylum entries. At the same time they seek means to regionalize the protection of Third World asylum-seekers (i.e. to expand refugee protection in regions *outside* of Western Europe) so that few will arrive.

The Council of Europe has drafted measures bearing on the

problem of refugee flows to industrialized countries. Pertinent among these is a 1982 Report of the Council's Committee on Migration, Refugees, and Demography that urged member governments to 'fight recent developments in several countries tending to assimilate the situation of the refugee with that of the ordinary alien or migrant worker and to apply refugee criteria too strictly'.[10]

In recent years the Council of Europe, through its *Ad Hoc* Committee of Experts on the Legal Aspects of Territorial Asylum (CAHAR), has devoted considerable attention to resolving the problem of refugees in orbit. CAHAR's mandate includes efforts to harmonize asylum eligibility procedures and this, in turn, has led that body to look critically at the issue of where jurisdiction lies for making asylum determinations. The United Nations Convention prohibits *refoulement*, but it does not preclude returning refugees or asylum-seekers to countries where they presumably would not face persecution. Governments have therefore increasingly tried to send asylum-seekers in their territories to the places presumed to be the countries of first asylum. CAHAR has sent to the Council of Europe's Committee of Ministers a draft resolution that sets down, among other things, standards for determining the 'country of first asylum'. No agreement has as yet been reached.[11] The practice of sending asylum-seekers from one country to another obviously has a negative effect on the possibility of their finding safe haven protection.

For the most part European governments developed their mechanisms for handling asylum determinations and providing 'safe haven' for those not meeting refugee criteria prior to the large-scale entries of the late 1970s and 1980s. Safe haven provisions were intended to provide humanitarian relief from deportation for non-refugees of national concern. To a large extent they were intended to benefit fellow Europeans, but at the present time these mechanisms serve a much wider range of persons, from all parts of the world.

The specific provisions for safe haven vary within Europe, as do

[10] 'Report in Reply to the 23rd Report on the Activities of the UNHCR', Council of Europe Doc. No. 4947 (7 Sept. 1982).

[11] The information for the 'refugees in orbit' discussion has been drawn in large part from an unpublished study prepared for the Refugee Policy Group by Clare Pastore of the Yale Law School, Lowenstein Human Rights Law Project, in 1986.

the names used (Class C refugee status; provisional admission, toleration, *Duldung*; extraordinary leave to remain). There is generally a good deal of administrative discretion given to national and, in some cases, local ministries to permit individuals to remain because of the conditions in their countries of origin. Unlike the administrative safe haven mechanisms in the United States, almost all those in Europe carry the possibility of eventual adjustment of status and integration. Whereas the United Kingdom designates national groups for safe haven protection in a similar fashion to the US extended voluntary departure, safe haven is determined in most West European countries on a case-by-case basis.

Safe haven responses in Canada

Canada remains one of the few industrialized countries that still encourages immigration. The Canadian Immigration Act of 1976, Section 3, pledges that immigration policy will recognize the need 'to fulfill Canada's international legal obligations with respect to refugees and to uphold its humanitarian tradition with respect to the displaced and the persecuted'.

In its refugee admissions and asylum programmes, Canada accepts ('lands') Convention refugees, and has also initiated Special Programmes for the nationals of countries 'experiencing adverse domestic events'.[12] There are special programmes for all (or certain categories) of nationals from Afghanistan, El Salvador, Guatemala, Iran, Iraq, Lebanon, and Sri Lanka (until recently the list included Chile, Ethiopia, and Poland as well). The special programmes permit immigration to Canada under relaxed criteria or, more often, protect members of the group from deportation once they have arrived. In addition to the special programmes, there have been long-standing 'no return' policies in effect for asylum applicants who are nationals of Albania, Bulgaria, Cuba, Czechoslovakia, Cambodia, North Korea, the GDR, Laos, the People's Republic of China, Romania, the USSR, and Vietnam. In 1987 the Canadian government lifted blanket national designations regarding 'no return', having received large numbers of Salvadorean aliens who feared the effects of the passage of the US Immigration Reform and Control Act. At present individuals must apply for permission to remain in Canada.

[12] Canadian Ministry of Employment and Emigration, *Immigration Manual*, ch. 26.

A Special Review Committee (SRC) receives the applications of refused refugee claimants and other persons who claim they would experience difficulties in returning to their countries of origin. The SRC may recommend that, because of special humanitarian circumstances, a person who is otherwise deportable be allowed to remain in Canada. SRC guidelines call for consideration to be given to persons in a variety of situations, including those whose return would be 'inhumane . . . because of severe oppression', persons who would suffer 'punishment of inordinate severity' for overstaying their visas, and persons 'who articulate a need to live in a democratic system and are prepared to sacrifice for this'. In practice individuals who are not from countries for which there are special programmes do not often benefit from these provisions.

While the list of countries for which there are special programmes is quite extensive, the Canadian government, at the same time, has imposed visa restrictions on the would-be entrants from these countries. The Canadian officials have done this in the hope that persons seeking to be refugees in Canada would make themselves known to Canadian consulates in their countries of origin or in another country outside of Canada. At the time of writing Canada is considering new legislation that would deter still further the entry of undocumented aliens, including would-be asylum-seekers.

Safe haven responses in the United States

Extended voluntary departure (EVD) is the principal mechanism by which the United States grants safe haven. It provides a temporary relief from deportation for both individuals and groups of people. As a remedy for groups, EVD has generally been applied to members of national entities physically present in the country, pursuant to a determination by State Department officials that conditions in the countries of origin are 'unstable' or 'unsettled', or show a pattern of 'denial of rights'. When members of the designated national groups who are subject to deportation express unwillingness to return to their countries of origin the deportation is not effected. Often members of these groups file political asylum applications which, if approved, afford them refugee protection. If asylum is denied, however, these applicants may remain in EVD status. EVD is presently being applied to groups of Ethiopians (who arrived prior to 30 June 1980), Poles, and Afghans and, on a case-by-case basis, to Lebanese as well.

EVD is a hybrid of immigration relief and political response. Formally, the decision to institute an EVD programme is made jointly by the State and Justice Departments. The State Department initiates the requests regarding a certain national group. The Department of State also takes the lead in determining when conditions in a country no longer warrant the continuation of EVD status for that country's nationals. The INS (Immigration and Naturalization Service) implements EVD programmes through its Office of Detention and Deportation. For their part, the members of the designated national group are not required to come forward and claim their EVD status unless they wish to obtain work permits. Although most do make themselves known to INS officials for this reason, it frequently occurs that the EVD candidates make themselves known only when threatened with deportation.

Beneficiaries of EVD are usually able to obtain work permits, but are eligible for few benefits. Except under special circumstances, recipients cannot obtain travel documents, nor can they bring their families to the United States. There is no provision for individuals with EVD to adjust their status, no matter how long they spend in the United States, unless they meet other criteria.

Of all the remedies presently in the US administrative cornucopia, EVD alone is tailored to provide temporary relief from deportation for persons who, while falling short of meeting an individual 'fear of persecution', as defined in the Refugee Act, would none the less probably face hardships or hazardous situations in their homelands. EVD, however, is and always has been a discretionary measure. No individuals or groups have a right to EVD, no matter how dangerous the situations they might face if deported to their homelands.

Past State Department requests for the application of EVD have been cast primarily in humanitarian terms related to conditions in the country of origin. Foreign policy issues and immigration impacts may also have been discussed and taken into account, but until recently only the humanitarian criteria have been cited to justify the grants. At the present time the nature of the balance between humanitarian criteria and these other factors has become an issue of considerable controversy in the face of the State

Department's continued use of EVD for some groups and refusal to grant it to Central Americans.

Safe haven comparisons

Although refugee procedures and safe haven responses differ, there seem to be two similar, if somewhat contradictory, tendencies in these responses between the countries of Western Europe and North America. First, these countries try, to the extent possible, to minimize large-scale entries of asylum-seekers from the Third World by imposing visa restrictions and policing of borders and international airports. Second, the industrialized countries of Western Europe and North America allow those individuals and groups already in the country to remain if it is believed they would face probable danger in their countries of origin, but the governments do not necessarily give the aliens formal status.

Nevertheless, pressures are growing throughout the region to deport a larger portion of the entrants who claim to be asylum-seekers. While authorities insist that they do not deport people to places where they face danger, evidence indicates that more people are being returned to their countries of origin, especially if they have entered with false documents. At the present time people acknowledged to be refugees are also frequently deported on the grounds that they had been given first asylum elsewhere. There have been public protests against deportations—especially of Salvadoreans and Tamils—in a number of countries. In Switzerland, where, in addition to Tamils, small groups of Zaïrians, Chileans, and Turks also have been expelled, some people have begun a sanctuary movement—similar to the US-based movement—in protest.

European governments remain committed to a policy of offering safe haven to Eastern Europeans. With regard to other national entities, European immigration officials, like their North American counterparts, wish to protect their borders from illegal entries, regardless of the motives of the people who seek entry.

Once people have entered and have initiated the asylum process, the Europeans (with the exception of the United Kingdom), and more recently the Canadians, differ somewhat from the United States in their approach to the question of safe haven. In the former, officials undertake individual status determinations rather than giving blanket designations to all members of a national group. In the United States, in contrast, asylum-seekers are tested individually, but EVD, the major form of safe haven, is generally given to all members of a national group.

Individual determinations, whether for asylum or safe haven, can take a long time—particularly when there are large numbers seeking to avoid deportation. The longer people spend in the adopted country, the stronger the humanitarian objections to obliging them to depart. In Europe there is greater likelihood that those receiving safe haven will be able to legalize their status. At first, people may be provided with humanitarian safe haven on political grounds; subsequently, the time spent in the country becomes the humanitarian factor assuring them of continued safe haven and eventual immigrant status. In the United States recipients of EVD remain indefinitely in illegal status unless they become eligible for permanent residence on some other immigration basis (for example by marrying a US citizen) or unless there is special legislation to permit adjustment of their status. Beneficiaries of EVD who arrived before 1982 may now be able to obtain permanent residence through the legalization provisions in the Immigration Reform and Control Act, but this amnesty programme is not likely to be repeated soon.

The difference between European and US perspectives is illustrated by detention practices on the two sides of the Atlantic. In both situations alien detention is perceived as a mechanism to control or deter illegal entry. Yet, types of, and attitudes towards, detention differ. European countries often assume that asylum-seekers will leave detention because they obtain some legal standing, whereas US policy assumes the continuation of illegal status until deportation occurs—an action made easier by maintaining apprehended aliens in detention.

Another major difference between North America and Europe is the immigration context in which policies about safe haven are made. The fact that it is relatively easy to reside in the United States without ever making oneself known to immigration officials increases the reluctance of the latter to implement safe haven policies. In Canada and in most of Europe (with the possible exception of France) registration procedures operate fairly effectively. Very few people live anonymously in these countries. Even in Spain and Italy, where thousands of aliens live without formal residence status, they have usually made themselves known to immigration officials at some point. Authorities in the United States candidly acknowledge that they cannot accurately estimate how many people are illegally residing in the United States, much less how many of these may be considered to have come for politically related reasons. Even with the immigration amnesty approved by the US Congress in October 1986, the number of undocumented aliens in the United States will remain controversial. However, through the imposition of sanctions on employers of undocumented aliens (authorized by the Immigration Reform and Control Act), the United States may join its industrial neighbours in having greater control over who enters and who works in the country.

Conclusions

For the most part, the countries of Europe and North America have not developed consistent public policies regarding safe haven. Major issues thus remain, such as: the criteria for granting safe haven; the extent to which it should be offered as blanket relief to all members of a nationality or should be based on individual criteria; mechanisms to deal with the immigration ramifications of safe haven decisions; the locus of responsibility for making decisions; the benefits to accrue to recipients of safe haven; the relationship between refugee policies and safe haven; or the international and regional ramifications of decisions on safe haven.

The reasons for leaving one's home country or for being afraid to return are far more complex than those covered in the refugee definition. Many migrants who do not have a well-founded fear of persecution nevertheless have a well-founded fear of injury, deprivation of human rights, and even death. They have left situations of civil war, civil strife, and repression where there is a good likelihood that they could be the victims of random or organized violence.

Seeking more coherent and co-ordinated safe haven policies is not without its dangers. A major concern about a more formal category of safe haven pertains to its relationship to asylum. Evident in several European countries with a status that falls short of full refugee recognition is a tendency to grant to applicants this lesser status rather than asylum. Those granted asylum are often given permanent status and may eventually become nationalized, whereas the safe haven status does not guarantee permanent residence. Thus, the availability of a safe haven status may create a population that remains in limbo for long periods and, in effect, is in a second-class position.

The absence of a safe haven status can also have negative repercussions on asylum, however. Some asylum applicants know that they do not have strong claims to asylum, but there are a few other ways to contest deportation to such countries as El Salvador or Sri Lanka. In such cases the asylum application is itself a form of safe haven since individuals will not be deported until they exhaust all appeals. As a result the asylum systems of many industrialized countries are overloaded with cases that are not likely to succeed on their merits. The public, seeing the large number of unmerited claims, then tend to view the asylum system as fraught with abuses.

Criteria are needed against which to measure the decisions made by governments regarding safe haven. The criteria to be used in determining the need for safe haven must take into account a variety of factors, including humanitarian concerns, the ramifications of immigration, and international relations. It is the weight that is given to the various factors that is the key.

Safe haven is essentially a policy of no return, based on humanitarian concern, not a form of immigration. It should be seen as a way to live up to humanitarian commitments, not as a means to return people to situations in which they may find themselves in danger. Concern about large-scale, negative impacts of safe haven stems from the perception that governments have not been able to control effectively the flow of undocumented aliens, and, therefore, will not be able to deal with the magnet effects of safe haven. What increases the concern is the view that aliens granted safe haven will not return to their countries of origin, even if political conditions permit, because of the economic differences between the industrialized world and the developing countries, from which many political migrants come.

Return will be difficult for many migrants, particularly those who have been out of their home countries for many years. Yet many political exiles proclaim their intentions to return to their homelands as soon as the violence abates and/or repressive governments are replaced. Research on the return home of economic migrants from the United States shows that there are a variety of factors that encourage repatriation—such as family considerations—and that 30 per cent or more of these migrants do go back to their home countries.

The situation of political exiles is more complicated, however. So long as violence and strife continue to endanger large numbers of people, and civil institutions are unable to protect them, it is unreasonable to expect that most exiles will return. Even when a change of government permits return, the home countries may be ambivalent about the return of their citizens. On the one hand, the willingness of people to repatriate is a potent symbol of the legitimacy of a new government, particularly one that is striving to show that it has established democratic institutions. On the other hand, politically active returnees may involve themselves in elections and be seen as unwelcome competition. Many developing countries do not have the economic resources to reintegrate their people—that is, find jobs, housing, etc. Also, people who have stayed on through the fall of one regime and the emergence of another may be antagonistic towards the expenditure of scarce resources on those who fled.

Until recently there were relatively few cases of change of government occurring in the refugee-producing countries that generated movements of people to the United States, Canada, and Europe. Most of those granted safe haven came from Eastern bloc countries that have had long-standing authoritarian governments. This situation has changed recently. Within the past few years several refugee-producing, developing countries have changed governments, including Argentina, Brazil, Uruguay, and the Philippines. Further research is needed to examine factors affecting the return migration of the nationals of these countries in order to develop informed policies regarding safe haven.

Finally, requests for the granting of safe haven should be considered in the context of efforts to internationalize refugee and related problems. By definition, refugee and refugee-like situations denote movement across national boundaries and therefore involve more than one country. In general there is need for greater effort to seek international or regional solutions to safe haven situations affecting the industrialized world.

Decisions regarding safe haven should also take greater account of the impact of these decisions on international standards for the protection of refugees and those in refugee-like situations. The unwillingness of the countries of North America and Europe to provide safe haven can have negative impacts on international practices and standards. Other countries of asylum, such as Thailand, Pakistan, and Mexico, which provide safe haven for thousands of individuals coming from neighbouring countries, may see the rejection of asylum-seekers as a justification for more restrictive policies on their part.

16. Early Warning of Refugee Incidents

Potentials and Obstacles

LEON GORDENKER

THE use of early warning better to prepare for the appearance of refugees seems to offer obvious advantages over the present situation. As it is now the arrival of forced migrants often surprises and even overwhelms everyone concerned. Even when the occasional clear warning is sounded, it may be disregarded for a number of reasons: because of questions about its source, questions about its authenticity, lack of confirmation, contradiction of apparently sound assumptions, or the political ramifications of reaction.

If an early warning system were effectively put to work, at least the arrival of refugees would be anticipated, and preparations perhaps made. Other advantages, such as the rapid mobilization of public concern, could also accrue.

On further examination, however, the idea of early warning presents some thorny difficulties. The following analysis proposes to expose some of these difficulties. It will examine some conceivable modes of early warning and explore the reasons for believing that such a system would be technically feasible. It will then treat the political and social factors which would inhibit its construction and use. Finally it will, hesitantly, suggest how progress towards its establishment might be made.

The nature of early warning

Early warning employs authentic information relevant to the development of a forced migration. The analysis of this information, the conclusions drawn as to the probable process of migration, and the transmission of the results of these analyses to those in a position to respond constitutes early warning. It can be distinguished from a programme of material response to refugees as well as from advocacy of particular policies for coping with refugees.

Early warning relates to a process, rather than an isolated event that sparks off forced migration. Any movement of people takes place over a period of time. In some instances a long period of gestation may precede any movement. Specific movements may vary in numbers, demographic and social composition, speed, degree of need, and distance travelled.

Strictly speaking, refugees represent only one form of forced migration. Defined by the United Nations Convention on Refugees of 1951,[1] they are people who have fled from their country, do not receive protection from its government, and have a well-founded fear of persecution. Those who do not fit into this definition are formally if not in fact excluded from the rather large-scale system of assistance and protection supervised by the United Nations High Commissioner for Refugees (UNHCR), and with which other inter-governmental and private voluntary agencies are associated.

While this formal definition may provide some reassuring limits on the commitment by governments that agree to take part in the system, it does not nearly cover the full range of forced migration.[2] Large numbers of people may be set on the move by government repression, malice, or incompetence. This may be combined with natural factors, such as drought, floods, plagues of insects, or disease. Yet only a few of the affected people may actually cross an international boundary, in order to meet the requirement that they be outside their own country. People may flee civil war, widespread civil disorder, an anticipated military attack from abroad, actual war, or merely the expectation of a grave worsening of their present situation. Once beyond their national borders, people who have left home may not qualify for refugee status even if, in every other respect, in terms of their needs they resemble refugees.

Partly as a consequence of humanitarian attitudes, and partly because forced migrants create an unavoidable impact on the societies they come into contact with, governments have rather

[1] 189 United Nations Treaty Series 150. For a brief, informal comment, see Guy S. Goodwin-Gill, *The Refugee in International Law* (Oxford: Clarendon Press, 1983), esp. 4–14, 17–19.

[2] Leon Gordenker, *Refugees in International Politics* (London: Croom Helm, 1987), ch. 3, 59–60.

often deliberately or quietly acceded to a fudging of the formal definition of the term refugee.[3] Assistance to forced migrants whose status as refugees could be dubious have been repeatedly improvised, sometimes under the supervision of those institutions created for the care of refugees, as narrowly defined.

Public awareness of a forced migration may only come after a long build-up.[4] In a ripe situation an isolated event may provide the sudden trigger for an unmistakable movement. It may begin, for example, against a background of repression by an arbitrary government. This repression could be complemented by the singling out of a particular group for special pressure, followed by the intensification of the campaign, by violence, and ultimately by the deprivation of any hope of a normal life. Alternatively, the migrants may comprise just a few individuals, who hold dissenting political views and who come under increasingly heavy repressive measures. Thus, long-term contributory factors may be separable from middle-term developments.

A complete early warning system should be able to compile useful information to cover refinements of the rather coarse formal definition of refugees used in most inter-governmental co-operation. Failure to do so would gravely limit the utility of the information. A successful system would assume the ability to make useful forecasts. The purpose of these forecasts would be to initiate a rapid, effective quick response.[5] Such responses could come from inter-governmental agencies, national governments, or private voluntary groups, or some combination of all these. The notion of quick responses, however, does not imply an immediate resolution of the difficulties which cause forced migration or those which follow it for both the migrants and the people and governments of the receiving territory. Rather, it is likely that chiefly emergency relief and protection would constitute the response, especially when considerable numbers of people are already on the move. Quick response, however, does imply

[3] See Goodwin-Gill, p. 73, n. 1 above. Resolutions of the General Assembly employ such circumlocutions as 'good offices' (e.g. UN General Assembly Resolution 1167 (XII), concerning refugees in Hong Kong in 1957); displaced persons (e.g. UNGA Res. 31/35); 'returnees' (e.g. UN Economic and Social Council Res. 1799 (LV), concerning southern Sudanese) and 'victims of man-made disaster' (e.g. in UNECOSOC Res. 2011 (LXI)).

[4] I am indebted to Lance Clark of the Refugee Policy Group, Washington, DC for pointing out that forced migration is a *process*.

[5] For further discussion, see Leon Gordenker, 'Early Warning of Disastrous Population Movement', *International Migration Review*, 20/2 (1986), 170–89; and in Gordenker, see n. 2 above, pp. 168–77.

the acknowledgement of a serious development. This would, it is presumed, be followed by appropriate action, including the operation of programmes of relief and protection. Effectiveness is determined by whether a response takes place and by how well calculated it is to produce a beneficial humanitarian effect.

This response could be directed to the long-term causes of forced migration, with a view to preventing the misery involved in displacement. The fundamental factors causing forced migration are likely to involve difficult issues of government repression or incompetence, or deep-seated social conflict.

Early warning involving middle-term developments would forecast an actual forced migration within a short time—perhaps a matter of weeks rather than months. During this time efforts to ameliorate the long-term causes could continue or be intensified. At the same time the imminence of migration could be emphasized to the authorities involved through diplomatic and other channels. Governments could prepare the necessary policy. Agencies, whether international or national, charged with the care and protection of refugees could prepare to receive migrants, including refugees. The location or stockpiling of supplies and transport could begin. The basic organization could be planned and administrative structures put into place. In some cases buildings might need to be constructed.

Then, if the forced migration were to actually happen, specific programmes could be put into operation. The early warning facility would have furnished short-term forecasts of movements of people, and if it were highly developed it would even include estimates of numbers, basic demographic analysis, and health status.

Assembling and analysing information

The idea of early warning depends on the availability and the timely compilation of relevant information. Since no such system exists at present, one cannot be certain that the necessary information could be assembled; but compelling reasons can be offered for believing that this could be accomplished.

Officials of the office of the UN High Commissioner for Refugees usually decline to make any public forecast of refugee flows.[6] A

[6] Both national and international officials working with refugees admit that forced migrations are part of world politics. Hints that further flows may be expected appear in official documents. 'Refugee situations are an integral part of political, social and economic developments in the world and of upheavals and divisions within the international

similar policy often constrains officials from other organizations, both national and voluntary. It is based on a fear that the government of a country from which refugees have come would resent such a forecast as impugning its humanitarian nature. That government would decline to treat with those who had made the forecast, perhaps closing down other projects already operating within its borders. The government most likely to receive the refugees might complain that the forecast had singled it out as the easiest point of asylum, encouraging migration in its direction. This could be seen as an unjust distribution of the burden. Furthermore, an erroneous warning would undermine the prestige of the organization issuing it and would deprive future refugees of protection and safety. Such errors would be highly likely, given the uncertainty of the information.

The above arguments have some merit. Some governments will certainly resent having to acknowledge responsibility for producing refugees. With the elaboration of an international standard of human rights that becomes increasingly better known, so inhumane activities by governments become more readily known. Even some states where police control is very harsh are formally bound by treaties protecting human rights. These governments and others hardly rush to admit that they even violate the rights of those citizens who leave behind family, friends, ancestral ties, and property, in their anxious rush for the nearest border. Merely pointing out the existence of such migration, let alone accurately forecasting it, may call down official displeasure on the heads of those persons responsible for the statement, and damage to their organization. Similar arguments have militated against open contingency planning for refugee movements.

Yet, officials of organizations especially concerned with refugees keep watch for indications of possible forced migrations. They also develop a talent for shrewd guesses about impending flows of asylum-seekers. Over the years since World War I a large corps of

community; as such they cannot be understood or treated in isolation [from] . . . the underlying causes of refugee movements.' UN General Assembly Executive Committee of the High Commissioner's Programme, Note on International Protection, Doc. A/AC.96/680, 15 July 1986, p. 14. That is a far cry from pointing out the next big movement, or a political situation, such as South Africa's, that seems likely before long to send out some refugees. The *UNHCR Handbook For Emergencies* (Geneva, 1982), 2, points out that much of that organization's work is an emergency response. There is no explicit treatment of procedures to anticipate an emergency caused by a sudden influx of refugees.

officials in national governments, voluntary agencies, and intergovernmental organizations has gained experience with emergencies involving migration and with the repatriation or resettlement of those who have left their native land. As a result of the large-scale forced migrations since the end of World War II in particular, an extended international network of people and organizations is in contact with displaced persons. This network serves to transmit the information collected by its members. The information may be fragmentary, not entirely accurate, slow in moving, and too formless for precise analysis, but shrewd observers may nevertheless know how to shape it into a pattern on which to base at least some predictions.

Occasionally estimates based on information gathered or put together in the field and subjected to intuitive examination do emerge publicly, even from the normally discreet circles of UNHCR. Thus, on one recent occasion a senior field official of UNHCR in Sudan openly predicted that 300,000 more refugees might be expected from Ethiopia within a few weeks.[7]

Less precisely, officials of the United States government have suggested from time to time that changing the interpretation of who qualifies as refugees from the turbulent situation of Central America would result in the northward flight of many thousands of people. Even now officials of several organizations are turning their attention to the possible forced migration of large numbers of people from South Africa.

News agencies, newspapers, and specialized periodicals, such as *Refugee Reports*, published by the US Committee on Refugees, carry substantial information on the subject. These are supplemented by publications and newsletters of voluntary organizations. Such public information sources clearly demonstrate the availability of data.

The flow of news, together with the specialists' practice of making educated guesses about the likely appearance of refugees, in themselves suggest that more systematic collection and analysis might yield valuable results. Some approximation to a systematic assembly of information, especially on current crises, probably

[7] Nicholas Morris, who was in charge of the programme in Sudan, the largest in Africa, remarked that this was a political declaration. Koert Lindijer, 'UNHCR faalde bij hulp in Soedan', *NRC Handelblad* (Rotterdam), 11 Feb. 1985, p. 4. Ethiopia protested. The refugees came.

takes place within the national governments concerned. For instance, the Bureau of Refugee Affairs in the United States Department of State closely watches developments. At the same time such efforts necessarily reflect national priorities and may not be based on the best conceivable scientific standards. Some voluntary organizations, moreover, may hesitate to furnish government officials with all the information in their possession.

If existing sources of information were systematically canvassed according to an explicit model, both a firmer factual base for forecasting could be built up and insights could be sharpened. The construction of such a systematic scheme of analysis would constitute the next step in raising the value of the information collected. Existing research on refugees suggests some elements of such an analytical scheme.

One such research approach relies on a metaphor drawn from the garden. Forced migrations are said to have root causes, from which intermediate factors sprout, eventually producing the evil flowers of forced migration. This metaphor emphasizes the social process involved in forced migration. The root causes may include political repression, social persecution, and a narrowing of social horizons for target groups or persons who will eventually become refugees. The intermediate factors include specific measures of repression, threats, occasional physical attack, etc. The situation is eventually reached where no escape from repression remains, where the pressure is extreme, and the outlook desperate.

This garden metaphor implies a temporal dimension. If the rate of deprivation increases, then the flight of the victims occurs sooner rather than later. The movement of repression or deprivation from the background to the foreground of daily life announces an approaching flight. The time span shortens. Desperation replaces hope. The longer span of time turns into a moment. This temporal dimension could also be roughly measured. Combined with an estimate of the degree of deprivation, it would provide a more systematic indication of forced migration.

This metaphor in fact uses a rough estimate of deprivation as an indicator. It implicitly assumes that deprivation leads to flight if the victims perceive their situation to be hopeless. It should be possible to measure deprivation with some accuracy and to estimate the psychological changes connected with perceptions of hopelessness. The forecast measurement of deprivation could be based on the gap that exists between the human rights promised in the UN Universal Declaration on Human Rights and the dynamic development of the existing situation.[8] By estimating the rate of derogation of rights it may be possible to forecast forced migration.

Another frequently-used metaphor likens refugees to a stream of water that begins as a few drops and eventually reaches to proportions of a flood. This metaphor involves dimensions of volume, pressure, and time. Changes in these dimensions could be measured and correlated to provide the basis of a forecast. The image of a flood also suggests spatial dimension. When the volume of water is sufficiently great, a flood rises over a dam, dike, or bank. What spills over will always be less than the total and perhaps of the volume contained behind the barrier. The point at which measurements are taken then has an important bearing on the results. In the case of refugees, measurements of those crossing an international boundary would fit with formal international definitions; but measuring the total flow of forced migrants would require observation at a point deeper in the country of origin, where they encounter a barrier.

The design of an analytical scheme could draw much from the increasingly sophisticated forecasting methods used in connection with food shortages in developing countries.[9] These employ data covering both macro and micro processes. At the macro level, forecasts of crop failures can be based on information gathered by satellite, by whole country crop forecasts relying on statistics collected by conventional cumulative methods, and even to some extent on meteorological data. These data can be scanned over an extended period of time. The analysis of such data provides a broad framework for anticipating disaster.

Data gathered at the micro level include the numbers of animals offered for sale and the appearance of family valuables on the market, and changes in the price level of grains and other foods. An unusual increase in the number of animals offered for sale reflects a

[8] The connection between mass exoduses, which I should call large-scale forced migrations, and human rights is emphasized in the study by former UN High Commissioner for Refugees Sadruddin Aga Khan, commissioned by the UN Commission on Human Rights. UN Doc. E/CN.4/1503.

[9] A condensed treatment of a considerable amount of technical exploration is Edward Clay and Elisabeth Everitt (eds.), 'Food Aid and Emergencies: A Report on the Third IDS Food Aid Seminar', DP 206, Institute of Development Studies at the University of Sussex (July 1985).

shortage of pasture and water, caused by drought, or perhaps by a plague of insects or a disease. Or it can reflect action by a government that induces a heavy sale of cattle. A rapid fall in the price of meat follows, succeeded by a period of slender supplies and higher prices. Continuing interference with normal agriculture soon results in a worse decline in animal sales in markets, and in steeply rising prices. The anticipation of higher prices may cause hoarding, which in turn sharpens their upturn. High prices mean that families try to sell their jewellery and other valuables in order to pay for food. As the process continues, farmers and herders may travel abnormal distances and paths in search of work, since they cannot till their own land or tend their own flocks. Their appearance announces the threshold of real hunger. The families left behind will begin to suffer severely unless relief is provided, either by those seeking work, or through outside souces, such as international agencies. If a response to the need for food fails to materialize in time some of those affected may seek asylum in other countries before long.

This famine forecasting technique employs concepts similar to those that would be required in early warning of forced migrations. The notion of a continuous process clearly underlies famine forecasting. The process extends over a considerable time and several intervening variables come into play at various stages. No single trigger determines the outcome. Data can be employed from a variety of sources, but however it is gathered, it has to be analysed and correlated in order to support a forecast.

Developing early warning capacity

Existing sources of information could conceivably furnish enough information of an appropriate quality to support a system of early warning. Yet, no rigorous test of this proposition has been attempted, or, if it has, no report has been published by the agency which made the attempt. Nor is there any specialized intellectual or material infrastructure for carrying out such experiments.

Despite its imperfections, the early warning mechanism for food disaster might serve as a model for use in forced migration. The model should trace a process. The indicator would be serious pressure by the authorities or by social groups on defined sections of a population. This pressure might be exerted in the course either of government decision-making, or the use of violence in internal disturbances, or against external forces. Thus, parts of the world where there is serious repression, or where it is threatened, or where fighting takes place, would be given priority. If forced migrations have previously taken place in the same area these might furnish clues to the possible pattern of a new movement.

By collecting and examining every possible piece of information relating to the process from such areas, it should be possible to fill in many boxes in an analytical scheme. These boxes could contain the data needed to estimate the depth of disturbance, the rate of movement, and the demographic character of those moving or about to move. Using the knowledge acquired during food crises, it would probably be possible to put together forecasts of nutritional deficiency among those people on the move. A similar estimate of health and other conditions of special interest in emergency relief might also be possible.

Although it seems probable that the collation of information from existing sources might go far towards improving prospects for successful early warning, the sources themselves might yet be improved. Consultations among voluntary agencies could be attempted, in an effort to standardize their information gathering and reporting techniques. Information published by governments and inter-governmental organizations about conditions in areas of potential forced migration could be scanned for material of special relevance to forced migration. These publications would include statistics on trade, agricultural and industrial production, health, and similar matters. A good deal of information that directly relates to the situation of human rights is published also through official sources. This includes periodic reports required by treaties or domestic laws, complaints made to human rights forums, statements and speeches in parliaments and in international assemblies, and even court cases. Furthermore, some governments would probably furnish confidential information to impartial fact-finders. This information, like any other, would have to be examined for its authenticity, comprehensiveness, accuracy, and possible bias.

Trials of early warning might also demonstrate how novel techniques of information gathering might serve to fill out available information. Future developments in information sources should emphasize the use of technological advances. Scanning by satellite—already used widely for agricultural, natural resources, meteorological, and military data—could conceivably be adapted for early warning of forced migrations. Presumably the movement of a considerable number of people would register even now in satellite-driven observation. No doubt governments that operate such systems would regard requests for data relevant to humanitarian affairs as of low priority, but there is nothing to indicate that they would absolutely decline ever to furnish any information. Timely data gathered from satellites that arrived at crucial stages of the analysis could bridge the gap between intuitive guesses and well-based estimates. Continuing access to every single piece of information would not be required, however. In any case satellite observation seems to be an under-used resource when viewed from the perspective of early warning.

As efficient early warning requires the rapid assembly and analysis of information, a better system would demand the speeding-up of data now flowing from the field to a central location for analysis. This could certainly be accomplished by greater use of modern telecommunications. Information could be rapidly transmitted in forms readily usable for computer analysis from the headquarters of organizations concerned with forced migration to the central analytical site. Furthermore, information could be transmitted from the field much more quickly and efficiently than it is now by standardizing its form and by employing telecommunications. Similarly, modern telecommunications make it possible to disseminate an early warning very rapidly to its targets, and also to amend or supplement warnings that have already been issued.

Although it could be argued that high technology involves high costs and that it is primarily financed for goals other than those of humanitarian assistance, the adaptation of existing information gathering for early warning of forced migration does not require capital investment on the scale of, say, a satellite launch. Moreover, the improvement of information gathering and analysis might well lead to greatly reduced costs both by reducing forced migrations and by eliminating unnecessary efforts when they do occur.

Obstacles to an early warning system

The obstacles to creating a good early warning system are formidable. They derive less from the problems involved in creating a conceptual structure for gathering information and analysing it than from the actual establishment and functioning of such a system. They include those problems wrongly lumped together as political—a word the connotations of which tend to cover up more than they disclose. If anything, 'political' is intended to point up conflicts over authority.

Forced migration over international boundaries can be viewed from the standpoint of a receiving local and national authority as forced immigration. If any subject is protected from extranational decision, it is immigration. Governments jealously guard it as their exclusive affair, and nationalistic attitudes reinforce this exclusiveness. Immigration policy receives virtually no attention in multinational forums, except for the occasional defence by a government that wishes to gain credit for its humanitarian policies, or that seeks to convince others that they should act to reduce the movement of refugees.

Early warning would very likely be seen by some governments as entering the forbidden preserve of immigration policy. An early warning of the forced movement of migrants could be understood as giving notice to governments that they might be faced with a challenge to their exclusionary or limiting policies regarding the entry of foreigners. Such governments can be expected to oppose early warning on principle. No one knows how many or how influential these governments may be.

The information required for accurate, reliable early warning touches on other profound areas of national policy. Governments that systematically violate the human rights of their nationals, or are so corrupt or incompetent as to damage their subjects sufficiently to induce them to flee, usually oppose outside attention. Similarly, information about military operations that may so threaten populations as to force them to move would probably be protected by the usual military secrecy. The collection and analysis of information bearing on such subjects at worst would be perceived as an intelligence operation on the part of enemies of the state. At best, it might be treated as gratuitous meddling.

Governments of some countries, often those which large numbers of forced migrants have fled, also would view the participation of voluntary organizations with scepticism. They decline to accept that such organizations can develop and act autonomously. Rather, voluntary agencies are treated as agents of foreign governments, including their intelligence organizations.

When exceptions are made, as they sometimes are for the International Committee of the Red Cross and a few other agencies, it is done for the purpose of gaining specific advantage or else avoiding some unpleasantness. An early warning system in which voluntary agencies were involved could be treated by some governments as additional proof that hostile intelligence operations were being contemplated.

Nevertheless, not all governments would be likely to react in this way. Some of those that have led efforts to cope with refugee situations might even welcome an early warning system. Others who have borne the weight of forced migrants might also support such efforts. What would probably be ruled out would be an inter-governmental early warning mechanism based on universal membership.

As an early warning system would almost certainly require the participation of several existing voluntary agencies, their attitudes towards it could also not be overlooked. No solid information on exactly how they might react is available; yet it might be expected that these agencies, like all organizations, would tend to protect their own integrity. Issues almost certainly would arise in regard to their relationships with host governments, with each other, and with their sponsors. Some clues to possible problems can be found in the difficulties involved in establishing and publishing *Refugee Abstracts*, a publication that began with joint sponsorship from the International Council of Voluntary Agencies and the UN High Commissioner for Refugees, with some of the financing for this venture coming from the Ford Foundation. Not every voluntary agency concerned with refugees acclaimed it, however. As it had difficulties in continuing as an independent publication, it has since been taken over by the UNHCR. Within that organization, changes attendant on a general administrative reorganization, set in motion by a new High Commissioner, have led also to uncertainties and readjustments. This affair provides a persuasive example of how even organizations with the best intentions may not react positively to co-operation on a controversial early warning effort.

Early warning has to be directed to organizations and persons who have the capacity to react to it. This, too, involves political issues. The reaction sought to an early warning is directed to the elimination of causes of forced migration and to more efficient reaction where such movements have begun. It would not serve these purposes to deliver early warnings in such a way as to obviate a positive response. At the same time no early warning can have much effect if it is possible merely to brush it aside without further notice.

Early warning could be addressed to a single government; to several governments; to no government, but to a single or several voluntary agencies; to one or more inter-governmental agencies; to individual participants in networks specializing in refugee matters; to an undifferentiated public; or to some combination of these. The choice of target would depend on the nature of the forced migration and on an estimate of the quality of reaction to it. Furthermore, the warning could be delivered in phases over a period of time; in each phase the audience could be either broadened or narrowed.

The targets of early warning and the phasing of the messages can probably not be set out in a precise scheme. In this part of an early warning operation timing and political insight would probably have greater importance than planning and standard analytical procedures. It is here that the most dramatic risks would be run in employing an early warning system.

These risks can be reduced by operating the early warning system in accordance with the best professional standards. Impartiality and sensitivity to the nature of the data used by the system should be obvious in the quality of the warnings. It is even more important, especially at first, that the warnings appear plausible and that they forecast with reasonable accuracy the sequence of events in a forced migration. The precision with which receivers of the early warning messages were identified would also bear on the acceptability of the system. Some would reject early warnings that entailed suggestions of culpability. Others would be interested only in warnings that were received in time for them to react effectively and that did not prove to be a waste of effort.

Overcoming the obstacles

Early warning of forced migration, it is clear, will encounter serious obstacles, which may prove to be insuperable. Yet the argument here suggests that some structure already exists for the collection of data, that it could be adjusted, expanded, and supplemented, and that a better conceptual basis for analysis could be constructed.

Furthermore, advanced technology offers real possibilities for an efficient, but modest, early warning system. The more formidable obstacles will be found in creating means for organizing, directing, and managing the system. These obstacles grow out of the very political structures and goals that induce forced migrations. They raise the question of whether any practical progress towards better early warning is conceivable.

In my judgement some progress would be possible. It hardly seems likely that a fully-developed early warning system could be brought into operation within a few months. That would require an inconceivable level of agreement among governments and large financial expenditure. Neither of these seems likely to arrive with the next sunrise. Moreover, appropriate personnel would have to be found to put together a sharp scheme of analysis if any successful operation were to follow. The rapid achievement of all this amounts to too large an order in a political structure that after some sixty years of formal attention to refugees still cannot in every particular instance agree on identifying them and cannot guarantee a right of asylum.

Some progress might however be possible in refining the conceptual scheme for early warning. This could be done in a university setting or within a public affairs research organization. It would require a mere handful of qualified researchers, advice from specialists with considerable experience in refugee affairs, and the use of computers adequate to the task of assembling the information and attempting simulations.

Once an analytical structure had been designed it could be subjected to two kinds of tests. The first of these is simulation, in which typical data are fed into the system. The second is a test of data about an actual forced migration. The latter would require access to some of the unpublished materials in the possession of voluntary agencies. Published materials would be available in any case. These sources might be supplemented by an experiment in gathering information in the field. Early experiments with the system would probably be best concentrated on the late middle term and final stages in a forced migration, because their analysis is less disputable than that related to fundamental factors.

The results of the experiments could be communicated to selected governmental and voluntary agency officials for their reaction. These reactions could in turn be studied. Later the results of the experiments could be published, and further comments invited from the members of the networks concerned with refugees.

Such an effort could conceivably be financed partly from within existing research establishments, partly from grants which might be obtained from philanthropic foundations, and partly from interested governments and inter-governmental agencies. Financing a study need not engage anyone in a commitment to policies. The researchers would be responsible for their own work and would not represent the policies of their organizations or sponsors.

If this initial effort proved successful it might be possible to put together a coalition of interested organizations—whether scientific, private, governmental, or inter-governmental—to sponsor a modest permanent organization. Or it might prove possible on the basis of positive experiments to find sponsorship for a well-based private institute.

This new mechanism would not undertake to watch the whole world. It would seek out situations in which its analytical capacities applied. Early warnings would be attempted only where they were well founded. Much would have to be learned about how and when to issue early warnings. This would probably have to proceed empirically.

The persuasiveness of early warning would be enhanced by the emergence, following the initial experiments, of a leader of recognized eminence. This person and his immediate associates would have to provide the insight into timing and targets necessary for the early warnings to have any effect. Such a leader might be attracted by the quality of the experimentation, or might be developed from the ranks of the experimenters. But every effort should be made by the sponsors of such an effort to prevent the creation of a conventional bureaucratic structure. A small, skilful early warning centre should provide a base for leadership in constructing the coalitions necessary for specific incidents of forced migration. It should not be the only source of leadership or formation of *ad hoc* networks.

In operation this modest early warning system would have available the necessary conceptual apparatus. The very process of putting it together and experimenting with it would train people who could then direct its operation. It would rely primarily on information sources now available but not fully exploited. It would not attempt to do everything at once, either in the experimental stage, or in actual situations. It would emphasize high-quality products, rather than notoriety. It would aim for overall effectiveness rather than for high profile. It would grow in scope only on the basis of its own competence and service.

17. Approaching the Refugee Problem Today

GERVASE COLES

THE increase in South–North refugee movements over the last few years would seem to signal a new period in refugee flows. This is a period with its own political dynamics and problems, significantly different from those of the two previous discernible periods following World War II. Updating the approach to refugee problems to take into account the new political dynamics and problems is now an urgent task.

The first period, characterized by East–West movement, lasted up to the end of the 1950s; the second, mainly by intra-South movement, into the late 1970s. Although the intra-South and, to a much lesser extent, East–West movements have continued into the 1980s, the South–North movement has attained prominence chiefly because the countries with the economic and political power to control or influence international approaches to the problem of refugees, i.e. the Northern (or Western) countries, have become increasingly preoccupied with this new movement. Inevitably, their preoccupation is affecting the approach to the entire problem.

A significant part of the difficulty the major actors have in dealing with the South–North movement stems from their inheritance of a way of thinking and acting which grew out of the circumstances of the two previous periods, but which is not suited to the different circumstances of the present period. A necessary adaptation is currently taking place, albeit slowly and painfully.

At the beginning of the first period, in the late 1940s, the Western countries which, together with their allies, formed a majority in the United Nations, were interested in establishing an approach to a much reduced but continuing European refugee problem. They were not interested in non-European refugees but, since they were using the United Nations as the means for dealing with their own problems, they were obliged to make at least some apparent concessions to universality.

These concessions, however, were inevitably arbitrary and fraught with problems since the new approach was specifically devised for a particular geographical problem at a particular time. Despite appearances, the approach was not universal, but regional and provisional: it was not a model for general application. A history of measures taken in relation to European refugee situations during the quarter of a century previous to this shows that each situation or time produced its own approach, suited to the particular circumstances of that situation or time. No general or consistent approach existed; indeed, there were major differences between those that were taken. In the five years preceding the adoption of the latest approach, two quite different approaches to the post-war European refugee problem were taken, each radically different from the other.

Old approaches to the refugee problem

A formal structure for the approach of the first period was finally codified in the 1950 Statute of the Office of the United Nations High Commissioner for Refugees (UNHCR) and in the 1951 Convention Relating to the Status of Refugees. Significant features of this Convention were that persecution was to be the essential characteristic of the new refugee; that the approach would be directed towards the individual, not to the group; that external settlement would be the normal solution; and that the refugee definition specified persons who were outside their country of origin.

Persecution was adopted as being the essential characteristic of the new refugee in the belief that this would satisfactorily define European asylum-seekers, the majority of whom were from Eastern Europe. Although the extension of the concept of persecution to include political opinion as well as religion and race made it quite broad, it was generally considered that the number of persons eventually involved would pose no problem since it was a time of renewed migration to the prospering continents of North America and Australia. Neither was the judgemental and polemical character of such a definition, when applied across an entire range of circumstances, seen as posing a serious problem, since it was the time of the Cold War, when such an approach would serve, from the Western point of view, as a useful way of stigmatizing the communist regimes of Eastern Europe as persecutors. Furthermore, it was also a satisfactory way of dealing with the historic concern of religious and racial minorities in Europe, especially the Jews, who were anxious to ensure that international arrangements existed to facilitate departure and resettlement elsewhere in the event of future persecution.

This approach had serious drawbacks, however. Above all, if the entire refugee problem was now to be seen as one of persecution, it was inevitable that countries of origin would not co-operate in any way. Indeed, since they would probably be hostile and tempted to retaliate, the only solution possible for the refugees would be permanent external settlement. Bridge-building between countries of refuge and countries of origin, even for such humanitarian purposes as family reunification or return, would become difficult, if not virtually impossible. In fact the annual reports of the United Nations High Commissioner for Refugees in the first half of the 1950s contained a number of statements about the lack of response to the numerous appeals addressed by the High Commissioner to the consular representatives of certain countries of origin.

Both in its conception, and in practice, the *ad hoc* and partisan character of this approach was incontrovertible. In 1949, only one year before the adoption of the 1950 Statute, the Western countries had favoured a quite different approach to the Palestinian refugee problem; there, they defined the Palestinian refugee as someone who, as a result of the conflict in Palestine in 1948, had lost his home. No particular motivation for leaving or remaining abroad formed part of the criterion for a Palestinian to qualify as a refugee; merely, the loss of home. The question of solution was left open and the mandate of the UN agency established to deal with the problem, UNWRA, was limited to providing assistance.

This latter approach reflected, in part, the fact that armed conflict was the immediate cause of the refugee situation. Indeed, the vast majority of all persons externally displaced by events occurring in Europe between the beginning of World War I and the end of World War II were 'war' refugees. Even the European refugee problem in 1950 was to some extent a consequence of the events of World War II.

Not surprisingly, many non-Western countries either rejected the Western approach or regarded it as relevant only to the European refugee situation. Almost all the socialist countries denounced the politics behind this approach, which were of course a diametric reversal of those that had led to the wholesale enforced returns organized by the Allies at the end of the war, and they vehemently criticized both the Statute and the Convention. The Arab states, also unhappy with the approach, inserted a provision in both instruments to ensure that neither was to be considered as applicable to Palestinian refugees. The Asian countries kept their distance, as did a number of major Latin American countries.

Early in the first period, however, problems considered to be refugee problems occurred as a result of events taking place outside Europe. They were to put the new approach to a revealing test.

Difficulties and limitations inherent in the old approaches

The first of these problems of major significance was the exodus of Chinese refugees from Communist China to Hong Kong. Because of the particular political and security factors involved and the lack of resettlement opportunity for Chinese refugees outside the territory of Hong Kong, the United Kingdom government considered that these refugees did not come within the purview of the Statute. In addition, it did not extend the application of the 1951 Convention to the territory of Hong Kong, although it did consider that it would be helpful if UNHCR provided certain assistance to the Chinese refugees. This episode illustrates well the provisional and pragmatic quality of the new approach to the refugee problem. For, as soon as a situation developed, the political dynamic of which did not correspond with that of the European situation, a different approach was devised for that situation.

Some of the Western countries, therefore, had no illusions about the limited character of the approach they had adopted in the Statute and Convention. Others, however, came to believe that an approach which had been devised for a European situation must necessarily also be valid for other regions of the world. But they had no real knowledge of regions outside Europe and no direct experience of large-scale influx. As soon as they themselves directly encountered the problems of vast numbers and of extra-regional origins, as they have recently, they showed a remarkable adaptability in the face of new circumstances.

The Chinese precedent was to be followed a few years later in the case of refugees from Algerian insurrection. On this occasion France opposed the application of the Statute to the Algerian refugees and stressed that the eventual solution could only be the return of the persons concerned. Eventually they were persuaded to accept a compromise designation of the situation to enable UNHCR to provide assistance to Tunisia and Morocco. As in the case of Hong Kong, UNHCR eventually concurred with the government position.

To take into account the new category of persons to whom UNHCR now extended limited help on an *ad hoc* basis, the concept of a 'good offices' role was advanced. This role related to persons who were not statutory refugees but who were considered to be refugees of concern to the High Commissioner. What the protection principles applicable to these refugees were was never stated and in the following years a number of different terms, none of them satisfactorily defined, were adopted to refer to extra-statutory persons or groups.

A situation somewhat different from that of the Chinese and Algerians resulted from the insurrection in Hungary in late 1956. On this occasion the Western countries decided on the immediate application of the Statute to the Hungarians and a resettlement programme was thus rapidly devised and implemented. However, when many thousands of refugees indicated that they wished to return once the security situation in Hungary had improved, it became clear that *persecution* had not been the universal factor behind the flight into Austria and Yugoslavia, that people had left for a variety of different reasons, some of them quite short-term. On this occasion, despite the acute political tensions of the time, Auguste Lindt the then UN High Commissioner took the initiative to establish contact with the new authorities in Budapest. This humane and courageous action did much to break the almost complete isolation of his Office from the socialist countries and to facilitate family reunion and the large return movement which took place in the succeeding months and years.

Approaches in the second period of refugee movements

During the second period the Western countries, now figuring mainly as donors and/or refugee-receiving countries, continued to dominate international refugee policy and action through their financial and political power. This was despite the fact that most of the refugee movement was now taking place within the Third

World and despite the fact that most of it was either the result of armed conflict between Western colonial powers and indigenous populations, or the result of the political and economic problems which developed in the new nations after they were granted independence by Western colonial countries.

To offset Western dominance at the international level, the African countries elaborated their own regional approach to take account of their particular problems. In the 1969 OAU Convention on Refugees, they adopted a much wider definition then persecution, which included compulsion to leave because of external aggression, occupation, foreign domination, or events seriously disturbing public order. This definition was so wide as, in many cases, to make individual determinations of status a mere formality. It also allowed for the promotion of voluntary repatriation. For the African countries, this was mainly a period of mass influx and their Convention included provisions for such matters as burden-sharing, voluntary repatriation, and subversive activities, which were not covered by the 1951 Convention. They invoked the principle of African solidarity to bring refugee-producing countries into the scheme of regional co-operation. Initially they also sought to develop the role of African organizations, such as the Organization of African Unity, but they were severely hampered by these organizations' lack of funds and were thus obliged to turn for assistance almost entirely to the Office of the UN High Commissioner for Refugees.

Most Arab states remained aloof behind the barrier of their traditional reserve, as did the Asian countries and some of the major countries of Latin America. When two of the Asian states most closely associated with the Western countries, Japan and the Philippines, acceded to the 1951 Convention at the end of the 1970s, they did so on the express understanding that they did not thereby undertake to afford more than temporary refuge to refugees under the Convention. Refugees who were admitted into their territories would have to be settled elsewhere. China, which also acceded to the Convention, made clear that refugee problems were essentially political and should be approached as such. In the case of India, a massive influx of nearly ten million refugees from what was then East Pakistan occurred in 1971, following the outbreak of internal conflict which was to result a few months later in the emergence of the new state of Bangladesh. The Indian government responded to the crisis by promptly making clear that the solution would be eventual voluntary repatriation, not local settlement, and took the necessary measures to ensure that this would in fact happen.

During this period most of the socialist countries retained much of their original hostility, but their attitude began to soften slightly when they saw the benefits that accrued to national liberation movements and left-wing groups from the international approach.

A political development of particular significance which occurred during this period was the perception by the states of the Third World of exile—in the context of national liberation struggles—as a denial of nearly all human rights, including the right of self-determination. The consequence of this was the stress put on the right to return in safety and dignity as fundamental to any approach to a refugee situation created by colonialism or by foreign occupation. Although this new perception was not reflected in the recommendations of the Third Committee of the UN General Assembly, which continued to be largely influenced by the Western group, it was amply expressed in the decisions of other Committees and UN bodies. The new emphasis on return was of course in strong contrast to the 'exile' bias of the Western approach which continued throughout most of this period.

The case of the Vietnamese boat people: a turning point

Another development of great significance, which proved to be a watershed, occurred towards the end of this period when the exodus of Vietnamese boat people was brought to international attention. For the first time during this period a major group of refugees had appeared for whom the Western countries, especially the United States, felt a serious responsibility for ultimately ensuring a solution. Moreover, political interests of major powers were directly involved, although the countries most directly and immediately affected were the littoral states of South-east Asia, Thailand, Indonesia, and Malaysia. These states, which had maintained a distance from the international approach to the refugee problem, were almost entirely unrepresented within UNHCR, the staff of which were still largely Western European.

At first the reaction of Western countries was to call these people not refugees but boat people, in the hope that the littoral states would accept responsibility for them; but the refusal of the South-east Asian states to settle them, and their plight as they were turned away from foreign shores, inevitably generated enormous Western media interest and public concern. The South-east Asian states skilfully exploited the new public interest, effectively evoking the Western concern for refugees and, by means of a dialectic of threat and response, they finally succeeded in almost entirely transferring the onus of settling these people onto the Western countries. They played both sides of the coin: on the one hand, they called the Vietnamese illegal immigrants and detained them as such; and, on the other, they facilitated their resettlement in the West by allowing them to be called refugees who had been granted first asylum— but only on the strict understanding that their resettlement elsewhere would ensue sufficiently speedily. Lest they be criticized too much for their action, it is only fair to remember that some Western European countries, as well as others, had done almost the same thing in an effort to ensure international burden-sharing. The Western countries and UNHCR created an unwise precedent, however, by calling refugees those persons who were illegal immigrants in the receiving countries, and by describing their detention as asylum. In trying to override sovereignty in so sensitive an area, they fashioned a two-edged sword, which was finally turned against them by the littoral states.

Although the major Western resettlement countries made an effort to screen the boat people, later, as their numbers became an increasing matter of concern, it was soon apparent that, by and large, they had to be treated as a group, even though economic factors were uppermost in many decisions to leave Vietnam. The political and economic situation in Vietnam made return impossible during this period, as the Vietnamese government's decided lack of interest in this solution was strengthened by the politicization of the refugee problem. At the insistent prompting of Western governments, UNHCR negotiated an Orderly Departure Programme; but, instead of being a way of bringing the exodus into more manageable proportions, it proved to be a means of facilitating family reunion and safe exodus. The divisions in the country that had led to a long and bloody armed conflict, and the long-standing tensions between the two main ethnic communities—the Vietnamese and the Chinese—made external settlement the only possible solution. The sharp politicizing of the refugee issue was also a contributory factor. Although, for the first time since 1945, some of the major resettlement countries began to emphasize repatriation as a solution, they encountered an almost complete lack of interest on the part of the Vietnamese government. As a result of the entire Indo-Chinese refugee drama, refugees became an 'in' cause in the West for the first time since the cold war. Last granted in 1954, the Nobel Peaçe Prize was once again awarded to UNHCR in 1981.

The African countries successfully exploited this development by means of an accusation of double standard in order to finally obtain the large sums of money for refugees in Africa that the West had not made available in the past. Shortly afterwards Latin American countries followed suit. Around the entire international refugee problem, a large. Western-based industry rapidly developed, almost all of it directed towards the Third World. Funding was sought by an increasing number of agencies, some of them in competition with one another. Public and private monies were made available on an unprecedented scale. By the end of the 1970s, UNHCR's assistance budget was nearly one hundred times what it had been less than ten years before. Almost overnight UNHCR became a major UN agency, whereas, in the first period, it had been mainly a small European migration agency and, for most of the second period, mainly a relatively modest assistance body.

A humanitarian approach to refugees: a donors' perspective

The focus of the new approach was humanitarian; that is, it was primarily concerned with the immediate needs of the refugees and not with questions of causes and solutions. It was essentially a rich and secure donors' perspective: it was about charity—and often very self-interested charity—not just about justice. Dependence was inherent in this humanitarian approach. Causes and solutions became politically relevant only later when, at the turn of the last decade, the refugee movements of the South began to spill over into the North and the new, large amounts of emergency aid appeared to be an indefinitely recurring expenditure. Then the themes of prevention and self-sufficiency became current, both of them reflecting concerns which, as they were expressed, were largely self-interested.

The significance of the donors' perspective served to impress the Western stamp deeply upon much of the international action for refugees—with predictable consequences. Afflicted with pressing economic problems, many Third World countries were sorely tempted to obtain from the new sources of largess as much financial and material assistance as possible. Obtaining further large grants became, for some of them, a significant consideration behind their approaches to their own refugee problems. They submitted refugee population figures which were open to challenge and which included nomadic groups for whom the description as refugees was also open to challenge. Newly-rich non-Western states declined to give large sums of money to organizations which they saw as mainly Western, preferring to leave the giving to the traditional Western donors of these organizations. Such sums as they did donate were mostly derisory. By and large, the non-Western governments also refused to involve themselves in international resettlement programmes, preferring to leave them mainly to what even some Western countries were accustomed to calling the 'traditional countries of resettlement'. Inadequately represented in a traditionally and mainly Western European organization, these resettlement countries became increasingly impatient with what they saw as the excessive Eurocentric character of so much of UNHCR's thinking, which they saw as unsuited to a large and complex world and as an additional source of complication.

Efforts made during this entire period to rationalize the international approach to the refugee problem finally foundered both upon the political expedience which had influenced so much of it from its origins and on the variable temporal and regional factors which made universalization so difficult. Expositions of international refugee law, which were mainly Western European, tended to pay insufficient attention to the political factors, presenting as universal what was often no more than a regional or temporal variable. In many cases an excessive positivist bias confined the legal enquiry entirely to the question 'what?', excluding the key question 'why?'. The results were expositions that were frequently if not usually unconsciously partisan or anachronistic. The conclusions of the UNHCR Executive Committee on protection, especially its Protection Subcommittee, tended to be not much more than an extension of the Council of Europe. In the highly politicized climate of so much international action for refugees, where short-term operational considerations tended to strongly supplant any longer-term ones, doctrine inevitably appeared largely irrelevant and, instead, there was finally none worth the name. However, lack of a clear and coherent set of aims and principles inevitably affected the quality and effectiveness of the action.

The UNHCR Statute shows its age

During this period the UNHCR Statute began to show its age badly and the 1951 Convention became largely irrelevant in many refugee situations, particularly in the Third World. No one, however, was willing to try to amend the Statute, and the Convention was widely seen as having at least some political or symbolic value. The Western countries, no longer in a majority in the UN General Assembly, were unwilling to renegotiate the Statute or to develop the international conventional law of refugees. By and large they saw their interests as served by a continuation of the status quo. No one else was interested in a global initiative, preferring regional means instead. An initiative taken in the 1970s by Sadruddin Aga Khan the then UN High Commissioner for Refugees to produce a Convention on Territorial Asylum was singularly unsuccessful, the original draft reflecting a mainly traditional Western approach, which attracted much socialist resistance and which finally foundered on a spate of amendments by a majority of Third World countries, which largely vitiated the original purpose of the exercise. The failure of the diplomatic conference, the only failure of its kind in the history of law-making in the United Nations, provided clear evidence of how political the whole question of the approach to the refugee problem had become.

The resolutions of the United Nations General Assembly during this period continued to direct the work of UNHCR and to recommend principles for state conduct, but they were vague and confusing, with rhetoric too often replacing clarity and logic. These resolutions were mainly incantatory political documents, reflecting in the 'mixed salad' of their content the ebb and flow of group political interests.

South–North movement ushers in a new period and new approaches

The emergence of a significant South–North movement at the end of the 1970s ushered in a new period. Numerically, this movement has been small, especially compared to the movements that have taken place in the Third World, but it is of concern to many Western countries because it comes from a number of different sources, and because some of the traditional champions of UNHCR and of the traditional approach are for the first time receiving significant numbers of asylum-seekers. For political and financial reasons, this concern weighs heavily on the deliberations and work of international bodies, as the history of recent discussions within the UNHCR Executive Committee shows.

As a result of the emergence of this South–North movement, virtually all of the Western countries are now in the process of changing their own traditional approach to the refugee problem. In response to the movement directed towards themselves, they are stressing the complex character of the movement of asylum-seekers, and especially the economic motivation of some of them; restrictive practices pertaining to recognition of status are being introduced in an attempt to keep the numbers down; return and prevention are now being emphasized; and arrangements with, or within, countries of origin or countries facilitating the transit of asylum-seekers are increasingly being made or at least advocated. Divisions are growing in their ranks as differences of interest and concern become apparent, and their first efforts to adapt their common position to new problems are proving difficult.

Western human rights advocates, concerned at this change of approach, are struggling to cope with the political complexity of the whole problem. Many of them suffer from the disastrous contemporary divorce of human rights from politics (in the sense of the art of government), with the result that different positive values are being placed in a fragmented context of conflicting relationships instead of in a holistic context of harmonization and equilibrium. The refugee industry is disconcerted too and is finding it hard to reconcile the comparative simplicity of the past Western approach to refugee problems in the Third World—with its concentration on care and maintenance—with the political complexity of the new Western approach to its own problems—with its emphasis on causes and solutions. Suddenly the politics of everything seem to have changed, unsettling those who have hitherto believed that their thinking at least was happily untarnished by politics.

The complex character of the South–North movement is scarcely deniable, but the phenomenon of immigration has always had varied and complex causes. Indeed, the experience of the European countries during this century has provided abundant evidence of the futility of trying to define a refugee by a particular motivation for departure. Not only is such an attempt inappropriate to a large-scale situation but its explanation is purely political in origin: the definitional approach was adopted by the Western countries to deal with Eastern Europeans during the cold war period and to meet the long-standing concerns of religious and racial minorities, notably Jews. It had no precedent in this century and proved inappropriate or unworkable in many subsequent situations.

In the case of the first large-scale refugee movement which had to be faced by the international community after the establishment of the League of Nations—that of Russians after the Bolshevik revolution and the ensuing civil war—the Secretary-General of the League came to the conclusion that the large and varied group of Russians who should be called refugees had in common only 'the general disorganization' in their homeland. To deal with the large European displacement problem after World War II, the IRO Constitution adopted a broad approach extending well beyond persecution and including a particular concept of displaced person to take into account some of the varied circumstances under which many persons found themselves outside their countries of origin. As we have seen, the approach adopted in the Palestinian case was similar to that adopted in the case of the Russian civil war. And even in Western practice after 1950 an interpretation was widely given to persecution in relation to Eastern Europeans that was so broad as to amount to a liberal immigration policy, a development necessitated by the overriding need to take account of the many people leaving for quite different and sometimes complex reasons who had to be settled outside their country of origin. If such an interpretation were given to asylum-seekers from the Third World today the potential number of refugees in the world would amount to hundreds of millions.

Furthermore, an approach directed to the individual asylum-seeker makes increasingly less sense as the numbers of asylum-seekers rise, to the point where it becomes entirely impossible, if only for practical reasons. As the history of refugee movement shows, increasing numbers gradually transform the problem of the individual into the problem of the group; and the larger the group, the more complex normally are the background circumstances of the many individuals who are included. In large-scale influxes practice has shown that it is essentially political or practical considerations which determine the decision to call the persons involved refugees or something else.

Leaving aside the problem of political or practical considerations which might militate against classifying an influx as a refugee movement, designating as refugee an alien who cannot return or be sent home because of conditions in his homeland makes sense in terms of a general approach which does not concern itself with particular questions such as status, the applicable principles of protection, or international institutional mandates. Such an approach makes sense not only in the varied and complex circumstances of a large-scale influx, but also in the circumstances of life generally, where a wide range of possibilities can explain why it is not possible for an individual to return home.

In this chapter therefore the term refugee is understood in the general sense used above, with its qualifications. In this broad sense, a refugee need not be an asylum-seeker, if by that is meant someone who has formally asked for asylum or refugee status; it suffices that the alien seeks to enter or remain in a country because living in his homeland is either impossible or intolerable. Where there are other ways of entering or remaining within a country, such as by a temporary visit or by enjoying tolerance status, an alien will often not make an asylum request, which sometimes, indeed, may not be in his best interests. In some cases, the receiving country does not provide asylum procedures for refugees, or deals with many of them in another way. Conversely, where an alien can only enter and remain by making a request for asylum, he will do so, even if it creates subsequent problems. The total number world-wide of those who do not seek asylum exceeds by far the total number of those who do.

On the basis of a narrow concept of a refugee as a victim of persecution, or of a narrow concept of persecution, it may be possible to maintain that many asylum-seekers or clandestine aliens do not suffer persecution; but what is more difficult to maintain in many cases is that they do not come from a society which is oppressive and/or seriously disturbed, even violent. Whereas the individual alien may not always be able to demonstrate a definite threat of harm, however that is defined, the facts surrounding the movement disclose the degree of adversity experienced in the country of origin. For many such aliens, transfrontier movement is not lightly engaged in; it usually carries a high personal cost, often setting them on a long, painful, and sometimes dangerous course. And, at the end of it, if residence is possible, whether on a regular, irregular, or tolerated basis, what awaits most of them is rarely El Dorado, but a hard and nerve-wracking life in a foreign community that is often coldly indifferent, if not openly hostile, and where the difficulties, deprivations, and humiliations encountered are hard to imagine.

Efforts to control the number of such aliens by the enforcement of immigration laws and procedures or by rendering more difficult the journey to the receiving country are proving by and large ineffective in situations where a major migratory movement is taking place. While it is possible in some cases to reduce drastically, at least for a time, the number of such aliens by tight immigration controls or by other dissuasive measures, or to reduce the number of such aliens in the country by recourse to expulsion, governments evidence a clear reluctance to proceed too far in this direction because of the fear of the negative consequences, internally as well as externally. In other cases making a reduction in the number of such aliens is proving impossible; instead, in some instances an actual increase in the number of such aliens seems inevitable. The problem also exists of the effective implementation of restrictive immigration laws and procedures by one country, which serves only to deflect that migratory movement to another country in the same region.

Ultimately, however, the modern refugee problem is not one of eligibility criteria or of immigration controls; the problem is, basically, that of the adverse conditions within the country of origin which are forcing people to flee. If the refugee problem is to be solved, the solution must basically be sought among those adverse conditions.

New necessities for new realities

If there is to be any hope of dealing effectively with the new realities today the first task is to free so much traditional Western thinking about the refugee problem of its 'exile' bias. This bias is inhumane and disastrously inapropriate in the circumstances of the modern refugee problem.

Because of the particular circumstances of the Cold War and because of the modern European history of the persecution of religious and racial groups, the assumption gained ground in the West that a refugee movement was a good thing. It provided the opportunity to attack an adversary, since the movement was the result of persecution, and it gave the persons involved the chance to find a new and better life. Sometimes too a refugee movement was a satisfactory way, though never proclaimed as such, of dealing with an internal problem. A refugee movement, however, is never a good thing: it may often be the lesser of two evils, but it remains an evil because it is, by definition, involuntary separation from the homeland—it is not voluntary migration.

It has even been asserted that refugees, unlike other human beings, do not want to return to their countries of origin. This could be true of only a relatively small number of refugees who have never had any real sense of belonging to their country of origin. For the vast majority of refugees the dream is of being able to return home one day. It is true that refugees normally have no desire to return to a country while the conditions that caused them to leave remain unchanged, but this is far from saying that in no circumstances in the future would they wish to return home. Indeed, the contrary is true, as the magnitude and rapidity of the occurrence of spontaneous return when conditions permit well demonstrates. In the bleak and bitter moments of exile the hope of return can be the one factor which sustains the refugee in a moment of trial.

For the vast majority of refugees today, the conditions of exile are far from good, even by the standards which normally apply to them at home. In some situations the conditions of exile can prove worse than the conditions experienced at home. Many do not get beyond the threshold of their countries of first asylum. They are detained in camps or treated as irregular aliens, forced to live in makeshift accommodation or wherever a roof can be found, under constant fear of expulsion or *refoulement*, dependent on hand-outs or the sale of tourist artefacts for survival, separated from their families and friends, often deprived of all news of them, vulnerable to the intense pressure of military or political groups and, finally, with a better future not even a light at the end of a long, dark tunnel of terrestrial existence. For the many millions of these people, exile is a painful trial, the occasion for heroism for many and the occasion for despair for some. Even for those who pass beyond the threshold and are eventually settled in areas of peace and prosperity, many still remain socially marginalized, often without employment, and prone to depression engendered by their sense of alienation.

In addition flight or expulsion as a result of social conflict usually amounts to a deteriorating situation in the country of origin. Often this deterioration directly affects other states, either because of their sympathy for the refugees or because they do not welcome them, and see their entry into their territory as a danger to their own internal stability and external security. Refugee situations can become a notoriously potent source of international tension and conflict, creating new problems as well as rendering more difficult the resolution of old ones.

Addressing Kampuchean refugees on the border of Thailand in 1984, Pope John Paul II said:

> There is something repugnant and abnormal in the fact that thousands upon thousands of human beings are forced to leave their country . . . transplantation cannot be a definite solution to the situation of refugees. They have a right to go back to their roots, to return to their native land with its national sovereignty and its right to independence and self-determination.

Accepting this view, therefore, it is unjustifiable—indeed it is profoundly wrong—that the prevailing international approach to the refugee problem should continue to have an exile bias. Yet this is unquestionably the case.

In the Western-inspired international instruments and documents on refugees and asylum, the emphasis has been mainly if not exclusively on exile. Although the UNHCR Statute mentioned voluntary repatriation as one of the durable solutions, it was only included, as the first High Commissioner Van Heuven Goedhart admitted, as 'the somewhat hypocritical compromise to which the interminable discussions in the United Nations had led'. In the 1951 Refugee Convention external settlement is the only solution contemplated, and there is no mention of the obligations (or rights) of the country of origin. When the United Nations General Assembly Declaration on Territorial Asylum was being debated in the Assembly's Sixth Committee in 1966, a proposal to include an article stating that 'nothing in the Declaration shall be interpreted to prejudice the right of everyone to return to his country as stated in Article 13, paragraph 2 of the Universal Declaration on Human Rights' was successfully opposed. And the draft Convention on Territorial Asylum prepared by a group of experts convened by the High Commissioner in the early 1970s included only a brief and passive provision on voluntary repatriation. In its own documentation, UNHCR refused consistently to accept the human right of return as the starting-point for a consideration of voluntary repatriation, and its documentation on protection persistently reflected its assumption that external settlement, not return, was the normal solution. The terminology employed revealed the exile bias; for example, 'exile' was always 'asylum' and 'homeland' was always the 'country of origin'. Expositions of international refugee law summarily dismissed the solution of return in a few platitudinous lines, which amounted to a complete evasion of the human rights issues involved, as well as of all the persistent promptings of some states; the subject of voluntary repatriation was considered and valuable recommendations were made, but some of them have yet to be implemented.

In addition UNHCR's operational weight has been primarily on care and maintenance and external settlement. A section existed for many years to deal with resettlement, but only *ad hoc* and often haphazard arrangements were made for voluntary repatriation. For much of the time UNHCR did not consider that it had any responsibility to take an initiative in favour of reconciliation or restoration. Whereas separation and alienation were humanitarian matters, reconciliation or restoration were political, and as such beyond UNHCR's mandate.

A new approach to the refugee problem

In recent years, however, an increasing number of Western governments have called into question this traditional bias and have sought to promote a new and positive approach to prevention and voluntary repatriation. It seems that we may now be reaching a watershed, a reorientation towards the key issue of a solution leading to a new conception of the purposes and principles of the approach to the refugee problem. In its comments to the UN Secretary-General on the General Assembly item on 'International Co-operation to Avert Further Mass Flows of Refugees', inscribed on the Assembly's agenda, on the initiative of the Federal Republic of Germany, the Australian government stated in 1981 that the assumption of external settlement as the correct durable solution to a refugee situation could not be justified on either humanitarian or political grounds. It would effectively relieve the country of origin of its serious responsibility to take whatever measures were possible and necessary to enable people who had fled its territory to return; it would also undermine the right of people who had fled their homeland to seek the support of the international community in obtaining the conditions which would make possible their voluntary return; and it would institutionalize exile at the expense of the fundamental right of the individual to return home and to enjoy their basic human rights. In some cases it would place an unrealistic burden on the country of refuge and result in 'solutions' which were highly unsatisfactory.

The international bias in favour of exile has prevailed not only for political reasons but as a consequence of the equation of the refugee to the victim of persecution; for, if the refugee is a victim of persecution, which is normally the deliberate and often systematic violation of the rights of the individual by a government, then the co-operation of the country of origin is either undesirable or unrealistic. Another consequence of this equation of course is that it ensures that the country of origin loses any interest in co-operating with other countries or international organizations which have declared its citizens to be the victims of its own grave and deliberate violation of their rights.

The international political response to events involving persecution, whatever the motivation of that persecution, has always been principally directed towards external settlement. Resettlement, however, involves more than just political questions. The international community also should take into account victims, which involves questions of human rights. This exile bias simply cannot be defended today in cases where the transfrontier movement is the result of such events as armed conflict, serious internal disturbances, or natural disaster. It is also quite unrealistic in cases such as mass influx, which are seen as threatening external security as well as internal stability.

Normally displacements as a result of armed conflict or natural disaster are of relatively short duration. Return in these circumstances is usually the solution and it would be inappropriate therefore to postulate external settlement as the solution for such displacements. In defence of the exile bias, it has sometimes been maintained that external settlement is in fact the normal solution for refugee movements and that return is the rare exception. The facts, however, prove the contrary to be true. If the problem of external displacement is seen as one that cannot be characterized simply as persecution but is one where armed conflict has been its principle cause, then it is external settlement which has been the exception, not return. For example, in the course of World War II, some thirty million people within Europe were displaced externally. Of this total, over nine-tenths returned to their homes. The problem of return concerned only a small percentage of this total. In the 1970s some fifteen million refugees returned to their countries of origin, including some ten million to the newly-formed state of Bangladesh. This last figure alone exceeds the present total of refugees throughout the world. Although the number of returns has not been nearly as high so far in this decade, return is nevertheless being considered on all sides as the eventual solution for the great majority of the refugees in the world. And, in all these cases, it is what the refugees themselves desire. It must be recognized that the available figures for return relate only to organized or assisted returns. No official figures are available for spontaneous (or non-assisted or non-organized) returns, but their number is clearly significant and over the last two decades runs into millions.

The exile bias of the traditional Western approach has been one of the main reasons why so many countries have kept their distance from it. In the case of Asia the bias poses grave political problems, since Asia is not much more than a geographic expression and, in an area which has been the birthplace of most of the world's religions and civilizations and where two-thirds of humanity is to be found, the problem of religious and racial discrimination is not one that can be easily solved by migration. It is in fact a highly complex and major political question.

Today it is of paramount importance that international co-operation in refugee situations be directed primarily towards the prevention of refugee movements and towards return. An approach to the refugee's problems, which amounts effectively to little more than one of separation and alienation, is not and has never been in anyone's long-term interest. Neither is it in accordance with the basic purposes and principles of the United Nations. Meaningful practical steps should be taken now to give effect to the primary concern for prevention and to the primary values of reconciliation and restoration. An invaluable first step would be to obtain a further objective and comprehensive study of the causes and dynamics of modern refugee movements. Recognizing the importance—indeed, the indispensability—of such a study in providing the pragmatic base for determining the modern approach to the refugee problem, a number of governments have called in recent years for such a study.

As mentioned earlier, in 1982 a valuable pioneering study was done by Sadruddin Aga Khan, at the request of the UN Human Rights Commission and on the initiative of Canada; but the factional character of so much of the forum limited what the study and subsequent debates could do. That study needs supplementing and developing. Although a number of political scientists and historians have made valuable contributions to this subject in recent years, further study and deliberation are necessary. Whereas it may not be possible for an inter-governmental organization to do this, a non-governmental body with a background of international humanitarian work could engage a broad range of independent expertise to produce a study which could be submitted for general deliberation.

It is remarkable that when states consider prevention they usually come forward with a more objective and comprehensive assessment of the causes of refugee movements than when they consider the question of the post-flow response. It is also notable that when a group of states is constituted on the basis of equitable geographical representation to consider the question of causes and prevention, they come forward on the basis of consensus, with a definition of a refugee or an attribution of the causes of refugee movements which is quite different from the traditional Western definition or attribution.

The 1986 report of the UN General Assembly Working Group on International Co-operation to Avert Further Mass Flows of Refugees, the members of which were nominated on the basis of equitable geographical representation, stated that the element of coercion which distinguished refugee movements from other kinds of transfrontier movements should be understood in a wide sense to cover a variety of natural, political, and socio-economic causes of situations which directly or indirectly forced people to flee their homeland. In examining the circumstances that had led directly to massive flows of refugees, the Group noted that wars and armed conflicts had been and continued to be a major cause of such flows. Colonialism and oppressive, segregationist, and racially supremacist regimes were identified, together with violations of human rights generally. Attention was also directed towards the practice of expulsions as well as to the phenomenon of spontaneous flight. The Group further noted that economic or social factors—sometimes the legacy of recent history, or aggravated by the international economic situation—were important factors in the creation of refugee situations. Several natural disasters, such as floods, prolonged drought, soil erosion, and desertification, could also cause refugees. Sometimes, the Group observed, mass movements could be attributed to one or a number of causes and factors—political, socio-economic, natural, or a combination of these.

The treatment of adverse conditions in the country of origin has hitherto been considered as falling entirely outside the scope of any approach to the refugee problem as such and as coming within the scope of some other concern, whether it be for the peaceful settlement of disputes, respect for human rights, or whatever. This view has always been untenable, however, and its tenacious retention in the past, by UNHCR in particular, has been a significant aspect of the modern refugee problem. It must now be changed if UNHCR is not to be part of the problem instead of part of its solution.

To justify the view that the refugee problem concerns only persons outside the country of origin and countries other than the country of origin, two related arguments have been advanced. First, it has been said that this limited view of the refugee problem is humanitarian, whereas any other view, requiring a broader approach, would inevitably be political—to mean partisan or factional. But there is another meaning of the word when it is used in a philosophical context, which signifies 'relating to the art of science of government'. In this sense, the refugee problem is entirely political, since it concerns an individual's relationship to a polity and the relationship of polities to one another. Also, the humanitarian value is not in conflict with the values that inform the art or science of government; on the contrary, it is, or should be, a basic value of that art or science. Too often the distinction between humanitarian and political has been made to avoid consideration of fundamental issues of justice or of long-term factors which surpass the simple issues of short-term charity that are more convenient to deal with.

Second, it has been said that the refugee problem, as a humanitarian problem, is quite distinct from a human rights problem: it is a separate area of concern, with different principles applying. This argument overlooks the fact that the accident of time or place should be irrelevant to a concern for the human being. Since the past and the future are both relevant to the present, the approach must finally take into account all of these aspects in determining what is best. Furthermore, the individual is always more than a refugee, for the individual remains a human being. General principles of human rights must therefore remain the basic principles which inform the entire approach to the refugee problem. An approach which divorces itself from human rights generally loses its proper orientation and sooner or later becomes inhumane and ineffective.

Again, the effort to distinguish humanitarian considerations from those of human rights is too often a shabby expedient to avoid examining fundamental human rights issues and their overriding implications for action. Neither argument stands up to a moment's careful, honest scrutiny, but the tenacity with which these arguments have been maintained and the frequency of their repetition indicates how deeply the exile bias has descended into the subconscious level of so much Western humanitarian thinking.

In the light of a broad perception of the refugee problem, an adequate approach should be seen as one aiming at the prevention of the loss of a homeland, the return to it, or the acquiring of a new country. In this view prevention is not different from the solution of the refugee problem but only an aspect of it. In considering preventive measures or remedial measures that will permit return, it is essential to be clear that a humane approach must exclude as unacceptable those measures which are designed to make transfrontier movement difficult or even impossible, regardless of the background circumstances of the individuals who might seek to leave. In a humane approach, prevention must be seen as concerning the avoidance or the remedy of conditions which, if left unchecked, would cause people to leave their country and to seek refuge elsewhere.

Action for the prevention of refugee movements can take a number of forms. In a general form it can be a warning to a country of origin or to other states, or to the international community as a whole that, if conditions are left unchecked, transfrontier movement will take place. This warning can pertain to a particular situation or to a general situation, e.g. to the world as a whole. Such a warning would not inevitably be regarded as unacceptable; it could be given confidentially if necessary, and in such a way as not to attribute any particular blame but simply to state a fact. It is also possible to recommend measures to check a situation in such a way as to avoid a negative confrontation with governments. At other times, however, it may be necessary to give the warning and to make specific recommendations in such a way that the responsibilities of govern ments are invoked, as in situations that involve clear violations of human rights, which are likely to lead to significant transfrontier movements. In the last case it is unconvincing to state that the action would necessarily be political in the sense of partisan or factional, for if the action is motivated by concern for human beings, it is necessarily humanitarian. Anyway, how is it consistent to refuse to evaluate an internal position prior to a flight but to proceed to evaluate it as persecution after the flight? Is not the explanation usually that there has been a dereliction of humanitarian responsibility before the flight—at a time when action was most needed?

It may suffice here to consider the situation in South-east Asia, where hundreds of thousands of citizens of a country leave by sea, tens of thousands drowning, and many others suffering various forms of severe distress during the outward journey. What can be said for an international approach in which strict silence is maintained—in the name of humanity—on the conditions which give rise to this problem, but public opinion inveighs against the littoral states for not receiving the refugees and protecting them in transit? Is it any wonder that the littoral states react negatively to this lop-sided approach and, in protest, limit their co-operation as much as possible?

A valuable contribution to prevention and to the goals of reconciliation and restoration would be made by speaking out honestly on the conditions which are experienced by most refugees today, and on their likely social consequences. In so many cases the suffering is immense but the sheer number of refugees detained in isolated camps or leading shadowy existences in vast urban agglomerations seems to have blunted public awareness of the suffering involved—almost as if the situation were seen to be irremediable. Too often, in the name of humanitarianism, a veil is drawn across this terrible but 'awkward' modern reality. The plain statement of the truth of these situations could serve to bring more sharply to international attention the destructive nature of the actions and policies which produce such situations.

Within the United Nations system the first cautious and overdue steps have now been taken to establish an early warning system. Although, regrettably, UNHCR originally resisted any involvement with this system, as it did with all prevention initiatives, it has now sought, under its new High Commissioner, to extend co-operation. More work needs to be done in this area, especially towards effecting general long-range forecasts of possible movements, and determining steps that could be taken to avoid or improve the conditions that could give rise to them.

Predictions about the future can serve fundamentally to determine action in the present. Concern for the human being requires that unreasonable fears should be shown to be such, or that reasonable fears should be met with anticipatory action which is the most humane and sensible in the circumstances. Largely because of its traditional exile bias, UNHCR has been seriously limited in not being prepared or able to make forecasts of further transfrontier movements, either world-wide or locally, but has preferred to confine its concerns to movements that have actually taken place. Since governments are always concerned about the future implications of their present actions or policies, and their attitude in the present is influenced by future expectations, this self-limitation of UNHCR has severely limited its relevance and usefulness. It is as if UNHCR has lacked any sense of direction.

An international presence, in the form, for example, of observers invited to confirm that as little as possible has been done to aggravate unnecessarily difficult conditions has in practice proved helpful. When a transfrontier movement is or is likely to become a major problem, as in the case of an armed conflict, one of the useful functions of an international presence should be to ensure that the displacement of civilians, whether externally or internally, is avoided as far as possible, and return permitted as soon as is feasible. The Nigerian civil war provided one encouraging precedent for such humanitarian action.

In 1982 a valuable contribution to the consideration of prevention and remedial measures was made by Sadruddin Aga Khan in his report on 'Mass Exodus and Human Rights' submitted to the UN Human Rights Commission. In this report Sadruddin Aga Khan, who drew on many years' experience as first Deputy High Commissioner and then High Commissioner, stated that the planning process pertaining to a refugee situation had to be solution-orientated from the beginning. While providing for immediate needs, attention had to be given to ensuring that a situation did not perpetuate itself. Both psychologically and politically, such an attitude, if adopted at the beginning, could have long-term beneficial effects, particularly if the root causes were to be investigated at the beginning of a mass exodus. When mass exodus did occur, it would be important to see the problem in the broad perspective of both 'refugee-producing' and 'refugee-receiving' countries. A simultaneous approach should help in identifying a long-term solution and in ensuring that humanitarian assistance in itself did not constitute a pull factor through any imbalance in the overall picture.

Sadruddin Aga Khan remarked on the obvious lack of contact, where the causes of an exodus were man-made, between the authorities of the country of origin and those of the country or countries of asylum. It would appear that those who left were 'written off' by their government—more often than not being labelled as traitors, criminals, undesirables, subversives, or at best misguided elements—while the receiving government was left to handle matters. To be sure, when the political situation changed and negotiated settlements could be initiated, bilateral talks were a prelude to any mass repatriation. Governments seldom co-operated while exodus was under way, however, and indeed might not be maintaining the normal diplomatic relations at the time which would permit them to do so. As a result the receiving countries, with the help of international agencies, mounted relief and resettlement operations which could develop and grow in a vacuum, without any relation to or detailed knowledge of the origins or causes of the problem or its likely resolution. Relief agencies, whether intergovernmental or non-governmental, continued to refrain from investigating the background to mass movements on the grounds that they had a humanitarian mandate to fulfil and could not concern themselves with controversial matters—matters which were usually political. Thus, the need for meaningful dialogue with those principally responsible on how to contain the problem remained unmet. Even if the countries of origin offered versions of the causes of refugee movement which some might see as biased, their responsibilities towards their own nationals had to be upheld, particularly if there were a danger of economic and social disruption in a receiving country and the undermining of peaceful relations between states which shared a common border.

Sadruddin Aga Khan added that, in the not infrequent cases where the reasons for an exodus were compounded by famine, the apportioning of aid and its timely distribution within the country of origin might help to circumscribe the flow. Conversely, in some situations, the availability of international assistance very close to the border but exclusively within the receiving country might help to precipitate the flow.

A serious defect in the organization of the UNHCR until recent times has been that it was not solution-oriented and that it did so little to initiate or even promote dialogue between refugee-producing and refugee-receiving countries. It was oriented too much towards care and maintenance and external settlement. The effect of placing the organizational weight on protection and assistance and of placing the question of solutions within the responsibility of the old Assistance Division was to ensure that a solution was usually dealt with superficially in the practical considerations of particular refugee situations, since solution is pre-eminently a political matter, not just one of protection or assistance, and the general consideration of solutions was quite inadequate, since it far transcended the limited scope of material assistance.

An improvement in the organization of UNHCR was made by Jean-Pierre Hocké the present High Commissioner when he liberated the Regional Bureaux of UNHCR from the dead hand of the old Protection and Assistance Division which, apart from their lack of political expertise as legal or material assistance bodies, sought to assume a global responsibility where the complexity and variety of particular circumstances required in-depth regional experience and expertise. Hocké has rightly entrusted the Regional Bureaux, as key action points within the new organization, with the main responsibility for solutions.

Efforts also have been made to establish a general dialogue with some refugee-producing countries. Such dialogue enables the High Commissioner not only to be better informed about the situation in the country of origin but also, if necessary, to act as a point of communication between the country of origin and other countries, or to exercise all round a helpful moderating influence. Often the refugee-producing countries have legitimate concerns in situations of transfrontier movement, and are disposed to engage in dialogue with a competent and impartial international agency. In addition, the interests of the individuals affected are served when dialogue leads to the lessening of tension, helps to prevent further forced movement or, at least, facilitates its accomplishment in the least unsatisfactory way, or makes possible such developments as family reunification and return. As far as possible, therefore, it would seem desirable to consider extending UNHCR posts or short-term missions to cover refugee-producing countries, some of which are also refugee-receiving countries.

The development of such a role for UNHCR requires special qualities of statesmanship. Today the High Commissioner is responsible for an organization which must be much more than an operational body charged with care and maintenance and external settlement: he must concern himself also with causes and prevention as well as with reconciliation and restoration. To advise and assist him in his key responsibility for seeking solutions, he needs a pool of staff with political experience, diplomatic background, regional expertise, and a wide range of international experience. Although his Office continues to need lawyers, assistance experts, and persons experienced in immigration work and social service, such persons cannot normally be entrusted with the specialized task of seeking solutions, which requires broad international political knowledge and diplomatic experience. Given its traditional role of providing mainly legal, assistance, and migration services, it would not be surprising if UNHCR had serious problems in adapting itself to the expanded role which is now required of it.

It would also be helpful to develop an international framework of principles for facilitating co-operation in refugee situations. The recommendations made in 1986 by the Group of Government Experts on International Co-operation to Avert New Flows of Refugees were a significant initial step, but the tone of recommendations is too polemical and censorious—insufficiently inviting, where co-operation is concerned. In addition, the recommendations were directed only towards prevention and not remedial measures. A general and flexible approach is needed which would better reflect the diversity and complexity of the causes of refugee movements and which would consequently be better suited to promoting co-operation. The question of where such an approach can initially be prepared is important; and the answer might be within the forum of a non-governmental body, with a background of international humanitarian concern. It is encouraging in this regard that a number of governments, within the context of the recent Romanian initiative in the UN General Assembly to consider the strengthening of good neighbourliness. have proposed principles governing co-operation in refugee problems.

To obtain rational and effective action, co-ordination is essential. Arrangements for the co-ordination of the actions of United Nations bodies have been made on various occasions, usually after a major man-made or natural disaster. These arrangements have been made largely on an *ad hoc* basis, however, the nomination of the co-ordinating point depending on the kind of action provided overall by the United Nations system. On many other occasions no arrangement for co-ordination has been made, either because the disaster has not attracted the same attention and the need for co-ordination has not been recognized, or because the limited and particular kind of action has not been seen as requiring co-ordination. Sometimes the co-ordination has been arranged too late. The question of the improvement of co-ordination is important, not only because each body tends to act on its own and is often not interested in how the entire system responds, but also because an improvement in co-ordination may ensure that the full potential for balanced and effective action is fully utilized.

In recent years governments on a number of occasions, including in the course of discussion of refugee problems, have stressed the need to improve co-ordination within the UN system, although they have discouraged the creation of new divisions or posts for this purpose. In the past there appeared at times to be an unfortunate tendency within UNHCR to consider itself as almost outside the United Nations system. Whereas, for example, resolutions of the Third Committee of the General Assembly were considered to be of direct concern, resolutions of other Committees which related directly to a refugee situation were frequently ignored as irrelevant or of no consequence. There was also a marked tendency within UNHCR to resist the involvement of the UN headquarters, as if such involvement were necessarily gratuitous interference in matters which properly concerned UNHCR alone. To no small extent this unfortunate attitude was the result of the exile bias of so much UNHCR thinking and of the false distinction made between 'humanitarian' and 'political'.

More extensive regional co-ordination is also possible, particularly in those situations where the combined political and financial resources of a region can bear significantly on a refugee problem. In recent years there has been a marked trend globally towards greater regional co-ordination of the response to refugee problems. It may be that a greater utilization of the capacity for regional action would significantly help to solve the problem of the limitations on action at the global level, particularly in promoting a more complete and balanced approach which addresses causes and solutions as well as care and maintenance and external settlement.

International law as part of the solution

A long overdue step would be to give more weight in international law and policy to the notion of belonging. Although the fact of belonging has not been mentioned explicitly in international human rights instruments as a source of rights, none the less, it basically underlies the proclamation of such rights as concerning return, as well as the related prohibitions contained in these instruments on expulsion, exile, and denationalization. Such rights as self-determination or participation in the government of a country are closely connected with belonging. Belonging in the full sense is a pre-condition for the enjoyment of rights generally, since the exiled national or the national deprived of all national protection in a foreign country enjoys only that modicum of rights granted to refugees or to aliens. In addition, the fact of belonging, or of social attachment, is a basic criterion for determining national jurisdiction and protection and, as such, is a basic principle of international political organization.

The human need to belong is more than a need for protection or for the means of individual development; it is also a need to be among one's own people. Although this latter need varies in degree according to individual circumstances and to such factors as age, it is normally a strong need, the satisfaction of which is conducive to individual and social well-being, and the denial of which is conducive to suffering and to social disorder.

One of the founders of modern international law, Francesco de Vittoria, rightly described exile as a capital penalty. To deny without justification an individual, a group, or a people the satisfaction of their need to belong by expelling or exiling, depriving of nationality or citizenship, by refusing return, or doing nothing to alleviate conditions which prevent return is to inflict a grievous injury on the persons concerned.

One possibility would be the preparation of a Protocol to the International Covenant on Civil and Political Rights which would deal more comprehensively than do the existing human rights instruments with the subject of belonging, including within itself provisions on such practices as expulsion, exile, de-nationalization, and the denial by one means or another of the right to return.

UNHCR as an initiator of reconciliation and restoration

There are cases where an international organization such as UNHCR can take the initiative in promoting reconciliation and restoration. In situations where there have been beneficial developments and where the moment is propitious, the High Commissioner can act as the catalyst by taking an initiative which sets in motion the discussions and practical measures necessary to achieve the reconciliation and restoration.

The High Commissioner's active involvement is necessary, more than ever today, as political pressures mount for effecting return as the solution to many mass influxes. The challenge to be active is not simply to be as co-operative as possible with governments that have constituted his office and have elected him, but also to ensure, in accordance with his mandate, that the interests of the refugees are safeguarded. Situations occur where there is pressure to return but where the circumstances are not conducive to this, such as where there has been no fundamental change in the circumstances which give rise to the refugee situation or where the conditions or guarantee relating to return are unsatisfactory. Situations also occur where the pressures are such that the refugees have no choice in the matter and proposals for 'assuring' the voluntary character of decisions to return are virtually meaningless. It is here that the High Commissioner needs all the authority and influence at his command to defend the interests of the refugees and to fulfil his mandate to protect. But it is unlikely that he will be able to fulfil this mandate successfully if he has the reputation of being unreasonably negative or passive where the principle of return is concerned. The problems surrounding the promotion of this solution are great, and the High Commissioner needs the best political and diplomatic advice available, as well as the support of governments, in steering a tricky course.

Whereas it is vital to maintain the fundamental principle of protection of refugees—that no one should be returned involuntarily where there is a reasonable possibility of harm—it is unbalanced and harmful to stress the significance of free will only in relation to conditions in the receiving country. As long as the refugee is unable to return he is not free to make any meaningful choice between returning and staying. For the refugee to be able to choose freely between returning and staying there must first be a fundamental change of circumstances in the country of origin.

To emphasize the importance of prevention and return is not in any way to weaken the protection and care of people who seek refuge in another country. Indeed, the emphasis on the broad range of human rights considerations can only serve to strengthen the case for refugee or settlement in another community where no other solution can be found. What would threaten the solution of external settlement would be to put the emphasis of international action on the obligations of actual or potential receiving countries, with little or no weight being attached to the obligations of the country of origin or of other countries in relation to that country. While not ruling out the necessity for some resettlement, an approach to the refugee problem which assumes that the normal solution should be external settlement and that the international approach should be directed primarily to this end is neither humane nor realistic. Until this concept is grasped, a more humane and effective approach to the international refugee problem will remain unattainable.

Temporary leave to stay and tolerated status

To ease the problem of numbers or of the geographical background of the refugees, two possibilities can be considered. Either those seeking entry or stay can be permitted to remain on a temporary basis, or they can be 'tolerated'. A number of situations exist where the request for refuge need not be considered a request for settlement. Such situations include armed conflicts, where the principal fear is of the indiscriminate violence of war, and natural disaster; in both cases the fear is often of relatively short duration and temporary refuge is all that is required or desired. Also, there are cases where a fundamental change in civil and political conditions is a real possibility in the not-too-distant future, or where resettlement in a third country is possible.

It has principally been to meet these situations and to provide general principles of protection that a concept of 'temporary refuge' has been proposed in recent years. The fact that this concept met opposition at the time was predictable in view of the exile bias which influenced so much Western thinking. So far this concept has not been considered applicable to conditions in most Western countries, but it has been applicable to many situations in the Third World; and it is currently being considered by some non-governmental groups in the United States as a possibility for meeting the protection problems of Central Americans.

Allowing admission or residence on a temporary basis is also in some circumstances a valuable way to buy time for finding a solution, whether by resettlement, return, local settlement, or by a combination of all three. Buying time eases the pressure to refuse admission to or to expel refugees out of hand. In a number of refugee situations the expedient of tolerating their stay has been found helpful. It reduces the number of asylum-seekers and, through the flexibility of a response which is not too structured, increases significantly the capacity of some communities to accept the aliens, whose numbers may sometimes range from hundreds of thousands to many millions. Today there are many instances of such situations, in the North as well as in the South, some of them appearing to be of long or indefinite duration. They will undoubtedly continue to occur in the future, with the likelihood of significant increases in numbers. These situations are mainly the result of the physical juxtaposition of countries with significantly different levels of economic and social development. In some cases in the Third World the difference is between that of intolerable physical conditions and conditions which are only marginally better but which are sufficient to induce transfrontier movement.

The main drawback of this approach is that these are just temporary expedients. They are not solutions. In the refugee context solution should be considered as retaining or regaining the normal benefits of a political community or, at least, the normal conditions of long-term or permanent residence. This concept of solution reflects the fundamental importance of human well-being of being in a community. As man is by nature a social being, he needs a community for fulfilment and protection. Without a community a human being is deprived and vulnerable. Conditions of temporary stay or 'tolerance' which fall short of the basic conditions of a solution can only be acceptable for a certain period of time since it is unacceptable to deprive a human being of a community for many years, especially where the person is denied the normal rights of prolonged or permanent residence or is forced to live under a continuing threat of expulsion.

The postulation of self-sufficiency as a solution, which has come into vogue in recent years, poses serious problems if this concept does not amount to settlement. The concept has not been sufficiently elaborated legally, and this should be done as soon as possible, to ensure that it is not inconsistent with concerns for protection. The answer to the problem of solution cannot be to drastically devalue this concept, the effect of which would be to create populations and quasi-homeless people.

Serious problems are being encountered today, however, not only in the absorption of refugees but also in the retention of migrant workers. In large part these problems are due either to the movement having taken place outside planned migration programmes or to the movement having been inadequately planned as regards longer-term considerations. Although precise figures are not obtainable, there are probably now world-wide some 30 million irregular migrants, some 20 million migrants who are part of a regular programme, but who do not have the right of permanent residence, and over 10 million refugees. Many of these people do not enjoy, in law or in fact, the normal conditions of residence. Essentially their presence is a temporary expedient. Others only have the right of temporary residence and after many years of stay are inevitably acquiring rights and interests which are increasingly at variance with the continued granting of temporary status.

There have been a number of recent instances of mass expulsion, and in other cases mass expulsions have been avoided only by international commitments to secure return or resettlement elsewhere within an acceptable time-scale. Increasing numbers of people who are seeking refuge or asylum from conditions which they find intolerable in their country of origin are finding it difficult, if not impossible, to obtain either admission or tolerable conditions of residence. And there is a widespread fear that an international recession will expose large groups of foreign populations to the risk of expulsion.

The seriousness of this situation, from both the individual and political perspectives, is undeniable. It leads to the exploitation of people and to the growth of racial antagonism. It also compounds the problem of the absorption of permanent migrants and threatens to become worse since the significance of transfrontier movement trends cannot be understood without a recognition of the great diversity in population growth trends between the more and the less developed regions.

The implications of this situation for the international response are clear. What is required is a broad range of measures commanding general support and relating to the causes of such movements as well as the response to them when they occur. The measures must relate to prevention and solution as well as to external settlement.

The purposes of these measures must be, primarily, to contribute to the establishment of conditions in the country of origin which are such that, by and large, movement will become voluntary, of a regular character, and the conditions of residence will be just and humane. They must not be adopted primarily to make transfrontier movement more difficult or, in some cases, impossible, for this would be to arrest, or even set back, the gradual process of developing an international community through freedom of movement—a process indispensable for planetary survival.

Wherein a real solution lies

What is indispensable to the success of these measures is a greater degree of general commitment to the purposes and principles of the UN Charter. Basically, because the refugee problem is the result of a lack of commitment to such purposes and principles, a broad notion of solution should relate to their promotion and realization and to the establishment of a more just and peaceful order in the world. Mankind must be liberated from the scourge of war; there must be faith in fundamental human rights, in the dignity and worth of the human person, in the equal rights of men and women, and of nations large and small; a sincere effort must be made to establish conditions under which justice and respect for the obligations existing under treaties and other sources of international law can be maintained; and a dedication to the promotion of social and economic progress and better standards of living, in greater freedom, must be reaffirmed.

It is not in the interests of Western states to dominate the international approach to the refugee problem to the exclusion or detriment of international co-operation. The co-operation of all states is indispensable. Domination leads only to the dominated exploiting the approach for their own gain at the cost of the dominators. The West does not have the economic capacity to support alone the financial and material burden of international assistance to the world's homeless. Nor does it have the political power to cope with the problem of homelessness, and as refugees from the South move towards the North to see if the northern countries practise what they have preached to the southern countries, a definite limit to its absorption capacity is also being witnessed.

The time has come to broaden not only the scope of the approach to the refugee problem but also the base of its support. It must become an international approach, at least as far as that is possible in a world of rivalries and conflicts. There are encouraging indications of a wide readiness to examine the development of international co-operation, and a common humanity and self-interest indicate that advantage should be taken of this readiness. After all it has been possible to develop international humanitarian co-operation in armed conflict and related situations through the conclusion of treaties and by support for the work of the Red Cross movement. Why can the same degree of international co-operation not be achieved in dealing with the modern refugee problem? It is useless and dishonest to pretend that one group of states is virtuous and alone worthy of telling the rest of the world what the approach to the refugee problem should be. The facts are plain to everyone: no group of states, especially the great ones of the world, are innocent. The basic issue, anyway, is self-interest, not virtue.

To achieve a more humane and effective approach it will be necessary to develop law and doctrine as well as international organization. The human being must be made the focus of concern, and the human being must be seen in the totality of human rights.

The approach must be solution-oriented, given primary emphasis to prevention and to reconciliation and restoration. As far as international institutional competence is concerned, the definitional approach must be pragmatic, giving due weight to political and practical factors. And, in the staffing of an international organization, the importance of international humanitarian co-operation and the principle of equitable geographical representation should be adequately reflected.

Finally, I would like to recall a long-forgotten letter which was written nearly fifty years ago by the then League of Nations High Commissioner for Refugees (Jewish and Others) coming from Germany Mr James G. McDonald. In this letter, which was addressed to the Secretary-General of the League of Nations and announced his resignation as High Commissioner, Mr McDonald referred to the state of affairs in the country of origin which was of direct concern to him, the national socialist state in Germany. Referring to recent events in that country Mr McDonald came to the following prophetic conclusions:

> The task of saving those victims calls for renewed efforts of the philanthropic bodies. The private organizations, Jewish and Christian, may be expected to do their part if the Governments, acting through the League, make possible a solution. But in the new circumstances, it will not be enough to continue the activities on behalf of those who flee from the Reich. Efforts must be made to remove or mitigate the causes which create German refugees. This could not have been any part of the world of the High Commissioner's Office; nor, presumably, can it be a function of the body to which the League may decide to entrust future administrative activities on behalf of the refugees. It is a political function, which properly belongs to the League itself. . . . The efforts of the private organizations and of any League organization for refugees can only mitigate a problem of growing gravity and complexity. In the present economic conditions of the world, the European states, and even those overseas, have only a limited power of absorption of refugees. The problem must be tackled at its source if disaster is to be avoided. This is the function of the League, which is essentially an association of states for the consideration of matters of common concern. The Covenant empowers the Council and the Assembly to deal with any matters within the sphere of activity of the League or affecting the peace of the world. The effort of the League to ensure respect for human personality, when not grounded in express provisions of the Covenant or of international treaties, has a sure foundation in the fact that the protection of the

individual from racial or religious intolerance is a vital condition of international peace and security.

At the end of his letter Mr McDonald justified his extraordinary action in referring in detail to the situation in the country of origin by stating:

When domestic policies threaten the demoralization and exile of hundreds of thousands of human beings, considerations of diplomatic correctness must yield to those of common humanity. I should be recreant if I did not call attention to the actual situation, and plead that world opinion, acting through the League and its member states and other countries, move to avert the existing and impending tragedies.

The message of the High Commissioner that the refugee problem must be tackled at its source if disaster was to be avoided can be applied with equal force to the present situation in the world. And as the High Commissioner also said, courageously and rightly, when policies threaten to demoralize and exile human beings—today, in their millions—considerations of diplomatic correctness must yield, finally, to those of common humanity.

Refugee Reference Guide and Selected Reading

Organizations and Documentation Centres

Academia Mexicana de Derechos Humanos, Filosofia y Letras 88, Colonia Copilco Universidad, Mexico D.F., CP 04360.
ALDOC, Arab League Documentation Centre, 37 Kheredine Pacha, Tunis, Tunisia.
AL-HAQ, Law in the Service of Man, PO Box 1413, Ramallah, West Bank, Via Israel.
All Africa Conference of Churches (AACC), PO Box 14205, Waiyaki Way, Westlands, Nairobi, Kenya.
Amnesty International (Research Department), International Secretariat, 1 Easton Street, London WX1X 8DJ
Association for the Study of the World Refugee Problem, A-6800 Feldkirch, Austria.
British Refugee Council, Bondway House, 3/9 Bondway, London SW8 1SJ.
Center for Migration Studies, 209 Flagg Place, Staten Island, New York 10304–1148.
Central America Resource Center, PO Box 2327, Austin, Tex. 78768.
Central American Human Rights Commission (CODEHUCA), Apartado 189, Paseo de los Estudiantes, San José, Costa Rica.
Centre for Documentation on Refugees (CDR), Office of the UN High Commissioner for Refugees (UNHCR), 1202 Geneva 10.
Church World Service, 475 Riverside Drive, New York, NY 10115.
Danish Refugee Council, Borgergade 10, 3, PO Box 53, 1300 Copenhagen K.
Department of Health and Human Services, Office of Refugee Resettlement, 330 'C' Street, Washington, DC 20201.
Ecumenical Migration Centre, 133 Church Street, Richmond, Victoria 3121, Australia.
European Consultation on Refugees and Exiles (ECRE), Bondway House, 3–9 Bondway, London SW8 1SJ.
France Terre D'Asile, 4–6 Passage Louis Phillippe, Paris 75011.
Human Rights Documentation Centre, Council of Europe, BP 431–R6, 67006 Strasbourg, France.

Independent Commission on International Humanitarian Issues (ICHI), 47 bis, avenue Blanc, 1202 Geneva.

Institut Africain pour le Développement Économique et Social (INADES), 08 BP 8 Abidjan 08, Ivory Coast.

Interaction, 1815 'H' Street NW, 11th Floor, Washington, DC.

Intergovernmental Committee for Migration, PO Box 71, 1200, Geneva 19.

International Catholic Migration Commission, 37–39, rue de Vermont, 1202 Geneva.

International Committee of the Red Cross (ICRC), 17 avenue de la Paix, 1202 Geneva.

International Council of Voluntary Agencies (ICVA), 13, rue Gautier, 1201 Geneva.

International Institute of Humanitarian Law, 5–7, avenue de la Paix, 1211 Geneva.

The Latin American Information Center on Migration (CIMAL), Intergovernmental Committee for Migration, Pedro de Valdivia 1224, Santiago, Chile.

Mexican Academy of Human Rights, Filosofia y Letras NBR 88, COL. Copilco Universidad, Mexico D.F., Mexico, C.P. 04360.

Office for the Commissioner for Refugees (COR), PO Box 1929, Khartoum, Sudan.

Office of the US Co-ordinator for Refugee Affairs, Department of State, Washington, DC.

Otto Benecke Stiftung, Bonner Talweg 57, 5300 Bonn 1, Federal Republic of Germany.

OXFAM, 274 Banbury Road, Oxford OX2 7DZ.

Refugee Documentation Project, York University, 4700 Keele Street, North York, Ontario, Canada M3J 2R6.

Refugee Policy Group, 1424 16th Street, Suite 401, Washington, DC 20036.

Refugee Studies Programme, Queen Elizabeth House, 21 St Giles, Oxford, England OX1 3LA.

Research Resource Division for Refugees, Centre for Immigration and Ethnic–Cultural Studies, Carleton University, Ottawa, Ont., Canada K1S 5B6.

Rights and Humanity, 65 Swinton Street, London WC1X 9NT.

Swiss Central Office for Help to Refugees (OSAR/SFH), Kinkelstrasse 2, CH-8035 Zurich.

United Nations High Commissioner for Refugees, Palais des Nations, 1211 Geneva 10.

United Nations Relief and Works Agency for Palestine Refugees in the Near East, Box 700, A 1400, Vienna, Austria.

University of Lund, Institution of International Law, PO Box 1165, S-22105 Lund, Sweden.

Universität der Saarlands, Sozial psychologische Forschungsstelle für Entwicklingsplanung. Im Fuchstalchen, D-66 Saarbrucken 11, Germany.

US Committee for Refugees, 815 15th Street NW, Suite 610, Washington, DC 20005.

World Council of Churches, 150, route de Ferney, 1211 Geneva 20.

World University Service, 5, chemin des Iris, 1216 Cointrin/Geneva.

Z.D.W.F., Hans Bockler Strasse 3, 5300 Bonn 3, West Germany.

Periodicals

Amnesty International Report.

Bulletin (New York: Lawyers Committee for International Human Rights).

Disasters (London: International Disaster Institute).

Foreign Affairs

Foreign Policy

Human Rights Internet (Cambridge, Mass.).

Human Rights Quarterly

ICVA (International Council of Voluntary Agencies) News.

International Journal of Refugee Law (Oxford University Press).

International Migration.

International Migration Review (Staten Island, NY: Center for Migration Studies, quarterly).

International Organization

Journal of Refugee Studies (Oxford University Press, quarterly).

Migration News (Geneva).

Migration Today (Geneva: World Council of Churches).

Monthly Dispatch (Geneva: Intergovernmental Committee for Migration).

Philosophy and Public Affairs

Political Science Quarterly

Refuge (York, Ont.: York University Refugee Documentation Project).

Refugee Abstracts (Geneva: UN High Commissioner for Refugees, quarterly).

Refugee Reports (Washington, DC: US Committee on Refugees).

Refugees (Geneva: UNHCR, monthly magazine).

RPG Review (Washington, DC: Refugee Policy Group).

UPDATE (Washington, DC: United States Catholic Conference).

Update: Latin America (Washington, DC: Washington Office on Latin America).

World Council of Churches, Refugees (Geneva: World Council of Churches, monthly newsletter).

World Politics

World Refugee Survey (Washington, DC: US Committee for Refugees).

Recommended Reading and Sources

Aga Khan, Sadruddin, *Legal Problems Related to Refugees and Displaced Persons* (The Hague: Academy of International Law, 1976).

—— *Study on Human Rights and Massive Exoduses*, ECOSOC doc. E/CN 4/1503, 1981.

—— 'Human Rights and Mass Exodus: Developing an International Conscience', 11th Annual Minority Rights Group Lecture, Royal Institute for International Affairs, London, 10 February 1983.

—— 'Towards a Humanitarian World Order', *Third World Affairs* (1985), 105–23.

Alienikoff, T. Alexander, 'Political Asylum in the Federal Republic of Germany and Republic of France: Lessons for the United States', *University of Michigan Journal of Law Reform*, 17 (winter 1984), 183–241.

Americas Watch Committee, *Guatemalan Refugees in Mexico 1980–1984* (New York: Americas Watch Committee, September 1984).

Amnesty International, *Allegations of Human Rights Violations in Democratic Kapuchea*, statement submitted by AI to UN Sub-Commission on Prevention of Discrimination and Protection of Minorities, August 1978.

Avery, Christopher, 'Refugee Status Decision-Making in Ten Countries', *Stanford Journal of International Law*, 17 (winter 1984), 183–241.

Bramwell, Anna (ed.), *Refugees in the Age of Total War* (London: Unwin Hyman, 1988).

Brown, Francis J. (ed.), *Refugees*, Special Issue of Annals of the American Academy of Political and Social Science, 203 (1936).

Buehrig, Edward H., *The UN and Palestinian Refugees: A Study in Nonterritorial Administration* (Bloomington, Ind.: Indiana University Press, 1971).

Carlin, James L., 'The Development of US Refugee and Migration Policies: An International Context', *Journal of Refugee Resettlement*, 1 (August 1981), 9–14.

Cels, Johan, *A Liberal and Humane Policy for Refugees and Asylum Seekers: Still a Realistic Option?* (London: European Consultation on Refugees and Exiles, 1986).

Chambers, Robert, 'Rural Refugees in Africa: What the Eye Does Not See', *Disasters*, 3 (1979), 381–92.

Clay, Jason, 'The West and the Ethiopian Famine: Implications for Humanitarian Assistance', in Gil Loescher and Bruce Nichols (eds.), *The Moral Nation: Humanitarianism and US Foreign Policy Today* (see separate entry).

——, and Holcombe, Bonnie, *Politics and the Ethiopian Famine, 1984–85* (Cambridge, Mass. Cultural Survival, 1985).

Coles, Gervase J. L., *Voluntary Repatriation: A Background Study*, for Round Table on Voluntary Repatriation [San Remo: International Institute of Humanitarian Law] (Geneva: UNHCR, July 1985).

Crisp, Jeff, 'Refugee Repatriation: New Pressures and Problems', *Migration World*, 14 (1987).

D'Souza, Frances, and Crisp, Jeff, *The Refugee Dilemma*, Minority Rights Group Report No. 43 (London: Minority Rights Group, February 1985).

de Zayas, Alfred M., *Nemesis at Potsdam: The Anglo-Americans and Expulsions of the Germans* (London: Routledge and Kegan Paul, 1979).

Dinnerstein, Leonard, *America and the Survivors of the Holocaust, 1941–1945* (New York: Columbia University Press, 1982).

Donnelly, 'International Human Rights: A Regime Analysis', *International Organization*, 40 (summer 1985), 249–70.

Douglas, Eugene, 'The Problem of Refugees in a Strategic Perspective', *Strategic Review* (Fall 1982), 11–20.

Elliot, Mark, *Pawns of Yalta* (Champaign: University of Illinois Press, 1982).

Fagen, Patricia Weiss, and Forbes, Susan, *Safe Haven Options in Industrialized Countries* (Washington, DC: Refugee Policy Group, 1987).

Far Eastern Economic Review, 'Asia's Refugees', *Asia 1979 Yearbook*, 126–8.

——'Asia's Refugees', *Asia 1980 Yearbook*, 110–15.

Ferris, Elizabeth G., *Central American Refugees and the Politics of Protection* (New York: Praeger, 1987).

——'The Politics of Asylum: Mexico and the Central American Refugees', *Journal of InterAmerican Studies and World Affairs*, 26 (August 1984), 357–84.

——(ed.), *Refugees and World Politics* (New York: Praeger, 1985).

Forsythe, David P., 'The United Nations and Human Rights, 1945–1985', *Political Science Quarterly*, 100 (summer 1985), 249–70.

Gallagher, Dennis (ed.), 'Refugees: Issues and Directions', *International Migration Review*, 20 (summer 1986).

——, Forbes, Susan, and Fagen, Patricia Weiss, *Of Special Humanitarian Concern: U.S. Refugee Admissions since Passage of the Refugee Act* (Washington, DC: Refugee Policy Group, 1985).

Ghoshal, Animesh, and Crowley, Thomas M., 'Refugees and Immigrants: A Human Rights Dilemma', *Human Rights Quarterly*, 5 (August 1983), 327–47.

Golden, Ronny, and McConnell, Michael, *Sanctuary: The New Underground Railroad* (Maryknoll, NY: Orbis Books, 1986).

Goodstadt, Leo, 'Race, Refugees and Rice: China and the Indochina Triangle', *Round Table* (July 1978).

Goodwin-Gill, G., *The Refugee in International Law* (Oxford: Clarendon Press, 1983).

Gordenker, Leon, 'Global Trends in Refugee Movements', in Lydio F. Tomasi (ed.), *In Defense of the Alien*, 5 (New York: Center for Migration Studies, 1983), 4–9.

—— *Refugees in International Politics* (London: Croom Helm, 1987).

Gorman, Robert, 'Coping with the African Refugee Problem: Reflections on the Role of Private Voluntary Organization Assistance', *Issue, A Journal of Africanist Opinion*, 12 (spring–summer 1982), 35–40.

—— *Private Voluntary Organizations as Agents of Development* (Boulder, Co.: Westview Press, 1984).

Grahl-Madsen, Atle, *The Status of Refugees in International Law* (2 vols.; Leiden: A. W. Sijthoff, 1966, 1972).

—— *Territorial Asylum* (Dobbs Ferry, NY: Oceana Publications, 1980).

Grant, Bruce, *The Boat People* (London: Penguin Books, 1979).

Hansen, Art, 'Managing Refugees: Zambia's Response to Angolan Refugees, 1966–1977', *Disasters*, 3 (1979), 375–80.

——, and Oliver-Smith, Anthony (eds.), *Involuntary Migration and Resettlement: The Problems and Responses of Dislocated Peoples* (Boulder, Co.: Westview Press, 1982).

Hanson, Christopher T., 'Behind the Paper Curtain: Asylum Policy v. Asylum Practice', *New York University Review of Law and Social Change*, 7 (winter 1978), 107–41.

Harrell-Bond, Barbara E., *Imposing Aid: Emergency Assistance to Refugees* (Oxford: Oxford University Press, 1986).

—— 'Repatriation: Under what Conditions is it the Most Desirable Solution for Refugees? An Agenda for Research', *African Studies Review*, 31 (1988).

Helton, Arthur, 'Political Asylum under the 1980 Refugee Act: An Unfulfilled Promise', *University of Michigan Journal of Law Reform*, 17 (1984), 243.

Hewlett, Sylvia Ann, 'Coping with Illegal Immigrants', *Foreign Affairs*, 60 (winter 1981–2), 358–78.

Hirschman, Albert O., *Exit, Voice, and Loyalty: Responses to Decline in Firms, Organizations, and States* (Cambridge, Mass.: Harvard University Press, 1970).

Holborn, Louise, *The International Refugee Organization: A Specialized Agency of the United Nations, its History and Work, 1946–52* (London: Oxford University Press, 1956).

——*Refugees, A Problem of Our Time: The Work of the United Nations High Commissioner for Refugees* (2 vols.; Metuchen, NJ: Scarecrow Press, 1975).

Hull, Elizabeth, *Without Justice for All* (Westport, Conn.: Greenwood Press, 1985).

Humphrey, Derek, and Ward, Michael, *Passports and Politics* (London: Penguin Books, 1974).

International Bibliography of Refugee Literature (Geneva: International Refugee Integration Resource Center, 1985).

International Refugee Integration Resource Centre, *A Selected and Annotated Bibliography on Women* (Geneva: UNHCR, 1985).

Jacques, André [with collaboration by his wife Geneviève Camus-Jacques, a contributor to this volume], *Lés Déracinés: Réfugiés et migrants dans le monde* (Paris: La Découverte, 1985).

Jaeger, Gilbert, *Status and International Protection of Refugees* (San Remo: International Institute of Human Rights, 1978).

Keely, Charles B., *Global Refugee Policy: the Case for a Development Oriented Strategy* (New York: The Population Council, Inc., 1981).

Keller, Stephen L., *Uprooting and Social Change: The Role of Refugees in Development* (New Delhi: Manohar Book Service, 1975).

Kennedy, David, 'International Refugee Protection', *Human Rights Quarterly*, 8 (February 1986), 9–69.

Kent, Randolph, *The Anatomy of Disaster Relief: The International Network in Action* (London: Pinter Publishers, 1987).

Keohane, Robert O., and Nye, Joseph S., *Power and Independence* (Boston, Mass.: Little Brown, 1977).

——(eds.), *Transnational Relations and World Politics* (Cambridge, Mass.: Harvard University Press, 1972).

Krasner, Steven D. (ed.), *International Regimes* (Ithaca, NY: Cornell University Press, 1983).

Kritz, Mary M. (ed.), *US Immigration and Refugee Policy: Global and Domestic Issues* (Lexington, Mass.: D.C. Heath, 1983).

——Keely, Charles B., and Tomasi, S. M. (eds.), *Global Trends in Migration Theory and Research in International Population Movements* (Staten Island, NY: Center for Migration Studies, 1981).

Kulischer, Eugene M., *Europe on the Move: War and Population Changes 1917–1947* (New York: Columbia University Press, 1948).

Kuper, Leo, *Genocide: Its Political Uses in the 20th Century* (New Haven, Conn.: Yale University Press, 1981).

Lawless, Richard, and Monahan, Laila (eds.), *War and Refugees: The*

Western Sahara Conflict (London and New York: Pinter Publishers and Columbia University Press, 1987).

Lawyers' Committee for International Human Rights, *The Haitians in Miami: Current Immigration Practices in the United States* (New York: Lawyers' Committee for International Human Rights, 1978).

Levy, Deborah M., *Transnational Legal Problems of Refugees: 1982 Michigan Yearbook of International Legal Studies* (New York: Clark Boardman, 1982).

Lichtenberg, Judith, 'Moral Boundaries and National Boundaries: A Cosmopolitan View'. Working Paper NB-4, University of Maryland Center for Philosophy and Public Policy, College Park, Md., 13 August 1980.

Loescher, Gil, 'Humanitarianism and Politics in Central America', *Political Science Quarterly*, 103 (summer 1988), 295–320.

——, and Nichols, Bruce (eds.), *The Moral Nation: Humanitarianism and US Foreign Policy Today* (Notre Dame, Ind. and London: University of Notre Dame Press, 1989).

——, and Scanlan, John (eds.), *The Global Refugee Problem: US and World Response* (Beverly Hills, Calif. and London: Sage Publications, 1983).

—— 'Human Rights, U.S. Foreign Policy and Haitian Refugees', *Journal of Inter-American Studies and World Affairs*, 26 (August 1984), 313–56.

—— *Human Rights, Power Politics, and the International Refugee Regime: The Case of U.S. Treatment of Caribbean Basin Refugees* (Princeton, NJ: Princeton University Center for International Studies, World Order Studies Occasional Paper Series, No. 14, 1985).

—— *Calculated Kindness: Refugees and America's Half-Open Door* (New York and London: The Free Press and Macmillan, 1986).

MacAlister-Smith, Peter, *International Humanitarian Assistance: Disaster Relief Organizations in International Law and Organization* (Dordrecht: Martinus Nijhoff, 1985).

Marrus, Michael R., *The Unwanted: European Refugees in the Twentieth Century* (New York: Oxford University Press, 1985).

Martin, David A., 'Large-Scale Migrations of Asylum-Seekers', *American Journal of International Law*, 76 (1982), 598–609.

Mason, Linda, *Rice, Rivalry and Politics* (Notre Dame, Ind. and London: University of Notre Dame Press, 1983).

McNeill, William, and Adams, Ruth, *Human Migrations: Patterns and Policies* (Bloomington, Ind.: Indiana University Press, 1978).

Melander, Goran, *Refugees in Orbit* (Geneva: International Universities Exchange Fund, 1978).

——, and Nobel, Peter (eds.), *African Refugees and the Law* (Uppsala: Scandinavian Institute of African Studies, 1978).

Meyer, Anne, *Annotated Bibliography on Sanctuary* (Champaign, Ill.: Urbana Ecumenical Committee on Sanctuary, 1986).

Morris, Benny, *The Birth of the Palestinian Refugee Problem: 1947–49* (Cambridge: Cambridge University Press, 1987).

Newland, Kathleen, *Refugees: The New International Politics of Displacement*, Worldwatch Paper 43 (Washington, DC: Worldwatch Institute, March 1981).

Nichols, Bruce, *The Uneasy Alliance: Religion, Refugee Work, and US Foreign Policy* (New York: Oxford University Press, 1988).

Nickle, James W., 'Human Rights and the Rights of Aliens', Working Paper NB-3, College Park, Md.: University of Maryland Center for Philosophy and Public Policy, 30 July 1980.

Osborne, Milton, 'The Indochinese Refugees: Cause and Effects', *International Affairs*, 56 (January 1980), 35–53.

——, Male, Beverly, Lawrie, Gordon, and O'Malley, W. J., *Refugees: Four Political Case Studies* Canberra Studies in World Affairs, No. 3. (Canberra: Australian National University, 1981).

Paludan, Anne, *The New Refugees in Europe* (Geneva: International Exchange Fund, 1974).

Paxton, Robert O., and Marrus, Michael, *Vichy France and the Jews* (New York: Basic Books, 1981).

Proudfoot, Malcolm J., *European Refugees, 1930–1952: A Study in Forced Population Movement* (London: Faber and Faber, 1957).

Refugee Policy Group, *The U.S.-Based Refugee Field: An Organizational Analysis* (Washington, DC: Refugee Policy Group, April 1982).

Refugees: The Dynamics of Displacement, a Report for the Independent Commission on International Humanitarian Issues [ICHI] (London: Zed Books, 1986).

Rogge, J., *Too Many, Too Long: Sudan's Twenty-Year Refugee Dilemma* (Totowa, NJ: Rowman and Allanheld 1985).

Rose, Peter I., 'The Business of Caring: Refugee Workers and Voluntary Agencies', *Refugee Reports*, 4 (1981), 1–6.

—— 'The Politics and Morality of U.S. Refugee Policy', *Center Magazine* (September-October 1985), 2–14.

Rudge, Philip, 'Fortress Europe', *World Refugee Survey 1986 in Review* (New York: US Committee for Refugees, 1987), 5–12.

Scanlan, John, 'Regulating Refugee Flow: Legal Alternative and Obligation under the Refugee Act of 1980', *Notre Dame Lawyer*, 56 (April 1981), 618–46.

——, and Loescher, G. D., 'Mass Asylum and Human Rights in American Foreign Policy', *Political Science Quarterly*, 97 (spring 1982), 39–56.

Schechtman, Joseph B., *European Population Transfers 1939–45* (New York: Oxford University Press, 1946).

——*Population Transfers in Asia* (New York: Hallsby Press, 1949).

——The Arab Refugee Problem (New York: Philosophical Library, 1952).

——Postwar Population Transfers in Europe 1945–55 (Philadelphia: University of Pennsylvania Press, 1962).

——*The Refugee in the World: Displacement and Integration* (New York: A. S. Barnes, 1963).

Segal, A., 'Haiti', in A. Segal (ed.), *Population Patterns in the Caribbean* (Lexington, Mass.: D. C. Heath, 1975), 197–204.

Shawcross, William, *Quality of Mercy: Cambodia, the Holocaust and Modern Conscience* (New York: Simon and Schuster, 1984).

Simpson, John Hope, *The Refugee Problem* (London: Oxford University Press, 1939).

Smyser, William R., 'Refugees: A Never Ending Story', *Foreign Affairs*, 64 (Fall 1985), 154–68.

——*Refugees: Extended Exile* (New York: Praeger, 1987).

Sobel, Lester A. (ed.) *Refugees: A World Report, 1979* (New York: Facts on File, 1980).

Stein, Barry, and Tomasi, Sylvano (eds.), 'Refugees Today', *International Migration Review*, 15 (spring-summer 1981), 331–93.

Stewart, Barbara McDonald, *United States Government Policy on Refugees from Nazism, 1933–1940* (New York: Garland Publishing, 1982).

Stoessinger, *The Refugee in the World Community* (Minneapolis: University of Minnesota Press, 1956).

Tabori, Paul, *The Anatomy of Exile* (London: George C. Harrap and Co., 1972).

Teitelbaum, Michael S., 'Right vs. Right: Immigration and Refugee Policy in the United States', *Foreign Affairs* (autumn 1980), 21–59.

——'Immigration, Refugees and Foreign Policy', *International Organization*, 38 (summer 1984), 429–50.

Tolstoy, Nikolai, *Victims of Yalta* (London: Hodder and Stoughton, 1977).

Tomaso, Lydio F., *In Defense of the Alien* (New York: Center for Migration Studies, annual since 1983).

United Nations High Commissioner for Refugees, *Collection of International Instruments Concerning Refugees* (Geneva: UNHCR, 1979).

——*Handbook on Procedures and Criteria for Determining Refugee Status under the 1951 Convention and the 1967 Protocol Relating to the Status of Refugees* (Geneva: UNHCR, 1979).

United States Department of State, *World Refugee Report*, A Report submitted to Congress as part of the Consultations on Refugee Admissions to the United States (Washington, DC: Bureau for Refugee Programs, 1986).

Vernant, Jacques, *The Refugee in the Post-War World* (New Haven, Conn.: Yale University Press, 1953).

Wain, Barry, *The Refused* (New York: Simon and Schuster, 1981).

Wasserstein, Bernard, *Britain and the Jews of Britain, 1939–1945* (Oxford: Clarendon Press, 1979).

Weis, Paul, 'Human Rights and Refugees', *Israel Yearbook on Human Rights*, 1 (1971), 35–50.

——'The 1967 Protocol Relating to the Status of Refugees and Some Questions of the Law of Treaties', *The British Yearbook of International Law* (1967), 39–70.

Woodbridge, George, *The History of UNRRA* (New York: Columbia University Press, 1950).

Wyman, David S., *The Abandonment of the Jews: America and the Holocaust 1941–45* (New York: Pantheon, 1985).

——*Paper Walls: America and the Refugee Crisis, 1938–41* (Amherst: University of Massachusetts Press, 1968).

Zolberg, Aristide, Suhrke, Astri, and Aguayo, Sergio, *Escape from Violence: Globalized Social Conflict and the Refugee Crisis in the Developing World* (New York: Oxford University Press, 1989).

Zucker, Norman L., and Zucker, Naomi Flink, *The Guarded Gate: The Reality of American Refugee Policy* (San Diego, Calif.: Harcourt Brace Jovanovich, 1987).

Index